COUPLE AND FAMILY ASSESSMENT

The field of family, child, and couple assessment continues to evolve and change since the first edition of this book appeared in 2004. *Couple and Family Assessment, Third Edition*, is a thoroughly revised and updated resource for anyone working with children, adolescents, couples, and families. It provides an in-depth description of an even larger number of clinically useful assessment tools and methods, including issue-specific tools, self-report inventories, standardized inventories, qualitative measures, and observational methods.

Each chapter provides strategies for systematically utilizing these various assessment methods and measures with a wide range of family dynamics that influence couples and families. These include couples conflict, divorce, separation, mediation, premarital decisions, parenting conflicts, child abuse, family violence, custody evaluation, and child and adolescent conditions, i.e., depression, anxiety, conduct disorder, bipolar disorder, obsessive compulsive disorder, autism, Asperger's syndrome, and learning disorders that can significantly influence family dynamics.

This third edition features the latest, most common and important assessment tools and strategies for addressing problematic clinical issues related to working with families, couples, and children. Chapters 3 through 11 include matrices that summarize pertinent information on all instruments reviewed, allowing readers to instantly compare more than 130 assessment devices. Finally, the book provides extensive clinical case material that illustrates the use of these various assessment tools and strategies in a wide array of clinical situations.

Couple and Family Assessment, Third Edition, will be useful to both trainees and practitioners as a ready reference on assessment measures and strategies for working with families, couples, and children.

Len Sperry, M.D. Ph.D., is Professor of Mental Health Counseling and Director of Clinical Training at Florida Atlantic University, Boca Raton, Florida, and Clinical Professor of Psychiatry and Behavioral Medicine at the Medical College of Wisconsin, Milwaukee, Wisconsin. He is a clinical fellow of the American Association of Marriage and Family Therapy, editor-in-chief of the *American Journal of Family Therapy*, founding associate editor of *The Family Journal,* and editorial board member of the *Journal of Marital and Family Therapy*. Among his 1000+ publications are eight books on families and couples.

The Family Therapy and Counseling Series

Series Editor: Jon Carlson, Psy.D., Ed.D.

For more information about this series, please visit: https://www.routledge.com

COUPLE AND FAMILY ASSESSMENT

Contemporary and Cutting-Edge Strategies

Third Edition

Edited by Len Sperry

Routledge
Taylor & Francis Group

NEW YORK AND LONDON

First published 2019
by Routledge
52 Vanderbilt Avenue, New York, NY 10017

and by Routledge
2 Park Square, Milton Park, Abingdon, Oxon, OX14 4RN

Routledge is an imprint of the Taylor & Francis Group, an informa business

Library of Congress Cataloging-in-Publication Data
A catalog record for this title has been requested

ISBN: 978-1-138-48460-3 (hbk)
ISBN: 978-1-138-48461-0 (pbk)
ISBN: 978-1-351-05162-0 (ebk)

Typeset in Minion
by codeMantra

This book is again dedicated to the memory of the late Kenneth I. Howard, Ph.D., a cherished mentor, colleague, and friend, and a major figure in psychological evaluation and clinical outcomes research. It is also dedicated to the memory of Luciano L'Abate, Lynelle Yingling, and Lisa Connolly, chapter authors of the second edition, who have since passed away.

CONTENTS

EDITOR

Len Sperry, M.D. Ph.D., Professor of Mental Health Counseling and Director of Clinical Training at Florida Atlantic University, Boca Raton, Florida, and Clinical Professor of Psychiatry and Behavioral Medicine at the Medical College of Wisconsin, Milwaukee, Wisconsin. He is a clinical fellow of the American Association of Marriage and Family Therapy, editor-in-chief of the *American Journal of Family Therapy,* founding associate editor of *The Family Journal,* and editorial board member of the *Journal of Marital and Family Therapy.* Among his 1000+ publications are eight books on families and couples.

CONTRIBUTORS

Dennis A. Bagarozzi, Sr., Ph.D., Couple and Family Therapist in private practice, St. Simons Island, Georgia.

W. Robert Beavers, MD, Director Emeritus, Family Studies Center, University of Texas Southwestern Medical Center, Dallas, Texas.

Vassilia Binenstzok, Ph.D., Instructor, Mental Health Counseling Program, Florida Atlantic University, Boca Raton, Florida.

Ronald J. Chenail, Ph.D., Professor of Family Therapy, Nova Southeastern University, Fort Lauderdale, Florida.

Alexandra (Ali) Cunningham Abbott, Ph.D., Assistant Professor, Lynn University, and Consultant, Florida Atlantic University Center for Autism and Related Disabilities, Boca Raton, Florida.

Maureen Duffy, Ph.D., Family Therapist, Consultant, and President of the International Institute for Human Understanding, Miami Shores, Florida.

M. Sylvia Fernandez, Ph.D., President and CEO, Council for Accreditation of Counseling and Related Educational Programs (CACREP).

Robert B. Hampson, Ph.D., Associate Professor of Psychology and Director of Clinical Training, Southern Methodist University Dallas, Texas.

Christine Sacco-Bene, Ph.D., Faculty in the Department of Counseling, Barry University, Miami Shores, Florida.

Sloane E. Veshinski, Ph.D., President, The Sloane Center, Inc., Hollywood, Florida.

Tiffany E. Vastardis, MS, Doctoral Candidate in Counseling, Florida Atlantic University, Boca Raton, Florida.

PREFACE*

The field of family, child, and couples assessment continues to evolve and change since the first edition of this book appeared in 2004. This third edition is a thoroughly revised and updated resource for anyone working with children, adolescents, couples, and families. It provides an in-depth description of an even larger number of clinically useful assessment tools and methods, including issue-specific tools, self-report inventories, standardized inventories, qualitative measures, and observational methods. Like the previous editions, it provides strategies for systematically utilizing these various assessment methods and measures with a wide range of family dynamics that influence couples and families. These include couples conflict, divorce, separation, mediation, premarital decisions, parenting conflicts, child abuse, family violence, custody evaluation, and child and adolescent conditions, i.e., depression, anxiety, conduct disorder, bipolar disorder, obsessive compulsive disorder, autism, Asperger's syndrome, and learning disorders that can significantly influence family dynamics.

This third edition brings together in a single publication the most common and important assessment tools and strategies for addressing problematic clinical issues related to working with families, couples, and children. Chapters 3 through 11 include a matrix that summarizes pertinent information on all instruments reviewed in that chapter. This feature allows the readers to instantly compare more than 130 assessment devices. Finally, it provides extensive clinical case material that illustrates the use of these various assessment tools and strategies in a wide array of clinical situations. In short, *Couple and Family Assessment: Contemporary and Cutting-Edge Strategies, Third Edition* will be useful to both trainees and practitioners as a ready reference on assessment measures and strategies for working with families, couples, and children.

Note

* The use of most of the inventories featured in this book are well within the scope of practice of licensed marriage and family therapists, mental health counselors, and other professional clinicians. However, there are a few standardized psychological instruments such as the MMPI-2 (Minnesota Multiphasic Personality Inventory), MCMI-III (Millon Clinical Multiaxial Inventory-III), and the Rorschach that, while they can be of immense clinical value, do require formal training and licensure as a psychologist, in most states, to legally and ethically administer, score, and interpret them.

1

CHOOSING EFFECTIVE COUPLE AND FAMILY ASSESSMENT METHODS

Len Sperry

For the past two decades, clinicians are increasingly being called on to deal with critical clinical treatment issues that require a working knowledge of couple and family assessment resources. These referrals may involve various challenges such as suitability for marriage, marital separation, divorce, mediation, family violence, and child custody for which couple and family assessment data and/or methods and strategies would be useful or essential.

Unfortunately, many graduate training programs continue to train clinicians to work with individual clients and conceptualize cases in terms of individual personality dynamics rather than in terms of systemic or couple and family dynamics. Accordingly, many have not had formal training or supervised experience in the use of couple and family assessment. Even those who have completed degrees in marital and family therapy may not have received much in the way of formal training and supervised experience in formally assessing couples and families. Thus, the discussion in this and subsequent chapters can be helpful in addressing such clinical considerations as marital issues, family violence, or child custody.

Recently, family therapy textbooks have begun listing common screening instruments with couples and families (Patterson, Williams, Edwards, Chamow, & Grauf-Grounds, 2018). This reflects the growing awareness of importance of the use formal screening instruments and measures in informing treatment decisions and for improving treatment. It also reflects the increasing emphasis on evidence-based practice in working with couples and families today (Bray & Stanton, 2010; Williams, Patterson, & Edwards, 2014). Among other things, it means the use of assessment instruments to quantify treatment outcomes.

Accurate assessment and screening instruments have become an essential element in the assessment of families. In the past, such instruments would have been used to identify specific family and couple issues and to set and achieve specific treatment goals and outcomes. Today, these instruments are also used to identify problem severity, risk factors, protective factors, family or couple readiness for change, and continuous assessment of the family-practitioner alliance. They are also invaluable in documenting the attainment of treatment goals and clinical outcomes (Thomlison, 2016).

> *Accurate assessment is essential for effective practice and to demonstrate effectiveness of services. To augment decision-making processes, practitioners need reliable instruments to increase quantity and quality of data collected during the provision of services. The use of data-collection instruments has become very important to insure individual goals as well as program goals are attainted.*
>
> *(Thomlison, 2016, p. 157)*

Fortunately, such resources are becoming discovered by clinicians and training programs available. For example, Corcoran and Fischer (2013) have compiled an extensive list of assessment and screening measures for evaluating specific issues common in families and couples, as well as childhood concerns. The actual measures are included so they can be examined for suitability for a given couple or family.

Now in its third edition, this book provides a general framework for couple and family assessment and an overview of various types of general and specific strategies for systematically and effectively collecting and coordinating interview data, self-report inventories, observational methods, collateral information, and so forth into the process of treatment planning and intervention. This chapter introduces the topic of couple and family assessment as an extension of individual assessment. It notes the diversity of views about assessment among the various family therapy approaches and considers whether formal family assessment is basically incompatible with such contemporary family approaches as narrative therapy and related social constructionist systems. It then provides a map of subsequent chapters by providing an overview of the issues and assessment methods and strategies that clinicians need to work effectively with individuals, couples, and families.

Next, it provides a clinically useful protocol for selecting and utilizing instrument as part of the assessment process. An extended case example illustrates this protocol. Finally, the Appendix provides a useful summary of the psychometric properties of such instruments, particularly their reliability and validity (Bolarinwa, 2015).

From Individual Assessment to Family Assessment

Why should a clinician be concerned with assessing family factors and dynamics, particularly if he or she is working primarily or entirely with individuals? A related question is whether family assessment (and, for that matter, couples assessment) is only of value to those conducting family therapy. This book endeavors to describe and illustrate the value of utilizing couple and family assessment for those who practice individual therapy as well as those who work therapeutically with couples and families.

The past few decades have witnessed a major shift in clinical assessment—from an exclusive focus on assessing personal attributes and individual pathology (i.e., symptoms and impaired functioning) to a greater awareness of the value of considering how family attributes, relationship patterns, systemic distress, and impaired functioning affect an individual's attitudes, behaviors, distress, and level of functioning. The reasons for this shift in thinking are many, although a principal reason is the recognition that an individual is inseparable from the system, which is the site of pathology.

Diagnosis means "to know," and understanding a problem situation can be called diagnosing. The process of diagnosing starts with observing data, forming concepts about the situation, and finally arranging the information in a particular way. All therapists have an epistemological base, and clinicians will diagnose differently according to this base (L'Abate, Ganahl, & Hansen, 1986, p. 34).

A traditional, non-systemic epistemology, which is the basis of the medical model, focuses on combining discrete clinician observations and individual dynamics; a systemic epistemology, which is the basis of family systems thinking, focuses on the whole system, including relational dynamics. In systemic assessment, diagnosis depends on the clinician's observation and elicitation of relational functioning, patterns, and styles rather than simply on the diagnostic criteria and individual symptoms and impairment characteristic of *Diagnostic and Statistical Manual of Mental Disorders, Fifth Edition,* (DSM-5) diagnostic thinking. "By bringing more people into therapy who are involved in the relational field of the identified patient, family therapy and diagnosis has moved more to the idea that the person within the system is part of the relationship system" (L'Abate et al., 1986, p. 34). In short, from a systemic perspective, an adequate assessment and diagnosis of an individual must necessarily involve the entire family system.

Differing Views of Couple and Family Assessment

Even though a systemic epistemology informs assessment and diagnosis in family therapy, it cannot be concluded that those who practice family therapy have reached a consensus about what constitutes appropriate and effective couple and family assessment. Nor does a consensus exist on training therapists in family assessment. Although some training programs in marital and family therapy provide students and trainees with formal instruction and supervision in using formal assessment methods with couples and families, others do not. This is not to say that assessment is less important in some approaches but rather that it is different. Why is this? Some insight into this query comes about by examining and comparing the place of assessment in the major approaches to family therapy. In a comparison of seven such approaches (behavioral, structural, strategic, Bowenian, experiential, solution focused, and collaborative), Yingling, Miller, McDonald, and Galwaler (1998) noted that each of these diverse approaches adopts a uniquely different theoretical perspective that "determines" which factors and variables are indicative of functionality or dysfunctionality; therefore, it should not be too surprising that what is assessed and how and when it is assessed in the course of treatment varies considerably from approach to approach. For example, formal assessment and history taking are essential in behavioral family therapy, but neither is typically a part of experiential family therapy. Nevertheless, assessment "is a natural part of the (experiential family) therapy process. It is accomplished through information given by the family as the therapist becomes acquainted with them as a group and individually" (L'Abate et al., 1986, p. 38). Furthermore, although goals and clinical outcomes are specified in terms of changes in family structure and boundaries in structural family therapy, outcomes that evaluate the efficacy of the relationship of family and therapists are more important in collaborative approaches. The question becomes, is an integrative approach to couple and family assessment possible? Many believe that such an approach will be possible to the extent that a set of common factors and dynamics involved in relational functioning is forthcoming.

Two encouraging developments in this regard are efforts to create a uniform system of relational diagnosis, the so-called Classification of Relational Disorders (CORD) that originated in the Group for the Advancement of Psychiatry (GAP) Committee on the Family (Kaslow, 1996) and the introduction of the Global Assessment of Relational Functioning (GARF) into DSM-IV (1994) and DSM-IV-TR (2000) and the various "Relational Problems" specified as V-Code diagnoses in DSM-5 (2013).

Family Assessment and Narrative and Social Constructionist Therapies

Striking at the very heart of family assessment is the concern that formal family assessment is incompatible with narrative and social constructionist therapies. Some would agree, claiming that formal assessment is a modernist convention focused on objective "truth" and as such is incompatible with a social constructivist, postmodern view. Some family assessment models, that is, the Beavers family systems model and its assessment methods, the Beavers Interactional Scales, and the Self-Report Family Inventory (SFI), have much in common with structural family therapy and related approaches; however, the traditional use of these models and related assessment methods appear to have little in common with narrative and other constructivist approaches. Nevertheless, Carr (2000) would contend that family assessment models like the Beavers model can easily be viewed as social constructions. Assessment models and methods that "have been found to be useful for solving problems, the hallmark of a valid social construction" (Carr, 2000, p. 127), can be compatible with social constructivism, depending on how they are utilized.

For example, scores on the SFI can be used, not as global knowledge of a family's or family member's cohesiveness or conflict but rather as specific, local knowledge and insights that a particular client might consider. Thus, it is one thing for a therapist to share assessment feedback and indicate that coaching, problem-solving, and communication skills might reduce the sense of distress and help solve presenting concerns more efficiently. It is another to imply or state the truth that the client is a poor communicator or poor problem solver. Finally, Carr notes that a commitment to social constructionism as a framework for clinical practice does not preclude a commitment to quantitative research grounded in empirical models of family functioning.

Recent Developments in Couples and Family Assessment

Since the publication of the first edition of this book, there have been several noteworthy developments in the assessment of couples and families. Perhaps the most obvious is the steadily increasing number of assessment devices aimed at children, adolescents, and parent–child relations. There have been a number of new instruments on children and adolescent functioning in several areas including academic achievement, psychopathology, personality, and social relations. Some are sensitive to social class and cultural diversity. There are also an increasing number of parent–child or parenting instruments that are available in the public domain and without cost. These are mostly in journal articles or researcher websites. In addition, there are a number of these assessment devices which are proprietary and involve a fee for its use. Assessment devices that have national norms continue to be in high demand. While academic researchers have and continue to produce useful instruments, they seldom have the financial resources to develop such norms. Because test publishers have such resources, they have been able to develop such norms. As a result, they are cashing in on the need for standardized instruments on various considerations of children and adolescents as well as child–parent relations. School counselors, school psychologists, forensic psychologists, and other clinicians have become ready consumers for instruments that have solid national norms, are culturally sensitive, and are acceptable in juvenile and family courts.

Indications for Utilizing Assessment with Couples and Families

Providing treatment or recommendations without adequate assessment can be problematic. Clinicians need to know where the couple or family has been, is now, and what direction they want to go. By understanding couples and families and their concerns, clinicians are more likely to intervene in helpful ways. In other words, assessment is both an event and a process. Couples and family assessment can be done for general or specific indications.

As a general indication, assessment is a guide and rationale for couple or family treatment, and it can become an intervention in and of itself. Assessment can clarify issues, specify symptomatic distress, identify level of impairment, and identify the goals and focus of treatment. As an intervention, clinicians can use assessment to support and validate couples and families as well as encourage their involvement in the treatment process. Accordingly, clinicians use assessment to welcome families into the treatment process and join with them, to give them feedback, to validate their concerns, and to engender hope. By asking questions, clinicians intervene by prompting couples and family members to think about issues and relationships in different ways. Finally, clinicians can use assessment techniques to track ongoing progress, re-evaluate goals, and stay in touch with the couple's or family's changing context and self-evaluation.

Specifically, assessment is used to address particular questions. These include the following: Has child abuse or domestic abuse occurred and what are the effects? Is divorce inevitable or can couples therapy help? Is divorce mediation indicated? What is the most appropriate custody arrangement when children are involved? Chapters 6 through 9 address such indications and considerations.

Types of Measures

Five broad types of measures are described and illustrated in this book. These are qualitative assessment, standardized assessment, observational assessment, ongoing assessment, and self-report assessment. This section briefly describes each.

Qualitative Assessment

Qualitative assessment is a type of evaluation that yields subjective data and narratives derived from unstructured methods of data collection, naturalistic observation, and existing records. In contrast to quantitative assessment, its methods tend to be holistic and integrated. Compared with standardized tests, qualitative assessment offers a more active role for clients, a more intimate connection between assessment and the treatment process, and greater adaptability to ethnic, cultural, age, gender, and other individual differences (Goldman, 1992). Qualitative methods are well suited for use with couples and families as they can foster mutuality, participation, and commitment and support communication and understanding in the treatment process. Examples of qualitative assessment range from unstructured interviewing and role playing to genograms and other graphic methods, such as photographs and collages. Chapter 2 provides a detailed discussion and illustration of qualitative assessment with families and couples.

Standardized Assessment

Standardized assessment is distinguished from other assessment types by the objectivity with which data are collected and analyzed and by its validity, reliability, and norms based on a large representative sample of the population. For many, the mention of standardized assessment brings to mind intelligence tests, such as the Wechsler Adult Intelligence Scale (WAIS), and personality inventories, such as the Minnesota Multiphasic Personality Inventory (MMPI), the Millon Clinical Multiaxial Inventory (MCMI), and the Millon Adolescent Clinical Inventory (MACI). However, there are several other instruments that are standardized or normed on large populations. These include the Rorschach, particularly the Exner-based system, and drawing tests, such as the Draw-A-Person test and Kinetic Family Drawing. While such instruments are considered devices for assessing individuals, they are also used in specific family situations, particularly child custody evaluations. A common assessment battery in child custody situations includes the MMPI-2, the MCMI-III, the Rorschach, and the Kinetic Family Drawing test. Chapter 3 provides a detailed discussion and illustration of the use of standardized assessment with families and couples.

Observational Assessment

Observational assessment is a type of evaluation in which observers are trained to watch and record individual, couple, or family behavior with accuracy and precision but without personal bias or interpretation. To facilitate comparisons between families, it is common to establish a specific task to be performed by each family. The form of the task chosen should reflect common problematic situations in average family life (e.g., discussing how to solve a discipline problem with a child or adolescent). Video recording, tape recorders, one-way mirrors, and other devices may be used to increase accuracy. The McMaster Clinical Rating Scale is one such observational rating instrument that is based on the McMaster Model of Family Functioning (Epstein, Ryan, Bishop, Miller, & Keitner, 2003). Chapter 4 provides a detailed discussion and illustration of the use of observational assessment methods with families and couples.

Ongoing Assessment

Ongoing assessment is a type of evaluation in which assessment is viewed as a continuous process throughout treatment rather than as a single or pre–post measure of individual, couple, or family functioning. Also called continuous assessment, treatment monitoring, and serial clinical outcomes assessment (Sperry, 2010), ongoing assessment influences the direction of treatment in two ways. First, goals identified during the initial assessment may need to be modified to meet the changing needs of the client system. Second, ongoing assessment assists in increasing treatment efficacy and efficiency by providing the clinician immediate feedback, which can alter the focus on direction of interventions. Using such feedback to refocus and modify treatment actually increases treatment outcomes and reduces premature termination (Lambert, 2010). The SFI and the Dyadic Adjustment Scale are two commonly used instruments for continuous assessment of families and couples. Chapter 5 provides a detailed discussion and illustration of ongoing assessment with families and couples.

Self-Report Assessment

Self-report measures are the most common means of assessing couple and family factors. Self-report measures include perceptions of the family by individual family members, ratings by family members of other family members' behavior or relationships, and self-reports of affect and emotions while engaging in certain behaviors. The value of self-report measures over other types of assessment is the ease with which ratings of partners or individual family members can be compared to ratings of the other partner or other family members regarding treatment issues. In the past decade, rapid assessment instruments were increasingly being utilized by clinicians.

Rapid Assessment Instruments. In this age of accountability, clinicians face increased demands to demonstrate the effectiveness of their evaluations and interventions. This can be accomplished with the use of rapid assessment instruments to measure a client's attitudes, beliefs, or level of functioning so that any subsequent change in functioning can be accurately detected over time. Rapid assessment instruments are typically short, self-report inventories for collecting information from couples or family members. These instruments are primarily in paper and pencil format and are usually quite easy and fast to administer and to score. The greater majority of measures described in Chapters 6 through 10 are of this type.

The Structure of Subsequent Chapters

There is a common structure underlying Chapters 6 through 10. It addresses both an assessment strategy for a particular area of family assessment, for example, child custody and divorce, as well as the use of specific methods and inventories. The purpose of the assessment strategy is to provide the reader with a specific plan and protocol for planning and implementing the assessment of a specific family or couple issue. This seven- to eight-step strategy reflects the way experts in the field think about the process of assessment from deciding on assessment methods and inventories to making recommendations and providing feedback to clients. It is then illustrated with an extended case example. A selection of the most useful and available assessment methods and inventories is provided with an outline common in each of these chapters. The outline is the following:

Instrument Name
Type of Instrument
Use–Target Audience
Multicultural/Translations
Ease and Time of Administration
Scoring Procedure
Reliability
Validity
Availability and Source
Comment

The purpose of this reader-friendly outline is to facilitate a rapid comparison of instruments from section to section and chapter to chapter. The following five-point structure (I through V) incorporates both the assessment strategy and specific inventories in Chapters 7 through 11.

I. *Issues and Challenges of Assessment.* This section describes and briefly illustrates the specific clinical, legal, and ethical (if relevant) issues and challenges associated with the chapter focus. Typically, the need for assessment of couple and/or family dynamics and functioning is described along with various technical and practical issues relevant to the topic.

II. *Instruments.* This section provides a brief, clinically relevant description of a number of common inventories used by clinicians and family researchers. These instruments have been chosen because of their psychometric characteristics (i.e., reliability and validity), availability, and ease of administration. For the most part, each instrument or assessment method follows a common format. **Table 1.1** summarizes this format.

III. *Strategy for Utilizing Assessment Results.* This section provides a step-by-step strategy for assessing a particular issue such as marital conflict, child custody, and so forth. For example, the assessment strategy might be (a) interview the clients, (b) administer specific inventories, (c) collect collateral data (school records, other interview data), (d) review and analyze the assessment data and various reports, (e) conceptualize the

case based on the review and analysis, and (f) plan treatment and interventions based on these data and the conceptualization.[1]
IV. *Case Example*. This section illustrates the use of specific instruments as
well as the assessment strategy. The case material demonstrates how one
or more of the specific inventories are incorporated as part of the preceding step.
V. *Inventory Matrix*. Finally, this very brief section summarizes pertinent
information on all the instruments, inventories, or methods in the chapter in the form of a matrix or chart. The matrix provides the reader with
a concise side-by-side comparison of each instrument.

Table 1.1 Format for Instrument Description

Name of Assessment	Indicates the authors or developers and date of publication and instrument or method revisions, if any, of the instrument or method.
Type of Instrument	Indicates type and form of the instrument or method, e.g., self-report, observational, clinician-rated, standard psychological instrument, outcome measure, etc.
Use–Target Audience	Specifies main use and targeted client, i.e., couple, family, parent–child, child custody, etc.
Multicultural	Indicates cultural applicability of the method; specifies other available language versions besides English that are available.
Ease and Time Of	Characterizes the ease of administration for the instrument of method, administration, i.e., easy, complicated, etc.; provides number of items and average time needed to complete the instrument; indicates if a manual is available.
Scoring Procedure	Specifies the (a) method, i.e., paper and pencil, etc. and (b) average time to score the instrument; if electronic or alternative form of administration or a computer scoring option is available, that information is indicated.
Reliability	Specifies types of reported reliability coefficients, such as test retest, internal consistency, i.e., Cronbach's alpha, and interrater (or scorer) reliability if applicable; also gives overall assessment: high, moderate, average, or below average reliability; if none reported, say: "no published or reported reliability data."
Validity	Specifies the types of reported validity, i.e., construct related, criterion related; if none reported, say: "no published or reported validity data."
Availability and Source	Provides information on availability and source of the instrument or method; if journal article provides assessment device, then journal reference is indicated; when only commercially available, name and/or address/phone number of supplier is indicated.
Comment	Provides chapter authors with opportunity to share professional evaluations of clinical utility and value of this instrument or method.

Selecting and Using the Results of Family Assessment Instrument

Following is a useful protocol in selecting and utilizing instrument as part of the assessment process. Clinicians trained in this protocol have found it helpful in working effectively with couples and families.

1. Background and Presenting Problem

    This part of the protocol prompts the clinician to provide sufficient background information and presentation that highlights the family and/or couple's symptoms or conflicts.

2. Clinical Questions

    This part of the protocol prompts the clinician to specify two or more clinical questions to be "answered" by the family assessment.

3. Rationale for Assessment Protocol

    This part of the protocol prompts the clinician to specify a rationale or reasons why and how the choice of specific assessment instruments will help "answer" the clinical questions.

4. Results of Assessment Instruments

    This part of the protocol prompts the clinician to score and report the results for each instrument, including ranges or norms if available. It is helpful to underline significant findings and double underline unexpected findings as these will need to be interpreted and incorporated in the family and/or couple case conceptualization.

5. Family or Couple Case Conceptualization

    This part of the protocol prompts the clinician to interpret the findings of the full assessment including clinical interview and family assessment instruments to answer the clinical questions (#.2). It also includes specifying the family's interaction pattern and/or, if applicable, the couple interaction pattern.

6. Planned Intervention

    This part of the protocol prompts the clinician to specify a treatment plan which addresses the presenting concerns (or a change in a previous treatment plan) in light of the assessment, instrument results, and family case conceptualization. It should specify short-term goals (typically first order change goals) and long-term goals (typically second order change goals).

Application of the Protocol

This case involves Rachel who is the identified patient. She is 11 years old, is the middle child in a single parent family, and lives with her mother, Jackie, and two female siblings, Jenny age 7 and Laura age 14. Rachel was diagnosed with Diabetes Mellitus Type I during an emergency hospitalization one year ago. It was previously called juvenile-onset diabetes, which means that because she is unable to produce sufficient insulin, she must do regular blood testing and take insulin injections. Jackie first sought individual therapy for Rachel. After 12 sessions, the therapist referred the family for a family evaluation and treatment. The family therapist utilized the family assessment instrument selection and utilization protocol and provided the following report.

1. Background and Presenting Problem

The onset of her Diabetes occurred within a few months after the family grieved two unexpected losses: the death of the girls' father and incarceration of the maternal grandfather. Rachel's diabetes symptoms are partially stabilized by insulin and diet restriction. Yet instead of encouraging Rachel's compliance with her medical treatment regimen, her mother is obsessed with finding a cure for this form of diabetes. As a result, she spends little time with her other daughters. They have reacted with jealous feelings (and other acting-in behavior), poor school performance, and other acting-out behavior. Rachel is shy, tall for her age, and awkward. She indicates that she is "adjusting" to her diabetes and the reactions of her siblings and peers; but she denies loss, grief, anxiety or depressive symptom reactions. Jackie and the children have been working with a family counselor for over a year. Lauren has been working with a counselor in individual therapy on sexual abuse issues, in an "on again, off again" manner for nearly two years. Only minimal changes, if any, can be attributed to both forms of counseling.

2. Clinical Questions

Three basic clinical questions were generated by the clinician. First, is there a connection of Rachel's diabetes and the family's trauma and experience of loss? Second, what accounts for family's specific reactions: mother's denial, Rachel's diabetes, and the other daughters' acting-out behaviors? Third, can the family be expected to effectively respond to professional help, and if so by what means?

3. Rationale for Assessment Protocol

In hopes of answering these three clinical questions, five family and child assessment instruments were chosen. The first was the *Beavers Interaction Scales* (BIS) which is a therapist observational measure. It was chosen to assess family style, level of competence–impairment, and family interactions patterns. The second was the SFI, a short paper and pencil, self-report measure. It was chosen to assess family competence and style from family's perspective and compare it to therapist's BIS ratings. The third measure was the *Family Hardiness Scale* (FHS). It was chosen to assess family's level of resilience, particularly Jackie's since specific norms are available for mothers dealing with medical conditions, like diabetes in a child. The fourth measure was the *Genogram* (GEN) chosen to identify any intergenerational patterns relevant to the clinical questions. Finally, the *Child Behavior Checklist* (CBCL), the teacher-rated version, was the fifth measure. It was chosen to assess the impact of Rachel's illness on herself, others and her adjustment since the diagnosis. A specific focus was on her scores on the following subscales: Somatic Complaints, Social Problems, and Anxious-Depressed.

4. Results of Assessment Instruments

The instruments were administered and scored. The following results can be reported. The therapist-rated BIS indicated a "midrange centripetal" family interaction pattern. The family competence score was 5.0 (midrange) while the family style score was 1.5 (centripetal). On the self-report SFI taken by Jackie, the score for family competence was 6.0 (midrange) and score for family style was 1.5 (centripetal). In other words, the same family interaction pattern was viewed the same by both a family member and the therapist. The FHS scores were particularly telling. Jackie's scores on the three subscales of family hardiness are commitment—19 (19.4), challenge—9 (12.7), and control—17 (14.2).

The mean scores are the ones in parentheses. In short, Jackie's scores were very similar to the mean scores and norms of mothers of children with diabetes, suggesting she has very similar levels of hardiness to those mothers. The GEN identified sexual abuse in previous two generations in Jackie's maternal family. Finally, the CBCL scores on the three most pertinent scales were Somatic—73, Social—67, and Anxious-Depressed—61. Note that there were high or unexpected scores (indicated by underlines) on GEN, CBCL, FHS.

5. Family Case Conceptualization

The following conceptualization is offered. The extent of the grief and the partially treated sexual abuse of Lauren has overly stressed this close-knit *centripetal* family sufficiently to "express" diabetes in Rachel, its physiologically most vulnerable member. Rachel's illness appears to serve the purpose of "restoring" the family's sense of cohesion by mobilizing family members in an effort to "control and cure" Rachel's symptoms (FHS-control). It is noteworthy that this family attempts to present themselves to others as healthier than they actually are, which is characteristic of a *midrange centripetal* family (SFI & BIS). The previous history of sexual abuse identified in the GEN may explain mother's denial behavior as well as the younger and older daughters' acting-out behavior. Until the mother is able to more equitably attend to the needs of these two family members, jealousy and discord will continue. Furthermore, both the mother and Rachel exhibit illness denial. Furthermore, the CBCL scores confirmed Rachel's social isolation, but "surfaced" her anxiety/depression which appeared to be "masked" by her fatigue and other diabetes symptoms.

Finally, the clinical questions can be answered: First, Rachel's diabetes appears to be directly connected to the family's trauma. Second, Jackie's denial and her daughters' acting-out and acting-in behaviors serve to restore the family's sense of cohesion. Third, because they are midrange centripetal family, there is a high likelihood they will respond to focused interventions in contrast to the treatment previously received.

6. Planned Intervention

The following treatment goals reflect this family case conceptualization. The short-term goal is for Jackie to re-establish giving equal "attention" to her older and younger daughters in place of "over-attentiveness" to Rachel's diabetes. Parent coaching is the suggested intervention. The long-term goal is to work with counselor/therapists who can best achieve the following focused treatment goals for effective care. For Rachel: individual health counseling to address her illness denial, her anxiety and depression, her body-image changes, and the development of a new, healthy self-view, i.e., "I'm an active teen who happens to have diabetes." This would replace her victim self-view: "I'm a suffering diabetes patient" and her illness denying self-view, i.e., "there's nothing wrong with me." For Lauren: specialized sex trauma therapy, and for the family: family work that includes educating them on diabetes and their role in Rachel's adherence to treatment, and a therapeutic focus on grieving and working together.

Case Commentary

Arguably, this family presents challenges for many therapists and most, if not all, therapists-in-training. The brittleness and impact of Rachel's chronic medical condition on the family system is a challenge in and of itself, while Lauren's sexual abuse adds a further level of complexity, as does the mother's over involvement with Rachel. As it turns out, the way the therapist framed the clinical questions and selected and utilized the five chosen assessment instruments greatly helped conceptualize the family dynamics and forge a reasonable treatment plan for this rather complicated case.

Concluding Comment

This chapter has begun the discussion of the need for and clinical value of couple and family assessment. We have described the shift that has occurred, and is still occurring, from individual assessment to family assessment. We have also noted that, owing to the diversity of viewpoints on the content and process of assessment, no single or integrative approach to family assessment currently exists. In addition, a basic incompatibility appears to exist between formal family assessment and the newer social constructivist approaches; however, assessment methods are quite compatible with such approaches, depending on the manner in which assessment information is framed with clients and families. Then, the common structure of subsequent chapters was briefly introduced. Finally, a protocol for choosing assessment instruments is provided. The case of Rachel and her family illustrates the clinical value of this protocol.

A Brief Overview of Reliability and Validity

As just noted, the technical description of each assessment instrument or method includes data on two key psychometric properties: reliability and validity. For some readers, this will be a review while for others it may be an introduction and overview of these two clinically useful constructs.

Because major clinical recommendations such as child custody are often based on clinical assessment, it is essential that the assessment instruments and methods on which these recommended courses of action are made are highly reliable and valid. It is also necessary that the clinician be sufficiently apprised of the appropriate use and limitations of such devices.

Even though this is a text on assessment, it cannot be assumed that all readers will be sufficiently familiar with these two key psychometric properties to appreciate the technical discussion on the various inventories and assessment methods adequately. Graduate training programs in clinical psychology, counseling psychology, and family psychology are likely to require formal instruction and experience in assessment that addresses psychometric issues. However, other graduate programs, such as marital and family therapy training programs, are less likely to emphasize these concepts. Accordingly, a brief overview of the concepts of reliability will be given as well as descriptions and illustrations of various types of each.

Reliability

Reliability is the extent to which a test or any assessment procedure yields the same result when repeated. In other words, reliability is the consistency of a measurement or the degree to which an instrument or assessment device measures the same way each time it is used under the same condition with the same individual (Bolarinwa, 2015). A measure is considered reliable if an individual's scores on the same test given twice are similar. Technically speaking, reliability is not measured but is estimated and represented as a correlation coefficient. The higher the reliability coefficient is, the more confidence one can have in the score. Reliability coefficients at or above .70 are considered adequate; those at or above .80 are considered good; those at .90 or above are considered excellent (Hambleton & Zaal, 1991). Three types of reliability can be described: test–retest, internal consistency, and interrater reliability.

- *Test–retest reliability*—the agreement of assessment measures over time. To determine it, a measure or test is repeated on the same individuals at a future date. Results are compared and correlated with the initial test to give a measure of stability. The Spearman–Brown formula is used for calculating this estimate of reliability.

- *Internal consistency*—the extent to which tests or procedures assess the same characteristic, skill, or quality. It is a measure of the precision between the observers or of the measuring instruments used in a study. This type of reliability often helps clinicians and researchers interpret data and predict the value of scores and the limits of the relationship among variables. For example, the McMaster Family Assessment Device (FAD) is a questionnaire to evaluate families in terms of seven functions including communication patterns. Analyzing the internal consistency of the FAD items on the Communications subscale reveals the extent to which items on this family assessment device actually reflect communication patterns among family members. The internal consistency of a test can be computed in different ways.
- *Split-half reliability*—a measure of internal consistency derived by correlating responses on half the test with responses to the other half.
- *Cronbach's alpha*—another, more sophisticated method. This method divides items on an instrument or measure and computes correlation values for them. Cronbach's alpha is a correlation coefficient, and the closer it is to one, the higher the reliability estimate of the assessment device.
- *Kuder-Richardson coefficient*—another means of estimating internal consistency. It is used for instruments or measures that involve dichotomous responses or items, such as yes/no, while Cronbach's alpha is used with Likert-scale types of responses or items. Finally, it should be noted that the primary difference between test–retest and internal consistency estimates of reliability is that test–retest involves two administrations of the measure or instrument, whereas internal consistency methods involve only a single administration of the instrument.
- *Interrater reliability*—the extent to which two or more individuals (raters) agree. Interrater reliability addresses the consistency of the implementation of a rating system. For example, interrater reliability can be established in the following scenario: Two clinical supervisors are observing the same family being treated by a counseling intern through a two-way mirror. As part of the observation, each supervisor independently rates the family's functioning on the GARF Scale. One supervisor rates the family at 62 and the other at 64 (on the 1- to 100-point scale). Because interrater reliability is dependent on the ability of two or more observers to be consistent, it could be said that interrater reliability is very high in this instance.

Validity

Validity refers to the ability of an assessment device or method to measure what it is intended to measure. Whereas reliability is concerned with the accuracy of the assessment device or procedure, validity is concerned with the study's success at measuring what the researchers set out to measure. Five types of validity can be described:

- *Face validity*—concerned with how a measure or procedure appears. Does it seem like a reasonable way to gain the information? Does it seem to be well designed? Does it seem as though it will work reliably? Unlike content validity, face validity does not depend on established theories for support (Fink, 1995).

- *Criterion-related validity*, or criterion-referenced validity—used to demonstrate the accuracy of a measure or procedure by comparing it with another measure or procedure previously demonstrated to be valid. For example, a paper-and-pencil test of family functioning, the SFI, appears to measure the same family dynamics and functioning as does a related observational assessment, the BIS. By comparing the scores of family members' self-report of family functioning with the therapist's observational ratings of family functioning, the SFI was validated by using a criterion-related strategy in which self-report scores were compared to the BIS ratings.

- *Construct validity*—seeks agreement between a theoretical concept and a specific measuring device or procedure. For example, a family researcher developing a new inventory for assessing marital intimacy might spend considerable time specifying the theoretical boundaries of the term *intimacy* and then operationally defining it with specific test items or a rating schema to achieve an acceptable level of construct validity.

- *Convergent validity* and *discriminate validity*—two subcategories of construct validity. Convergent validity is the actual general agreement among ratings, gathered independently of one another, whereas measures should be theoretically related. Discriminate validity is the lack of a relationship among measures that theoretically should not be related. To understand whether an assessment device has construct validity, three steps are followed. First, the theoretical relationships are specified. Next, the empirical relationships between the measures of the concepts are examined. Finally, the empirical evidence is interpreted in terms of how it clarifies the construct validity of the particular measure being tested (Carmines & Zeller, 1991, p. 23).

- *Content validity*—based on the extent to which a measurement reflects the specific intended domain of content (Carmines & Zeller, 1991, p. 20). Content validity can be illustrated using the following example: Family researchers attempting to measure a family structural dimension, such as adaptability, must decide what constitutes a relevant domain of content for that dimension. They may look for commonalities among several definitions of adaptability or use the Delphi technique or a similar strategy so that a consensus opinion or conceptualization of family adaptability from a group of recognized experts on the topic can be reached.

- *Predictive validity*—assesses the capacity of the instrument to forecast or predict future events, behavior, attitudes, or outcomes. It is assessed using correlation coefficient. In short, predictive validity is the ability of a test to measure some event or outcome in the future (Bolarinwa, 2015). An example of predictive validity is the use of the Adverse Childhood Experiences (ACE) Questionnaire to predict a child or adolescent's likely medical history and health care utilization in mid-life (Chartier, Walker, & Naimark, 2010).

Correlation coefficients can be derived for criterion-related and construct validity. Validity coefficients for assessment devices tend to be much lower than reliability coefficients. For example, validity coefficients for the MMPI-2 are about .30.

Note

1 Plan treatment and interventions based on these data and the conceptualization.

References

Bolarinwa, O. A. (2015). Principles and methods of validity and reliability testing of questionnaires used in social and health science researches. *Nigerian Postgraduate Medical Journal, 22*(4), 195–201.

Bray, J., & Stanton, M. (Eds.). (2010). *The Wiley-Blackwell handbook of family psychology.* Oxford, UK: Blackwell.

Carmines, E. G. & Zeller, R. A. (1991). *Reliability and validity assessment.* Newbury Park, CA: Sage Publications.

Carr, A. (2000). Editorial: Empirical approaches to family assessment. *Journal of Family Therapy, 22,* 121–127.

Chartier, M. J., Walker, J. R., & Naimark, B. (2010). Separate and cumulative effects of adverse childhood experiences in predicting adult health and health care utilization. *Child Abuse and Neglect, 34*(6), 454–464.

Corcoran, K. J., & Fischer, J. (2013). *Measures for clinical practice: A sourcebook. Volume 1: Couples, families, and children* (5th ed.). New York, NY: Oxford.

Epstein, N. B., Ryan, C. E., Bishop, D. S., Miller, I. W., & Keitner, G. I. (2003). The McMaster model: A view of healthy family functioning. In F. Walsh (Ed.), *Normal family processes* (3rd ed., pp. 581–607). New York, NY: Guilford Press.

Fink, A. (1995). *The survey handbook.* Thousand Oaks, CA: Sage Publications.

Goldman, L. (1992). Qualitative assessment: An approach for counselors. *Journal of Counseling & Development, 70,* 616–621.

Hambleton, R. K., Zaal, J. N., & Pieters, J. P. (1991). Computerized adaptive testing: Theory, applications, and standards. In *Advances in educational and psychological testing: Theory and applications* (pp. 341–366). New York, NY: Springer.

Kaslow, F. (Ed.). (1996). *Handbook of relational diagnosis and dysfunctional family patterns*. New York, NY: Wiley.

L'Abate, L., Ganahl, G., & Hansen, J. (1986). *Methods of family therapy*. Englewood Cliffs, NJ: Prentice Hall.

Lambert, M. (2010). *Prevention of treatment failure: The use of measuring, monitoring, and feedback in clinical practice*. Washington, DC: American Psychological Association.

Patterson, J., Williams, L., Edwards, T. M., Chamow, L., & Grauf-Grounds, C. (2018). *Essential skills in family therapy: From the first interview to termination* (3rd ed.). New York, NY: Guilford.

Sperry, L. (2010). *Core competencies in counseling and psychotherapy: Becoming a highly competent and effective therapist*. New York, NY: Routledge.

Thomlison, B. (2016). *Family assessment handbook: An introductory practice guide to family assessment* (4th ed.). Boston, MA: Cengage.

Williams, L., Patterson, J., & Edwards, T. M. (2014). *Research methods in family therapy: Foundations of evidence-based practice*. New York, NY: Guilford.

Yingling, L., Miller, W., McDonald, A., & Galwaler, S. (1998). *GARF assessment sourcebook: Using the DSM-IV global assessment of relational functioning*. Washington, DC: Brunner/Mazel.

2

ASSESSMENT AND CASE CONCEPTUALIZATION WITH COUPLES AND FAMILIES

Len Sperry

Effective, therapeutic work with families and couples begins with a comprehensive assessment and case conceptualization. Such an assessment may include the use of various assessment instruments, devices, and procedures. This chapter provides a context for the use of the assessment methods that are detailed in the chapters that follow. It focuses on two areas. The first involves a review of the common factors in the assessment of families and couples. These include presenting concerns, relational history, relational or interaction pattern, as well as strengths, explanations, and expectation for treatment. The second describes three types of case conceptualization: individual, couple, and family case conceptualizations for planning and implementing treatment.

Assessment

This section focuses on the assessment process in couple and family therapy. Key elements of this assessment are assessment of the family or couple's presenting problems or concerns, their relational history, relational dynamics, cultural dynamics, relational patterns, and couple strengths, their expectations for therapy, as well as their explanations of presenting concerns. Such a comprehensive assessment and family and couple assessment instruments, if they are utilized, are the basis for developing a family or couple case conceptualization.

Presenting Concerns

Assessment usually begins with presenting concerns of one or both partners or of one or more family members. Since these concerns are typically the reason for seeking treatment, one of the partners or family members is usually eager to disclose such concerns. The therapist does well to identify who and how these concerns affect that and the other partner or other family members (Taibbi, 2017). The goal is to encourage the engagement of all parties engaged in the process without uncontrolled emotional outbursts and blaming.

Relational History

Next, the history of the family or couple's relationship is addressed. In couple format, this is accomplished conjointly, whereas in a family treatment format, the information in the next several sections is best discussed in a separate session with the parents. For couples, eliciting families of origin information of the partners is useful. For families, a review of the milestones of the family's history can be valuable. Then, the assessment focuses on important system factors such as boundaries, power, and intimacy, as well as stressors, health, and financial issues, and level of social interest and cooperation. Eliciting the relationship history begins with questions such as How did you meet? What attracted you to each other? How did your dating go? How did you decide to formalize your relationship (marriage)? How did things go when you were first married? How have things changed since then?

Exploration of the couple's history or parent's history in relation to their families of origin can be very useful. It can explicate issues and bringing them into the therapy process. The genogram is a powerful tool for understanding the influence of a couple's families of origin, as well as providing feedback to the client about these dynamics. It is a simple, graphic way to trace the multi-generational influences on an individual or family's present-day functioning. It can easily highlight relational patterns that repeat themselves, particularly with regard to unresolved emotional issues. They can trace addiction history, patterns of divorce, abuse, and diseases within the family of origin. Additional information about influential life events, significant deaths in the family, and coalitions in the family of origin, which may be difficult to directly assess in an interview, are readily discussed in a genogram (McGoldrick, Gerson, & Petry, 2008). In the context of couples work, the therapist constructs a genogram of one partner and encourage the other partner to fill in information and make comments. Then the process is reversed

Relational Dynamics

A critical component of assessment involves relational dynamics in both couples and family work. This involves boundaries, power, and intimacy. To elicit information on structure or boundaries, as questions like: Who else is considered to be part of the couples system? What is being excluded from the couples or parent's relationship and assigned to children or others? Who and what events or things are intruding into the parent's or couple's relationship? For power, the therapist asks: Who is in charge? How do partners deal with power in their relationship? For intimacy, some questions are How near, how far, and how do the partners tolerate or respond to each other's needs and desires for intimate contact and closeness? How do partners use emotional and geographical distance when struggling with their need for closeness? Answers to such questions provide significant data for the therapist in assessing the couples system.

Cultural Dynamics

Assessment of the couple or parent subsystem wherein one or both partners or parents are from different cultures is also essential. It is important to include questions about the presenting problem and how the parents or partners view the problem from their unique cultural perspective. Ask both parents and partners about their roles within the home and within their family. Inquire about the role of each partner's family of origin, as influenced by their cultural norms. Other areas of assessment with culturally diverse parents or partners include a wide range of norms for the marriage relationship. The therapist should also inquire issues such as the usual age for men and women to marry within the partner's diversity group, expectations regarding husband/wife prior to and after marriage, and the basis for mate selection. Finally, inquire about each partner's understanding of their sexual relationship, and expectations for interaction with outsiders, including in-laws and extended family members (Bhugra & De Silva, 2000).

Parents or Partners Strengths and Resources

Now that history and dynamics have uncovered parent's or partner's concerns and issues, it is important to identify the strengths and resources that they possess to deal with these concerns and issues. This part of the assessment is crucial for tailoring treatment to the strengths of each partner and to the couple as a whole. Accordingly, the therapist would do well to assess the level of support, appropriate role models, emotional energy, and cognitive ability to make the kind of changes that are necessary. It is also important to identify their past successes and failures and each partner's sense of personal responsibility for the condition of the relationship. In addition, their level of readiness for change, resistance to treatment, and expectations for therapy are elicited.

Treatment Expectations

Effective therapists attend to the expectations that parents or partners have for therapy. Recent research treatment expectations of couples demonstrates the following. They expect to discuss problems, the events that led up to their problems' development, and the ways in which those problems impacted individual and couple functioning (Tambling & Johnson, 2010). They also expect to recover from their problems (Froude & Tambling, 2014). Accordingly, begin this inquiry by asking about what each partner expects from therapy.

Explanatory Model

Understanding the parent's or partner's explanation of their presenting problems is important because it provides the therapist with a client-focused context on how to approach discussions about the problems during the course of treatment (Froude & Tambling, 2014). These client explanations are referred to as the client's case conceptualization in contrast to the therapist's expectation (Sperry, 2010). Research on such explanations has considerable clinical value for therapists. Understanding such explanations provides the therapist with a client-centered context on how to approach discussions about the problems during the course of treatment. Furthermore, it suggests that most individuals explain their problems from an individualistic standpoint and they tend to internalize problems (Froude & Tambling, 2014).

Explanation or explanatory model is their "theory" or best guess for what is causing their presenting problems or personal or relational issue. It is akin to the therapist's case conceptualization (Sperry, 2010). Trainees are often surprised to learn that clients have come up with their own case conceptualizations. Because individuals are often aware of their conceptualization, therapists need to understand it since the greater it differs from the therapists' conceptualization, the more likely treatment will be negatively impacted. This can be manifested in many ways: tardiness or no-shows for appointment, failure to do homework, or even premature termination. Accordingly, the therapist would do well to elicit individual's explanatory model particularly since it often reflects their expectations for treatment. Then, after eliciting the explanatory model and sharing the therapist's case conceptualization, a mutually agreeable conceptualization can be negotiated (Sperry, 2010).

Individual Dynamics and Systems Dynamics

When working with couples and families, effective therapists focus on both individual and systems dynamics. A basic premise is that each partner's or member's behavior reflects their personal maladaptive pattern (Sperry, 2010). A second premise is that, irrespective of whether the client reports an individual symptom or a relational issue, it is embedded in the couples' systems dynamics and that the symptom or issue serves to maintain the homeostasis or sense of normalcy of the system (Gehart, 2010).

Assessment of Systemic Dynamics and Patterns

Virtually all couples and family therapy approaches involve the assessment of system dynamics particularly "relational interaction patterns" within the system (Gehart, 2017). Assessing this pattern involves identifying the problematic interaction pattern underlying the presenting problem. Usually, couples have one or two such patterns that are reflected in their presenting problem. The therapist traces such patterns by noting one partner's emotional and behavioral response and then the other partner's response until a sense normalcy. "Neither partner sees the mutually reinforcing pattern, nor if they do, it is seen as 'caused' by the other" (Gehart, 2017, p. 257). Assessment of such interaction patterns, along with the identification of each partner's own maladaptive pattern, is central to developing a couple case conceptualization and planning effective interventions.

Case Conceptualizations

This section introduces case conceptualization and its clinical value and utility. Then it describes the centrality of patterns in conceptualizing cases, as an introduction to discussing individual and couple case conceptualizations. Let's begin with a definition and description of their clinical value.

Case conceptualization is a method and strategy for obtaining and organizing information about a partner or couple, understanding and explaining maladaptive patterns, focusing treatment, anticipating treatment challenges and roadblocks, and preparing for termination (Sperry, 2010). In short, a case conceptualization reflects how a therapist thinks about, or conceptualizes, the clients' presenting problems and concerns. It informs all aspects of treatment, including who should attend sessions, the type of therapeutic relationship, and the choice of therapeutic interventions (Gehart, 2017)

Clinically useful and valuable case conceptualizations provide therapists with a coherent treatment strategy for planning and focusing treatment interventions to increase the likelihood of effecting change. They emphasize the unique context and the needs and resources that the individual or couple brings to treatment. Such case conceptualizations can be informed by a theoretical framework (e.g., CBT, Narrative, Solution-focused, etc.) or integrative approaches that incorporate biological, psychological, social, and cultural factors (Sperry, 2011).

At a minimum, clinically useful case conceptualization includes the client's presentation, precipitant, predisposition, pattern, and personality style. The presentation is the client's presenting problem, often a response to a precipitant that is congruent with the client's pattern. Presentation can include specific symptoms and their severity, personal and social functioning, medical and *Diagnostic and Statistical Manual of Mental Disorders* (DSM) diagnoses, as well as the history and course of symptoms. Precipitants include triggers that activate the client's pattern, leading to the presenting problem. These are antecedents to symptoms, upsetting thoughts, and problematic behaviors. The key to understanding this interaction between presentation and precipitant is identifying the client's maladaptive pattern, or consistent style of problematic thinking, feeling, and behaving. The predisposition refers to factors that foster and lead to either maladaptive or adaptive patterns. Biological, psychological, and social factors can all contribute to the predisposition. Finally, perpetuants are factors that maintain the presenting problem.

Many clinicians and researchers consider case conceptualization as one of the most challenging clinical competencies to master (Eells, 2010; Sperry & Sperry, 2012). The perceived difficulty in developing an effective case conceptualization may be one reason why many therapists neither develop nor use case conceptualizations or they lack confidence in their ability to conceptualize cases. My experience is that both experienced therapists and trainees can easily and confidently begin to master this competency in as little as 2–3 hours of formal training. The training approach involves learning an integrated model of case conceptualization based on common and distinctive elements; and that emphasizes the element of pattern, i.e., maladaptive pattern. A basic premise underlies this integrative model. It is that individuals unwittingly develop a self-perpetuating, maladaptive pattern of functioning and relating to others. Inevitably, this pattern underlies the individual's or couple's presenting issues. Effective treatment will involve a change process in which the client and therapist collaborate to identify this pattern, break it, and replace it with a more adaptive pattern. At least two outcomes result from this change process: increased well-being and resolution of the individual's or couple's presenting issues.

Centrality of Pattern

Central to the case conceptualization, whether it is a conceptualization of one partner or of the relationship itself, referred to as an individual case conceptualization or a couple case conceptualization, pattern is the central and defining feature. Pattern is defined as the predicable, consistent, and self-perpetuating style and manner in which individuals think, feel, act, cope, and defend themselves (Sperry, 2010). Patterns can either be maladaptive or adaptive. Patterns that are maladaptive tend to be inflexible, ineffective, and inappropriate and cause symptoms and impairment in personal and relational functioning, as well as chronic dissatisfaction. When a pattern is sufficiently distressing or impairing it can be diagnosed as a personality disorder. In contrast, an adaptive pattern reflects a personality style that is flexible, effective, and appropriate.

Effective individual therapy requires changing maladaptive patterns (Livesley, 2003). A critical part of this change is for clients to become adept at recognizing the patterns, particularly the maladaptive patterns, that overwhelmingly influence their lives. Clients readily accept the idea that there is a "pattern" underlying their behavior. The word is reassuring, for it suggests that there is order and meaning to behavior and experience. Educating clients about their patterns helps them to distance themselves from events, increases self-observation, and promotes "integration by connecting, events, behaviors, and experiences that were previously assumed to be unconnected" (Livesley, 2003, p. 274).

Individual Patterns

Individual partners are likely to bring longstanding problems and maladaptive patterns into their relationships. Their faulty thinking patterns and negative affective reactions can wreak havoc on partners' efforts to enjoy intimate contact and maintain a positive attachment with the other partner. These individual patterns inevitably reflect a partner's personality style or DSM, Fifth Edition (DSM-5) personality disorder.

Relational Patterns

Relational patterns, whether adaptive or maladaptive, tend to be learned by modelling well before the couples meet. Such patterns often reflect the relational patterns of the parents of both partners and appear to be part of the attraction process of the couple. Relational patterns evolve from the personality patterns of each partner. An effective case conceptualization specifies and explains how these factors operate and explains the couples' relationship.

These maladaptive patterns are evident in every aspect of the relationship: the amount of time spent together, the type of communication, amount, type, and timing of sexual intimacy, how problems and challenges are handled, etc. Not surprisingly, relational patterns have predictable outcomes.

Unfortunately, when fully operative, as in a major disagreement, these patterns can polarize partners so that the situation seems hopeless then when their differences are only a matter of degree. Or, they can protect and insulate the partners from getting too close to each other. Maladaptive relational patterns make the partners appear to be more incompatible than they might otherwise seem by polarizing the partners until they seem to represent opposite ends of the continuum of intimacy. Five different relational patterns are described below.

Individual Case Conceptualizations

The author advocates for developing and writing three case conceptualizations when working with couples: individual case conceptualizations for each partner and a couple case conceptualization for the relationship. At a minimum, clinically useful individual case conceptualization includes the personality style/disorder and maladaptive pattern of each partner. For example, a partner with an attention-getting pattern typically reflects a histrionic personality style or disorder. Similarly, a partner with overly conscientious and perfectionistic pattern usually reflects an obsessive compulsive personality style or disorder.

Couple Case Conceptualizations

While every therapeutic approach has its own unique method of case conceptualization, most approaches for working with couples involve relational interaction patterns as part of the couple case conceptualization. "Specifically, therapists focus on identifying the couple's interaction pattern related to the presenting problem. Typically, couples and families have one or two basic patterns of interaction that characterize the presenting problem" (Gehart, 2017, p. 256). Thus, the couple case conceptualization reflects and emphasizes the couple's relational pattern(s) and explains their presenting problem or concern with this pattern in the context of their relational history.

Each partner plays a role in their relationship, as each displays one or two habitual and cyclical patterns of relating that each has learned over time to cope. In the couples therapy literature, these patterns are referred to as couples interaction patterns or relational patterns (Christensen & Shenk, 1991). Because these patterns are central to couple case conceptualization, they are described in the case conceptualization section.

Couple relational interaction patterns are central to developing an effective couple case conceptualization. When the pattern is negative, the relationship is unable to grow and thrive. At best, that pattern allows the relationship to survive, at least for a while. Presumably, couples work can break and replace these patterns with more adaptive ones. Here are brief descriptions of five of the most common negative relational patterns and one positive pattern.

1. Demand/Withdraw

   This pattern develops when one partner blames, criticizes, or demands (*demand*) change from the other partner. In response, the other partner gives in, defers, surrenders or complies (*withdraw*). It is also known as the pursuer–distancer pattern and is the most common relational pattern (Christensen & Shenk, 1991). It is correlated with partner hostility and aggression, relationship dissatisfaction, and divorce. All other negative relational patterns are variants of this one.

2. Demand/Submit

This pattern develops when one partner blames, accrues, criticizes, or demands [*demand*] change from the other partner. In response, the other partner avoids, fails to respond, is defensive or silent, or essentially refuses to discuss the concern [*submit*]. While this is a relatively common interaction pattern, it has not received as much research attention as the Demand/Withdraw pattern (Knobloch-Fedders et al., 2014).

3. Withdraw/Withdraw

This pattern develops after a couple has exhausted the demand/withdraw pattern. Both partners are hesitant to engage emotionally and, in the face of conflict, both withdraw further. They feel hopeless over their situation and begin to give up. In these cases, the pursuer may be a "soft" pursuer who is hard to recognize because he or she does not show the overwhelming anxious energy seen in a lot of pursuers and who, despite being a pursuer, gives up easily. The other possibility, which is more common, involves a "burnt out" pursuer who has now given up reaching for the other partner. Withdrawal then can be the beginning of grieving and detaching from the relationship (Kasting, 2015).

4. Attack/Attack

This pattern involves a sequence in which an attack is responded to with an attack. Not surprisingly, this pattern results in an escalation of relational discord. The escalations are a variant of the demand/withdraw pattern. In response to the demanding partner [*attack*], the withdrawing partner becomes sufficiently provoked and erupts in anger [*attack*]. Following the fight, the withdrawer is likely to revert back to the withdrawing role until he or she feels sufficiently provoked again. This pattern is also referred to as the "high conflict couple" (Fruzzetti, 2006).

5. Reactive Demand/Withdraw

This pattern develops when a couple reverses a previous long-standing pattern. This occurs with a role change in one of the partners. For example, a demanding wife [*demand*] gradually gives up and limits her investment in the relationship. Increasingly, she withdraws and distances herself [*withdraw*]. Typically, her work-obsessed partner fails to notice this change. She may even leave the relationship. In this reactive pattern, the husband will frantically pursue the wife to prevent a separation. The withdrawing wife refuses to commit to the relationship. Then, the withdrawer takes on the demand role and aggressively pursues his wife. In short, this is a reversal of their previous long-standing pattern of her demanding and his withdrawing.

6. Constructive Engagement

This pattern develops as partners express issues that bother them in a "non-attacking way that accurately reflects what they feel, think, or want, including accurate expression of primary emotions. The other partner listens, brings curiosity, tries to understand, and communicates understanding, even if he or she disagrees" (Fruzzetti & Payne, 2015, p. 609). This pattern fosters problem-solving and validation. It requires that both partners are aware of their emotions and wants and effectively regulate their emotions.

Family Case Conceptualizations

A family case conceptualization is one that incorporates family system dynamics. As with an individual case conceptualization, a useful family case conceptualization focuses "on the unique contexts, needs, and resources of the individual family members and the system as a whole" (Bitter, 2009, p. 374). It should describe the relational interactions of the family. Over the past 40 years, research and clinical experience with the Beavers Systems Model of Family Functioning (Beavers, 1981; Hampson & Beavers, 2012) has demonstrated its value in conceptualizing the relational patterns in families.

This model nicely conceptualizes family relational patterns in terms of family competence and family style, its two main dimensions. The competence dimension consists of five levels of relational functionality ranging from highly effective to severely dysfunctional. The levels are as follows: optimal, adequate, midrange, borderline, and severely dysfunctional. The style dimension ranges from centripetal (characterized by clinging and internalizing) to centrifugal (characterized by attacking, demanding, and externalizing) in families that are lower functioning than the optimal and adequate types. When these two dimensions are combined, they result in nine distinct family types of which the last six are sufficiently problematic to require clinical intervention.

1. Optimal Families
   Their relational functioning is highly effective. Members are aware of multiple influences on each other's' behavior and reciprocity. They have the capacity to solve family problems easily using different approaches, and they seek and usually achieve intimacy. Parents share power flexibly, and boundaries between members are clear and respected. Whenever conflict arises, it tends to be resolved quickly.
2. Adequate Families
   Their relational functioning is moderately effective. Parents strive for overt power, are less able to feel intimate and trusting, and less spontaneous and happy. Children seem to be as capable as those from optimal families. Members experience pain and some loneliness for which they are usually able to cope sufficiently.

3. Midrange Centripetal Families

   Their relational functioning is somewhat impaired. They use direct control, repress hostility, but can express caring. Rules and authority are emphasized while spontaneity is diminished. They work hard, keep their pain inconspicuous to their neighbors, develop transference nicely, and pay their bills.

4. Midrange Centrifugal Families

   Their relational functioning is somewhat impaired. They use indirect control, manipulation, intimidation, and blame but seldom express warmth. Members have difficulty with and contempt for authority in the home and outside. Parents spend little time at home and children move into neighborhoods and streets much earlier than the norm.

5. Midrange Mixed Families

   Their relational functioning is somewhat impaired. They have alternating and conflicting centripetal and centrifugal behavior. In this mixed group, the parental coalition typically varies in one interview from dominance/submission to petty bickering and blaming; the children alternate between accepting and resisting parental control.

6. Borderline Centripetal Families

   Relational functioning is moderately impaired. Their chaos is more verbal than behavioral, and control battles are intense but usually covert. Open rebellion or covertly expressed rage is not expected, that is, not within the family rules. Severely obsessional and anorectic patients may sometimes be found in these families.

7. Borderline Centrifugal Families

   Relational functioning is moderately impaired. They are much more open in the expression of anger. The parental relationship is non-supportive and stormy battles occur regularly. Children learn to manipulate their parents. They sometimes receive the diagnosis of borderline personality disorder.

8. Severely Dysfunctional Centrifugal Families

   Relational functioning is severely impaired. They are seen as strange by neighbors. Parental rules and expectations are often unclear and ambivalence is denied. Children are seriously limited in finding their own individuality and functioning independently. A schizophrenic break is one way of solving this dilemma.

9. Severely Dysfunctional Centripetal Families

   Relational functioning is severely impaired. Interactions are characterized by open hostility and contempt. Parents seldom provide nurturing and tenderness. Instead ambivalence is denied, and negative feelings are expected. Children's development is emotionally and relationally stunted, resulting in antisocial personality. Child abuse, sexual deviance and drug abuse are common.

Concluding Comment

The purpose of this chapter was a theoretical context for the use of the family assessment methods that are detailed in the chapters that follow. It first reviewed the common elements in the assessment of families and couple including presenting concerns, relational history, relational or interaction pattern, as well as strengths, explanations, and expectation for treatment. It then described and differentiated individual, couple, and family case conceptualization. All these elements are essential in the selection and use of family assessment instruments as part of the assessment-case conceptualization process.

References

Beavers, W. R. (1981). A systems model of family for family therapists. *Journal of Marital and Family Therapy, 7*(4), 299–307.

Bhugra, D., & De Silva, P. (2000). Couple therapy across cultures. *Sexual and Relationship Therapy, 15*(2), 183–192.

Bitter, J. (2009). *Theory and practice of family therapy and counseling*. Belmont, CA: Brooks/Cole.

Christensen, A., & Shenk, J. (1991). Communication, conflict, and psychological distance in nondistressed, clinic, and divorcing couples. *Journal of Consulting and Clinical Psychology, 59*(3), 458–463.

Eells, T. D. (2010). The unfolding case formulation: The interplay of description and inference. *Pragmatic Case Studies in Psychotherapy, 6*(4), 225–254.

Froude, C., & Tambling, R. (2014). Couples' conceptualizations of problems in couple therapy. *The Qualitative Report, 19*(13), 1–19.

Fruzzetti, A. (2006). *The high-conflict couple: A dialectical behavior therapy guide to finding peace, intimacy, and validation*. Oakland, CA: New Harbinger Publications.

Fruzzetti, A., & Payne, L. (2015). Couple therapy and borderline personality disorder. In A. Gurman, J. Lebow, & D. Snyder (Eds.), *Clinical handbook of couple therapy* (5th ed., pp. 606–434). New York, NY: Guilford.

Gehart, D. (2010). *Mastering competencies in family therapy*. Belmont, CA: Brooks/Cole.

Gehart, D. (2017). Clinical case conceptualization with couples and families. In J. Carlson & S. Dermer (Eds.), *The SAGE encyclopedia of marriage, family, and couples counseling* (pp. 256–260). Thousand Oaks, CA: Sage Publications.

Hampson, R. B., & Beavers, W. R. (2012). Observational assessment. In L. Sperry (Ed.). *Family assessment: Contemporary and cutting-edge strategies* (pp. 83–114). New York, NY: Routledge.

Kasting, A. (2015). Withdraw-withdraw pattern. University of Tennessee. Retrieved from https://relationshiprx.utk.edu/2015/05/19/withdraw-withdraw-pattern/

Knobloch-Fedders, L. M., Critchfield, K. L., Boisson, T., Woods, N., Bitman, R., & Durbin, C. E. (2014). Depression, relationship quality, and couples' demand/withdraw and demand/submit sequential interactions. *Journal of Counseling Psychology, 61*(2), 264–279.

Livesley, W. (2003). *Practical management of personality disorder*. New York, NY: Guilford.

McGoldrick, M., Gerson, R., & Petry, S. (2008). *Genograms: Assessment and intervention.* New York, NY: Norton.

Sperry, L. (2010). *Core competencies in counseling and psychotherapy: Becoming a highly competent and effective therapist.* New York, NY: Routledge.

Sperry, L., & Sperry, J. (2012). *Case conceptualization: Mastering this competency with ease and confidence.* New York, NY: Routledge.

Taibbi, R. (2017). *Doing couple therapy: Craft and creativity in work with intimate partners.* New York, NY: Guilford.

Tambling, R. B., & Johnson, L. N. (2010). Client expectations about couple therapy. *The American Journal of Family Therapy, 38,* 322–333.

3

QUALITATIVE STRATEGIES IN COUPLE AND FAMILY ASSESSMENT

Maureen Duffy and Ronald J. Chenail

The most significant development in the past ten years affecting couples and family therapists, and health care in general, has been the rapidly growing momentum of the evidence-based practice movement. Interestingly, the rise of evidence-based practice has happened at the same time as the traditional hierarchical relationships between health care providers and patients have yielded to more collaborative relationships. During the same time health care providers, including couples and family therapists, have found themselves increasingly accountable to administrative requirements to demonstrate that their practice is evidence-based (Gabbay & Le May, 2011).

The influence of the evidence-based practice movement has generated professional and policy discussions that have focused on questions of meaning within the movement and that have challenged narrow understandings of evidence-based practice as representing only the results of formal scientific research, in particular, randomized controlled trials. As a result of these conversations, a fuller understanding of evidence-based practice now includes not only formal scientific research evidence, but also the evidence gleaned from clinical practice, with both kinds of evidence being subjected to ongoing individual and community professional conversation and evaluation (Gabbay & Le May, 2011; Lemieux-Charles & Champagne, 2008). Both low context scientific evidence and high context practice evidence are needed to provide quality care.

Evidence-based practice, which includes practice-based evidence, is about generating, making sense of, and utilizing knowledge that is of high quality and that has the greatest likelihood of helping consumers to obtain positive, desired outcomes for their routine and crisis healthcare needs. The couples and family assessments that are detailed in this chapter outline ways that skilled and conscientious couples and family therapists can utilize qualitative assessments to generate and apply high context evidence needed to gather critical information about their clients, make sense of that information in collaboration with their clients, and use the information to develop effective collaborative interventions grounded in practice-based evidence.

While culture has always been an important focus of qualitative assessment and research, recent global political developments have placed issues of migration and immigration in high relief. Movements of people and the cultural heritages that they bring with them to new countries are important factors that must be addressed in couple and family assessment. Likewise, assessing strengths, coping skills, and resilience are important for all couple and family assessment but take on vital significance when considering issues of migration and immigration. Therefore, we have added two qualitative assessments focusing on (1) cultural formulation and (2) emotion mapping that can help address current challenges which clinicians are likely to face in our present social environment.

Use of qualitative assessments in couples and family therapy provides many of the same advantages that qualitative research provides in human science inquiry. Qualitative strategies are flexible and nonreductionist, focused on meaning and on understanding and interpretation of experience and relationships. The complexity and multiple perspectives present in couples and family therapy provide rich opportunities for the clinician interested in qualitative assessment to represent family members' thoughts, actions, interactions, conversations, realities, motivations, beliefs, and lives in terms of words, figures, pictures, diagrams, matrices, drawings, observations, and stories. Qualitative assessment strategies span the continuum from noninterventive, observational strategies to interventive, prescribed activities and tasks. The clinician can make qualitative diagnostic assessments single-handedly or, more commonly, can include the couple or family in a collaborative process of assessment (Jordan & Franklin, 2011). This chapter will present a number of clinically useful qualitative assessment strategies and provide detailed descriptions of each method and clear procedures for its use, interpretation, and evaluation.

Observational Strategies

Observing Structure, Hierarchy, and Interactions

Qualitative assessment name. Observing structure, hierarchy, and interactions is grounded in the work of Salvador Minuchin, who developed the structural model of family therapy, and Jay Haley, who developed the strategic model of family therapy. Minuchin and Haley are considered founders of family therapy and began to publish their work in the 1960s and 1970s.

Type of assessment. This is an observational assessment of family structure and organization, hierarchy, family subsystems, boundaries, coalitions, and alliances.

Use–target audience. This strategy is particularly suitable for family groups, including multigenerational families; it may also be used with couples and parts or subsystems of families.

Multicultural. Observation of structural, hierarchical, and interactional patterns of particular couples and families encourages therapist attention to the culturally specific and unique aspects of each couple and family.

Ease and time of administration. This strategy requires therapist understanding of the theoretical concepts underlying the observation; observation is continuous over the course of treatment. The therapist need not identify primarily as a structural or strategic family therapist to find these observations useful.

Scoring procedure. Scoring comprises clinical judgment and decisions based on observations.

Reliability/validity. Trustworthiness of structural/strategic model-based observations has been established by use over time. Outcome effectiveness has been scientifically validated by National Institute on Drug Abuse (NIDA) grant-supported work of Jose Szapocznik (Szapocznik & Coatsworth, 1999) and Howard Liddle (Liddle & Dakoff, 1995) at the University of Miami with drug-abusing adolescents.

Availability and source. For detailed information, see the works of Salvador Minuchin, Jay Haley, Charles Fishman, Harry Aponte, Cloe Madanes, and James Keim. Selected references include Aponte (1994); Haley (1991); Madanes, Keim, and Smessler (1995); Minuchin and Fishman (1981); and Minuchin, Lee, and Simon (1996).

Comment. One of the significant contributions of the structural/strategic models is the emphasis on observation and assessment of truly interactional sequences and phenomena as opposed to the observation and assessment of individual affect and behavior. Assessments, interventions, and outcomes based on the structural/strategic models are among the most widely researched of the systemic approaches.

Conducting and Utilizing Observational Assessment of Structure, Hierarchy, and Interactions

Assessment of family or couple structure, hierarchy, and interactions is begun at the initial clinical interview and continues throughout therapy. This form of assessment is used to conceptualize the case, to develop appropriate interventions, and, during the termination phase of therapy, to evaluate clinical outcome and effectiveness. Assessment of structure, hierarchy, and interactions is integrated within the therapeutic process. No formal and separate assessment phase is used in this method. Much of the structure, hierarchy, and interactional patterns can be observed from how family members respond to clinical questions and interact together during the session. The therapist may also need to ask the couple or family particular questions related to the following indicators if additional information is required to make a fuller assessment.

The structure of a family refers to the members of the couple or family, including extended family members, and their patterns of interaction, closeness, distance, conflict, conflict management, expressions of affect, problem-solving style, and rules and regulations (whether covert or overt) that govern their ways of relating to one another. The therapist assesses the family's structure by observing and assessing the following indicators:

- who sits close to whom and who sits furthest away from whom
- who initiates conversation about key family issues and who remains quiet
- who speaks spontaneously and who speaks only when spoken to
- who identifies the problem or goals for the therapy
- who agrees and who disagrees with the identified problem or goals
- what topics are permitted to be spoken about and who is allowed to talk about or comment on them; what topics seem to be off-limits for family members to discuss
- who can interrupt or disagree and who cannot
- how emotion is expressed and responded to by various family members
- whose opinion counts most and whose does not; who attempts to solve problems and who is less involved
- who is effective and competent at handling particular family tasks and who seems less effective
- who teams up with whom to get something done or to take a position

Carefully observing and assessing these indicators will provide the couple and family therapist with a wealth of interactional information about the family's structure and boundaries between individual members as well as subsystems within the family. This information can then be utilized to develop appropriate systemic interventions and treatment plans.

Hierarchy is a concept related to the concept of family structure but is important to consider and observe specifically because of its connection to issues of power, decision-making, and roles within a couple or family. The therapist assesses hierarchy and other interactional patterns within the family by carefully attending to the following:

- who is in charge of which activities and functions within the couple or family
- who is in charge of discipline and who is in charge of fun

- who can make independent decisions and who must be consulted
- who has veto power over important decisions
- how family roles are tied to traditional gender roles
- who gets nurtured and by whom; who gets less nurturing from other family members

---

Case Example

Janice and Tom were parents of two small children, a four-year-old boy, Billy, and an eight-month-old girl who had just started sleeping through the night. Janice and Tom complained of being chronically exhausted and frazzled. They were up most nights because Billy would not stay in his bedroom at night and routinely came into their room, fidgeting and crying, shortly after they attempted to go to bed. During the initial family therapy session, the therapist observed the parents' weak and ineffectual attempts to manage Billy's demands for attention. Billy repeatedly interrupted conversation between the therapist and Billy's parents by whining or by persistently asking them to play with the toys he had brought with him to the session. Billy's parents tried to pacify him without clearly telling him to be quiet and entertain himself. In the same way, Billy's parents felt powerless and expressed disagreement over how to handle the increasingly intolerable nighttime situation. Their only point of agreement was that they disagreed with their pediatrician's suggestion to lock Billy in his room at night.

The therapist was able to support Billy's parents in their efforts to take charge of the situation and clearly enforce the "must stay in your own bed rule." The therapist also encouraged Janice and Tom to develop a variety of ways of taking charge—learning how to take charge by being firm and consistent and also learning how to take charge by being playful and comforting.

Summary

Since the development of the structural and strategic models of family therapy, multiple new theories and models of couple and family therapy have been developed. However, the relational assessment of a couple or family's structure, hierarchy, and patterns of interaction remains a cornerstone of sound systemic work and can enhance case conceptualization and treatment planning by therapists practicing from many different systemic models. It is significant that clinical research has established the success of structural/strategic assessment and intervention with adolescent drug abusers—a large population that is difficult to treat.

Interviewing

Diagnostic Interviewing

Qualitative assessment name. Diagnostic interviewing refers to the general method of interviewing clients within a framework of pre-existing criteria that will then be used to make clinical assessments. In individual therapy, interviewing from within the framework of the *Diagnostic and Statistical Manual of Mental Disorders, Fifth Edition* (DSM-V) to arrive at a clinical diagnosis is an example of diagnostic interviewing. In couples and family therapy, diagnostic interviewing is used to identify areas that couples or family members experience as problematic and as sources of strength. Identifying psychopathology of an individual member of the couple or family may be a part of the diagnostic interviewing process, if, in the judgment of the clinician, the presence of individual psychopathology is compounding the relational problems.

Type of assessment. This interview format is open ended. In diagnostic interviewing for couples, the following interpersonal domains are explored in order to arrive at a clinical diagnosis of the relational problems: Commitment to the Relationship, Emotional Expressiveness, Sexual Functioning, Development of Shared Goals and Aspirations, Gender Roles and/or Role Functioning, Communication Skills and Styles, Perceptions of Intimacy, and Conflict Management. In diagnostic interviewing for families, these domains are explored: Goal Setting, Hierarchy and Distribution of Power, Boundaries, Problem-Solving Skills, Role Functioning, Emotional Expressiveness and Responsiveness, Communications Skills and Styles, Social Support, and Conflict Management.

Use–target audience. Couples and families are the target audience.

Multicultural. The therapist bears the responsibility for ensuring that the interview is conducted in a multiculturally sensitive way.

Ease and time of administration. In most couples and family therapy, initial diagnostic interviews take between 1 and 2 hours. Additional sessions are scheduled as needed. Keep in mind that many family therapists purposefully do not make a clear distinction between "diagnosis" and "intervention."

Scoring procedure. Responses to the interview questions are compared to the criteria used by the therapist and a qualitative clinical assessment is then made. The assessment may be in the form of a problem description, a resource or strength description, and/or a score on the Global Assessment of Relational Functioning (GARF) Scale (American Psychiatric Association, 2000).

Reliability/validity. The particular diagnostic framework used by the clinician determines these. The diagnostic interviewing work with couples of John Gottman (1999a, 1999b), for example, is based on rigorous empirical study and has resulted in a reliable model identifying couple behaviors predictive of marriages that fail or those that succeed.

Availability and source. Resources for diagnostic interviewing are ordinarily found in the theoretical literature describing a particular family therapy approach. Additional excellent resources to enhance diagnostic interviewing are also available, among them are the works of Atkinson (1999), Carlson and Sperry (1997), and Gottman (1999a, 1999b).

Comment. Diagnostic interviewing requires the therapist to clearly think through and articulate the theoretical framework within which he or she is working.

Utilizing Diagnostic Interviewing with Couples

The sample interview questions included here are based on the work of Gottman (1999a) and Atkinson (1999). The first set of questions is designed to assess the commitment of each partner to the marriage and the strength of the marital bond. The second set is designed to assess the couple's management of conflict and the presence of behaviors predictive of marital failure.

These samples are broad-based general questions that, in practice, would need to be broken down into smaller questions focusing on particular aspects of the general theme. These questions should be asked in a conjoint session.

Commitment and Strength of Marital Bond Questions:

- Does your partner know what your hopes and dreams are for your marriage?
- Do you have a shared set of hopes and dreams that you can talk about or do you think that your hopes and dreams for your relationship are different from one another?
- Do you know your partner's pet peeves, current interests and hobbies, likes and dislikes?
- Does your partner know what you are most worried about now?
- Does your partner know how things are going for you at work and what challenges you experience there?
- What memories from the past and experiences from the present do you have that are closest to your image of what being together in a good way is like?
- When your partner wants to make you happy or laugh, what kinds of things is he or she likely to do?

These questions are important because they provide information about the commitment to the relationship, each partner's level of awareness of the other's internal world, and whether the couple has a shared vision for who they are together and for their future. Shared vision, friendship and reliance upon the other, and awareness of the other's thoughts and feelings are predictive of marital success.

Conflict Management Questions:

- Can you describe what happens (what you say and do and how you feel) when you get into a disagreement?
- What do you see your partner saying and doing and how do you imagine he or she is feeling?
- How do you try to resolve arguments or problems once they have come up?
- What behaviors (include verbal and physical behaviors) of your partner hurt or upset you most?
- Do both of you try to resolve problems once they have come up or does one of you wind up doing more than the other to fix things?
- Do you feel that your partner values your opinions about things?
- If you have an idea about solving a problem or doing something differently in your relationship, is your partner open to hearing and trying out your suggestion or advice?

These questions are also important because they reveal how a couple fights and makes efforts to repair the relationship after the fight. They also reveal the presence of what Gottman (1999a, 1999b) calls the "four horsemen of the apocalypse," namely, criticism, defensiveness, contempt, and stonewalling. Contempt is the behavior in marriage most definitively predictive of marital failure, and Gottman clearly identifies it as a form of abuse that must not be empathized with but that must be named as abusive and stopped.

Case Example

Wanda wanted the racy new Infiniti that she was crazy about. She loved it and knew that a lot of people called it the sexiest car on the face of the earth. Craig was very uncomfortable with the idea, complaining that they did not have $50,000 to spend on a car and repeatedly asked her in a mocking kind of way who she was trying to impress and attract. Wanda countered that "you only live once" and they would manage to pay for the car somehow. She was outgoing, a little flamboyant, and loved beautiful clothes, furnishings, and cars that were a little out of reach, financially. Craig grew up with the injunction not to "make a show of yourself or stand out." Wanda's desire for the car was highly symbolic for Craig in terms of their sexual functioning, financial goals, and as a challenge to the values of his family of origin.

In this case, the therapist could actively help each partner to understand the internal world of the other around the issue of the car by asking each to reflect upon and share what meanings buying that car would hold for each, including exploring Craig's fears and insecurities and Wanda's needs and desires that she was seeing the car as fulfilling. This kind of therapeutic conversation would address what is at stake for each partner in the marriage in this situation and help unfold the maps of each one's internal world, thus making these maps more available to the other. Additionally, the therapist would directly address Craig's derisive behavior by naming it as contempt, explain the research findings on contempt, and strongly suggest that Craig discontinue any practices of contempt. The therapist would point out that Craig had already expressed his admiration for Wanda in many ways to which he could reconnect and also help Craig learn ways of expressing a different point of view clearly without resorting to insults.

Summary

Diagnostic interviewing is a theoretically driven method of obtaining information from client couples and families in order to arrive at a clinical description of the client's problems and strengths. This information forms the basis for developing targeted interventions that utilize the client's resources to manage problems differently in a more effective and satisfying way.

Interventive Interviewing

Qualitative assessment name. Interventive interviewing is based on the idea that any relationship or involvement is interventive in that it changes the system. Interventive interviewing refers to the use of a variety of categories of questions designed not only to obtain information for assessment but also to initiate therapeutic change simultaneously. The categories of questions include circular questions (Fleuridas, Nelson, & Rosenthal, 1986), reflexive questions (Tomm, 1987a, 1987b, 1988), solution-focused questions (Berg & De Jong, 1996; de Shazer, 1988), and narrative questions (White & Epston, 1990). The Milan Group introduced the idea of circular questioning and Tomm introduced the phrase "interventive interviewing."

Type of assessment. The interview format is open ended.

Use–target audience. Individuals, couples, and families are the target audience.

Multicultural. Interventive interviewing is multiculturally respectful because it elicits information unique to the client's culture and worldview and makes no normative presuppositions.

Ease and time of administration. This interviewing method requires theoretical understanding of interventive interviewing and skill in question construction.

Scoring procedure. No formal scoring is done; "scores" are clients' responses to interventive questions that trigger changes in perception and/or behavior.

Reliability/validity. These are determined by trustworthiness demonstrated pragmatically through clinical effectiveness of technique over time.

Availability and source. An excellent "primer" on the use of circular questioning is the article by Fleuridas, Nelson, and Rosenthal (1986). Tomm's (1987a, 1987b, 1988). *Family Process* series on interventive interviewing is the landmark articulation of the method and rationale.

Comment. Interventive interviewing has changed the landscape of family therapy by operationalizing the second-order cybernetics view (von Foerster, 1981), namely, that one is part of the system that one observes or "assesses" and changes the system by virtue of doing so.

Utilizing Interventive Interviewing with Couples and Families

Interventive interviewing with couples and families is marked by the therapist's reliance on the question rather than on the statement, on the interrogative form rather than on the declarative form. Statements communicate the worldview and preferences of the therapist, but questions invite clients to reflect on their experiences and to communicate their worldviews. Questions are seen as having the potential for triggering client change by inviting clients to see things differently within the context of the interaction between therapist and client. Interventive questions are non-blaming questions that invite clients to reflect on their beliefs, feelings, and behaviors, thus freeing them to think about themselves and their relationships with others in less defensive, more exploratory ways. Questions, framed nonjudgmentally, also have the potential for increasing clients' awareness of and concern for the other. The major categories of interventive questions are circular questions, reflexive questions, solution-focused questions, and narrative questions.

Circular questions. In contrast to linear questions, circular questions focus on the relationships among persons and among the beliefs and views held by an individual person. Linear questions assume a sequence of actions, such as cause and effect. The question "Why are you so angry?" is a good example of a linear question because it presumes that there is a knowable cause for the anger that the cause precedes in time. Examples of circular questions are "How does your partner begin to reconnect with you when you have been arguing with each other?" or "When you get upset and raise your voice, which of your children seems to be most concerned and which seems to be least concerned?" or "How do they know that you have cooled down?" Circular questions invite clients to reflect on the relational effects of their thinking and acting. Such questions shift the client's view from that of actor to that of observer, from first or second person ("I" or "you") to third person ("he," "she," or "they"), bringing the presence of the other into much greater focus.

Reflexive questions. Reflexivity refers to a blurring between subject and object, self and other. It is the presence of the observer in all description. For example, assigning a *DSM, Fifth Edition* (DSM-5) diagnosis results in a particular description of a client, but it also reveals that the diagnostician has some alignment with the assumptions and theories supporting the DSM-5. Reflexive questions invite clients to think about how they experience and describe themselves, how they present themselves to others, how others perceive them, what a change would mean to their lives and relationships, and how that change might be accomplished. Because reflexive questions are relational, they are also circular, but Tomm (1987b) distinguishes reflexive questions from circular questions by suggesting that "reflexive questioning focuses more heavily on an explicit recognition of the autonomy of the family in determining the outcome" (p. 182).

Examples of reflexive questions are "In the midst of the monumental job of caring for your dying adult son, how are you maintaining your own sense of balance so that you can continue to be there for him?" and "In that so much of what you are saying to your son is said by your being there for him now, what things would upset you if you did not get to say them to him in words before he died?" and "Even if it never happens, what conversation do you imagine would be most helpful for your son's father to have now so that after your son's death his father would be less angry and less hurt?" These questions are gently suggestive of possible alternatives for action and reflection for the family to consider.

Solution-focused questions. Solution-focused questions play to the strength and resilience side of the court and are grounded in the postmodern constructivist view of knowledge. This view holds that individuals bring forth knowledge by their language practices and that western language practices are predominantly problem-focused. As a result of problem-saturated talk, the strengths and solutions to problems that people utilize in their daily lives go unnoticed and are not brought forth in language to the same extent that problems are. Solution-focused questions are designed to bring forth exceptions to problem saturation and to emphasize competence, resilience, and strength.

Several categories of solution-focused questions exist:

- *Pre-session change questions*—ask what differences occurred between the time the appointment was set and the first session, capitalizing on the hope and positive change that often occur before the first session.
- *Exception questions*—ask about when the problem is less intense or less of a concern for the client or when it could have occurred but did not.

- *Miracle questions*—ask clients to describe how they would know the problem was not there anymore if they went to sleep and a miracle happened and the problem went away—but they did not know that the miracle had happened because they were sleeping. This question encourages clients to focus, in a detailed and specific way, on how life would be different in the absence of the problem and how they would be feeling and living differently.
- *Scaling questions*—ask clients to consider how they would know they had made some progress from baseline toward their goals and what they would need to do to move another point or half point forward. The scaling question breaks goals down into manageable, realistic steps.
- *Coping questions*—ask how clients have been able to do what they have done, emphasizing the strength and dignity in surviving and managing life's hardships and obstacles.

Narrative questions. Narrative questions are rooted in the metaphor of the story and are designed to help clients represent their lives, relationships, and life experiences as part of an expanding and richer narrative or storyline. The work of White and Epston (1990) has been pivotal in providing family therapists with a theoretical framework and question construction guidelines to develop narrative practices. White and Epston drew from French philosopher Michel Foucault's analysis of knowledge in which persons were seen as being recruited into particular ways of thinking about the world and themselves and then measuring themselves and their lives against this dominant view. An example of a dominant discourse is the contemporary western representation of female beauty as young, thin, and unblemished. This dominant discourse provides an unyielding and agonizing standard against which young girls and women measure themselves and find themselves wanting.

Narrative questions help clients to reflect on their unwitting participation in this dominant discourse and to separate themselves from it. Clients are encouraged, through narrative questions, to think about their lives and relationships differently and to develop their own preferred stories and accounts of their life and relationships. Dominant narratives box people in. Narrative questions can be seen as a form of protest against the anonymous but powerful requirements of collective social knowledge and as an opportunity for clients to free themselves from the restrictions of such knowledge. Examples of narrative questions are "What does being a 'good enough' mother as opposed to a 'perfect' mother mean for you?" "How would a 'good enough' mother think about the problems your teenage daughter is having?" "What would a 'good enough' mother tell a 'perfect mother' about being gentler on oneself?"

Summary

Understanding the systemic and nonnormative, nonpathologizing nature of circular, reflexive, solution-focused, and narrative questions and practice at question construction are the key skills required for effective interventive interviewing. Interventive interviewing involves therapist and client in a process of ongoing collaborative assessment and change.

Adult Attachment Interview

Qualitative assessment name. The Adult Attachment Interview (AAI) was developed by George, Kaplan, and Main through the Department of Psychology at the University of California, Berkeley, in 1985; the third edition was developed in 1996 (George, Kaplan, & Main, 1985, 1996). Both are unpublished manuscripts.

Type of assessment. The AAI is a semistructured interview designed to identify attachment representations in adults by examining narrative accounts of adults' early childhood experiences with parents or other primary caregivers for coherence, quality of presentation, and level of remembered detail.

Use–target audience. The AAI is intended for use with adults. Because early key attachment experiences are conceptualized as influencing emotion and behavior in later significant relationships, the AAI is particularly useful in couples work.

Multicultural. Emerging research (Rodrigues, Wais, Zevallos, & Rodrigues, 2001) is suggesting the universality of attachment scripts across cultures and therefore supports the use of the AAI with diverse populations.

Ease and time of administration. The AAI takes between 45 min and an hour and a half to complete. It consists of 20 open-ended questions, many requiring clarifying and/or probing follow-up questions. Administering the AAI requires specific training in the method and general skill in interviewing.

Scoring procedure. Scoring of the AAI is a complex process and requires completion of a two-week intensive training course in the scoring and coding procedures developed by Main and Goldwyn. Each interview is transcribed verbatim and is rated on 14 nine-point scales. Certification in the administration and scoring of the AAI requires an additional 18 months, consisting of three tests taken at six-month intervals. Each test requires the trainee to code a set of approximately ten AAI transcripts.

Reliability/validity. Test–retest reliabilities of 78% (Bakermans–Kranenburg & Van IJzendoorn, 1993) and 90% (Benoit & Parker, 1994) have been reported.

Availability and source. The AAI protocol is available on the Web at: www.psychology.sunysb.edu/attachment/measures/content/aai_interview. pdf. It is made available on the Web only to provide context and access to the interview questions for those interested in the AAI and research surrounding it. The scoring manual is only available to those who have completed the specialized AAI training.

Comment. Data from this assessment interview is now being linked to developments in neuroscience (Cozolino, 2002; Siegel, 2007). The quality of brain integration of neural networks is hypothesized to be linked to the quality of early attachment relationships with parents or primary caregivers—the more secure the attachment, the better the integration of neural networks.

Utilizing the Adult Attachment Interview in Couples and Family Therapy

The AAI is a semistructured interview in which the interviewer asks the respondent a series of questions primarily focused on recollections of the relationship with his mother and father. The bulk of the interview concentrates on the respondent's memories of early childhood and adolescent experiences and whether he experienced a parent as threatening or coercive. The interview includes specific questions about whether the respondent feels that any early childhood experience was negative or served as an impediment in life. For example, Question #8 of the AAI is *Did you ever feel rejected as a young child? Of course, looking back on it now, you may realize it wasn't really rejection, but what I'm trying to ask about here is whether you remember ever having rejected in childhood.* The interview shifts to the present when the interviewer asks how the respondent thinks his childhood experiences have affected the development of his personality in general, what the quality of the respondent's current relationship with his parents is like, and how the respondent feels when he is separated from his children now. For example, Question #10 reads: *In general, how do you think your overall experiences with your parents have affected your adult personality?* The interview also includes questions about loss of a loved one or other traumas and invites the respondent to speculate on why his parents acted as they did when the respondent was a child. The interview ends with a future focus in which the respondent is asked questions about his hopes and wishes for his children. The interview is taped and a verbatim transcript is made.

The respondent's answers to the questions compose a narrative of understanding and meaning or lack of it and of coherence or confusion about childhood experiences. Persons specifically trained in the coding of the AAI code the transcript according to the conventions of qualitative discourse analysis. The results of the coding are classified into one of four categories:

- (F) Secure—freely autonomous when the transcript narratives are internally coherent and consistent. Those with traumatic childhoods as well as those with stable, loving childhoods may be classified as secure because the criteria for classification are narrative coherence not the nature of the childhood experiences.

- (D) Insecure—dismissing when the narratives give evidence of minimization or denial of the significance of early childhood experiences and of relationships with parents or show idealization of parents.
- (E) Insecure—preoccupied when the narratives show confusion and inconsistency about early childhood relationships, experiences, and their meaning. The transcripts also give evidence of preoccupation with parents and/or current relationships with parents characterized by anger or by efforts to please.
- (U) Unresolved—narrative disorganization about a loss or trauma within the context of a narrative that meets the criteria for one of the three preceding categories and would be so classified if it were not for the evidence of intense mourning, guilt, or irrational beliefs surrounding a loss or trauma.

The quality of early attachment experiences is increasingly being linked to brain development and neural integration (Schore, 2003). Narrative coherence and therefore secure attachment as scored on the AAI are hypothesized as reflecting better integration of neural networks in the brain (Cozolino, 2002; Siegel, 2007).

Case Example

A mother whose AAI score is (E) insecure–preoccupied may oscillate between anger at her parents and attempts to please them, thus preoccupying her so that she has difficulty identifying and responding to the emotional needs of her young child. Her attachment template oscillates between overvaluation and derogation of her parents, negatively affecting her ability to think clearly and making her vulnerable to emotional overreactions to her child's behavior.

Summary

The AAI is an instrument that has been widely used and researched by developmental psychologists and is gaining wider attention as neuroscience links early attachment experiences to brain development and integration. For family therapists, the attachment profiles obtained from the AAI provide information about the primary attachment pattern influencing a parent or spouse. For those who are insecurely attached, interventions can be appropriately targeted to help dismissive clients identify and respond to the emotional needs of others, to help preoccupied clients individuate and react less intensely to the behaviors of others, and to help those with unresolved trauma make sense and construct meaning around their experience of loss or abuse.

Cultural Formulation Interview (CFI)

Qualitative assessment name. The CFI was developed by a sub-group of the American Psychiatric Association (American Psychiatric Association, 2013) to increase clinical understanding of how cultural factors affect clients'defintions of their problems; their presenting explanatory models; their levels of functioning, social support, and coping; and their help-seeking behaviors both past and present.

Type of assessment. The CFI is a brief semistructured interview composed of 16 questions that address both individual experience and social context. The CFI emphasizes four domains of assessment: the cultural definition of the problem (Q1–3); cultural perceptions of cause, context, and support (Q4–10); cultural factors affecting self-coping and past help-seeking (Q11–13); and cultural factors affecting current help-seeking (Q14–16).

Use–target audience. The tool is suitable for adults and can be used in all patient, outpatient, emergency, and transitional settings. Couple and family therapists can administer individually to each adult in couple or family therapy contexts.

Multicultural. The CFI is intended to obtain cultural views and practices from persons of all cultural backgrounds.

Ease & time of administration. Conducting the CFI can take from 30 to 90 min, and clinicians should be skilled in both diagnostic and interventive interviewing.

Scoring procedure. The qualitative responses from the CFI are used in clinical assessment and treatment planning.

Reliability/validity. 80% interrater reliability was found using deductive content analysis (Lewis-Fernandez et al. (2017).

Availability & source. The CFI is included in Section III of the *DSM-5 and can be obtained from the American Psychiatric Association DSM-5 website:* https://www.psychiatry.org/File%20Library/Psychiatrists/Practice/DSM/APA_DSM5_Cultural-Formulation-Interview.pdf

Utilizing the CFI in Couples and Family Therapy (Brief Case Example)

A couple who had emigrated from Haiti to South Florida ten years earlier was referred by the school counselor for couples/family therapy to discuss their 16-year-old son who had been having both personal and school problems. The father only showed up for the session because of the intervention of his local pastor whom the mother had asked for help. The therapist administered the CFI in conjunction with standard clinical interviewing protocols. The therapist interviewed both parents together using the CFI but recorded their responses separately. The therapist was careful to ask the father first for his responses after each question. Both parents, but especially the father, seemed relieved to be able to talk about how their son's problems would be understood and handled in Haiti. It quickly became clear that the father would not easily accept understandings of his son's problems that included any description of them as mental illness and that he would not easily be supportive of his son receiving help from a psychiatrist or psychotherapist. The father was willing to accept help for his son from a coach or maybe a counselor and described his son's problems as the result of not working hard enough at school. The information gleaned from the CFI was essential in helping the therapist to frame the sons' problems in a culturally acceptable way and to collaboratively develop an initial treatment plan for the family.

Graphic Methods

Genogram

Qualitative assessment name. The conceptual foundation for the use of genograms was advanced by Murray Bowen. The graphic and interpretive techniques for constructing and using genograms were developed and elaborated by McGoldrick and colleagues at the Multicultural Family Institute of New Jersey.

Type of assessment. A genogram is a graphic representation of a person's family, interpersonal relationships among family members, and family history over multiple generations. The genogram is typically co-constructed by the therapist and client and represents key life-cycle events (e.g., birth, marriage, divorce, death) as well as the nature and intensity of relationships among family members. For example, it can be used in family assessment from a normative and a nonnormative clinical standpoint. Used by Bowenian therapists, the genogram can be used to track family patterns of enmeshment and disengagement—concepts that are normative within Bowen family systems theory. On the other hand, the genogram can also be used in a nonnormative way by solution-focused therapists to identify family patterns of strength, resilience, and problem-solving skill.

Use–target audience. The genogram can be used in couples and family therapy to represent family relationships visually and to identify or construct patterns of relationship, feeling, and behaving across a number of generations. In couples' therapy, genograms can be constructed for each partner; major family patterns and themes can then be compared and discussed. For therapists working with individual clients who wish to introduce a family perspective, the use of a genogram can be particularly helpful in invoking the wider influence of family and context. In addition to the uses of genograms described elsewhere in this section, genograms have been used and recommended for understanding couples and family spirituality (Hodge, 2005), for use in addressing trauma and trauma-inscribed memories (Jordan, 2006), and very recently for use with military families (Weiss, Coll, Gerbauer, Smiley, & Carillo, 2010). Genograms have been utilized in solution-focused work (Weiss, Coll, Gerbauer, Smiley, & Carillo, 2010) and in collaborative, narrative, and social constructionist-informed practices (Dunn & Levitt, 2000; Milewski-Hertlein, 2001; Rigazio-DiGilio, Ivey, Kunkler-Peck, & Grady, 2005) as well as in their classic use in Bowen family systems work (Kerr & Bowen, 1988).

Multicultural. The genogram is a culturally sensitive and culturally specific assessment tool. The cultural genogram and cultural context of the family and of individual family members is considered a fundamental part of using and interpreting the genogram (Hardy & Laszloffy, 1995; Shellenberger et al., 2007).

Ease and time of administration. This is a simple method requiring that the therapist use pencil and paper and have a basic knowledge of the symbols and conventions used in genogram construction. A basic genogram can be developed in only several minutes; adding detail and complexity may require that the therapist encourage the client to gather more information about family history.

Scoring procedure. Representing and interpreting family history and family patterns of feeling and behaving is a process of co-construction between the client and therapist. Factual information about marriages, significant relationships, births, divorces, deaths, and so forth is obtained from the client and represented graphically. As information about individual members of the client's extended family is gathered, patterns of feeling and behaving may become evident and may be identified or suggested by the client or the therapist. The process of interpretation is akin to thematic analysis in qualitative research in which recurring and dominant themes are identified.

Reliability/validity. The trustworthiness of the genogram is demonstrated by its consistent use over time by family therapists to identify family patterns and themes and the consistent perceived usefulness of the tool by therapists and clients. The use of the genogram has expanded to include a focus on strengths, resilience, culture, spirituality, and problem-solving skills, as well as its traditional use to identify pathology and family emotional themes. Reliability and validity issues do emerge with respect to the role of memory and the accuracy of retrieved family history data.

Availability and source. McGoldrick's books on genograms (McGoldrick, Gerson, & Petry, 2008; McGoldrick, Gerson, & Shellenberger, 1999) are basic references for developing skills in the construction and use of the genogram in therapy. Various computer software programs to facilitate production of professional quality genograms are available.

Comment. Irrespective of preferred family therapy modality, a focus on a client's family history through the use of the genogram immediately expands the frame to include larger cultural themes and context.

Utilizing the Genogram in Couples and Family Therapy

Constructing a genogram is similar to building a family tree. The first step in developing a genogram is to identify the index person. The index person is typically the identified patient in family therapy or each partner in couples therapy. Squares are used to identify males and circles to identify females. Birth and death dates are written above the symbol on the left and right, respectively. An "X" inside the symbol indicates the family member is dead. Marriage is indicated by a solid horizontal line connecting the symbols for male and female; living together is indicated by a dotted horizontal line connecting the symbols for the partners. Lesbian couples in a committed relationship are indicated by two circles with inverted triangles inside them connected by both solid and dotted horizontal lines. Gay couples in committed relationships are indicated by two squares with inverted triangles inside them connected by both solid and dotted horizontal lines. The solid and dotted horizontal lines used together represent unmarried committed relationships. Divorce is indicated by a double hash mark on the horizontal line connecting the couple, with the dates of the marriage and divorce next to it. Children are listed from oldest to the youngest, from left to right, with the symbols for male or female on vertical lines descending from the horizontal line between the couple. A solid vertical line indicates a biological child; a dotted vertical line indicates a foster child; and a dual solid and dotted vertical line indicates an adopted child. Other symbols indicate pregnancy, miscarriage, stillbirth, and identical or fraternal twins. Substance abuse is indicated by a horizontal line bisecting the symbol for male or female with the bottom half of the symbol shaded in. A significant mental or physical problem is indicated by a vertical line bisecting the symbol for male or female and the left side of the symbol shaded in.

In the genogram, the index person is indicated by a double circle or square and marriage or living together is then indicated as described earlier, with any children also symbolized. Parents and siblings of the index person are then symbolized, as are grandparents, aunts, uncles, and cousins as the family history becomes known. Each generation occupies its own line or latitude on the genogram, similar to a family tree, with the older generations (great grandparents, grandparents) on the upper part of the genogram and the children and subsequent generations on the lower part.

Relationships within a generation (for example, between siblings) or across generations (for example, between a grandmother and granddaughter) are also indicated by specific symbols. Two solid lines between two people on the genogram indicate a close relationship; a dotted line indicates a distant relationship; a zigzag line indicates a conflicted or hostile relationship; and two solid lines with a zigzag line between them indicate a close, conflicted relationship (Figure 3.1).

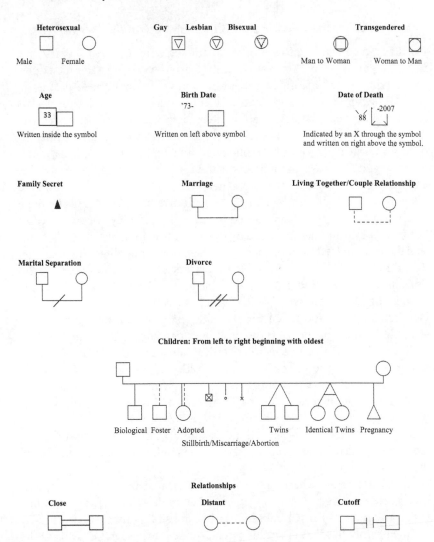

Figure 3.1 Basic Genogram Symbols

Source: Based on McGoldrick et al. (2008).

A basic genogram can be constructed within a single therapy session using the knowledge of family history that the client brings with him or her. The therapist may ask the client to interview various family members in order to find out more information about family members, particularly in preceding generations. A sufficiently detailed genogram will immediately reveal patterns of marriage and divorce, family size, multiple marriages or relationships, separation and divorce, and substance abuse or physical illness. The therapist will then use the genogram to help the client develop an enhanced understanding of larger family patterns. These patterns would include family vulnerabilities like addiction or depression, losses, and traumas, as well as family strengths, resources, and resiliencies, like adapting and prospering as an immigrant family without the support of extended kin.

Case Example

Eric and Joy had been married for 18 months when they sought therapy because of increasing arguments and tension over money and communication. Eric complained that Joy was not as warm and close as she once was and that she did not pay attention to the cost of things; Joy complained that Eric wanted to spend too much time at home and was becoming boring. Eric was building his own spin-off business, with his father's help, from his father's successful insurance agency. Joy had a degree in advertising and was signed up with a professional temp agency. She worked 3 or 4 days most weeks. When she did not feel like working, she turned down the temporary jobs.

Eric's Genogram

Eric was the older of two boys. His mother and father had been married for 31 years; in the early years of their marriage, Eric's mom worked in the insurance agency that her husband had started. Gradually, as the business became more successful, she turned her attention to the children and their school and extracurricular activities. Eric's dad was very focused on doing the right thing, working hard, being a good provider, and living by the book. His father was a career military officer who bred this sense of duty and consistency into him. Eric was protected by his mother and tried very hard to receive approval from his father, who was not emotionally expressive.

Joy's Genogram

Joy was the third child of five, with one older brother and sister and one younger brother and sister. Joy's mother and grandmother worked as professionals—her grandmother as a physician and her mother as a pharmacist. Joy's father was an investigative journalist for the leading newspaper in their city. Family life was rough and tumble with boisterous dinner conversations and a steady stream of friends and

(Continued)

her father's talkative newspaper colleagues throughout the house. Joy's mother participated in rock climbing, sailing, and white-water rafting whenever she could. Joy was interested in everything but had a hard time focusing on anything in particular. She worshipped her father and had little time for her mother, whom she saw as self-centered and aloof.

Interpretation and Therapeutic Use

Eric valued the pattern of hard work, commitment, and loyalty that he saw in his family when considering his genogram. He also saw the multigenerational father–son pattern of seeking approval and lack of emotional expressiveness. Joy relished the intellectual vigor that characterized her multigenerational family. In thinking about her genogram, Joy also began to see the women in her family in a new light. Although she had always valued her father's curiosity, love of life, and brashness, she began to appreciate her mother and grandmother as trailblazers and independent spirits in their own, more quiet ways.

In discussing Joy's genogram, Eric was vividly reminded of how Joy's own free-spirited ways were what had attracted him to her in the first place. Eric also recognized that he did not want to spend the rest of his life waiting for his father's approval and began to see himself as a "good enough" son already. In so doing, he moved closer to Joy and began to accept her invitations to have more fun and play in their relationship. For her part, Joy began to see herself as a strong woman in a line of strong women, although not as quiet or solitary as her mother, and started to focus on her career aspirations, which pleased Eric. Joy also began to see Eric's steadiness and loyalty as a reflection of his commitment to her rather than as a boring and plodding personality trait. She saw that, in overvaluing her father's unpredictable hours and activities, she had undervalued Eric's reliable presence and pleasure in the ordinary things of domestic life.

Summary

The genogram is a basic family therapy assessment tool that has numerous applications in clinical practice. The genogram enables therapist and client to identify family patterns of strength and deficit quickly and to locate an individual's life within the multigenerational family and wider community and culture.

Emotion Maps

Instrument name. The emotion map is a graphic participatory method developed by Jacqui Gabb in her research of everyday family relationships in 2008. Emotion maps enable clinicians to effectively "see" the dynamic experience and emotional repertoires of family life.

Type of instrument. Gabb (2008) designed this graphic participatory method to examine everyday materiality, temporality, and emotionality in their relationships. Emotion maps are designed to elicit information on family processes as experienced through interactions located in the family home. The therapist and family members typically co-construct an emotion map as a floor plan of the family's living space and utilize emoticon stickers to locate their feelings and interactions in the home.

Use–target audience. The emotion map can be used in couples, family, and children's therapy to represent family relationships visually. Individuals can identify or construct patterns of relationships, feelings, and behaviors within various locations of their home. Emotion maps have been utilized in families and couples counseling (Gabb & Singh, 2015).

Multicultural. The emotion map is culturally sensitive in that individuals can emotionally represent their homes in their own terms. As emotion maps are not reliant on literacy or language skills, they can be equally completed by parents and children alike, enabling children's perspectives to be heard.

Ease & time of administration. This is a simple method that requires the floor plan or picture of a home and stickers with facial expressions. A basic emotion map can be completed in minutes; adding detail and complexity is up to the therapist. The therapist is encouraged to discuss the map with the individual family members to gain further insight on where, when, and how family members describe the emotionality of their everyday interactions.

Scoring procedure. Representing and interpreting family patterns of feelings and behaving is a co-construction process between the individual family members and therapist. Together they explore the relationships between familial interactions and the emotions they connect to these processes. Therapists can ask families to create new emotion maps throughout the course of therapy so that recurring and/or changing themes in the maps can be discussed.

Reliability/Validity. Although there are no published or reported reliability or validity data, the clinical trustworthiness of emotion mapping comes from its use over time by family therapists to compare and contrast recurring and changing themes in the emotion maps with clinical observations on family interactions in sessions.

Availability & source. Researching Intimacy in Families provides information for developing skills in the construction of an emotion map. Additional resources: youtube video https://www.youtube.com/watch?v=eYfvrPErRSU and Enduring Love? website: www.open.ac.uk/researchprojects/enduring love/

Comment. Provides further information about perceived emotions and the interactions among family members in a home. The graphics method will help to expand on cultural themes and family dynamics.

Utilizing the Emotion Map in Couples and Family Therapy (Brief Case Example)

The Diaz family consisting of Maria and Gonzalo, wife and husband, and their nine-year-old son, Miguel, came to therapy with concerns regarding recent increases in arguments between the couple and Miguel's acting-out behaviors. As the opening session unfolded, the therapist asked the family members if they would like to construct an emotion map so she could have a better idea of where and when in the Diaz home these problematic behaviors had been taking place. Mother, father, and son agreed, so the therapist brought a large piece of paper and a set of emoticons depicting happy, sad, angry, and other feelings. There were three sets of emoticons in different colors so Gonzalo selected red emoticons, Maria chose blue ones, and Miguel picked out the orange ones. Gonzalo sketched out the floor plan of their three-bedroom, two-bathroom house. Over the next 20 min, the therapist asked family members to place emoticons in the house to signify the feelings they have had recently experienced in the house and to describe the events the emoticon represented. Miguel placed red and blue angry emoticons in the living room to represent his parents and an orange sad emoticon for him in his room. When asked about the mapping of his emotions, Miguel was able to explain how his parents' arguments made him feel. Gonzalo and Maria added their stickers and stories, and a clearer picture emerged for them and their therapist how their individual actions affected each other.

As therapy progressed and the family members reported improvements, the therapist asked if they would like to draw another emotion map. The family agreed and their new emotion map revealed more happy emoticons throughout the home for mother, father, and son.

Summary

The emotion map is a simple tool to help individuals, couples, and families visualize their interactions and articulate aspects of their situation which might have been challenging for them to do verbally. Emotion maps can also help family members to emphasize things they are doing outside of the therapy room which contribute to their progress.

Discursive Methods

Recursive Frame Analysis (RFA)

Qualitative assessment name. RFA, developed by Bradford Keeney in 1987 (Keeney, 1991), is a qualitative tool designed to assess the flow of communication in couple and family members' interactions. RFA was originally created as a real-time coding system to help couple and family therapists track clinical conversations and has been developed into a micro and macro qualitative assessment system (Chenail, 1991; Rambo, Heath, & Chenail, 1993).

Type of assessment. RFA is used to conduct three separate but connected types of discursive analyses: semantic, sequential, and pragmatic (Chenail & Duffy, 2011; Cotton, 2010). In the semantic assessment, the analyst listens to conversations and/or reads the transcript and notes how the individual speakers contribute the creation of meaning. This is done by noting small units of meaning, known as frames, and then grouping frames of semantically similar meaning into larger semantic groupings known as galleries. Galleries can be grouped into larger semantically similar groupings known as wings, which in turn can be grouped into still larger collections known as museums. In the semantic analysis, the analyst makes note of which family members contribute frames to which galleries and which family members do not. In the sequential assessment, the analyst listens to conversations and/or reads the transcript and notes when the individual family members shift the conversational flow from one frame or gallery to another new or old frame or gallery. These shifts are noted as openings from one frame or gallery to another frame or gallery. In the pragmatic analysis, the analyst makes note of how family members (a) maintain conversation presence in a particular frame or gallery, (b) generate an opening to a new frame or gallery, (c) connect one gallery or frame to another frame or gallery, or (d) reverse the relationship between a gallery and its frames.

Use–target audience. RFA can be used to assess individual, couple, family, and group conversations.

Multicultural. RFA can be used with individuals, couples, and families from all cultures.

Ease and time of administration. RFA used as a conversational scoring method to assess semantic/sequential flows can be done in real-time by a trained analyst. To conduct more micro-analyses, it may take the analyst one to two weeks to produce a detailed assessment of the semantic/sequential/pragmatic patterns in a one hour conversation.

Scoring procedure. Conversations are coded in terms of (a) frames, galleries, wings, museums for semantic analyses; (b) openings, frame-to-frame, frame-to-gallery, and gallery-to-gallery for sequential analyses; and (c) conversational moves or speech acts for pragmatic analyses. These renderings can be conducted and presented in textual presentations: Gallery 1: Frame 1a, Frame 1b or in graphical displays:

Gallery 1: Problems with Son	Opening 1: Exceptions	Gallery 2: Son's good Acts
Frame 1a: Son doesn't clean room	⇒	Frame 3a: Son helps set the table
Frame 1b: Son doesn't obey father		Frame 3b: Son looks after little sister

With either the textual or graphical approach, the analyst could include excerpts from the conversation to support the frame and gallery constructions (Chenail & Duffy, 2011).

Reliability/validity. RFA employs a number of techniques to increase the rigor of its analysis: (1) Incorporation of the constant comparative method of analysis from grounded theory that requires individuals conducting the analysis to return continuously to the transcript to validate the coding process (Corbin & Strauss, 2007), (2) Utilization of multiple analysts to conduct the RFA's and multiple judges to assess the individual RFA's to produce consensual RFA's (Hill et al., 2005), and (3) Use of member checking by presenting the RFA's to the clients for their validation of the results (Patton, 2002).

Availability and source. Information on RFA can be located at the Recursive Frame Analysis Home Page (http://www.nova.edu/~ron/rfa.html).

Comment. RFA has been used to analyze a variety of clinical discourse including family therapy sessions (Cotton, 2010) and written clinical discourse (Chenail, Somers, & Benjamin, 2009).

Utilizing RFA in Couples and Family Therapy

Whether utilizing RFA in real-time conversational scoring or in its more macro-analytical forms, the analyst can write observations on a piece of paper or use software applications such as Microsoft Word or PowerPoint to record the RFA (Chenail & Duffy, 2010). Whether by pencil or keyboard, the analyst starts by listening or reading what each family member says. As the first family member speaks, the analyst makes a determination as to the meaning of the words being spoken. Similar to open coding in grounded theory (Corbin & Strauss, 2007), the analyst attempts to keep an open mind as each word is spoken until a declaration of meaning can be assigned to the words, or in RFA, a frame is created (Chenail & Duffy, 2010). From that initial framing of the family member's word, the analyst continues to track the conversation so what family members are saying from point to point in the talk can be noted as words that convey something similar in meaning to what had been previously uttered (e.g., talk continuing in the same frame) or something different in meaning to what had been prior to that time (e.g., a new frame or a return to a previous frame).

For example, upon hearing the following words from a mother, "I am worried that our daughter Ellen is having trouble at school. She is not getting good grades. Her teacher says she doesn't pay attention in class. And we have noticed some changes with her at home too," the analyst could create these frames: Frame 1: Mother worries about daughter's (Ellen) trouble at school; Frame 2: Ellen not getting good grades; Frame 3: Teacher says Ellen doesn't pay attention in class; and Frame 4: Mother and father notice changes with Ellen at home. As these frames are generated, the analyst can group frames with similar meanings into galleries. In the case of these four frames, the analyst could group Frames 1, 2, and 3 into one gallery: Gallery 1: Ellen's School Problems and then could create a second gallery for Frame 2: Gallery 2: Ellen's Problems at Home. The analyst could decide to group both Gallery 1 and Gallery 2 into one Wing called Wing 1: Mom's Worries about Ellen.

As the father joins the conversation, the analyst notes how this parent joins in with the mother's talk or possibly speaks differently about Ellen. For example, if the father reports, "Yes, I have heard what Ellen's teacher has said, but I'm not sure if I agree. I think Ellen is just going through a phase." From an RFA perspective, the father's opening frame appears to be spoken within the context of Gallery 1: Ellen's School Problems, but as the talk continues "...but I'm not sure if I agree," his talk suggests that the focus of the conversation is shifting from Ellen's School Problems (Gallery 1) to a new gallery: Gallery 3: Father's Disagrees about Ellen Having School Problems. As the father continues to speak, the analysts can note the conversation seems to be leaving Wing 1: Mom's Worries about Ellen and entering a new Wing, Wing 2: Father's Sees Ellen Going through a Phase.

Besides noting these semantic frames in relationship to each other, the analyst can focus on how the speakers maintain conversation within one gallery or shift the talk to new ones. For example, the father's use of a "Yes, but" way of speaking can be noted as a speech act known as an opening up closing (Chenail & Duffy, 2010) by which a speaker can speak initially within one topic or gallery (e.g., Gallery 1: Ellen's School Problems) but then close down that part of the conversation while opening up a new flow to the talk (e.g., Gallery 3: Father's Disagrees about Ellen Having School Problems). Over the course of the conversation, the analyst continues to frame the meaning of speakers' words, to frame the meaning of frames into galleries, to frame the meaning of galleries into wings, and to frame the meaning of wings into museums while also noting how the conversation opens into new frames and returns to existing ones.

Summary

RFA can be used to assess the flow of family members' conversations in real-time and to conduct more micro-analyses of semantic, sequential, and pragmatic patterns of communicative interactions. It can be used with naturally occurring family conversations, with therapy sessions, and with scenarios or role playing.

Protocol for Using Qualitative Assessment
Strategies with Couples and Families

The following protocol provides summative guidelines for using the preceding qualitative assessment strategies with couples and families:

1. Select qualitative assessment strategies appropriate for the couple or family and their presenting problem(s). Considerations: Are the strategies selected compatible with the therapist's theoretical framework and clinical operating assumptions?

2. Determine whether the assessment strategies to be used will be diagnostic only or iterative (diagnostic and interventive). Considerations: Will the selected strategies be used at intake only or throughout therapy on an ongoing basis? Diagnostic interviewing and the AAI should be used primarily during intake and as part of a formal assessment process. The CFI is also most useful when used initially during intake, but the results should be referred to throughout therapy. Emotion maps can be

constructed in an initial session, as a homework assignment, and repeated throughout therapy. Observing structure, hierarchy, and interactions; interventive interviewing, genograms; and RFA are typically used iteratively.

3. Implement the selected qualitative strategy in a two-step process of data collection and data analysis and interpretation.

4. Collect additional collateral information about the couple or family, as needed. Possible collateral information could include review of clinical records, interviews with significant others in the client's relational system (e.g., teacher, physician, probation officer, family member, or friend), and results of other clinical or psychological assessments (e.g., inventories of personality, family, self-report, family violence or child abuse, or divorce or child custody). Collecting data from several sources (e.g., multiple family members, other assessments, clinical records, etc.) is a process called *triangulation* in qualitative research and is a method of confirming and verifying results.

5. Review the preceding information and develop an initial qualitative report for the couple or family assessed. The report may summarize the couple or family system from a relational perspective only or it may additionally provide assessment information about each individual member of the couple or family. Individual family member reports should be akin to "within-case" analyses in qualitative research and relational or systemic reports akin to "cross-case" analyses. Some reports include within-case and cross-case analyses, whereas others include the cross-case or relational perspective only. The clinician determines the most appropriate report form based on the clinical purpose for the report.

   Reports can be oral, written, and/or graphic in format. Reports based on observing structure, hierarchy, and interactions are often oral. Reports based on diagnostic interviewing, the AAI, and the CFI are typically written. Reports based on interventive interviewing may be oral or written; if written, such reports may be in the form of letters to the client and may include reflections of the therapist about the client's new understandings or positive life changes. Reports based on the genogram and emotion maps should include a graphic component, and reports using RFA may include both a narrative and graphic component.

6. Present preliminary assessment results/report to the couple or family before revising the qualitative report. Use of qualitative assessment strategies involves a collaborative process of verification of results. What this means is that the clinician presents preliminary results and interpretations to the couple or family for their comments and feedback prior to revising or summarizing the results. In qualitative research, this process

is called member checking. The revised report incorporates the results of this member checking process.

7. Review preliminary report and feedback from member checking and develop a revised report. This can be an iterative report reflecting the interactional effect between the therapist's use of the qualitative strategies and movement in the couple or family since the beginning of the clinical assessment process or it can be a summative report more reflective of the clinician's diagnostic impressions.

Extended Case Example

Background Information and Presenting Problem

Elaine, a 43-year-old paralegal, and her 45-year-old husband Sam, the owner–operator of a small house-repairs business, came to therapy requesting help for their 14-year-old son, Brian, who expressed fear and resentment about transferring to a new middle school. The family had recently moved to a new neighborhood because they wanted Brian and his ten-year-old sister, Danielle, to benefit from the better schools in this new location. The parents described Brian as quiet and "into himself," but they said they had never thought much of it and were happy that he had not been a behavioral problem at school or home. Brian's academic performance at his previous middle school was average. The family moved to their new neighborhood about six weeks before the start of the school year. During the first three weeks of school, Brian attended school for only seven full days. On the other days, Brian came home sick or did not go to school in the first place because of stomach pain and headaches. The school's attendance office had contacted the parents about Brian's situation; his parents had taken him to their primary care doctor who could not find anything wrong with him and referred him for therapy.

Based on the presenting problem, and on the therapist's systemic theoretical framework, the therapist decided to utilize the following qualitative assessment strategies: observation of structure, hierarchy, and family interactions; interventive interviewing; construction of a genogram; and conducting an ongoing RFA to note the shifts in family-therapist discourse throughout the therapy encounter (Step 1). She elected to use the strategies iteratively (diagnostically and interventively) with the goal of facilitating rapid change (Step 2) (**Table 3.1**).

Table 3.1 Matrix: Qualitative Assessment Strategies with Couples and Families

Assessment Instrument	Specific Couple and Family Applications	Cultural/ Language	Instructions/Use: T = Time to Take S = Time to Score I = Items	Computerized a = Scoring b = Report	Reliability & Validity	Availability
Observing Structure, Hierarchy, & Interactions	Parents, Partners, or Children; Provides Visual & Language-Based Profile of Relational Patterns.	Administer in Any Language.	T = 60–120 min. S = 60–120 min. I = n/a	a = no b = no	Triangulation.	Books, Journal Articles.
Diagnostic Interviewing	Parents, Partners, or Children; Provides Visual & Language-Based Profile of Relational Patterns.	Administer in Any Language.	T = 60–120 min. S = 60–120 min. I = responses to questions	a = no b = no	Triangulation, Member checks.	Books, Journal Articles.
AAI	Parents or Partners; Provides Narrative Accounts of Relational Patterns.	Administer in Any Language.	T = 45–90 min. S = several hours I = 20	a = no b = no	Test–retest Reliability: .70–.90	AAI Workshops, AAI Websites.
Interventive Interviewing *Circular Reflexive Solution- Focused Narrative*	Parents, Partners, or Children; Language-Based; Used to Identify and Change Relational Patterns.	Administer in Any Language.	T = 60–120 min. S = 60–120 min. I = responses to questions	a = no b = no	Triangulation, Member Checks.	Books, Journal Articles.

(Continued)

Assessment Instrument	Specific Couple and Family Applications	Cultural/ Language	Instructions/ Use: T = Time to Take S = Time to Score I = Items	Computerized a = Scoring b = Report	Reliability & Validity	Availability
CFI	Parents, Partners, Caregivers.	Administer in Any Language.	T = 30–90 min. S = 30–90 min. I = responses to questions	a = no b = no	Interrater Reliability: .80	DSM-5 Website.
Genogram	Parents, Partners, or Children; Provides Graphic of Multigenerational Relationships and Family Themes.	Administer in Any Language.	T = 10–30 min. S = 20–60 min. I = n/a	a = no b = yes	Triangulation, Member Checks.	Books, Journal Articles, Computer Software.
Emotional Mapping	Parents, Partners, or Children; Provides Graphic of Emotions, Family Themes, & Relationships.	Administer in Any Language.	T = 30–60 min. S = 60–120 min. I = responses to questions	a = no b = no	Triangulation, Member Checks.	Books, Journal Articles, www. open.ac.uk/ researchprojects/ enduringlove/
RFA	Parents, Partners, or Children; Provides Semantic, Sequential, and Pragmatic Discourse Analysis of Conversations, Interviews, Scenarios, or Role-playing Sessions.	Administer in Any Language.	T = Real-time conversational scoring S = several hours for microanalysis I = n/a	a = no b = no	Consensual, Member Checks, Constant-comparative Method.	Books, Chapters, Journal Articles, www.nova. edu/~ron/rfa.html

During the initial 90-minute session, the therapist observed the family's structure, hierarchy, and interactions. In her RFA of the session, the therapist created a "Brian's School Difficulties" gallery and filled it with the frames shared by the parents. Although the parents expressed concern for Brian and his obvious difficulty in going to school, they were not emotionally expressive with each other or towards Brian. They easily lapsed into a pattern of bewildered silence, shrugging their shoulders and waiting for the therapist to say something. When Brian's parents asked him if there were any problems at school, Brian said that he did not know and the family lapsed into silence again. The therapist observed that the "Brian's School Difficulties" gallery lacked any frames contributed by Brian himself and that the individual family members had not added new frames to build upon previous generated frames by the other family members in the session. The therapist quickly concluded that the parents had limited skill in providing emotional support to each other or to their introverted 14-year-old son and that the family was floundering in the domain of emotional expressiveness. Family members were having difficulties providing support to one another. The therapist utilized interventive interviewing in order to help the family members give voice to their unexpressed feelings and worries and lived experiences within their family. In her RFA, the therapist noted a new opening as she asked each family member to describe what he or she imagined the other family members were most worried about as they sat in the room finding it hard to say anything. The therapist added family member frames she placed into the new gallery she entitled, "Other Family Members' Worries" (Step 3).

The therapist recorded the parents' hopeful talk in a "Mom and Dad's Hopes for Brian" gallery. In a series of openings to new galleries, the therapist asked the parents to think back to their early teenage years and to describe a time when an older person had given them some encouragement or helped out and what that had meant to them. She also asked the parents to share their perspectives on how being a teenager today is different from being a teenager when they were growing up. The frames and galleries the therapists noted from the family through the process of interventive interviewing provided the basis for her further assessment of Brian's and his parents' worries and fears and also began to open up space for connection between them through sharing of meanings and reflections about adolescence and getting support from adults. To make these connections, the therapist drew a side-by-side rendering of the problem wing populated by

(*Continued*)

galleries such as "Brian's School Difficulties" on one side of her paper and a hopeful wing with galleries such as "Family Members' Shared Adolescent" on the other side of the page (Step 4).

Building upon the emerging themes of isolation versus mutual support, and bewilderment versus active encouragement and emotional expressiveness as noted across the "Brian's School Difficulties" and "Family Members' Shared Adolescent" galleries, the therapist helped the family to construct their genogram and locate themselves within the wider context of their larger family and cultural history, at least as much of it as they were able to pull together. Brian's parents were second-generation Irish immigrants and were part of the Irish Diaspora, with close relatives whom they had never met in Australia, England, and other parts of the U.S. As they constructed their genogram, the family began to see that their enduring work ethic and "suffer in silence" style made sense given the challenges and lack of support that their grandparents and great-grandparents contended with as immigrants to the southern U.S. without extended family or an Irish exile community to depend upon. Brian began to express an interest in his cultural history and his parents began to reflect on how difficult it had been for their families without active support from other relatives or a community.

The qualitative assessments that the therapist had selected worked synergistically and helped the family to reflect on themes of isolation, support, encouragement, and expressiveness. From within these "problem" galleries, the therapist began to construct new, more solution-focused frames as Brian's parents began thinking about and commenting upon their cultural heritage of "suffer in silence" and were questioning how they could change that history for Brian and Danielle. A fuller assessment of Brian's particular fears about school and his relationships was critical. The therapist decided to involve the family fully in that assessment because the context had now been set for greater reflection and sharing with one another through use of the other qualitative assessments described.

The therapist used oral and written reports to Brian and his family in an iterative process throughout therapy and worked collaboratively with the family to develop graphic assessments through the use of the genogram (Step 5 and Step 6). The oral reports consisted of summarizing and commenting upon the wings, galleries, and frames derived from the qualitative assessment data—namely, isolation versus mutual support and bewilderment versus active encouragement and emotional expressiveness. The therapist invited Brian and his parents to reflect on these themes and to add their own comments and meanings to them in an ongoing collaborative and iterative process. The therapist added these new frames to her RFA of the case.

The therapist developed written reports in the form of letters to Brian and his parents after each session. In the letters, the therapist would include her RFA drawings and reflect on the most recent therapy session by posing interventive questions to each family member related to the major theme discussed in the session. In this way, more data for ongoing iterative assessment and intervention were collected. Through building a genogram, the family created a more coherent and articulated history than they had constructed previously and they were able to stand back from that history and see themselves and their own challenges within it. Through the RFA scoring of their session, the therapist was able to show the family how their work in therapy allowed them to present the important problems they were facing individually and collectively while also identifying some hopeful and solution-focused directions they could take together (Step 7).

Concluding Comment

The qualitative assessment methods included in this chapter consist of classic assessments like the genogram and structural and strategic observations and innovative methods like RFA as well as the recently developed CFI and Emotion Maps. The postmodern perspective on interpersonal assessment is represented in the section on interventive interviewing. Additionally, an overlooked resource, the AAI has been included for family therapists interested in using this assessment to guide therapy toward repair of insecure attachments in the service of brain integration, consistent with the latest findings in neuroscience. Use of RFA can help the therapist to identify the most promising areas for intervention by tracking conversational themes and shifts in themes. RFA provides the therapist with a map of family members' conversations so that the easy to overlook openings to new and more desirable ways of thinking and acting can then be amplified.

The role of theory in assessment selection has been emphasized and assessment techniques representing multiple philosophical paradigms have been presented. Qualitative assessments in couples and family therapy are the cornerstone of the work of practicing family therapists; in fact, some therapists also suggest that the use of qualitative approaches can have therapeutic benefits for clients (e.g., Gale, 1992). In addition, the qualitative assessments described in detail above provide a highly legitimated avenue for developing high context, rapidly usable practice-based evidence. It is hoped that this chapter has been a review of methods with which the reader is already familiar as well as an invitation to explore some new ones.

References

American Psychiatric Association. (2000). *The diagnostic and statistical manual of mental disorders* (4th ed., text revision). Washington, DC: Author.

American Psychiatric Association. (2013). *The DSM-5 handbook on the cultural formulation interview.* Washington, DC: Author.

Aponte, H. J. (1994). *Bread and spirit: Therapy with the new poor: Diversity of race, culture, and values.* New York, NY: Norton.

Atkinson, B. (1999). Brainstorms: Rewiring the neural circuitry of family conflict. *Family Therapy Networker, July/August*, 23–33.

Bakermans–Kranenburg, M. J., & Van IJzendoorn, M. H. (1993). A psychometric study of the adult attachment interview: Reliability and discriminant validity. *Developmental Psychology, 29*, 870–880.

Benoit, D., & Parker, K. C. H. (1994). Stability and transmission of attachment across three generations. *Child Development, 65*, 1444–1456.

Berg, I. K., & De Jong, P. (1996). Solution-building conversations: Co-constructing a sense of competence with clients, *Families in Society, 77*, 376–391.

Carlson, J., & Sperry, L. (Eds.) (1997). *The disordered couple.* New York, NY: Taylor & Francis.

Chenail, R. J. (1991). *Medical discourse and systemic frames of comprehension.* Norwood, NJ: Ablex.

Chenail, R. J., & Duffy, M. (2011). Utilizing Microsoft® Office to produce and present recursive frame analysis findings. *The Qualitative Report, 16*(1), 292–307. Retrieved from http://www.nova.edu/ssss/QR/QR16-1/rfa.pdf

Chenail, R. J., Somers, C. V., & Benjamin, J. D. (2009). A recursive frame qualitative analysis of MFT progress note tipping points. *Contemporary Family Therapy, 31*(2), 87–99. doi:10.1007/s10591-009-9085-7

Corbin, J., & Strauss, A. (2007). *Basics of qualitative research: Techniques and procedures for developing grounded theory* (3rd ed.). Thousand Oaks, CA: Sage.

Cotton, J. (2010). Question utilization in solution-focused brief therapy: A recursive frame analysis of Insoo Kim Berg's solution talk. *The Qualitative Report, 15*(1), 18–36. Retrieved from http://www.nova.edu/ssss/QR/QR15-1/cotton.pdf

Cozolino, L. (2002). *The neuroscience of psychiatry: Building and rebuilding the human brain.* New York, NY: Norton.

de Shazer, S. (1988). *Clues: Investigating solutions in brief therapy.* New York, NY: Norton.

Dunn, A. B., & Levitt, M. M. (2000). The genogram: From diagnostics to mutual collaboration. *The Family Journal, 8*(3), 236–244.

Fleuridas, C., Nelson, T. S., & Rosenthal, D. M. (1986). The evolution of circular questions: Training family therapists. *Journal of Marital and Family Therapy, 12*, 113–127.

Gabb, J. (2008). *Researching intimacy in families.* Basingstoke, UK: Palgrave Macmillan.

Gabb, J., & Singh, R. (2015). The uses of emotion maps in research and clinical practice with families and couples: Methodological innovation and critical inquiry. *Family Process, 54*(1), 185–197.

Gabbay, J., & Le May, A. (2011). *Practice-based evidence for healthcare: Clinical mindlines.* London, UK: Routledge.

Gale, J. (1992). When research interviews are more therapeutic than therapy interviews. *The Qualitative Report, 1*(4). Retrieved from http://www.nova.edu/ssss/QR/QR1-4/gale.html

George, C., Kaplan, N., & Main, M. (1985). *The attachment interview for adults* (Unpublished manuscript). University of California, Berkeley.

George, C., Kaplan, N., & Main, M. (1996). *Adult attachment interview* (Unpublished manuscript, 3rd ed.). Department of Psychology, University of California, Berkeley.

Gottman. J. M. (1999a). *The marriage clinic: A scientifically based marital therapy*. New York, NY: Norton.

Gottman, J. M. (1999b). *The seven principles for making marriage work*. New York, NY: Crown Publishers.

Haley, J. (1991). *Problem-solving therapy* (2nd ed.). San Francisco, CA: Jossey–Bass.

Hardy, K. V., & Laszloffy, T. A. (1995). The cultural genogram: Key to training culturally competent family therapists. *Journal of Marital and Family Therapy, 21,* 227–237.

Hill, C. E., Knox, S., Thompson, B. J., Williams, E. N., Hess, S. A., & Ladany, N. (2005). Consensual qualitative research: An update. *Journal of Counseling Psychology, 52*(2), 196–205.

Hodge, D. R. (2005). Spiritual assessment in marital and family therapy: A methodological framework for selecting between six qualitative assessment tools. *Journal of Marital and Family Therapy, 31*(4), 341–356.

Jordan, K. (2006). The scripto-trauma genogram: An innovative technique for working with trauma survivors' intrusive memories. *Brief Treatment and Crisis Intervention, 6*(1), 36–51.

Jordan, C., & Franklin, C. (2011). *Clinical assessment: Quantitative and qualitative methods* (3rd ed.). Chicago, IL: Lyceum Books.

Keeney, B. P. (1991). *Improvisational therapy: A practical guide for creative clinical strategies*. New York, NY: Guilford.

Kerr, M. E., & Bowen, M. (1988). *Family evaluation*. New York, NY: Norton.

Lemieux-Charles, L., & Champagne, F. (2008). *Using knowledge and evidence in healthcare: Multidisciplinary perspectives*. Toronto, ON: University of Toronto Press.

Lewis-Fernandez, R. et al. (2017). Feasibility, acceptability and clinical utility of the cultural formulation interview: Mixed-methods results from the DSM-5 international field trial. *The British Journal of Psychiatry, 210*(4), 290–297.

Liddle, H. A., & Dakoff, G. A. (1995). Family-based treatment for adolescent drug use: State of the science. In E. Rahdert & D. Czechowicz (Eds.), *Adolescent drug abuse: Clinical assessment and therapeutic interventions* (pp. 218–254). National Institute on Drug Abuse Research monograph 156. NIH Pub. No. 95–3908. Rockville, MD: National Institute on Drug Abuse.

Madanes, C., Keim, J., & Smessler, D. (1995). *The violence of men: A therapy of social action*. San Francisco, CA: Jossey–Bass.

McGoldrick, M., Gerson, R., & Petry, S. S. (2008). *Genograms: Assessment and intervention* (3rd ed.). New York, NY: Norton.

McGoldrick, M., Gerson, R., & Shellenberger, S. (1999). *Genograms: Assessment and intervention* (2nd ed.). New York, NY: Norton.

Milewski-Hertlein, K. (2001). The use of a socially constructed genogram in clinical practice. *American Journal of Family Therapy, 29*(1), 23–38.

Minuchin, S., & Fishman, H. C. (1981). *Family therapy techniques*. Cambridge, MA: Harvard University Press.

Minuchin, S., Lee, W.-Y., & Simon, G. M. (1996). *Mastering family therapy: Journeys of growth and transformation.* New York, NY: Wiley.

Patton, M. Q. (2002). *Qualitative research & evaluation methods* (3rd ed.). Thousand Oaks, CA: Sage.

Rambo, A. H., Heath, A. W., & Chenail, R. J. (1993). *Practicing therapy: Exercises for growing therapists.* New York, NY: W. W. Norton.

Rigazio-DiGilio, S. A., Ivey, A. E., Kunkler-Peck, K. P., & Grady, L. T. (2005). *Community genograms: Using individual, family and cultural narratives with clients.* New York, NY: Teachers College Press.

Rodrigues, L. M., Wais, D. P., Zevallos, A., & Rodrigues, R. R. (2001, April). *Attachment scripts across cultures: Evidence for a universal script.* Poster session presented at Society for Research in Child Development, Minneapolis, MN.

Schore, A. N. (2003). *Affect dysregulation and disorders of the self.* New York, NY: Norton.

Shellenberger, S., Dent, M. M., Davis-Smith, M., Seale, J., Weintraut, R., & Wright, T. (2007). Cultural genogram: A tool for teaching and practice. *Families, Systems, and Health, 25*(4), 367–381. doi:10.1037/1091–7527.25.4.367

Siegel, D. (2007). *The mindful brain: Reflection and attunement in the cultivation of well-being.* New York, NY: Norton.

Szapocznik, J., & Coatsworth, J. D. (1999). An ecodevelopmental framework for organizing risk and protection for drug abuse: A developmental model of risk and protection. In M. Glantz & C. R. Hartel (Eds.), *Drug abuse: Origins and interventions* (pp. 331–366). Washington, DC: American Psychological Association.

Tomm, K. (1987a). Interventive interviewing: Part I. Strategizing as a fourth guideline for the therapist. *Family Process, 26,* 3–13.

Tomm, K. (1987b). Interventive interviewing: Part II. Reflexive questioning as a means to enable self-healing. *Family Process, 26,* 167–183.

Tomm, K. (1988). Interventive interviewing: Part III. Intending to ask lineal, circular, strategic, or reflexive questions? *Family Process, 27,* 1–15.

von Foerster, H. (1981). *Observing systems.* Seaside, CA: Intersystems.

Weiss, E. L., Coll. J. E., Gerbauer, J., Smiley, K., & Carillo, E. (2010). The military genogram: A solution-focused approach for resiliency building in service members and their families. *The Family Journal, 18*(4), 395–406. doi:10.1177/1066480710378479

White, M., & Epston, D. (1990). *Narrative means to therapeutic ends.* New York, NY: Norton.

4

STANDARDIZED ASSESSMENT WITH COUPLES AND FAMILIES[1]

Len Sperry

Just as there have major advances in every assessment mode and application described in this third edition, there have been notable advances in standardized assessments used with families. One of the most obvious advances is that standardized assessment has rapidly moved from paper and pencil and offline software administration to internet-based, online administration. Before describing test-specific developments, it may be useful to begin with a brief explanation of standardized assessment and testing. Standardized tests are unique as assessment devices in that they are designed to have consistent items and scoring procedures and are administered in a consistent or "standard" manner. This means that certain rules and specifications are followed so that testing conditions are the same for all those being assessed.

When a family assessment includes a standardized assessment or a full test battery, the assessment applies scientifically sound psychological instruments that have stood the test of time with practicing clinicians. Although most of these tests were originally developed to evaluate individuals, the instruments discussed in this chapter have considerable value with couples and families. This chapter will describe four well-known and highly regarded instruments that are commonly used in assessing couples and families. These tests are the Minnesota Multiphasic Personality Inventory-2, the Millon Clinical Multiaxial Inventory-IV, the Rorschach Inkblot Test, and the Kinetic Family Drawing Test. Current advances of these instruments and applications to couples and families are described. Then, a seven-step clinical strategy for effectively utilizing these instruments is provided. Finally, a detailed case example that illustrates the tests and the clinical protocol. This chapter reflects the basic orientation of A. Rodney Nurse's *Family Assessment: Effective Uses of Personality Tests with Couples and Families* (1999).

While these four instruments are often used together as a test battery, it has become increasingly common to selectively utilize one or more depending on client needs. As these instruments are increasingly computer administered and scored, clinicians can focus more on test interpretation conserving professional time and reflecting current economic realities.

Instruments

Minnesota Multiphasic Personality Inventory-Revised Version (MMPI-2): Assessing Symptoms, Moods, and Couple Types

Instrument name. The MMPI is the most widely used clinical testing instrument in the United States. It was developed by Starke Hathaway and Charnley McKinley, named after the University of Minnesota, and first published in 1943. A revised version, MMPI-2, was published in 1989. In 2008, the MMPI-2-RF (Restructured Form) became available (Ben-Porath & Tellegen, 2008/2011). It is a streamlined version of the MMPI-2. It contains 338 of the original 567 items and has 51 scales including two new Validity Scales. MMPI-2-RF is reported to perform as well or better than the MMPI-2 (Ben-Porath, 2012; Friedman, Bolinskey, Levak, & Nichols, 2015; McCord, 2018). A useful addition is the Marital Distress Scale (MDS) which is a subscale of the Generalized Emotional Distress Scale. The MDS contains 14 items that correlate with scores on the Dyadic Adjustment Scale. Accordingly, high scores on the MDS are likely to reflect dissatisfaction with marriage or a romantic relationship (Friedman et al., 2015). For clinical pattern interpretation purposes, these versions are sufficiently similar to justify applying the couple pattern research described here.

This application is particularly appropriate with well-defined, high two-point clinical scores above T of 70 or close (Butcher, 1990, 2002; Greene, 2000). Recently the MMPI-2 normative sample was updated psychometrically, major scales restructured, the number of items reduced to 338, and other changes made to capitalize on the strength of the instrument. Additionally, some wordings were normalized.

Type of instrument. MMPI-2 is a standardized personality inventory providing, at its original core, a quantitative measure of psychological symptoms, emotional adjustment indications, and psychopathological patterns: 1-Hypochondrisais, 2-Depression, 3-Hysteria, 4-Psychopathic Deviate, 5-Masculinity/Femininity, 6-Paranoia, 7-Psychasthenia, 8-Schizophrenia, 9-Hypomania, 10-Social Introversion. Because these names are either obsolete or convey distorted meanings of the present understandings of these dimensions, these scales are ordinarily referred to by numbers.

Use and target audience. The MMPI-2 is intended as a personality screening tool for individuals 18 and older. A related instrument, the Minnesota Multiphasic Personality Inventory–Adolescent (MMPI-A), is designed for use with 14- to 18-year-olds and is useful with parents or partners for a variety of purposes. Five common couple clusters have been articulated and are described in this chapter.

Multicultural. The MMPI-2 is available in English, Spanish, Hmong, French, Chinese, Hebrew, Korean, and Italian. Computer-generated interpretive reports are available only in English.

Ease and time of administration. An easy-to-administer inventory, the MMPI-2 calls for the client to respond "true" or "false" to 567 items and takes 60–90 min to complete. The MMPI-2 may be taken in paper-and-pencil format, audiocassette, or in a computer format and requires a sixth- to eighth-grade reading level.

Scoring procedure. The MMPI-2 is always scored on at least ten scales measuring various clinical or personality dimensions and three scales related to validity and test-taking attitude. Ordinarily, four additional validity scales are scored together with more than 80 additional clinical scales, including two germane to marital and family issues. It may take 15–20 min to hand score and chart the basic clinical profile. Computerized scoring, however, is typically the standard, not only because it easily scores the large number of additional scales, but also because accuracy is guaranteed, additional hypotheses are generated, and basic research-grounded interpretive statements may be provided.

Reliability. As indicated in the MMPI-2 manual, moderate test–retest reliabilities are reported, ranging from .67 to .92. Split-half reliabilities are also moderate median correlations of .70 (Groth-Marnat, 2016).

Validity. An unweighted mean validity coefficient of .30 is reported (Weiner, Spielberger, & Abeles, 2002).

Availability and source. Several scoring and interpretive computer programs are available, including the version generated by the developers of the MMPI-2 distributed by Pearson Assessments (formerly National Computer Systems) to qualified professionals. Pearson sells the test manual (Butcher, Dahlstrom, Graham, Tellegen, & Kaemmer, 2001). Although basic interpretive hypotheses are provided in addition to scoring, clinicians interested in an in-depth, research-grounded dynamic interpretive report may utilize the Alex Caldwell report system (2001).

Comment. This is the most widely used standardized psychological test and has considerable value with couples and families, as noted in the following sections.

Using the MMPI-2 with Couples

Because work with couples typically focuses first on dysfunctional relationships, the MMPI-2—which measures behavioral symptoms and mood states that may have an impact on a partner, stem from a partner's impact, or both—has considerable usefulness as an initial assessment device. Two new scales have been developed that have particular relevance to family and couple assessment:

- *Family Problems Scale* (FAM). Families with high scores on this content scale are described as lacking in love and being quarrelsome and unpleasant. Their childhoods may be portrayed as abusive and their marriages seen as unhappy and lacking in intimacy and affection. FAM is a gross measure reflecting problems, past and present, in the family as a whole. It is useful in initial screening to ascertain the degree of seriousness of family problems.
- MDS. This scale has the advantage of focusing on measuring distress or discord in close relationships, rather than measuring more global family problems as with the FAM. The MDS is described as an efficient discrimination of maladjustment in marriages at a T score of 60 or above.

Five-Cluster MMPI Classification of Couples Seeking Therapy

Research on the original MMPI cited by Nurse (1999) suggests that as many as 50% of couples with marital problems fall into one of five recognized MMPI clusters. Renaming them slightly from the original research, Nurse labels these clusters as openly warring couples; unhappy, problem-focused couples; husband-blaming couples; psychologically disordered couples; and distant, calm couples. Each of these couples and MMPI codes is briefly described in terms of interactional dynamics and unique treatment issues. Wives' codes are presented first, husbands' second, in the parentheses next to the name of the couple pattern.

Openly Warring Couples (4-3/4-9 Codes) Warring wives present with poorly controlled anger and hostility that is expressed in a cyclical fashion, as reflected in their 4-3 high-point code. Following a submissive, suppressive phase, a build-up of tension can result in a loss of control seen in angry, aggressive acting-out. This may be triggered as much by internal stimuli as by externally based stress. Between stormy bouts of anger expressions, they are models of (older generational culturally stereotyped) "femininity," displaying passivity and submissiveness (but demonstrating periodically complaining behavior) as they defer overtly to their husbands. Not surprisingly, this submissive behavior adds to suppressed resentment that, in time, erupts.

Warring husbands act regularly on their impulses and are frequently rebellious against the restraints of authority and usual socially accepted standards. This reflects their high Scale 4. Integral to this personality style is a high level of energy, indicated by Scale 9, which serves to provide fuel to the acting-out. Because of their freedom from anxiety, worry, and guilt, these husbands often make a comfortable, smoother, and socially facile appearance initially. At the same time, they are impatient with anything deeper than a superficial relationship consistent with their craving for action and excitement. A seemingly submissive wife, who follows the husband's lead uncritically and without question, as well as satisfying needs for attention and sex, fits the husband's comfort with someone to cater to his impulses and action orientation. Therapy with this couple tends to be volatile, and the therapist's challenge is to join with their fighting style and help them learn to fight fairly or to identify this overall repetitive conflict pattern and work with conflict resolution skills. However, this is not typically a couple that excels at communicating verbally or reasons well with problems. Instead, this is an action-oriented couple that, if they can fight fairly to resolve conflicts, may be able to reach reasonable solutions to their problems, despite their overall pattern, and may stay together satisfactorily.

Unhappy, Problem-Focused Couples (2-1-3/2-7 Codes) This couple is seen quite commonly in couples therapy, often presenting with unhappiness or depressive features and high levels of marital dissatisfaction. They typically present with a problem-solving orientation and an openness to self-appraisal. Unhappy, problem-focused husbands tend to have 2-7 codes and present with unhappiness, worry, and tension. They blame themselves; easily feel inadequate despite their achievements; and, interestingly, have the capacity for satisfying and rewarding interpersonal relationships because they are turned in on themselves. They seek advice and help from therapists and are likely to follow therapeutic suggestions. Unhappy, problem-focused wives tend to have major symptoms of depression. Their overall code is often 2-1-3, which is known as the neurotic triad configuration. Like their husbands, they are anxious and self-doubting and tend to be dependent and immature. They seem capable of maintaining a long-suffering, unhappy role in the relationship; consequently, their motivation for change may be less than optimal. Not only will a worsening of the relationship present a crisis, but positive change can also upset the couple or family homoeostatic balance. In couples therapy, therapists may find that intimacy is the core issue for these couples and that they deal with intimacy issues by maintaining some degree of disengagement. Thus, efforts to increase their interaction and intimacy may increase conflict and their perception that therapy "makes things worse." Accordingly, the strategy is to focus gently on the dynamics of interaction, without blaming, and concentrate on the couple's ability to work on practical solutions to identified problems. Such couples do maintain longstanding marriages, solving problems somehow with avoidance and yet resolving them nevertheless. If therapy goes even reasonably well, these couples have the potential to move past their avoidant pattern, interact more directly, and evolve into a positive, growing marriage relationship.

Husband-Blaming Couples (4-6/2-4 Codes) In these couples, angry husband blaming (4-6) by the wives is linked to apologetic, although sometimes resentful, acceptance of blame by the husbands (2-4). These women attempt to present themselves as psychologically healthy yet are guarded, as reflected in L and K scores elevated above the F score. They tend to see the world in right–wrong, black–white terms and are reluctant to engage in self-criticism, which is consistent with the 4-6 code. When Scale 1 is also elevated, "whining somatization" can be noted. A blaming woman is also wary and suspicious; if there is verified reason for this suspiciousness and no history of delinquency or past major difficulty in social relations, it may well be that she is reacting to the present couple dispute instead of this being a characterological problem.

The striking feature of the husbands' typical profile (2-4) is depression; these men are suffering from a generally unhappy, dysphoric mood accompanied by feelings of inadequacy, lack of self-confidence, self-depreciation, and strong guilt feelings. For the husbands, their wives' blaming and perceived nagging may provide justification for their resentfulness and self-destructive behavior (e.g., alcohol abuse and suicidal ideation). Therapy needs to focus on both partners learning to take responsibility for themselves, avoiding blaming, and understanding more of their own psychological make-up. Therapy can help them learn to be more empathic with their partners. To this end, a couples group could prove useful. If the husband's depression continues, a medication evaluation should be considered. For wives, a group separate from their husbands could also provide a place to learn to modify the extreme black-and-white thinking and to learn how to shoulder more responsibility without blaming.

Psychologically Disordered Couples (1-2-3/2-4-6-8 Codes) These couples have the greatest conflict potential of all five couple clusters. Psychologically disordered husbands are clearly seeking help and may even be exaggerating symptoms to attract attention. However, they appear to be seeking help for good psychological reasons. Their clinical scale profile is a saw-toothed pattern in which Scales 2, 4, 6, and 8 are significantly elevated above the other scales. These husbands are depressed, angry, and distrustful as well as feeling alienated from others; others view them as moody and unpredictable. They are likely to be ruminative, preoccupied, and inflexible in problem-solving. In contrast to the overly acute nature of their husbands' presentation, psychologically disordered wives are attempting to avoid, deny, and generally not deal with unacceptable feelings and impulses. However, despite this effort, they appear to have a chronic neurotic condition and are usually diagnosed with somatoform disorders, anxiety disorders, depressive disorders, or all of these. They are unsure, rather inept females who may have grown accustomed to a high level of unhappiness and considerable discomfort. When in therapy, these wives are seldom highly motivated for treatment because of their melancholy adjustment to a chronic condition and their pattern of denial, which contrasts with their husbands actively seeking help. However, because of the unstableness of their condition, the husbands may have difficulty in persevering in treatment. Unlike couples in the four other clusters, these couples may need intensive individual psychological evaluation, including a psychological testing battery, and they may require collateral psychiatric evaluation for medication.

When therapy is undertaken, the therapeutic plan, including goals, objectives, and intermediate tactics, must be thoroughly delineated with as much collateral help as appropriate (e.g., psychiatry, support groups, and provisions for emergencies). If these couples make changes, the changes will be even more threatening than for many couples with other dysfunctional patterns. If the disordered husband behaves in a more sane way, he must take more responsibility for his actions. At the same time, the disordered wife must tolerate the anxiety of looking at herself psychologically and assuming more responsibility for herself without focusing as much on her husband. Not surprisingly, psychophysiological stress reactions are to be expected.

Distant, Calm Couples (Within Normal Limits 4-8/8 Spike Codes) Typically, the MMPI profiles for these couples fall within normal limits. Compared to other couple clusters, these couples are relatively satisfied with their marriages. They tend to be older and have been married longer than other couple clusters. These distant, calm husbands are likely to think somewhat differently from others (mild 8). This may reflect their creativity, avant-garde attitude, or schizoid or avoidant personality structure. They tend to avoid reality through daydreaming and fantasy. Their distant, calm wives also have some sense of differentness and avoidance, yet they may be more genuinely concerned about social problems and issues. The couple's distancing pattern may reflect their response to situational conflicts, or it may reflect their habitual level of social and interpersonal relatedness. Their apparent lack of acute distress does not mean that they are not silently suffering the angst of emptiness, separation, deprivation, and lack of meaning associated with their high Scale 8 scores. Nevertheless, therapists who come across such seemingly normal MMPI profiles, suggesting the couple is without symptoms and is not demonstrating any obvious psychopathology, might look to other instruments such as the Millon Clinical Multiaxial Inventory (MCMI-III) or the Millon Index of Personality Styles (MIPS; Millon, 1994) for further diagnostic understanding and for treatment planning. Among MMPI-2 interpreters, such "normal" profiles can sometimes mean that the couple has become adjusted to their chronically ingrained problems and issues.

Interpreting Couple MMPI-2s Outside the Five Clusters

Some of the MMPI-2 couple patterns falling outside the five groupings will have one partner who does fit a pattern in one of the five groups. The reader is referred to descriptions of other code types in Greene (2000) and Groth-Marnat (2016). The evaluating therapist should also be cognizant of certain red flag warnings about potentially dangerous problems. These include high elevations on Scale 9 (Mania), which can indicate narcissistic, grandiose, and overly active (hypomanic) behavior, and high elevations on Scale 6 (Paranoid) that could indicate suspicious hostility, blaming, or projection of negative feelings onto others. See Nurse (1999) for a discussion of other red flags and interview suggestions related to following up on them. Nurse (1999) also discusses gender issues related to two MMPI-2 scales, as well as scale indicators of spousal dominance and submission issues.

Summary

This section presented an approach for interpreting couple MMPI-2s based on an elaboration of probable interactional dynamics of an MMPI-2 typology of five types of couples originally identified in MMPI research. Because up to 50% of couples with marital problems fall into this typology, therapists would do well to become familiar with these types and their therapeutic implications for couples treatment. Suggestions were also made for considering other patterns and the clinical utility of other specialized and content scales relevant to working with couples.

MCMI-IV: Assessing Personality Styles or Disorders of Couples

Instrument name. The MCMI-IV, in its fourth edition, was developed by Theodore Millon (1977, 1996, 1997a, 2008, 2015) and became available in the fall of 2015 (Millon, Grossman, & Millon, 2015). It is keyed to *Diagnostic and Statistical Manual of Mental Disorders, Fifth Edition* (DSM-5) and consists of 15 personality pattern scales, ten clinical syndrome scales, and five validity scales. New to this edition is the Grossman Personality Facet Scales which were added to improve the test's overall clinical utility (Choca & Grossman, 2015).

Type of instrument. The MCMI-IV is a standardized personality inventory that includes 25 clinical scales and five scales concerning reliability and validity, on which every test taker is scored. Twelve clinical scales measure clinical personality patterns and three indicate severe personality patterns, with very high scores similar to DSM-5 personality disorders. Moderate clinical personality pattern scores reflect personality traits, while a slightly elevated score represents personality features. Seven clinical syndrome scales assess DSM-5 clinical syndromes (i.e., anxiety, somatoform, bipolar, dysthymia, alcohol dependence, drug dependence, and posttraumatic stress disorder) and three reflect serious clinical syndromes (i.e., thought disorder, major depression, and delusional disorder). In addition, the Grossman Personality Facet Scales identify personality processes that underlie overall scale elevations on the 15 Personality Pattern Scales but are activated only when a Personality Pattern Score reaches a significantly high level.

Use and target audience. This instrument is used for assessing and making treatment decisions in adults (18 years and older), focusing on personality style and disorders, and is unique among tests. An adolescent version, the Millon Adolescent Clinical Inventory (MACI), is available and has been normed on 13- to 19-year-olds.

Multicultural. English and Spanish versions are available. Computer-generated interpretive reports are available only in English.

Ease and time of administration. The inventory consists of 175 statements about personality and behavior to which the individual responds "true" or "false" as applied to him or her. It can be completed in 20–30 min and may be taken directly on a computer or in paper format. An eighth-grade reading level is specified.

Scoring procedure. Computer scoring takes only a few minutes to provide a simple profile with minimal interpretive comments or a full interpretive report.

Reliability. Moderate levels of reliability have been noted. Test–retest reliabilities have been reported in a range from .67–.91 to .67–.69 for one year as well as an internal consistency of .80 (Groth-Marnat, 2016).

Validity. Although the positive predictive power of the MCMI-II ranged between .30 and .80, predictive values for the MCMI-III were not reported in the test manual (Millon, 1997a).

Availability and source. This inventory can be obtained from Pearson Assessments (formerly National Computer Systems, Inc.).

Comment. The MCMI-IV, developed empirically from a theoretical base, has accrued over 600 references, including a number of books. Over the course of a quarter of a century, it has reached an established place among clinicians, including those working with couples in whom DSM-5 issues are suspected in one or both partners.

Using the MCMI-IV with Couples

At the present time, the MCMI-IV is the only major and widely used psychological inventory that assesses qualities of personality styles and personality disorders within the context of an empirically derived theory consistent with DSM-5. This makes it a core instrument for a comprehensive assessment battery. Even used alone for screening, the inventory is extremely useful in arriving at hypotheses about the personality structure and interactive pattern of the underlying immediate conflicts, overt anxiety, and depressive, or acting-out, features that partners present with in couples therapy.

The Process of Couple MCMI-IV Analysis

1. Check for satisfactory validity and response style scores.
2. Next, note significant scores on the profile of each spouse so that indications of personality disorders or styles (traits or disorders indicated by elevated scores falling at a level below disorders) and any clinical syndromes are compared with other information collected, such as the

clinical interview and previous records or collateral data. Beyond comparing family history of psychiatric and substance dependence, information on the partners' family-of-origin histories, attraction to each other, and courting history can be usefully compared with their scores on the 15-personality style/disorders scales.

3. After completing this overall analysis, an in-depth analysis of the personalities and interaction patterns needs to be undertaken. This can be done with the help of Millon's *MCMI-IV Manual* (2015) or, in greater depth, Millon's *Disorders of Personality* (1996). The most recent comprehensive MCMI-III reference material may be found in Millon's second edition of *The Millon Inventories* (2008). Consistent with the purposes of this writing, we recommend the chapter in that book by Nurse and Stanton.

Using the MCMI in Treating Couples

With couple interpretations, it is particularly important to look at the behavioral level, that is, expressive behavior and interpersonal behavior. From this level, inferences can be systematically drawn about linkages with features or domains falling at other levels. These levels include the polarities of pleasure–pain, active–passive, and self–other. Identifying where couples fall with reference to these polarities (especially self–other) and their personality styles/disorders can be most clinically useful in understanding the homeostatic function of these balances. This is because the couple or family system tends to make adjustments to maintain the status quo, thereby preserving the relationships between individuals that meet some individual needs. This analysis permits a more detailed description of the interactive pattern of the personality expressions of the couple and provides the basis for planning and therapeutic treatment, which can be sharpened by reference to personality-guided therapy (Millon, 1999). A detailed example of this analysis process applied to the dependent/narcissistic couple may be found in Nurse's (1997) chapter in *The Disordered Couple* (Carlson & Sperry, 1997). See also the Nurse and Stanton chapter in *The Millon Inventories* (Millon, 2nd ed., 2008) and the Stanton and Nurse chapter (2009), which provide illustrations of the process.

Prototypic MCMI Couple Relational Patterns

This section briefly describes six MCMI couple relationship patterns commonly seen in outpatient treatment settings.

Narcissistic Male/Histrionic Female Males with a very high score on the Narcissistic scale (5) may act in an arrogant fashion with a tendency irresponsibly to ignore social norms and standards. They may show little empathy and act in an interpersonally exploitive manner, seemingly unaware of the negative impact on others. These males may have self-glorifying fantasies of success, yet may move from job to job always looking for employment that meets how they think they should be treated. Yet, narcissistic males maintain a cool aura, seemingly not shaken by anything. However, it is particularly important on this scale to determine whether a high score represents a style or a disorder (Craig, 1999). With a narcissistic style, subtle attitudes may be reflective in a moderate way of these characteristics, except under pressure when the attitudes and behaviors can become significantly more pronounced. Females in this relational pattern often show a marked peak on the Histrionic scale (4). They convey an engaging, fleeting, and often theatrical attitude, conveying a high level of excitement and activity. Histrionics seek to be the center of attention, developing ways of being socially stimulating, but they avoid reflecting on even fleeting unwanted emotions, seeking to deny contradictory feelings as they are constantly in action. At the trait level, they may be dramatic and energetic but can enter more into relationships with some success. Given the frequent lack of any symptoms evident on the MCMI clinical syndrome scale scores, some with slight scale elevations appear to have simply histrionic features and are upbeat and free from indications of maladjustment. If an elevation on the Compulsive scale (7) occurs, their general emotional style is likely to be balanced by some capacity to be organized, thorough, and conscientious while remaining expressive and outgoing, as reflected in a moderately elevated Histrionic scale score. This pattern suggests a person functioning relatively effectively.

In the couple relationship, the truly histrionic female will likely be attracted to the narcissistic male because of his sureness, command, and seeming interest in her. He is likely to be attracted to her, however, because of her apparent attraction to him and his own fantasies of how enhanced his life would be and how others will see him with her on his arm. They are likely to become disillusioned, periodically fight, and sometimes even triangulate a child or other individual in a struggle to gain power and make up for what they do not have with each other. Because these patterns represent some gender stereotypes, it may be useful for the couple to be seen by a male–female co-therapy team. Each therapist in individual sessions prior to some of the couple sessions could prepare his or her same-gendered client by acknowledging strengths and achievements coupled with setting structured goals. For the female, these sessions could include practicing on channeling of controlling feeling expressions; for the male, they could focus on empathy practice (with the therapist avoiding mirroring, which serves to reinforce narcissism). For the more moderate, normal-appearing histrionic/narcissistic couple, it may be that that couple's difficulties lie more in relationship communication problems than in the personality structure of either.

Compulsive Female/Dependent–Avoidant Male Females with a high elevation on the Compulsive scale (7) appear excessively disciplined and maintain a highly structured, organized life. They see themselves as conscientious, devoted to thoroughness, and fearful of not doing things in the best possible way. They maintain an inner world that is cognitively constricted (i.e., narrow and rule bound, anticipating that others will behave similarly). Sometimes using reaction formation as a major defense, they appear super-reasonable, not dealing with contrary feelings, and fearful of underlying feelings such as anger. Although their lives may be full of tension and tight control of emotions, research suggests that an elevated compulsive score may indicate more conscientiousness than compulsivity (Craig, 1999), an effective and rewarded style in many environments. Males with an elevation on the Dependent (3) and Avoidant (2A) scales have a need for close relationships but hesitate about approaching others out of a fear of rejection. Their style is interpersonally submissive but not expressive. They may be seen as cognitively naive, avoiding confrontation; sometimes they experience themselves as weak and alienated. They may feel a need to become involved with, if not devoted to, others; they introject others' views and maintain relationships through the use of fantasy in order to avoid significant anxiety. At a level of personality style, moderate-level scores point to a person with a significant emotional neediness who, because of the importance of relationships, is hesitant to take action without being sure of acceptance.

Couples therapy with couples demonstrating more pronounced score patterns needs to proceed slowly and may benefit from accompanying individual sessions. Conjoint sessions must appeal to the female's need to do the right thing and the male's need for a close relationship with reassurance of acceptance. In couple sessions, the goal is for the male to become more assertive and capitalize on his abilities developed outside the home and to become more active in the home. The goal for the female is to modify her sometimes too conscientious pattern so as to be in more control of it, thus turning it to positive use and being less constricted by it, and to move from being passive and only (restrictively) nurturing others to paying increased attention to her own needs as well as those of others.

Narcissistic Male/Narcissistic Female As noted earlier, males with a marked peak on the Narcissistic scale (5) may act in an arrogant, condescending fashion with a tendency to irresponsibly ignore social norms and standards. They likely possess an interpersonally exploitive manner, seemingly unaware of the negative impact on others. They tend to view themselves as special and have fantasies of love and success that drive them to high levels of achievement, yet they may repress and/or reshape affect and distort facts to maintain their self-illusions in the face of failures. Typically, they maintain a cool aura of self-possessed optimism unless their confidence is shaken. Females with very high elevations on the Narcissistic scale (5) may present much as narcissistic males. They are interested in others in large part for what they can gain from them in terms of their own self-esteem, and thus they can behave amorously. Nevertheless, they tend to be self-deceptive, self-centered, and rational; until their confidence is shaken, they present with a cool, imperturbable demeanor.

As a couple, narcissistic males and females tend to have similar blind spots: repressing and denying the same negative aspects of their personalities. This means that they cannot easily confront each other without being aware of similar self-aggrandizing traits in themselves. Although they believed earlier in their relationship that they were "made for each other" (because they reflected each other), with the arrival of a child or other shifts in their interpersonal balance, each misses the other's focused attention. Their intense attachment can switch from positive to negative, blaming each other and pointing out the negative parts of the other's personality, and thereby warding off confronting themselves with their own experiences of deprivation and recognition of their shortcomings. By recognizing the couple's interlocking narcissistic styles, a couples therapist can more easily avoid responding negatively to these individuals' self-focused approaches to life and instead can support their effectiveness while gently helping them gain more empathy with each other. A couple demonstrating narcissistic traits (rather than disorders) may have developed a broader base and a better interpersonal connection, giving the therapist a platform to assist them in building a sounder marriage relationship despite the arrival of a child, loss of a job, illness, or other unbalancing occurrence.

Histrionic–Narcissistic Female/Compulsive Male In this profile, the Histrionic pattern (Scale 4), mixed with Narcissistic features (Scale 5) of superiority and entitlement, increases the possibility of irresponsible, acting-out behavior considerably beyond that of the prototypical histrionic personality disorder in females. These individuals tend to be attracted to Compulsive (Scale 7), that is, conscientious, males whom they view as stable, goal oriented, and secure. However, with time they experience such men as boring and rigid. These females may have sought out other types of relationships but, after being wounded, may have retreated to safe kinds of husband–father relationships with a compulsive male in order to lick their wounds.

Males with a compulsive or conscientious personality (Scale 7) are likely to have been excited and attracted to these affectively dominated females, whom they typically view as intriguing, colorful, and vivacious. Yet, with the passage of time and relational demands, these males become disconcerted with their partners, whom they now view as flighty, irresponsible, and supremely selfish and vain. Relationally, these females will be the source of feeling expressiveness in the relationship, while these males will be the voice of reason. Couples therapy stressing improved communication could focus on having these couples get to know each other as specific, unique individuals. Unfortunately, without the benefit of couples therapy or other corrective experiences, neither partner is likely to move beyond these limiting roles without expressing his or her humanity.

Antisocial Female/Antisocial–Narcissistic Male Clinicians inexperienced with the MCMI-IV may improperly conclude that both partners are antisocial or psychopathic personalities because of elevated 6A Scales. In keeping with Millon's clinical formulation of this scale as primarily a measure of aggression, such scale elevations (particularly at a moderate level) reflect the competitive, aggressive attitude and style associated with successful entrepreneurs. These are the "antisocial" style individuals who are likely to come in for couples therapy. It would be surprising if true psychopaths, who comprise only a minority of antisocial personality disorders, came for therapy.

Couples with this pattern who show up for therapy typically take risks, exploit (usually within the limits of the law), and shade the truth to meet their own needs. Yet, they view themselves as law-abiding individuals. When they become involved in close romantic relationships, they can carry some of these antisocial qualities into that relationship. Thus, they can be competitive and can view their relationship as a game in which they match wits with each other. They may admire each other's ability to succeed in business; however, they can be tough, argumentative, and insensitive to each other's feelings. With this couple, an imbalance can be anticipated because of the male's narcissistic (Scale 5) entitlement. His partner will become incensed at his self-centeredness. When she finds ways to puncture his confident front, he may respond with hurt, rage, and vindictiveness. Their motivation for coming for couples therapy is probably so that each can gain an advantage over the other. When the therapist does not express judgment of who is right, they can impatiently join in turning on the therapist, only to seek a new one. Therapists need to be aware that this therapy could be the first stage in a long divorce battle in which neither gives because winning is everything for them.

Dependent Male/Dependent Female Dependent partners (Scale 3) tend to be so "nice" to each other that they inevitably tread lightly in their relationship. Unfortunately, treading lightly allows little opportunity for openly dealing with their problems. Consequently, problem-solving only appears to occur when one partner quickly acquiesces in order to avoid being criticized. At some level, each partner may be looking for a good parent and thus may develop considerable resentment, although each tends to squelch this; if irritation comes out unexpectedly, that partner may hurriedly apologize. Each partner has the capacity to be kind, loving, and caring with each other. If they begin to develop personally outside the relationship—through work experiences, for instance—and maintain their same way of couple relating, this dissonance in their lives may bring them to couples therapy. By helping each recognize his or her growing resentment and assisting each in learning to communicate feelings more directly, the therapist can help these needy people experience developing together. When dependent style couples seek help, the therapist needs to discover what has unbalanced their relationship, for example, the personal growth of one more than the other, a new child, a promotion, a relationship external to the marriage, and so forth.

Summary

The MCMI-IV uniquely provides informational, descriptive hypotheses about personality structure as well as syndromal indications. The MCMI-IV profile helps the couples therapist draw understandable hypotheses about the couple relationship and interactive pattern in guiding planning for interventions.

The Rorschach: Application to Families

Instrument name. The Rorschach Inkblot Test, usually called the Rorschach, was named after the Swiss psychiatrist who developed and first published it in 1921. While the content and administration of this projective test has remained constant for nearly a century, its scoring and interpretation has improved dramatically with the Rorschach Performance Assessment System (R-PAS). R-PAS is a scoring system for the Rorschach that is empirically based and easier to use than Exner's Comprehensive System (Viglione, Blume-Marcovici, Miller, Giromini, & Meyer, 2012).

Type of instrument. It is a projective test consisting of ten inkblots.

Use and target audience. This test is used with all ages (except the youngest of children) for gathering information describing personality as reflected in the perceptual processes of the person and the associational dynamics related to content. It is particularly valuable for in-depth personality evaluations of parents or partners with issues involving child custody, child abuse, and divorce, as well as in planning psychotherapy with adults, adolescents, and children.

Multicultural. This instrument can be administered in any language. A Spanish language manual is available from the publisher of Exner's Comprehensive System for the Rorschach; however, computer-generated interpretive reports based on Exner's system are available only in English.

Ease and time of administration. In administering the Rorschach using Exner's Comprehensive System (Exner, 1993, 2001; the most extensively used system), the examiner sits side by side with the examinee, thus avoiding distractions or unconscious shaping of responses caused by an examiner's inadvertent changes of facial expression or body posture. The examiner presents each blot with the instructions to respond to the question: "What might this be?" A follow-up inquiry using carefully delineated questioning helps the examiner to be clear about the location of the response, what went into making the response, and a sense of the nature of the content of the response.

Scoring procedure. Using the Comprehensive System, responses are categorized by using scoring procedures painstakingly developed to maximize consistency of assessor scoring. Entered into a computer, these resulting scores are combined based on research-derived procedures. A computer program provides not only the combinations of scores but also a lengthy narrative of research and clinically based hypotheses for the assessor to use as an interpretive base (Exner et al., 2003). As already noted, the R-PAS scoring system is empirically based and easier to use than Exner's system (Meyer & Eblin, 2012). The R-PAS manual provides information for administering, scoring, and interpreting the Rorschach. A website supplements the manual. Initial research supports R-PAS as an evidence-based assessment method (Meyer, Viglione, & Giromini, 2014).

Reliability. Test–retest reliabilities are reported in the range of .75–.85, while intercoder agreement is in the range of .79–.88 (Groth-Marnat, 2016).

Validity. An unweighted mean validity coefficient of .29 is reported in more than 2,200 Rorschach protocols. This suggests that the Rorschach "is generally as valid as the MMPI" (Weiner et al., 2002, p. 9).

Availability and source. Materials for the comprehensive system are distributed by Psychological Assessment Resources, Inc., to qualified professionals.

Comment. Despite this empirically based comprehensive system protocol, crafting a clinical report requires intensive instruction and supervision. It also requires extensive experience with the Rorschach, coupled with interview data about the examinee, typically complemented by the results of other psychological tests and inventories.

Using the Rorschach with Families

The Rorschach has a unique, significant, and often essential place in family treatment situations in which a thorough, in-depth understanding of personality is required on which to base decisions with far-reaching effects on the lives of family members, particularly children. For example, when an appraisal is sought about the mental state of parents and children in a heated, drawn-out, child custody dispute, the Rorschach can be a crucial source of uniquely salient information. It can also be helpful in complicated family situations when a puzzling child problem presents. Notably, the Rorschach findings in these situations may uncover processes not readily apparent, such as a thought disorder, the discovery of depression and its depth, or the dynamics of acting-out problem behavior.

Response styles (Exner, 1993) have particular relevance for understanding family behavior because they consistently influence or provide direction for various and sometimes diverse personality features manifest in family interaction. As such, they form major anchoring points for the therapist in searching for family system patterns. At the same time, the therapist must pay attention to consistent, pervasive behaviors on the part of each individual. These dominant Rorschach features are the Lambda Index, Experience Balance, Reflections, the Passive/Active Relationship, and the Hypervigilance Index. Nurse (1999) provides a cogent description of each of these dominant Rorschach features and suggests how each may have an impact on the family process and the strategy of the family therapist.

In considering the interpersonal, family-related implications of Rorschach findings, Exner's handbook on interpretation can serve as a primary reference (Exner, 2001). Research has resulted in identifying 11 key variables or clusters that provide substantial core information on the individual's personality and point the way toward organizing the remaining Rorschach data. Nurse (1999) offers a clinically useful discussion of these key variables.

Summary

The Rorschach is particularly applicable in situations requiring in-depth personality evaluations because at that time a family is facing situations that have far-reaching effects on its members, especially those involving children. In addition to diagnostic assessment and treatment planning, these issues include separation, divorce, abuse, and identifying psychosis and clinical depression. This section focused on the dominant interpersonal style and key characteristics of the Rorschach and their implications for understanding family interaction and for developing targets for therapeutic change.

The Kinetic Family Drawing Test (KFD): Clues to Family Relationships

Instrument name. The KFD follows in the tradition of other family drawing tests described since 1950. Robert Burns and S. Harvard Kaufman are credited with adding the highly important "kinetic" conception to the family drawing test (Burns & Kaufman, 1970). By adding the word kinetic to the test-taking instructions, they "force" the test taker to draw an action picture of relationships among all family members. Alternatively, the family members may be asked to draw one KFD representing the entire family. Either way, useful hypotheses about the family system can be generated in the process of discussions with the family. Understanding the family system is fundamental to the work of the family practitioner. By contrast, neither the Draw-A-Person (DAP) nor the House Tree Person (HTP) has this focus. While the content, administration, and scoring if KFD have remained constant, recent research has significantly increased its cultural applicability and clinical value.

Type of instrument. This test is a projective drawing measure of family dynamics.

Use and target audience. The KFD is utilized with children, adolescents, and adults individually to ascertain an individual's view of his or her family system. A second purpose is to obtain a family drawing as drawn together by the entire family.

Multicultural. Because culture and family structure influence children and their parents, research in the past decade on the KFD has increasingly focused on cultural considerations. One such study used the KFD with first and second graders with different family structures: traditional families, single-parent families, and new immigrant families. Some distinct differences on various categories, i.e., "action of and between figures" and "distance between figures, barriers," were noted suggesting that the KFD has clinical value for school counselors and family therapists particularly in working with students from single-parent and new immigrant families (Fan, 2012).

The influence of culture has been noted in children's responses to the KFD. Among very young children, the influence of culture appears to be minimal across the globe.

This changes with the progression of age and is reflected in the developmental sequences of their drawings (Di Leo, 2015). Owing to the unique instructions for administration, this test can be administered in any language.

Ease and time of administration. The KFD is easy to administer: Simply provide the family member with a plain sheet of ordinary size white paper and a number-2 pencil and say, "Draw a picture of everyone in your family, including you, doing something. Try to draw whole people, not cartoons or stick people. Remember, make everyone do something—some kind of action" (Burns & Kaufman, 1970, pp. 19–30). When asking the entire family to complete one drawing, it is best to provide one large sheet of art paper with pencils or crayons, paraphrasing the instructions to fit the family context (Thompson & Nurse, 1999, p. 127). As noted, the instruction to have everyone "doing something" added to instructions to draw a family has turned out to be a very important contribution. The testing procedure usually takes 20–30 min.

Scoring procedure. There is no generally accepted scoring procedure even though a formal scoring system that focuses on actions, styles, and symbols has been proposed (Burns & Kaufman, 1972; Handler & Habenicht, 1994). Some contend that the proposed scoring system has not proven particularly useful and a more integrative, holistic approach has been offered instead (Thompson & Nurse, 1999). One holistic approach is for the therapist/evaluator, after the drawing system, to try to duplicate physically the actual postures and imagine the actions indicated on the KFD. These kinesthetic experiences can trigger feelings and thoughts for the therapist/evaluator that may be akin to the client's. For instance, acting out a child's smile with arms out toward family members, compared with duplicating a scowling, hiding child crouching in a corner, would certainly elicit different feelings and thoughts for the clinicians.

Reliability. Test–retest reliabilities have been low, which is not surprising because this instrument is often scored or interpreted qualitatively. However, when quantitative scoring was used, interscorer agreement is reported in the range of .87–.95 (Groth-Marnat, 2016).

Validity. Overall validity has been rather low and variable (Groth-Marnat, 2016).

Availability and source. The KFD and the Kinetic School Drawing (KSD; Knoff, 1985), comprising the Kinetic Drawing Systems (KDS; Knoff & Prout, 1985), are distributed by Western Psychological Services, Inc. Of course, it is possible to follow the instructions provided here if no scoring system is desired.

Comment. Although it lacks the extensive empirical and experimental data that would provide it the validity of such clinical instruments as the MMPI-2, the MCMI-III, or the Rorschach, the KFD is included in this chapter because it is the only widely used drawing method that attempts to elicit responses pertaining directly to understanding the family system from the perception of the person drawing. It has been noted that the KFD is considered a pictorial analog of "family sculpting" as described by Satir (1967).

Using the KFD with Families

The KFD can be utilized with families in various ways. The standard way is to collect and analyze the KFD from the child or children at the onset of treatment and use it in conceptualization of, and treatment planning for, the case. Thompson and Nurse (1999) suggest some other uses of this assessment tool. One is to have everyone in a family session do a KFD by him- or herself, then have the family discuss the different drawing perceptions of the family members with the guidance of the therapists. Such discussion of similarities and differences can stimulate talk about affectionate family bonds and significant differences among family members.

Alternatively, the therapist may have family members work together to draw one KFD on a large sheet of art paper with crayons rather than on a regular sheet of paper with a pencil. The instructions are the same except that family members are asked to decide together what each member is to draw and where on the large sheet of paper each member will accomplish the drawing task. This step is particularly important because it gives the observer examples of family interaction. The therapist–observer pays attention to such questions as who leads, who has the final say, and how the drawing is executed by those involved. These observations can be shared in subsequent discussions with the family to ascertain if these family patterns are representative outside the consulting room and, if they are, what the implications of these patterns might be. Or, the therapist can request the family to complete one KFD as a family and simply observe how the family goes about doing the task and, afterward, question them. An additional approach is for the family to act out the actions depicted in the family KFD. Finally, the KFD can serve as a starting point for a general family discussion, with the drawer or drawers of the picture alone or involving the entire family.

Summary

KFD is a useful method for family therapists. Although it currently lacks the impressive psychometric properties of other standard assessment measures, the KFD is the only drawing method that consistently identifies family interrelationships. Because it can provide clues about family relationships, it is particularly helpful as one instrument in a battery of tests, although it can be used by itself. Given its simplicity of administration and increased cultural sensitivity and clinical value, it will continue to be used worldwide.

Strategy for Using Standardized Tests with Couples and Families

The following protocol can be useful when utilizing the MMPI/MMPI-2, MCMI-III, KFD, and the Rorschach with couples and families.

1. Select psychological tests that are appropriate to the questions raised that call for the psychological assessment, and are appropriate for the couple or family.
2. Administer and score the tests.
3. Collect additional information on the couple or family through interview, observation, clinical records, collateral information, or other self-report measures.
4. Review and develop an initial test report for each partner or each family member tested.
5. Review and develop a final test report with a focus on the couple and/or family relationships.
6. Feed data back to the couple or family as appropriate.

It is useful to keep in mind that, when developing an initial test report (Step 4) involving the MMPI/MMPI-2, MCMI-III, KFD, and Rorschach, a concurrence of results on these instruments may or may not occur. Differences may reflect the need to over-report symptoms to gain some advantage or to under-report symptoms to put the best foot forward (e.g., the parent seeking child custody in a divorce proceeding). Finn (1996) and Nurse (1999) have offered some clinically useful guidelines for reviewing such test results. A modified version of these guidelines is presented here. When disturbance is present on the MMPI/MMPI-2 and the Rorschach, most probably the client is aware of difficulties in coping on a day-to-day basis and ordinarily has a history of confirming that difficulty. When the MMPI/MMPI-2 clinical scale scores fall within the normal range while the Rorschach shows significant disturbances, the clinician needs to consider the possible uses of the test as viewed by the client carefully. For example, if the client has something to gain by appearing "normal," his MMPI scores may simply mean under-reporting. If it appears that nothing is to be gained for under-reporting, it is likely that psychological disturbances appear under stressful, unfamiliar circumstances despite ordinarily maintaining an adequate adjustment in familiar surroundings, or there may be a conscious denial of disturbance by the family member.

When the disturbance is high on the MMPI/MMPI-2 and low on the Rorschach, two possibilities exist. The client may be over-reporting on the MMPI/MMPI-2, which may reflect malingering or a call for help, probably for assistance with an immediate situation. Alternatively, if the Rorschach is defensive, constricted, and generally shut down, it may be that the client can respond accurately on the impersonal MMPI/MMPI-2, while needing to be protective in the interpersonal, emotionally arousing context of the Rorschach. In this instance, high MMPI/MMPI-2 scores do not necessarily represent over-reporting, particularly if the situation involves no anticipated gain for expressing psychopathology.

Very rarely, low disturbances are noted on the MMPI/MMPI-2 and on the Rorschach. Although this is not common in clinical settings, it does occur occasionally in marital evaluations. For example, both partners may have little in the way of psychological disturbance yet may need to enhance their relationship, or they may be so ill-matched that they need to find a more effective way of relating, coexisting, or divorcing.

When data on the MMPI/MMPI-2 and the Rorschach diverge, a review of the MCMI-III may clarify matters. For example, the narcissistic person may have great difficulty consciously describing himself in other than self-aggrandizing terms on the MMPI/MMPI-2 with accompanying minimizing awareness of psychological problems. In contrast to this under-reporting, the Rorschach may pick up considerable psychological disturbance. Similarly, the identification of a dependent personality on the MCMI-III may indicate a propensity to over-report symptoms on the MMPI/MMPI-2 to establish a therapeutic relationship. The anticipation of the dependent personality may be that appearing needy is necessary to be cared for and loved; however, the Rorschach may indicate relatively little disturbance.

In the process of developing a final test report on the couple or the family (Step 5), individual test reports are reviewed along with interview, observational, and other sources of data. This information is then synthesized and integrated and forms the basis for feedback and possible modification of the original treatment plan.

Providing feedback to the couple or family is an important part of the assessment process (Step 6). Under the ethics code of the American Psychological Association, a clinician or evaluator who is a psychologist would have an obligation to discuss test findings with clients. Typically, the clinician or evaluator meets with individual partners or parents to discuss their own results.

Reviewing results individually with the clinician and without the presence of the other partner or parent provides an environment more conducive to exploratory discussion, including considering the implications for the couple relationship or family. A joint meeting with partners or parents and the clinician follows. At that meeting, each partner or parent is encouraged to share as much about his own test feedback, as he is willing. The clinician then focuses on key couple or family dynamics that have emerged from the evaluation and discusses relevant treatment or decisional implications and recommendations.

If a family evaluation is involved and the child tested is below the age of 13, feedback on the child's testing would be provided primarily to the parents. However, if the individual is an adolescent, feedback would be provided first through a private discussion with him or her. Then the adolescent would be helped in a joint session with the therapist and parents to tell the parents what he or she considered most important about the test results. The therapist would support the adolescent and fill in important gaps in feedback for the parents.

Case Example

The following case report, involving issues of divorce and child custody, delineates the use of traditional psychological assessment methods with a family in counseling. The case illustrates the protocol for using tests with couples and families wherein each step is noted in parentheses.

Background Information and Reason for Testing

Jack S., a 31-year-old engineering technician, and Jill S., his 30-year-old wife who works in a clerical managing position, are separated and have initiated divorce proceedings. Both have begun new live-in relationships. Their nine-year-old daughter, Mary, has witnessed many of the couple's fights over the years. Her teacher has raised concern that she is functioning below her intellectual potential and does not relate well to her classmates. As part of the child custody evaluation, each family member is given a battery of tests (Step 1 and Step 2), and additional information is gathered from a number of sources, including their new partners, interviews, home visits, discussions with collaterals, letters, legal documents, and other data sources (Step 3). Jack is requesting primary custody of Mary and is open to liberal visitation by the child's mother.

Individual and Family Testing Summary

MMPI-2 and Rorschach results for Jack suggest a test pattern (Step 4) of low disturbance levels on both, while his MCMI-III profile indicates little if any disturbance and is consistent with an overall controlled, organized, and constricted person. His style is to sidestep dealing with his feelings by pushing them away or avoiding any awareness of them. Complementing this conscientious/avoidant style is a perceptual processing style in which he narrows and simplifies information as it comes to him; thus he can maintain an appearance of composure, work efficiency, and conventionality in his behaviors. Nevertheless, this suppressive defensive process feeds underlying resentment that can periodically break through. There is also some indication that he is ruminating about some self-perceived negative features in his personality and behavior. The testing also suggests that he has some positive parenting skills and attitudes.

MMPI-2 results for Jill indicate low disturbance, whereas the Rorschach points to a significant level of disturbance. Her MCMI-III also indicates psychological disturbance characteristic of individuals with anxiety disorders in the context of a histrionic personality disorder. Despite the appearance of putting up a good front, indications are that she is grief stricken about an emotional loss. Testing reveals a personality style that has important implications for her parenting (Step 4). She behaves socially in an often charming and effective way consistent with her histrionic and (mildly) narcissistic style. Unfortunately, this appearance of focusing on others seems motivated less by her interests in them than in what they can do for her. She is fearful of rejection and needs constant reassurance that she is the superior, effective person she strives to be. This self-focus may be so strong that it can interfere with her ability to extend herself toward her daughter as her daughter evolves into an increasingly independent person. Furthermore, her readiness for underlying hostility to break through would be expected to stimulate at least uneasiness and a readiness to be annoyed with other household members. The potential violence of her verbal and possibly physical outbursts is at a level to be potentially damaging for a child. The ubiquity of her underlying hostility means that her relationships with adults and children are likely to be more superficial, and she is likely to put others off. Finally, she has not developed a workable problem-solving style in that, faced with a problem, she vacillates and is unsure about which choice is better for her. She reverses decisions, thus having a hard time depending on herself; others also find it difficult to depend on her.

On the KFD, Mary identifies her family as her father, stepmother (father's new partner), her aunt and uncle (who are temporarily staying with her father), and their son. Strikingly, Mary does not include her mother in her drawing. Based on all information gathered, Mary is a very angry girl. As reflected by her anger, her distress is marked. Its power and its pervasiveness are such that it impairs her ability to think things through without internal disruptions. Her inconsistent decision-making patterns create an unsettled state, and she suffers from poor reality testing accompanied by distortions in her ways of thinking about the world. Perhaps it is this internal disorganization that makes her feel so vulnerable, resulting in hypervigilance. Mary clearly needs help in dealing with her anger and to alleviate negative feelings about herself. Testing reveals that her sense of personal worth is very poor and

(Continued)

her need for safety is significant. A concern that needs to be addressed is that her mother views Mary as very disturbed, seeing her as acting-out and acting-in, with depression and probably high anxiety. This relationship between mother and daughter is reinforced by the fact that Mary does not include her mother in her family drawing. Interestingly, her father does not see a disturbance in Mary. Their different views of Mary may reflect their different relationships with her. That is, mother–daughter relationships may reflect conflict and difficulty, whereas the relationship with her father may be relatively free of problems.

Based on these test interpretations, which primarily reflect individual dynamics, an integrative, synthesis interpretation of family dynamics and relationships can be articulated (Step 5). The overriding feature of this family grouping is that of angry expression. The mother, Jill, has not only a temper but also a ubiquitous angry quality underlying her relationships, despite an overt orientation to charming others. This readiness to break through her social, other-oriented exterior is made worse by her inadequate controls over expression of feelings, particularly anger. Her anger seems matched by her daughter's marked hostility, also characterized by lack of adequate controls, even in comparison with other nine-year-olds. Collateral information confirms a long history of flare-ups between mother and daughter that have become increasingly frequent since the parental break-up.

It is likely that Mary's fear of abandonment, stimulated when the mother left, significantly fuels these flare-ups, even though the mother has returned to visit regularly. Despite Jill's action in leaving the family home, her sense of loss and accompanying loneliness are probably related to her frayed connection to her daughter. She cannot acknowledge her ambivalence at not having more contact with her daughter and thus fights in a custody "battle" for her, precipitating this evaluation. Were she not to fight so strongly, she would need to confront her ambivalence about her daughter, manage her anxiety, and deal with the guilt for, in many ways, rejecting her daughter. Jack, as father, does not have the same problem of ubiquitous anger that his wife displays. Rather, he holds in all feelings, including anger, until, rarely, the provocation is strong enough that he can explode. He can pick Jill's most extreme behavior to righteously express his own and thereby not need to look at his own role in the family conflict. The mix of anger between them has developed and serves to maintain a cyclical fight dynamic.

Mary was traumatized and responded with her fearfulness by identifying with her aggressive mother even while being very angry with her. Mary's anger overwhelms her, disrupting her thinking process, particularly when confronted with her mother's anger or in the wake of it. Mary's reaction generalizes to others. She is hyperalert, wary, and mistrustful and does not easily mix with other children. This standoffish attitude means that she cannot benefit from the day-to-day feedback from peers so necessary for adequate development. Thus, her personality development is faltering at the present time.

Treatment and Custody Recommendations

Based on these findings, Mary needs some individual play therapy to handle her built-up trauma. Jill, her mother, likewise needs individual therapy to learn to manage her anger and find more constructive ways to respond under pressure. The two of them need sessions with a family therapist to work on their relationship. A final healing process is for mother, daughter, and father to meet with the family therapist to rework the child's trauma with them and establish a working co-parenting relationship. In the meantime, the recommendation is for the father to continue to have primary physical custody and the parents to have joint legal custody. Relatively short, two- to four-hour mother–daughter visits are recommended, perhaps three times per week. Jill can utilize long-term therapy to help her modify her histrionic style and narcissistic traits.

Feedback of Results

The clinician/assessor provided feedback to the parents (Step 7). The evaluator first met individually with Jack, and then with Jill, to review their individual results, but each parent's individual results were not discussed with the other parent. However, in a joint session with the evaluator, each parent was encouraged to share as much as he or she was willing with the other. With the parents together, the circular problem of the anger dynamic with the three of them and the mother–daughter conflict was discussed, and feedback to the parents about Mary's testing was provided. Mary's results were not discussed with her because of her age.

Concluding Comments

This chapter has described the use of standard psychological tests in the process of evaluating couples and families. Four such tests and new developments and applications were discussed: MMPI-2, MCMI-IV, Rorschach, and KFD, as well as a protocol for utilizing these instruments in clinical practice. The instruments and the protocol were illustrated in a detailed case example, suggesting how therapists might use such instruments, as long as their use is within their scope of practice, or the alternative of referring to a family-experienced, systemically oriented psychologist for such an evaluation (**Table 4.1**).

Table 4.1 Matrix: Four Standard Psychological Tests with Families and Couples

Assessment Instrument	Specific Couple and Family Applications	Cultural/ Language	Instructions/Use: T = Time to Take; S = Time to Score; I = Items	Computerized: a = Scoring; b = Report	Reliability(R)/ Validity (V)	Availability
Minnesota Multiphasic Personality Inventory (MMPI-2)	Parents or Partners/ Adolescent Version; Provides Symptoms and Mood States; Five Common Couple Clusters are Described	English; Spanish; Hmong; French	T = 60–90 min; S = 2–3 min for Computer Scoring; I = 567	a = yes; b = yes	R = .70 Split-Half; R = .67–92 Test–Retest; V = .30	National Computer Systems, Inc.
Millon Clinical Multiaxial Inventory (MCMI-IV)	Parents or Partners; Provides Personality Style/Syndromal Data; Six Common Couple Relational Patterns	English; Spanish (Interpretive Reports Only in English)	T = 20–30 min; S = a Few Minutes for Computer Scoring; I = 175	a = yes; b = yes	R = .67–.91 Test–Retest; R = .80 Internal Consistency; V = Low to .30	National Computer Systems, Inc.
Rorschach (Comprehensive System Version)	Parents or Partners; for In-Depth Personality Evaluations, e.g., Child Custody, Abuse, Divorce, etc.	Administer in Any Language (Interpretive Reports Only in English)	T = 45–60 min, Including Inquiry; S = Variable; I = 10 inkblots	a = yes, with Clinician Input; b = yes	R = .75–85 Test–Retest; R = .79–88 Intercoder Agreement; V = .29	Psychological Assessment Resources, Inc.
Kinetic Family Drawing (KFD) Test	Children and/or Adolescents, or Whole Family to Assess Family Relationships and Interaction	Administer in Any Language	T = 20 min; S = Variable Time to Score/Interpret; I = n/a	a = no; b = no	R = .87–95 Interscorer Agreement; V = Low and Variable	Journal article; Western Psychological Services, Inc.

Note

1 The results of standardized psychological instruments such as the MMPI-2, MCMI-III, and the Rorschach can be of immense clinical value. However, these instruments do require formal training and licensure as a psychologist, in most states, to legally and ethically administer, score, and interpret them.

References

Ben-Porath, Y. S. (2012). *Interpreting the MMPI-2-RF*. Minneapolis, MN: University of Minnesota Press.

Ben-Porath, Y. S., & Tellegen, A. (2008/2011). *MMPI-2-RF (Minnesota Multiphasic Personality Inventory-2-Restructured Form): Manual for administration, scoring, and interpretation*. Minneapolis, MN: University of Minnesota Press.

Burns, R., & Kaufman, S. (1970). *Kinetic Family Drawing (KFD)*. New York, NY: Brunner/Mazel.

Burns, R., & Kaufman, S. (1972). *Actions, styles, and symbols in kinetic family drawings (KFD)*. New York, NY: Brunner/Mazel.

Butcher, J. (1990). *MMPI-2 in psychological treatment*. New York, NY: Oxford University Press.

Butcher, J. (2002). *Clinical personality assessment* (2nd ed.). New York, NY: Oxford University Press.

Butcher, J., Dahlstrom, G., Graham, J., Tellegen, A., & Kaemmer, B. (2001). *MMPI-2: Manual for administration and scoring*. Minneapolis, MN: University of Minnesota Press.

Caldwell, A. (2001). *Caldwell MMPI-2 report*. Los Angeles, CA: Author.

Carlson, J., & Sperry, L. (Eds.). (1997). *The disordered couple*. New York, NY: Brunner/Mazel.

Choca, J. P., & Grossman, S. D. (2015). Evolution of the Millon Clinical Multiaxial Inventory. *Journal of Personality Assessment, 97*(6), 541–549.

Craig, R. (1999). Overview and current status of the Millon Clinical Axial Inventory. *Journal of Personality Assessment, 72*(3), 390–406.

Di Leo, J. H. (2015). *Children's drawings as diagnostic aids*. New York, NY: Routledge.

Exner, J. (1993). *The Rorschach: A comprehensive system. Basic foundations* (vol. 1, 3rd ed.). New York, NY: Wiley.

Exner, J. (2001). *A Rorschach workbook for the comprehensive system*. Asheville, NC: Rorschach Workshops.

Exner, J., & Weiner, I. (2003). Rorschach interpretation assistance program: Odessa, FL: Psychological Assessment Resources.

Fan, R. J. (2012). A study on the kinetic family drawings by children with different family structures. *The International Journal of Arts Education, 10*(1), 173–204.

Finn, S. (1996). Assessment feedback integrating MMPI-2 and Rorschach findings. *Journal of Personality Assessment, 673*, 543–557.

Friedman, A. F., Bolinskey, P. K., Levak, R. W., & Nichols, D. S. (2015). *Psychological assessment with the MMPI-2/MMPI-2-RF*. New York, NY: Routledge.

Greene, R. (2000). *The MMPI/MMPI-2: An interpretive manual* (2nd ed.). Boston, MA: Allyn & Bacon.

Groth-Marnat, G. (2016). *Handbook of psychological assessment* (6th ed.). New York, NY: Wiley.

Handler, L., & Habenicht, D. (1994). The kinetic family drawing technique: A review of the literature. *Journal of Personality Assessment, 633*, 440–464.

Knoff, H. (1985). *Kinetic drawing system for family and school: Scoring booklet.* Los Angeles, CA: Western Psychological Services.

Knoff, H., & Prout, T. (1985). *Kinetic drawing system for family and school: A handbook.* Los Angeles, CA: Western Psychological Services.

McCord, D. M. (2018). *Assessment using the MMPI-2-RF.* Washington, DC: American Psychological Association.

Meyer, G. J., & Eblin, J. J. (2012). An overview of the Rorschach performance assessment system (R-PAS). *Psychological Injury and Law, 5*(2), 107–121.

Meyer, G. J., Viglione, D. J., & Giromini, L. (2014). An introduction to Rorschach-based performance assessment. In R. Archer & S. Smith (Eds.), *Personality assessment* (2nd ed., pp. 301–370). New York, NY: Routledge.

Millon, T. (1977). *Manual for the Millon Multiaxial Inventory (MCMI).* Minneapolis, MN: National Computers Services.

Millon, T. (1994). *Millon index of personality styles.* New York, NY: Psychological Corporation.

Millon, T. (1996). *Disorders of personality: DSM-IV and beyond.* New York, NY: Wiley.

Millon, T. (1997a). *Manual for the Millon Multiaxial Inventory-III (MCMI-III).* Minneapolis, MN: National Computers Services.

Millon, T. (1999). *Personality-guided couple therapy.* New York, NY: Wiley.

Millon, T. (2008). *The Millon inventories* (2nd ed.). New York, NY: Guilford Press.

Millon, T., Grossman, S., & Millon, C. (2015). *MCMI-IV: Millon Clinical Multiaxial Inventory Manual.* Bloomington, MN: NCS Pearson.

Nurse, A. (1997). The dependent/narcissistic couple. In J. Carlson & L. Sperry (Eds.), *The disordered couple* (pp. 315–332). New York, NY: Brunner/Mazel.

Nurse, A. (1999). *Family assessment: Effective uses of personality tests with couples and families.* New York, NY: Wiley.

Nurse, A., & Stanton, M. (2008). Using the MCMI in treating couples. In T. Millon & C. Bloom (Eds.), *The Millon instrument* (pp. 347–368). New York, NY: Guilford Press.

Satir, V. (1967). *Peoplemaking.* Palo Alto, CA: Science and Behavior Books.

Stanton, M., & Nurse, A. R. (2009). Personality-guided couples psychotherapy. In J. H. Bray & M. Stanton (Eds.), *The Wiley-Blackwell handbook of family psychology* (pp. 258–271). New York, NY: Wiley-Blackwell.

Thompson, P., & Nurse, R. (1999). The KFD test: Clues to family relationships. In A. Nurse (Ed.), *Family assessment: Effective uses of personality tests with couples and families* (pp. 124–134). New York, NY: Wiley.

Viglione, D. J., Blume-Marcovici, A. C., Miller, H. L., Giromini, L., & Meyer, G. (2012). An inter-rater reliability study for the Rorschach performance assessment system. *Journal of Personality Assessment, 94*(6), 607–612.

Weiner, I., Spielberger, C., & Abeles, N. (2002). Scientific psychology and the Rorschach inkblot method. *Clinical Psychologist, 55*(4), 7–12.

5

OBSERVATIONAL ASSESSMENT WITH COUPLES AND FAMILIES

Robert B. Hampson and W. Robert Beavers

L earning about people by watching them behave is perhaps the oldest assessment tool in evaluating human behavior. Direct observation of humans in context allows an undiluted behavior sample untainted by verbiage, self-report social desirability, or purposeful distortions. However, as will be demonstrated, the behavior must be interpreted and rated within a context and within the theoretical bounds of an assessment model. The observer is provided a conceptual framework, and specific behaviors, to observe and rate. Hence, the observational rating is a product of the tool, so understanding the model and tool is a necessary step in choosing and using an assessment model.

In the past decade since the first edition of this chapter was written, most of the major models presented at that time have remained on the forefront of clinical and research utility as measures of whole-family functioning. In terms of newer instruments, the tendency is toward briefer and more specific observational assessments, including marital instability, couples' intimate behavior ratings, and parenting behaviors. Many of these more specific measures are attempts to measure and predict response to treatment, need for intervention, and improvements through the course of treatment. It should also be noted that there are available self-report scales for most of the major general family models, including the Beavers, Circumplex, and McMaster models (Dai & Wang, 2015).

This chapter will describe several well-known and frequently used clinical rating scales and observational assessment tools designed for the overall evaluation of couples and families. We will not be covering observational assessment tools designed to measure highly specific individual or interactional behavior in research studies (Kerig & Lindahl, 2001; Pinsof, Zinbarg, &

Knobloch-Fedders, 2008). The instruments and more global clinical models include the Beavers Interactional Competence and Style Scales, the Circumplex Model Clinical Rating Scale (CRS), the McMaster Model CRS, and the Global Assessment of Relational Functioning (GARF). The instruments and underlying models will be discussed, and then two detailed case examples will be provided to illustrate how assessment can be used as a guide in planning intervention in family therapy.

Beavers Interactional Scales (BIS):
Competence and Style

Instrument name. The Beavers Interactional Competence Scale and Interactional Style Scale were derived originally from the Beavers-Timberlawn Scale. These scales were refined and standardized by W. Robert Beavers and Robert B. Hampson (Beavers & Hampson, 1990; Lebow & Stroud, 2012).

Type of instrument. These scales are presented as Likert-type ratings. Subscales are rated from 1 to 5, and the global competence rating is a 1–10 scale. The ratings are based on family interaction observed over a 10-min period.

Use–target audience. The intended target group is a two (or more) generational family system, usually parent(s) and child(ren). The scales can and have been used for couples, but several of the subscales do not apply to single-generational systems.

Multicultural. The scales have been used (and norms published) on various ethnic groups in the United States (Hampson, Beavers, & Hulgus, 1990). The scales have also been used in Finland, Sweden, Denmark, Italy, France, Germany, China, Pakistan, Mexico, and Japan. The accompanying self-report scale (Self-Report Family Inventory [SFI]) is also available in several foreign languages. This instrument has been studied and used with clinical and nonclinical families.

Ease and time of administration. Once a rater has been trained to reliability, the actual time of administration is 10 min. Prior to an initial session, the family is instructed to "Discuss together what you would like to see changed in your family," while the interviewer leaves the room. Ten-minute segments are usually videotaped. Rater teams (for research) or the therapist views the tape, or the live interaction, and the ratings are done immediately following the 10-min interaction.

Scoring procedure. The interactional scales are hand-scored immediately after the 10-min observation.

Reliability. Interrater reliability coefficients of .85 or above have been noted for global ratings of competence and style. Reliability of individual Likert subscales range from .74 to .93.

Validity. The Beavers Interactional Competence Scale correlates +.72 (Canonical correlation) with the self-report scale (SFI). The Competence scale also correlates favorably with other measures of family functioning (McMaster). (Beavers & Hampson, 1990).

Availability and source. These rating scales have been made readily available through the authors' book, *Successful Families: Assessment and Intervention* (1990).

They can also be ordered from Dr. Hampson directly: Psychology Department, P.O. Box 0442, Southern Methodist University, Dallas, Texas 75275-0442 (rhampson@smu.edu). There is no charge for the use of the observational scales or the accompanying SFI. The authors request results from studies using the scales.

Comment. The BIS have evolved over 45 years of observation of clinical and nonclinical families of a wide variety of structure, ethnicity, and nationality. The scales are based on the Beavers Systems Model, which has studied family competence as well as dysfunction. The model also can identify family system lacks and needs at different levels of disturbance and suggested strength-building procedures and guidelines for therapy at different levels. The Style scale, unique to this model, provides a rating of Centripetal (internalizing) and Centrifugal (externalizing) forces, which is also useful in therapy planning.

The Beavers Systems Model

The dimensions of competence and style provide a useful map for identifying levels of family health and dysfunction. Figure 5.1, below, illustrates this model.

Family competence ranges from Optimal to Severely Dysfunctional and is plotted along the horizontal axis. From left to right, the continuum of family competence ranges from extreme rigidity (chaotic, noninteractive), through marked dominance–submission patterns, to greater capacity for egalitarian and more successful transactions.

The vertical axis represents family Style, a dimension unique to the Beavers Model. It ranges from highly Centripetal (internalizing, lower end) to highly Centrifugal (externalizing, upper end). The representation is intended to depict more rigid and extreme styles to be found in more dysfunctional families and a more blended and flexible style in the more competent families. The resultant arrow shape shows the clinical and empirical findings that healthy families show a flexible and blended family style, such that they can adapt stylistic behavior as developmental, individual, and family needs change over time. At the most dysfunctional end of the competence dimension are the most rigid and extreme family styles; these families' extreme rigidity and limited coping skills disallow variation in interactional behavior. The V-shaped "notch" on the left represents the finding that severely disturbed families show more extreme and rigid styles, with no moderation or blending of stylistic behavior.

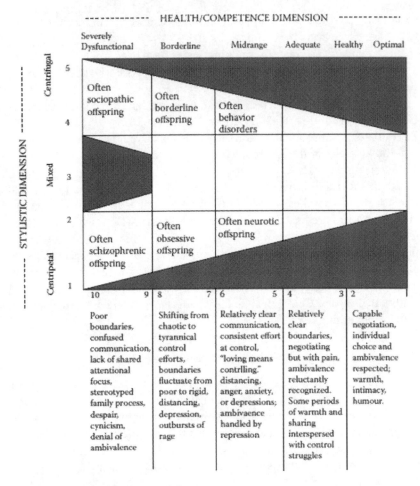

Figure 5.1 Beavers Systems Model

The Rating Scales

The Competence Scale has a global rating, which is based on the ratings on 12 subscales. These are (with interrater reliabilities in parentheses):

1. Structure of the family:
   Overt Power: chaotic to egalitarian (.83)
   Parental Coalition: parent–child to strong parental bond (.85)
   Closeness: indistinct boundaries to close, distinct boundaries (.72)
2. Mythology: reality perception: incongruent to congruent/realistic (.86)
3. Goal-directed negotiation: inefficient to efficient problem-solving (.83)
4. Autonomy:
   Clarity of Expression: indirect to direct expression of feelings/thoughts (.82)

Responsibility: disowning versus owning responsibility for personal issues (.86)

Permeability: open versus unreceptive to other members (.86)

5. Family Affect:

Range of Feelings: taboos to wide range of feeling expressed (.84)

Mood and Tone: open/optimistic to cynical/pessimistic (.89)

Unresolvable conflict: chronic unresolved to ability to resolve (.77)

Empathy: empathic versus inappropriate responses (.88)

6. Global Health/Pathology: optimal to dysfunctional (.85)

The Beavers Interactional Style Scale has a global rating, as well as seven subscales. Middle ratings on each scale are representative of mixed/blended style in more competent families, while extremes of style are more characteristic of the rigid (either/or) styles found in more dysfunctional families:

1. Dependency needs: encouraged (CP) to discouraged (CF) (.81)
2. Adult conflict: covert/hidden (CP) to open/direct (CF) (.74)
3. Physical proximity: very closely spaced (CP) to distant (CF) (.83)
4. Social presentation: overly concerned (CP) versus unconcerned (CF) about their impression (.74)
5. Expression of closeness: high (CP) versus denial (CF) of closeness (.77)
6. Agressive/hostile expression: discouraging (CP) versus solicitation/encouragement (CF) (.81)
7. Types of feelings: warm/positive (CP) versus angry/hostile (CF) (.83)
8. Global CP/CF rating: extreme CP to mixed to extreme CF (.80)

Using the Beavers Scales with Families and Couples

The ten-minute observation usually precedes the first therapy session, after which the therapist trained in the use of the Beavers system begins to work with the family. The Beavers Model offers specific guidance for developing a therapy plan for the family, based on the observational assessment. The assessment of family competence and style provides for seven different clinically useful groupings of families, which have been described in detail elsewhere (Beavers & Hampson, 2003); each require a somewhat different therapeutic stance (Hampson & Beavers, 1996a, 1996b). A brief summary of family types typically encountered in a clinical setting follows.

Midrange families: These are the most frequently occurring families in the general population and represent a substantial number of clinical families. They are of quite traditional structure and are invested in maintaining a consistent rule structure ("loving means controlling"). Cultural stereotyping of sex roles is predominant in these families.

Midrange Centripetal families are characterized by concern for rules and authority; no overt defiance is expected. They expect control efforts to be successful. Family members keep their anger and dissention in check; there is no allowance for expression of overt disagreement or hostility. Hence, internalizing and repression will manifest as anxiety and depression. Only modest levels of spontaneity are seen, and sex role stereotyping is rigid and traditional. These families need therapists who will join them, model straightforward expression and negotiation of differences, encourage clarity and honesty, and promote nonverbal awareness of affect. Paradoxical techniques often backfire, since trust is so vital to these families. If there is a clinical patient, most likely that individual will be the symptom-bearer and manifest an internalizing disorder.

Midrange Mixed and Midrange Centrifugal families also attempt to control by authority, but that control is less effective in producing consistent and internalized behavior control. To deal with behavioral transgressions, these families use criticism, blame, and anger expressed overtly. In these families, no one person is to blame, and everyone feels the brunt of power and control struggles. Adults spend little time together, and satisfaction is sought outside the family. Individual manifestations of psychiatric disturbance are manifest as acting-out disorders. Centrifugal families rarely present voluntarily for treatment, since they have more reliance on action than words as a means of dealing with human distress. They require therapists who can maintain some control over conflict situations and help the family verbalize conflict issues. Eventually, the therapist helps the family redefine bad behavior as needy and conflict as desire for nurturance. These therapists cannot "join" the family as "warm and fuzzy"; they need to exert more structuring and control.

Borderline-level families are more concerned about control issues than are midrange families, to the near exclusion of concerns for happiness, intimacy, or satisfaction. Individual family members find little emotional support in these rigid and fluctuating systems, yet separation and individuation issues are often unresolved.

Borderline Centripetal families are rigid control-oriented systems that are often rigidly organized. They alternate between rigid control efforts to attempt to stem chaos, and chaotic interaction. Offspring are typically rigidly obsessive or compulsive (including anorexia), which mimics the family pattern of little joy and an illusory level of control over self and the world. Observers of these families will see fluctuations between effective domination and disintegration into chaos. Scapegoats in these families are often symptom bearers of the system itself (rigid control). Others are rebels from the tight reins and are the "fallen saints" of the system. Hence, some acting-out behavior may be seen in some of these families. This is why therapists for this family group need to maintain a power differential with the family and physically set boundaries for intrusions. They need to focus on satisfaction and possibilities and with the possibility of satisfaction and enjoyment in relating. Paradoxical procedures can be useful in interrupting vicious cycles of behavior (this is perhaps the only clinical group where this is effective).

Borderline Centrifugal families are much more open in the direct expression of anger and hostility; there is frequent leave-taking. Control themes are overt blaming and direct emotional assaults; the cyclical chaos is more overt than covert. Nurturance is not available to parents or children, and satisfaction is sought outside the family. Each person is on his/her own to try to get whatever they need. In these families, there is no single "fallen saint"; multiple members act out like a "pack of like sinners." Psychiatric disorders typically include externalizing disorders (conduct, substance abuse) and cyclical disorders that reflect the rigid-to-chaos fluctuations (Borderline Personality Disorders are often members of these families). They need therapists who can maintain effective control, limit the number of members attending, focus on the basic, help the family organize simple actions and activities, organize generational boundaries, and help members take risks with neediness and emotional pain.

Severely Dysfunctional families are the most limited in making adjustments for developmental needs of offspring, in negotiation and basic communication skills, and in clarity and contextual coherence. Boundaries are vague and amorphous, and parent–child coalitions may supplant adult coalitions in these families. Expressions of coherent affective tone are missing, and family members typically look bewildered and feel considerable despair. Because of the limited degree of autonomy and differentiation (indeed, these were the families Murray Bowen described in his work), people cannot resolve conflict or offer intimacy. These systems flounder like a ship without a rudder.

Severely Dysfunctional Centripetal families are vague and indistinct structures where verbal incoherence and chaos predominate. There is little if any sense of individuation; members frequently speak for each other; children do not progress through normal patterns of separation and autonomy. Crises and losses are not handled through sharing; emotional isolation and taboos about dealing with crisis issues are firmly felt. Children in these families are inhibited and overcontrolled; some of these families have schizophrenic offspring (obviously with strong biological loadings). The adult coalition is nearly nonexistent, and often there are covert parent–child alliances. Therapists who work with these families must structure and organize; promoting contextual and communicational clarity is job one. Through every session, the therapist must facilitate encounters, demand coherence, promote clarity, block intrusions, and reinforce collaboration among family members.

Severely Dysfunctional Centrifugal families are characterized by chaos of a different sort; their boundary with the outside world is diffuse (the definition of who constitutes the family is often ambiguous), and the internal chaos is more behavioral than verbal. Family interaction is characterized by negative exchanges: disrespect, name-calling, put-downs, and overt hostility. Leave-taking is frequent, and when satisfaction (which is sought away from home) is not attained, family members may return home even more cynical than when they left. There is no nurturance provided for offspring, and they develop a hostile attitude toward others, often manifest as sociopathy or extreme aggression. Family members spread out across the room, keeping both physical and emotional distance. Hopelessness pervades these families. These families seldom come to therapy on their own; for those that do, or are court ordered to attend therapy, they need a therapist who can keep firm control of the session, including seating arrangements and determining who shall attend. Eventually, the therapist has to help family members pair words with behavior, coordinate basic activities, and emphasize risk taking with positive feelings.

Using the Beavers Model observational rating scales can provide a useful roadmap, not only for the classification of families, but also in anticipating a given family's basic lacks and needs. An appropriate "match" of therapist orientation with the competence and style level of the family (Hampson & Beavers, 1996a) or couple (Hampson, Prince, & Beavers, 1999) can facilitate greater gains in therapy than an apparent mismatch can. Family competence is a much stronger predictor of therapy outcome (Hampson & Beavers, 1996b) or dropout status (a study currently in progress) than any other factor, including family structure, income and socioeconomic status, and ethnicity. Family competence has also been related to health outcomes; a recent study using the Beavers scales found that obese adolescents in the most competent families were able (with family support) to lose the most weight while participating in a family-based weight loss and nutrition program (Kitzman et al., 2009). In studies with adolescent drug users, families who received Multidimensional Family Therapy were substantially improved on family competence during treatment and at follow-ups (Liddle et al., 2001).

We also use the scales to monitor a family's progress. For example, on the "Closeness" dimension, a Severely Dysfunctional Centripetal family will be seen as having "Amorphous, vague and indistinct boundaries among members." If a family is making progress, we will see the next higher level, as the family members show "Isolation and distancing." This is therapeutic progress, even though family members fear being lost to each other.

When subjected to a confirmatory factor analysis (Lee, Jager, Whiting, & Kwanted, 2000), there were mixed results in terms of Competence or Style being unitary constructs. However, this fits with the clinical foundations of the scales, in that summatively, family competence is defined by structure, affective tones, communication skills, and autonomy of members. Hence, it is not surprising that the subscales of the Competence and Style dimensions were not unitary dimensions.

The observational scales can be used in conjunction with the self-report instrument from the Beavers Model, the SFI. This is a brief (36 items) and reliable instrument that measures family Competence, Style (Cohesion), and three additional scales: Conflict, Leadership, and Emotional Expressiveness. It is often informative to see which family members view the family as more or less competent in planning therapeutic goals and strategies. The SFI also shows a high level of convergence with the observational scales in a clinical sample (Hampson, Beavers, & Hulgus, 1989).

The McMaster Model CRS

Instrument name. The McMaster CRS is an observational rating scale based on the McMaster Model of Family Functioning (Epstein, Ryan, Bishop, Miller, & Keitner, 2003). The original model was developed by Epstein while at McMaster University. More recently, the CRS, its sibling self-report scale (FAD: Family Assessment Device; Lebow & Stroud, 2012), and structured interview (McSIFF: McMaster Structured Interview for Family Functioning; Bishop et al., 2000) have been studied by the Brown University group (Miller, Ryan, Keitner, Bishop, & Epstein, 2000).

Type of instrument. The McMaster CRS is a Likert-type rating scale designed to measure overall Family Functional (a global rating). There are also six subscales, each rated from 1 (very disturbed) to 7 (superior): Problem-Solving, Communication, Roles, Affective Responsiveness, Affective Involvement, and Behavior Control. The rating is based on observation (or conducting) a detailed family interview.

Use–target audience. The McMaster CRS is designed to be used on whole families, following a detailed clinical interview.

Multicultural. The self-report FAD has been translated into 14 different languages and has been used on a wide variety of ethnic and socioeconomic groups in this country (Aarons, McDonald, Connelly, & Newton, 2007; Mansfield, Keitner, & Dealy, 2015). The CRS, however, has been studied primarily with clinical and nonclinical families mostly of middle-class status (Miller et al., 2000).

Ease and time of administration. The CRS can be completed by trained raters in a matter of minutes. However, since it is based on the observation of a detailed clinical interview, that time must be factored into the total administration. The McSIFF and its precursor, the McMaster Model Structured Interview (Bishop et al., 1987) can take 90 min to administer. The authors indicate that individuals at various levels of training can become reliable on the CRS, but the interview needs to be conducted by a more experienced clinician.

Scoring procedure. Each scale is rated from 1 (Very Disturbed) to 7 (Superior). A manual describes concise anchor descriptions for points 1, 5 (nonclinical range) and 7 on each scale.

Reliability. Miller et al. (1994) report acceptable test–retest reliabilities (.81–.87) across subscales and good interrater reliabilities (.68–.87).

Validity. The CRS has shown adequate correspondence with the self-report FAD scales for a variety of clinical groups (Miller et al., 1994). In one study of discriminative validity, the CRS scale scores were significantly more disturbed for patents' families during the acute phase of depression than at post-acute follow-up.

Availability and source. The McMaster CRS is $15.00, and the McSIFF interview protocol is $40.00. The scales are available from Christine Ryan, Ph.D. or Ivan Miller, Ph.D., Brown University Family Research Program, Rhode Island Hospital—Potter 3, 593 Eddy Street, Providence, RI 02903 (phone: (401) 444–3534; FAX: (401) 444–3298).

Comment. The McMaster CRS is based upon 30 years of clinical observation and research. Descriptors of disturbed families are based firmly upon collective observations in clinical settings. The scale does not attempt to measure all aspects of family life, but the dimensions deemed to be most predictive of disturbance versus competence in families in clinical settings.

Using the McMaster CRS

Following the detailed clinical interview (McSIFF), the McMaster CRS ratings quantify and summarize the major findings that were probed during the interview. The questions in the interview deal with family functioning, by asking the family members directly a question about how they operate. For example, under the domain of family roles, the interviewer asks directly who is involved in grocery shopping, laundry, repairs, etc. The clinical interview takes from 90 to 120 min.

The CRS has six family functioning domains, and a summary Overall Family Functioning. By providing summary ratings from 1 (very disturbed) to 7 (Superior), a profile of family strengths and needs is constructed, which then allows the therapist to construct goals.

Problem-Solving is the first dimension rated. Effective problem-solving refers to family behavior that resolves problems to a degree that the family can move along effectively. The most effective families do not have fewer problems but are able to solve them readily. The McMaster model offers seven steps in effective problem-solving (Epstein et al., 2003). Families that are more disturbed are less able to resolve differences and solve problems effectively, so there are more unresolved problems.

Communication refers to the exchange of verbal information within the family. Communication within families is subdivided into instrumental (task) and affective areas. More competent families utilize clear (coherent) and direct (spoken to the intended recipient) verbal messages. At lower levels of competence, the communication becomes more masked (unclear) and indirect (deflected or divert to/through someone else).

Role Functioning has to do with consistent role maintenance within the family. This dimension addresses the assignment of roles in the family (allocation) and the ability to maintain stable role performance over time (accountability). Families that are more competent have more stable, predictable performance and maintenance of key family functions, while families that are more disturbed show more fluctuation and less accountability in performance of key family functions.

Affective Responsiveness has to do with the range and appropriateness of family members' emotional interaction. Healthy families are able to experience and respond to a full range of human emotions, in a context appropriate to that emotion, while more disturbed families show limitation on the range and type of feelings expressed, as well as some inappropriate emotional responses (laughing at someone's sorrow).

Affective Involvement refers to the level and type of dyadic relationships within the family structure. This addresses the manner in which family members show interest and investment in each other. The model presents six types of involvement, ranging from lack of involvement to symbiotic involvement, with "empathic involvement" in the middle as a descriptor of the more competent families. The extremes of involvement represent the relationships in more disturbed families.

Behavior Control refers to the family's means of shaping and directing members' behavior in three major domains: dangerous situations, development of socialization skills, and satisfying/regulating biological needs and drives. Families differ in the way in which they are consistent, direct, and fair. More competent families employ "flexible behavior control," which represents reasonable and negotiable methods of discipline. More disturbed families are of two extremes: "rigid behavior control" (narrow, rigid, non-negotiable) and "laissez-faire behavior control" (lax, no standards, no a priori rules).

Identifying a family's strengths and weaknesses can alert a therapist what problem areas are most pressing as therapy begins. Therapists derive a family profile of strengths and needs and then follow the McMaster Model's treatment approach, as described in the Problem Centered Systems Therapy of the Family (Hamilton & Carr, 2016). Subsequent evaluations can be used in research studies evaluating the effectiveness of family therapy or can be used individually to monitor the progress of a given case.

Circumplex Model CRS

Instrument name. CRS for the Circumplex Model of Marital and Family Systems is an observational rating scale based on the major theoretical dimensions of the Circumplex Model (Olson & Gorall, 2003). It was initially developed in 1980 and has evolved over several modifications of the Circumplex Model, with revisions in 1983, 1985, and 1988.

Type of instrument. The CRS is a checklist-type rating scale, with descriptors for each dimension at each rating point. It is to be used following observation or direction of a semistructured family interview.

Use–target audience. The Circumplex CRS is designed to be used by trained raters for observing couples and families.

Multicultural. The scales of the Circumplex Model, including the self-report Family Adaptability and Cohesion Evaluation Scales (FACES I, II, III, and IV), have been used in many foreign countries and have been translated into several languages. The FACES instruments are estimated to be the third most widely used family scales in couple and family therapy outcome research (Sanderson et al., 2009). The CRS is less widely used than the FACES.

Ease and time of administration. The completion of the rating scale itself takes only a few minutes for trained raters. The clinical interview on which the ratings are based is of an unspecified length. The clinical interview can be semistructured yet should cover the basic dimensions of the model (Cohesion, Flexibility, and Communication). It is also important for the family to dialogue with each other, for example, asking them to describe what a typical week is like and how they handle their daily routines.

Scoring procedure. Each of the three major theoretical dimensions of the Circumplex Model, and composite subscales, are rated by the observer following the interview. The scales and their composites will be described below. Cohesion dimensions are rated from 1–2 (disconnected) through 5–6 (connected) to 9–10 (enmeshed). Flexibility dimensions are rated from 1–2 (inflexible-rigid) through 5–6 (flexible) to 9–10 (overly flexible-chaotic). Communication dimensions are rated from 1–2 (low) through 3–4 (facilitating) through 5–6 (high). The first two scales are based on a curvilinear distribution, where competence is theoretically in the middle; communication is a unidimensional scale, from low to high.

Reliability. The Circumplex CRS has good internal and interrater reliability. Alpha coefficients for the three dimensions include .95 for Cohesion, .94 for Adaptability (Flexibility), and .97 for Communication (Thomas & Olson, 1993). Test–retest reliabilities have also been reported: .83 for Cohesion, .75 for Adaptability (Flexibility), and .86 for Communication.

Validity. Support for the curvilinear distribution of Circumplex rating scale scores has been demonstrated via regression analysis. Both Cohesion and Flexibility have been curvilinearly related to family communication and family satisfaction (both linear). Hence, the CRS more closely fits the Circumplex theory than do the self-report FACES instruments.

Availability and source: The Circumplex CRS is available for $30.00 from Life Innovations, 2660 Arthur Street, Roseville, MN 55113 (www.facesiv/ studies/family_scales.html). There is also a Circumplex Training Package, containing a training manual, training video, and the CRS; it costs $50.00. Finally, the revised self-report scales are available in the Family Inventories Package (FIP; Olson, Gorall, & Tiesel, 2006): www.facesiv.com/studies/fip.html.

Comment. The CRS is a less widely used instrument than the Circumplex Model self-report scale, the FACES. There have been challenges in the past regarding the curvilinear nature of some of the scales, especially the Flexibility Scale (and its predecessor, "Adaptability"). Other models (Lee, 1988) state that Chaos and Rigidity are closely related in evolution of system development, rather than polar opposites.

Using the Circumplex CRS with Couples and Families

Following an interview or detailed discussion task, raters (or therapists) rate the family on specific dimensions of each of the subscales of the major dimensions of Cohesion, Flexibility, and Communication. The Cohesion subscales, which range from Disconnected (1–2) to Overly Connected/ Enmeshed (9–10), include dimensions of Emotional Bonding, Family Involvement, Marital Relationship, and Parent–child Relationships. The Cohesion dimension also provides ratings for Internal Boundaries (time, space, and decision-making) and External Boundaries (friends, interests, and activities). Descriptive rating points for each level of Cohesion are provided.

The Flexibility scales, representing a curvilinear distribution from Inflexible (rigid) through Flexible to Overly Flexible/Chaotic, provide the following subscales: leadership (authoritarian to limited leadership), discipline (autocratic to laissez-faire), negotiation (imposed decisions to impulsive decisions), roles (rigid to shifting roles), and rules (inflexible to changing rule structure).

The Communication scale is a directional, linear rating from Low to High levels of communication skills. The dimensions rated include listeners' skills (empathy, attentive listening), speakers' skills (speaking for oneself, speaking for others), self-disclosure, clarity, continuity, and respect & regard. Olson's view of communication is that it is a facilitating dimension within the various family types as described by the Flexibility and Cohesion dimensions. Communication is also an important part of the PREPARE/ENRICH assessment for premarital and married couples.

GARF Scale

Instrument name. The GARF scale is an appendix in the current *Diagnostic and Statistical Manual of Mental Disorders, Fourth Edition* (DSM-IV) and DSM-IV Text Revision (DSM-IV-TR), to assist clinicians in their evaluation and diagnosis of individual patients by emphasizing their relational context. The current instrument evolved through multi-organization collaboration. Spearheaded by a critique of the DSM system lacking a family or relational axis by Lyman Wynne, the GAP Committee on the Family began developing such a rating scale. In 1989, after key DSM-IV chairpersons endorsed the development of such a scale, a multi-organization task force was convened by Robert Beavers (then president of American Association for Marital and Family Therapy (AAMFT), on the Group for the Advancement of Psychiatry (GAP) Committee, and on the board of American Family Therapy Association (AFTA)). The result was the Coalition on Family Diagnosis, co-chaired by Florence Kaslow and Herta Guttman; that coalition, with participation from 12 different organizations, developed the GARF (Yingling, Miller, McDonald, & Galewater, 1998).

Type of instrument. The GARF is a dimensional rating scale analogous to the Global Assessment of Functioning (GAF) Axis in DSM-IV. Ratings are based on a 1–99 rating. The most satisfactory family ratings are 81–99; less satisfactory, 61–80; predominantly unsatisfactory, 41–60; rarely satisfactory, 21–40; and chaotic, 1–20. These ratings are done for the global family/couple interaction. Separate sub-ratings of the family/couple's Problem-Solving, Organization, and Emotional Climate can also be made using the same number line.

Use–target audience. The GARF is intended to be used for rating the contextual relationship for a given patient/client, regardless of the formal definition of that relationship. This not only includes couples and families, but can also include life partners, key friendships, and support networks for single/unattached people.

Multicultural. Most of the published reports regarding the GARF are set in clinical settings, primarily with English-speaking clients.

Ease and time of administration. The GARF can be completed in a matter of minutes by trained clinicians. The rating most typically follows the completion of a family/couple therapy session, although less formal interactions can be rated. It is even possible to rate a family based on a client's *report* of the relational system.

Scoring procedure. Following the session or interaction observed, the rater completes a GARF rating scale for Global functioning, as well as the subscales addressed above. A single number is assigned to each dimension.

Reliability. Reliability analysis of the GARF has shown a broad spectrum of interrater reliability scores. Since the GARF presents a 20-point range within each of the five levels of functioning, exact-number reliability between pairs of raters has ranged from .34 to .75 (Gordon, 1997). However, when the range of ratings was broadened to within five rating points within the same level, the reliability estimates (*kappa* coefficients) were consistently higher: Global +.79, Problem-Solving +.73, Organization +.86, and Emotional Climate +.83 (Gordon, 1997). There is evidence that raters with higher levels of training in family systems theory and therapy have higher agreement and generalizability ratings (Motarella, Philpot, & Fritzsche, 2001).

Validity. The relationship between GARF ratings and other ratings of family/couple functioning indicate generally adequate construct and clinical validity. For example, GARF and Beavers Interactional Competence were correlated—−.69 (different directions of scores) at the initial session and −.54 with mother's Self-Report Family Inventory competence (Henney & Hampson, 1994). GARF change scores (pre–post GARF ratings across therapy) have correlated well with therapists' ratings of change (.47) and clients' report of change (.36). In addition, initial GARF ratings have been associated with severity ratings of the client at intake (−.52) (Ross & Doherty, 2001).

Availability and source. The GARF is printed in the DSM-IV and DSM-IV-TR as an Axis Provided for Further Study. Family-related problems are listed primarily as V-codes in DSM-5. A good resource is *GARF Assessment Sourcebook: Using the DSM-IV Global Assessment of Relational Functioning*, 1998, by Yingling and her co-authors (Brunner/Mazel).

Comment: The GARF is a brief and fairly simple instrument that can be used by therapists and researchers. It can be used on a session-by-session basis to track progress in relational functioning. It addresses only the "competence" dimension of family/couple functioning.

Using the GARF with Couples and Families

GARF ratings may be performed by therapists or non-participating raters. Although the particular interaction task or setting is not specified, it is typical that the raters provide global and subscale ratings following the first therapy session, rather than after a specified interaction sequence. Yingling et al. (1998) provide several excellent examples of the use of the GARF to monitor session-by-session progress in family therapy cases. It is important that the rater be the same person every session, since between-rater variance for exact-point numerical ratings can be rather large (Henney & Hampson, 1994). Recent validation research has shown the GARF to have adequate interrater reliability (Denton, Nakonezny, & Burwell, 2010).

The functioning categories and ranges of scores help classify families from dysfunctional to satisfactory. Based on the history of the couple/family, it is often useful to classify not just current relational functioning, but past relational functioning. The GARF authors recommend rating the highest level of functioning and the lowest level of functioning within the past year, much like the GAF rating in the DSM-IV.

Ratings are performed for the overall level of family functioning. The GARF developers also recommend subscale ratings for more specific behaviors. *Problem-Solving* refers to the relational unit's ability to negotiate rules and differences, adapt and cope with stressful events, provide clear and direct communication, and resolve conflict. *Organization* refers to the clarity and ongoing distinctness of roles and interpersonal boundaries, power distribution and hierarchical functioning, behavioral control, and personal responsibility for actions. *Emotional climate* represents the family's overall mood and tone; quality of caring, attachment, and empathy; respect and valuing; and quality of sexual relating. While it is true that there are not going to be large differences among these ratings (Beavers & Hampson, 1990), these ratings can be useful in determining specific family/couple lacks and needs.

The highest level of functioning, satisfactory relational functioning (81–100), describes a relational context that is structured and predictable, yet flexible in the face of the need to adapt. Conflicts are typically resolved successfully. Each member is unique, and the power distribution is shared. These relational units appear satisfied, optimistic, and therefore can display a wide range of feelings as the situation dictates.

Somewhat unsatisfactory relational units (61–80) demonstrate adequate, mostly normal patterns of relating but with more pain and struggle than the satisfactory group. Some conflicts are not resolved. While decision-making is competent, there may be control struggles that interfere with egalitarian relationships. There is a masking of some feelings; warmth and caring are present but not as unconditional as in the satisfactory units. Parenting is adequate but less spontaneous than in the former group.

Predominantly unsatisfactory couples and families (41–60) demonstrate more difficulty with clarity, problem-solving, and transitory adaptations to change. Control themes predominate, and an emphasis on rules is common. Decision-making is intermittently effective; these families are either rigid or lack sufficient structure to enforce rules (see Beavers' Style dimension). Different feelings are disallowed; pain and anger are typically not handled well. While there is some warmth and support, it is often contingent and unequally distributed.

Rarely satisfactory units (21–40) provide relatively low levels of support. Expectations for behavior are rigidly and obsessionally held to or are largely ignored. These units do not handle change and transition well. Obvious emotional distancing or physical leave-taking and hostility prevent smooth communication and negotiation. The emotional climate is quite barren or openly hostile. Alternations between attempts at rigid control and chaotic functioning disallow continuity in these families.

Chaotic relational units (1–20) lack coherence and continuity. Day-to-day routines are negligible, and communication is indirect and incoherent. Relationships are overly dependent (cf. "Centripetal") or overly distant and hostile (cf. "Centrifugal"). Relational boundaries fluctuate, and no one knows where he/she stands with other family members. Despair, cynicism, and lack of hope predominate, so there is little emotional nurturance provided.

By rating a family or couple on global functioning and the individual subscales, a profile of family strengths and needs can be mapped (Yingling et al., 1998).

Marital Instability Index (MII)

Instrument name. MII measures proneness to divorce by taking cognitions as well as behaviors into account.

Type of instrument. The MII makes use of a 14-item dichotomous in Part I. It also has five Likert-scale questions in Part II which measures other risk factors and adds to the accuracy of this assessment. It is most useful the more recently it is administered in relation to specified cognitions and behaviors. It holds promise for predicting with greater accuracy, the outcome of marital relationships.

Ease and time of administration. It can be easily administered by a single interviewer.

Scoring procedure. The number of divorced prone answers are summed and recorded at the bottom of the measure where a corresponding "chance of divorce" figure is presented. Part II is scored by adding or subtracting a given number of points to the "divorce proneness" score based on the answers to questions in part II.

Reliability. The MII has excellent internal consistency with an alpha of .93.

Validity. The MII has good predictive validity. Only 3% of people who showed no signs of marital instability divorced three years later compared to 27% of those who scored at the other extreme. It also has good construct validity, correlating positively with measures of marital problems and marital "disagrees."

Availability and source. The MII is available by journal article and was written by John N. Edwards, David R. Johnson, and Alan Booth. Coming apart: A prognostic instrument of marital breakup, *Family Relations*, 36, 168–170.

Comments. There are no norms or demographic data reported for this instrument. However, this instrument is valuable because it is short, so it would be good for a retest during follow-up. In addition, 2,034 people were included in the sample, but because we do not know the demographics, one must be careful when interpreting results with various populations.

Environmental Assessment Index (EAI)

Instrument name. EAI assesses the educational/developmental quality of children's home environment.

Type of Instrument. The EAI is a 44-item instrument (22 items in the short version), used in homes of children 3–11.

Ease and time of administration. The EAI is relativity easy to administer. How long it takes to administer this scale will be determined by whether the observer answers questions by direct observation, which will take longer than just asking mother.

Scoring procedure: Score yes or no for each item based on direct observation or information from mother. Each "yes" is scored 2 and each "no" receives a score of 1. The total score is the sum of all items. The scores on the long form range from 44 to 88 and 24 to 48 on the short form.

Reliability. Cronbach's alpha is .84 for the long form and .82 for the short form suggesting good internal consistency. The correlation between the long and short forms is .93, which suggests alternate form reliability. Test–retest reliability ranged from .67 to .96.

Validity. The EAI has good concurrent and predictive validity with significant correlations between the scale and intellectual functioning.

Availability and source. The EAI was written by Robert H. Poresky and is available by journal article. Environmental Assessment Index Reliability, stability and validity of the long and short forms, *Educational and Psychological Measurements*, 47, 969–975.

Comments. The EAI is viewed as being useful in assisting with child placements, assessing the effectiveness of home interventions, and understanding the home environment's influence on children's development. It was normed with nonurban two parent Midwest families. Therefore, its use may be limited in metropolitan areas like South Florida. Some items in the questionnaire need to be updated.

Couples' Intimate Behavior (CIB) Rating System

Instrument name. The CIB rating system assesses the depth of factual, emotional, and cognitive self-disclosure of the speaker and understanding, validation, and caring expressed by listener in each interaction.

Type of Instrument. The CIB rating system is a global system in which ratings of each type and class of behavior is made on a five-point Likert scale.

Ease and time of administration. This system is somewhat time consuming due to the fact the rater must watch video of couple's discussion two times. However, the segments rated are each only five minutes long (Mitchell, A., personal communication, 2011).

Scoring procedure. Raters look at type twice to rate first the speaker on factual, emotional, and cognitive disclosure. Then s/he watches it again to rate the listener's understanding, validation, and caring. Higher ratings reflect greater depth of disclosure.

Reliability. Interrater reliability ranged from .79 to .92

Validity. Unavailable.

Availability and source: Mitchell, A. E., Castellani, A. M., Herrington, R. L., Joseph, J. I., Doss, B. D., & Snyder, D. K. (2008). Predictors of intimacy in couples' discussions of relationship injuries: An observational study. *Journal of Family Psychology, 22*(1), 21–29.

Comments. This rater system has not been normed and was developed for the primary purpose of researching couple intimacy.

Child and Adult Relational Experimental Index (CARE-Index)

Instrument name. CARE-Index is an observational measure of parenting behavior (Crittendon, 1988).

Type of instrument. This measure was specifically designed to distinguish at-risk from adequate parenting behavior. Mothers' ratings on the measure also were associated with children's interactive behavior and with an estimation of risk based on a multifaceted, comprehensive assessment. The measure's relation to estimation of risk remained significant when two other predictors of risk, maternal caregiving attitudes, and insight into mental illness were considered. Taken together, the findings suggest that the measure can provide reliable, valid, and independent information on parenting behavior that could inform comprehensive, multifaceted assessments of parenting risk.

Ease and time of administration. Easy to administer and can be used in different settings.

Scoring procedure. Raters weighed the various risk and protective factors, assigning each parent into a high- (3), moderate- (2), or low- (1) risk category. Higher risk scores were given when the evidence indicated that even if a mother was offered interventions, the prognosis for her being able to provide adequate parenting to her child in a reasonable time frame was poor. A lower risk score meant that there was a reasonable likelihood that the mother could successfully parent her child effectively if specific interventions were offered and accepted

Reliability. Independent and trained raters achieved a high level of reliability on the measure. Interrater reliability was high ($\kappa = .95$).

Validity. Mothers' scores on the CARE-Index were associated in many ways with children's behavior. Maternal sensitivity was linked to cooperative child behavior. Maternal hostility/intrusiveness was linked to difficult child behavior in children up to 18 months of age and only to compulsive compliant child behavior in children aged 18 months and older. Unresponsive maternal behavior was associated with passive child behavior and was not linked to compulsive compliant or difficult child behavior. Unresponsive maternal behavior also predicted adult attachment problems 20 years later in a longitudinal study (Zayas, Mischel, Shoda, & Aber, 2010).

Availability and source. See Crittendon (1988).

Comments. With the high incidence of mental illness, and the increasing incidence of maltreatment of children, this instrument could be used with greater frequency. As it is used more, norms will continue to be developed.

Family Alliance Assessment Scales (FAAS)

Instrument name. FAAS assess the interactive relationship between mother, father, and infant. The scales assess co-parenting, affective relating, and organizational styles of interaction.

Type of instrument. The FAAS are eleven rating scales based on the observation of video-recorded interaction segments in which parents and infant play together for around ten minutes (Lausanne Trilogue Play, LTP). In one segment, one parent plays with the child while the other watches, and then the parents switch roles in the second. The third segment involves both parents playing with the child, and then in the final segment the parents interact with each other only. Fifteen scales measure seven major constructs: Participation (postures and gazes, inclusion of partners), Organization (role implications, structure), Focalization (co-construction), Affect Sharing (family warmth, validation, and authenticity), Timing/synchronization (interactive mistakes during activities and during transitions), Co-parenting (support, conflicts), and Infant (involvement, self-regulation).

Ease and time of administration. This system is economical in terms of time to administer. The interactional period lasts approximately ten minutes, and one trained rater typically does the ratings. In the reliability study, two additional raters were added for that purpose.

Scoring procedure. Solo raters watch the video once and rate each scale on a 0, 1, or 2 index.

Reliability. Interrater reliability (ICC) ranged from .61 to .90, with an average of .80. The Cronbach alpha for all scales was .92

Validity. Normative families had significantly higher (better functioning) ratings than did clinical families on 12 of the 15 scales. Ecological validity of the interaction task showed a high level of couple ratings (3.7 of 5) that the interaction being observed was typical of day-to-day behavior at home.

Availability and source. Favez, N., Scaiola, C.L, Tissot, H., Darwiche, J, and Frascarolo, F. (2011). The Family Alliance Assessment Scales: Steps toward validity and reliability of an observational assessment tool for early family interactions. *Journal of Child and Family Studies, 20*, 23–37.

Comments: This rater system has not been normed and was developed for the primary purpose of researching couple intimacy.

Protocol for Using Observational Assessments with Couples and Families

The following protocol can be useful when utilizing any of the whole-family assessment rating scales addressed in this chapter. Some require more time and detail in terms of administration, and some require a videotaped assessment segment.

1. Obtain written consent for the observational procedure and consent for videotaping (when used). Assure the family that no one outside the clinical supervisors and direct therapists will be viewing the tape.
2. Select an assessment tool that fits the needs of the clinic or practice that is using the instrument. For example, the Beavers Model rating scales can be used within a rather brief time period at the beginning of the first session. The McMaster Model provides much more overt detail (McSIFF interview), which is then summarized through the rating scales.
3. An interviewer or therapist introduces the discussion task. For the Beavers Scales, it is "For the next ten minutes, I would like you to discuss together what you would like to see changed in your family," while the interviewer leaves the room. For the McMaster Model, the detailed clinical interview (McSIFF) is used, conducted by an experienced clinician. For the Circumplex Model, there is no one specific task, but the family is asked to engage in interactive dialogue, such as asking them to describe their typical week. No set procedure or task is specified for the GARF.
4. Rate the family, based on the observed interactional sequences. Raters typically are trained and well versed in the particular model they are using. For example, it takes approximately 15 hours of rater training to reach interrater reliabilities of +.90 using the Beavers scales.
5. When possible, use the self-report version of the model with individuals, to compare each member's perception of the family with the overall ratings. These are the SFI (Beavers), FAD (McMaster), and FACES III or IV (Circumplex).
6. Use the family ratings to help set therapeutic goals. The identification of specific lacks and needs of the family helps provide an operational list of what tasks need to be accomplished. The identification of family competence and style (Beavers) also helps therapists tailor their approach to each family, in terms of control (power differential), partnership, and disclosure of strategy with the family (see **Table 5.1**).

Table 5.1 Matrix: Observational Family Ratings (Beavers & Hampson, 1990)

Assessment Instrument	Specific Couple and Family Applications	Cultural/ Language	Instruction/Use: T = Time to Take S = Time to Score I = Items	Computerized a = Scoring b = Report	Reliability (R) Validity (V)	Availability
Beavers Interactional Competence & Style; SFI	Whole Families; Classifies Family Competence and Behavioral Style, and Suggestions for Appropriate Therapy	English, Spanish, Italian, Portuguese, Greek, Chinese, Japanese, German, French, Urdu	T = 10 min S = 10 min I = 12 Competence 8 Style	a = no b = no	R = .85 (Interrater) R = α = .88 V = .72 (Canonical)	Directly from Dr. Hampson (Dallas, Texas) rhampson@smu.edu
McMaster CRS	Whole Families; Classifies Families on General Functioning and Composite Behaviors	English, French, 12 Other Languages	T = 90 min with Interview S = 10 min I = 7 Scales McSIFF Interview Has 35 Pages of Questions	a = no b = no	R = .68–87 (Interrater) R = .81–87 (Test-retest) V = Good Clinical Validity	Brown University Family Research Program
Circumplex CRS	Whole Families; Couples. Measures Cohesion, Change (Adaptability), and Communication	English, Spanish, Several Other Languages	T = 45–60 min S = 10–15 min I = 3 Global Scales, 13 Subscales	a = no b = no	R = α = .95–.97 R = .75–.86 (Test-retest) V = Good Support for Circumplex Theory	Life Innovations, Inc, Minneapolis, MN. www.lifeinnivations.org

Instrument	Purpose	Language	T/S/I	a/b	Scoring	Reliability / Validity	Source
GARF	Any relational Unit: Family, Couple, Partner, Support System	English	T = 15–60 min; S = 10 min; I = 4 Global Ratings	a = no; b = no		R = .73–.86 (Interrater); V = .69 (with Beavers Competence)	American Psychological Association (DSM-IV-TR)
FAAS	Measures Co-parenting and Infant–parent Relationships	French and English; sample Caucasian Europeans (Switzerland)	T = Short (10.5 min); S = Short; I = 15 Scales	a = no; b = no		R = .80 (Interrater Average), Range = .71–.90; α = .92; V = 10 Scales Show Significantly Higher Ratings for Norm versus Clinical Families	Author: Nicolas. favez@unige.ch
EAI	Measure Quality of Family's Home Environment for Children	English	T = Not Given; S = Not Given; I = 44 (22 for Short Form)		Hand scoring	R = α = .84 (.82 for Short Form); V = Good Predictive & Concurrent Validity	Journal article
CIB Rating System	Assesses the Depth of Factual, Emotional, and Cognitive Self-Disclosure of the Speaker and Understanding, Validation and Caring Expressed by Listener in Each Interaction	English			Hand scoring	R = α = .79–.82; V = Not Specific	Journal article
CARE-Index	Measure of Parenting Behavior	English	T = 1½ hours		Hand scoring	R = Interrater Reliability was High (κ = .95). V = Passed Several Tests of Validity	Journal article

7. Rerate the family at several points along the therapy time line to monitor progress and check on the therapeutic alliance. In our clinical setting, families are rated again at the sixth session and every six sessions thereafter. In several studies using the GARF, these ratings are provided after every session (Yingling et al., 1998).
8. Provide feedback to the family about the assessment, where they appear to be having problems, and the fact that certain goals can be established right there in the initial session.

Whenever rating scales are used, there may be a certain degree of subjectivity, so the decision about who will perform the rating is important. In our studies, the therapist is always one of the family's raters, since it is done at the outset of the first session. We also have neutral research rating teams view the tapes during the week, and these ratings are added to the case files prior to the second session. Interestingly, and much like the findings of Kolevzon, Green, Fortune, and Vosler (1988), we have found that therapists tend to rate the families they are beginning to treat as slightly more dysfunctional than the neutral raters do in the beginning. Family members' ratings (on the SFI) tend to line up more with the neutral raters. At the close of therapy, the therapists' ratings put the family in a more competent direction than the neutral raters and line up more with the family members' views.

It is also informative to see which family member(s)' rating on the SFI rates the family as more or less disturbed than the outside raters. Our studies have found that adolescents in general, and acting-out adolescents in particular, rate their families as more disturbed than the raters. However, in certain internalizing (CP) patterns, it is not uncommon for the symptomatic adolescent (e.g., anorexic adolescents) to paint a picture of perfection in their families. These varying perspectives can provide a therapist some important insights into family dynamics.

Case Example: A Centrifugal Family

The Redd family was referred by the children's hospital following the second hospitalization of their daughter, Jessie, age 15. She had a tentative diagnosis of Bipolar Disorder II, although the referring counselor termed her a "pre-Borderline" personality disorder. The presenting problems were frequent fits of rage and non-suicidal self-injury (cutting), followed by a suicide attempt with her mother's sleeping pills.

This working-class Caucasian family consisted of Jessie, her father Jimmy (an auto mechanic), mother Deena (stay-at-home mom), brothers Cody (14) and Brady (8), and sisters Michelle (10) and Darlene

(6). The family reported frequent conflict within the home and regular school-based concerns of behavior problems with Michelle and both boys. Cody (14) had also been written up for truancy from junior high school.

The family arrived for the initial assessment interview in two cars and both were late for the initial assessment. After initial forms were completed (Step 1: obtain informed consent for evaluation), the family was introduced to the family discussion task ("What would you like to see changed in your family?"), based in the Beavers Interactional Scales (Steps 2: choose an appropriate instrument and model & 3: introduce the discussion task). Initially, Jimmy and Deena sat on opposite sides of the room, and the children were up and moving around for most of the session. The identified patient, Jessie, sat on the couch and assailed her parents for having no control over the family and even grabbed Brady by the hair at one point when he was acting up. Mother spent most of the time following the young children around, straightening out chairs, and trying to get them to sit and listen. The older son cruised the room and made gestures at the video camera. At any given time, multiple people were speaking, calling each other names ("butthead" was rather frequent), or moving around the room. Finally, Jimmy attempted to organize the group, by barking for one and then a second child to come sit in the circle, which lasted less than a minute until chaos erupted again. Mother just looked defeated, and the family never did get to the discussion task. "What do we want to change as a family?" Jimmy barked out finally, and a few people detachedly called back "nothing." Finally, Jimmy resigned himself to isolated silence.

Almost every family member had a way of blaming everyone else for his or her problems. Jessie tried to take on the burden of managing the younger children, but her influence was lost very quickly. Allies were fleeting or nonexistent. The family affect fluctuated from rather cynical to fleetingly hopeful and unresolved conflict abounded. The family was rated as "Borderline" in competence on the Beavers Interactional Competence Scale (Step 4: rate the family's interaction).

In terms of stylistic behavior (also Step 4: rate the family's interaction), there were consistent indicators of Centrifugal family behavior: open conflicts, behavior problems at home and at school, some open hostility, and discouraged dependency needs in the offspring. The family also spaced themselves physically apart, especially Jimmy, who was all the way across the room from his wife and oldest daughter. They also appeared unconcerned about their social presentation to outsiders.

(Continued)

The family was rated "Borderline Centrifugal," which, according to the Beavers Model, are open in the direct expression of anger and hostility; there is frequent leave-taking. Control themes are overt blaming and direct emotional assaults; the cyclical chaos is frequent. Nurturance is not available to parents or children, and satisfaction is sought outside the family. Psychiatric disorders typically include externalizing disorders (conduct, substance abuse) and cyclical disorders that reflect the rigid-to-chaos fluctuations (Borderline Personality Disorders are often members of these families). They need therapists who can maintain effective control, limit the number of members attending, and focus on the basic, help the family organize simple actions and activities, organize generational boundaries, and help members take risks with neediness and emotional pain.

On the SFI, taken by Deena and Jessie (Step 5: use self-report scales related to the observational model), there were similar results except that Jessie graded the family somewhat lower in competence than her mother. They both rated the family Style ("Cohesion" factor) as disengaged/Centrifugal. Jessie's lower Competence rating is quite characteristic of the "symptom bearer," indicating lower levels of family satisfaction and higher levels of unresolved conflict, as well as greater emotional distance from the rest of the family.

The combined results placed the family in the borderline CF group. In the six sessions we had with this family, it was necessary to focus on reasonable goals (Step 6: set reasonable goals based on the assessment). The therapist established that Jimmy and Deena work together on some basic family rules, starting with some behavior controls for the younger children. Several fundamental behavioral tasks were developed. We worked on small successes in overt behavior rather than verbal awareness, since Centrifugal families often do not trust words and discussion as a means of solving anything.

Task one was to help establish more effective teamwork with the parents. The first session was held with just the couple at a time the children were in school. They were asked to choose a behavior in one of the younger children that they could address and develop a plan for working together. They chose Brady's lying about brushing his teeth, since they were told not to choose anything that would take too much time or too much mutual reliance on each other. The session was relatively brief but long enough to whittle down the behaviors they considered that could be too demanding. These families need to be able to take baby steps and experience some success. They were instructed to report back on their progress at the next session.

Task number two (task number one attended to make this goal easier to accomplish) involved having the parents work together with Jessie, who felt pressure and was critical in regards to lack of parental leadership. The session started with a brief discussion about the teamwork related to Brady's lying, which appeared to be at least partially successful. Since Jessie was unaware they were working on something together, she witnessed, perhaps for the first time, her parents discussing something together. The therapist then introduced the idea that Jessie might feel less pressure and could become less conflicted, if she knew her parents could handle some of the younger children's behavior problems. The three family members began talking with each other. It was comforting for Jessie to have her parents seemingly agree, and for her father to be participating, in family activities.

Task number three involved bringing more family members into the mix. In sessions three and four, both parents and the two oldest children attended. Cody remained rather aloof and disconnected, and the parents and Jessie continued to develop a connection. During this phase, Jessie and her mother started talking more about some personal concerns (Jessie about a boy at school who was bothering her, Deena about how tiring it was to take care of little children). While remaining purposely disconnected, Cody and his father were making some connections, even though they consisted of occasional barbs and even snide remarks to each other. During these sessions, clinical aides kept and played with the younger children, also keeping behavioral records of conflict and acting-out behaviors. Eventually, in sessions five and six, Michelle was brought in, and the parents were coached in conducting a family meeting, where they were able to start the much-avoided process of confronting anger and perceived rejection that had built up over the past several years. Jimmy was on the verge of leaving the room on several occasions but was congratulated each time he stayed, having the "guts": to stay and hear what was obviously painful. The family came back two more times, roughly a month apart, to deal with Jessie's building tensions, indicating they were taking steps to keep her from going back to the hospital. A follow-up phone call a month later found that Jessie was not in the hospital, and had begun individual therapy (as recommended by our therapists) at the school district's Youth and Family Canter.

The Borderline CF style dictated the necessity for a more directive approach to help the family clear up confusion and focus on the "do-able." Across their eight sessions, the family was rated as improved in communication, teamwork of the parental coalition,

(Continued)

and overall mood and tone, whereby they were functioning at the midrange CF level.

Because our Family Studies Center contracts for a six-session family model with our grantors, the SFI is a better instrument for evaluating results than is the GARF. The SFI reflects changes more rapidly (Step 7: re-evaluate the family periodically). Our use of the GARF is limited to longer-term treatment. In both of these case histories, there was significant increase in reported family competence, though the style did not change with the CP family and only modestly with the CF family. The use of the SFI with school children, school reports of behavior and functioning offer better and quicker evidence of improvement (Step 8: share the results to help the family plan future goals).

Case Example: A Centripetal Family

The Lee family referred themselves to the sliding fee clinic because of acting-out behavior in their younger daughter, Michelle, who was 18 and a senior in high school. The family consisted of the father, Benny, his wife, Grace, their older daughter, Rosa (22), and Michelle. The family was Filipino; they moved from the Philippines when Rosa was a baby; Michelle was born in the United States. Mr. Lee was an educated professional. Mrs. Lee held a college degree but did not work outside the home.

Mr. Lee had been fed up with Michelle's increasing tendency to defy her parents. His blood pressure was up, and tension headaches were common; he had three auto accidents in the past two months. Some of her behaviors involved sneaking out in the middle of the night, taking the car without permission, and running up charge cards to the maximum. Michelle constantly complained that her parents were too strict and she had to sneak out and defy in order to have a halfway "normal" life. The Lees referred to their expectation of compliance as "the Filipino way" and thought Michelle was entirely "too American."

The entire family presented for the initial family assessment. Mr. Lee had trouble with the fact that a videotape was being made of the family's interaction. He consented (Step 1) to participate only if the therapist remained in the room (she said that would, but she would not talk) and he remained off camera. The family discussion task (again, "What would you like to see changed in your family?" Steps 2 and 3) revealed a number of key interactions. First, Mr. Lee controlled every exchange in the family, from directing who was to talk to correcting the perspective of individuals who had a divergent view. His wife, no patsy, would occasionally redirect or contradict his comments. However, these exchanges were all done with little emotion, in a very mechanical tone. When Michelle disagreed or tried to defend her behavior as "normal", he would lecture on about how she was threatening to blow the family apart by not following the Filipino way. The older daughter, Rosa, was a passive, sad, and ineffectual person who deferred to her parents. She also had a negative relationship with Michelle, who referred to Rosa as "the narc." There was a tone of invasiveness on both parents' part, who labeled the behaviors of their daughters as "American" and "little mama." It was clear, however, that the scapegoat in this system was Michelle. While many CP families have individuals with only internalizing disorders, this "fallen saint" pattern is another variation on the scapegoating theme.

From the observation of the family, and their description of the circular nature of the interaction (act out, ground her, more acting out, etc.), that the control themes in the family were quite rigid and that rigid control gave way to chaos as the effectiveness of parental control was defied. The family was stuck. The operating themes within the family were expectations for perfect behavior, condemnation for not following the "correct" culture, and dominance/submission. This family was rated as "Borderline" in competence on the Beavers Competence Scale (Step 4), and as Centripetal in Style (Step 4 also), given the emphasis on compliant and "correct" behavior and the suppression of the expression of negative feelings. Michelle was clearly the "fallen saint" in this system.

The Borderline Centripetal family system, according to the Beavers model, is a control-oriented structure that lacks intimacy and spontaneity. They are stuck in control efforts. When these families seek help, it is to help further control the fallen saint, not to relinquish control. Any effort on the therapists' part to increase the control (shape the offender) or challenge the control of the tyrant is doomed to failure. The former solidifies the cyclical control themes, and the latter will result in the controlling member pulling the family out of treatment. Instead, the therapist needs to go below the control issues, to the underlying feelings of the family members. They are upset, disappointed, and probably very lonely. Hence, getting family members to address what they miss and long for can be a powerful tool.

(Continued)

Second, there will be strong attempts of different factions to pull the therapist into their side of the struggle. The therapist needs to avoid judgments and side taking. As the focus on relationships and lost hopes and dreams progresses, it becomes clear that there is not a specifically defined villain and victim. They are all hurting. It is a good idea to cater to the emotional needs of the most powerful person in the family initially, so he/she feels understood. This can go a long way to preventing the powerful member from pulling the family out of therapy. The SFI (Step 5) was not administered to the Lees.

For the Lee family, the therapeutic goals were several (step 6). One was to develop a focus on the feeling level, especially with family members asking for more of what they liked, rather than rigid rule structures. A second was to shift the "blame" for behavior from the clash of cultures to the individual level. A third was for the parents to learn cooperation and negotiation skills, so they could share parenting roles and duties. A related theme had to do with helping Rosa develop some sense of autonomy, in that the parents would view her strivings to be more independent as a sign of individual competence and not defiance. Finally, Michelle would learn that as control themes softened, she needed to rely less on rebellious tactics to get what she wanted. When the family began dealing with Task 1, it became clear that each member was feeling isolated and lonely. The guilt-inducing and controlling exchanges that characterized the family began to be interspersed with questions such as "Well, what would you like to see more of?" It was much harder for Mr. Lee than the others to address the feeling level. He also had more difficulty with the second task, that of personalizing rather than culturalizing the deviant behavior. However, there was an important breakthrough when the parental dyad began addressing working as a team (task 3). The more Mr. Lee observed that his wife was reasonably competent in talking with the girls, and even soliciting cooperation from them, the more he felt that he could back off. In fact, he soon "allowed" his wife and daughters to continue counseling without him, a major step in altering his rigid control efforts.

Once this step was reached, the three women were able to negotiate on some key matters, including a more modest social schedule for Michelle, and some independent maneuvering for Rosa. Rosa began taking some classes at the Community College and had begun joining several activity groups at the church. The three women/family subset attended a total of 15 sessions and reported a much higher degree of satisfaction. From their reports, Mr. Lee was also happier and was significantly less stressed out at home.

Re-evaluation (Step 7) at the 12th session involved only Mrs. Lee, Rosa, and Michelle. The discussion was productive and respectful. It was clear that there was less testy behavior on Michelle's part, and the respect for each other was higher. However, since Mr. Lee was not present, it was not possible to tell whether this same interaction would have occurred had he been there. By their reports, however, negotiation and overall interaction was much smoother at home, especially since Mr. Lee had decided that he did not need to control everyone and everything. The rating at the 12th session found this family at the higher Midrange level of competence, still with a modestly Centripetal style, so there was a noticeable improvement in their functioning level.

Concluding Comments

The various family observational assessment systems in this chapter focus on the "macro" level of assessment, examining the "big picture" of family functioning. As mentioned earlier, there are a wide variety of more "micro" assessment procedures that measure highly specific behaviors within family interaction sequences, but these may be less amenable to therapy planning and intervention than the models presented here.

There are probably more similarities than differences across the global assessment models presented in this chapter. The Beavers Model addresses family competence, which refers to structure, autonomy, communication clarity, and boundaries. In a similar vein, the McMaster Model addresses overall family functioning, which is also a linear, more-is-better dimension consisting of important family tasks and communication skills. The GARF is also a linear rating scale, comprised of dimensions of emotional climate, problem-solving, and organization. The Circumplex Communication rating is also a linear scale, ranging from low to high. However, the Flexibility dimension is a curvilinear scale, ranging from polar opposites of Rigid to Chaotic; these dimensions are close kin in the Beavers Model, representing dysfunctional to borderline levels of competence.

The Style dimension of the Beavers Model describes the behavioral climate of the family and is highly associated with the nature of behavior disorders in family members. This is more of a curvilinear dimension, in that middle levels of style are associated with healthy family functioning, and extremes are found in families that are more disturbed. This maps on to the Circumplex Model Cohesion factor, where extremes of Disengaged and Enmeshed are associated with family disturbance. This dimension is addressed on the Affective Involvement rating on the McMaster Model, where "empathic involvement" is optimal, and the extremes of "lack of involvement" and "symbiotic involvement" are more pathological. This dimension is not addressed directly on the GARF.

References

Aarons, G., McDonald, E., Connelly, C., & Newton, R. (2007). Assessment of family functioning in Caucasian and Hispanic Americans: Reliability, validity, and factor structure of the family assessment device. *Family Process, 46,* 557–569.

Beavers, W. R., & Hampson, R. B. (1990). *Successful families: Assessment and intervention.* New York, NY: W.W. Norton.

Beavers, W. R., & Hampson, R. B. (2003). Measuring family competence: The Beavers systems model. In F. Walsh (Ed.), *Normal family processes* (3rd ed., pp. 549–580). New York, NY: Guilford Press,

Bishop, D. S., Epstein, N. B., Keitner, G. I., Miller, I. W., Zlotnick, C., & Ryan, C. E. (2000). *McMaster Structured Interview of Family Functioning (McSIFF).* Providence, RI: Brown University Family Research Program.

Crittendon, P. (1988). Relationships at risk. In J. Belsky & T. Nezworski (Eds.), *Clinical implications of attachment* (pp. 136–174). Hillsdale, NJ: Lawrence Erlbaum.

Dai, L., & Wang, L. (2015). Review of family functioning. *Open Journal of Social Sciences, 3,* 134–141.

Denton, W. H., Nakonezny, P. A., & Burwell, S. R. (2010). Reliability and validity of the Global Assessment of Relational Functioning (GARF) in a psychiatric family therapy clinic. *Journal of Marital and Family Therapy, 36,* 376–387.

Epstein, N. B., Ryan, C. E., Bishop, D. S., Miller, I. W., & Keitner, G. I. (2003). The McMaster model: A view of healthy family functioning. In F. Walsh (Ed.), *Normal family processes* (3rd ed., pp. 581–607). New York, NY: Guilford Press.

Favez, N., Scaiola, C. L, Tissot, H., Darwiche, J., & Frascarolo, F. (2011). The family alliance assessment scales: Steps toward validity and reliability of an observational assessment tool for early family interactions. *Journal of Child and Family Studies, 20,* 23–37.

Gordon, E. D. (1997). *The Global Assessment of Relational Functioning (GARF): Reliability and validity* (Unpublished masters' thesis). Southern Methodist University, Dallas, TX.

Hamilton, E., & Carr, A. (2016). Systematic review of self-report assessment measures. *Family Process, 55,* 16–30.

Hampson, R. B., & Beavers, W. R. (1996a). Family therapy and outcome: Relationships between therapist and family styles. *Contemporary Family Therapy, 18,* 345–369.

Hampson, R. B., & Beavers, W. R. (1996b). Measuring family therapy outcome in a clinical setting: Families that do better or worse in therapy. *Family Process, 35,* 347–361.

Hampson, R. B., Beavers, W. R., & Hulgus, Y. F. (1989). Insiders' and outsiders' views of family: The assessment of family competence and style. *Journal of Family Psychology, 3,* 118–136.

Hampson, R. N., Beavers, W. R., & Hulgus, Y. F. (1990). Cross-ethnic family differences: Interactional assessment of White, Black, and Mexican-American families. *Journal of Marital and Family Therapy, 16,* 307–319.

Hampson, R. B., Prince, C. C., & Beavers, W. R. (1999). Marital therapy: Qualities of couples who fare better or worse in treatment. *Journal of Marital and Family Therapy, 25,* 411–424.

Henney, S. M., & Hampson, R. B. (1994). *Social desirability effects on family self-report ratings.* Presented at American Psychological Association Convention, Los Angeles, CA.

Kerig, P., & Lindahl, K. M. (2001). *Family observational coding systems: Resources for systematic research.* Mahwah, NJ: Erlbaum.

Kitzman, H., Hampson, R. B., Wilson, D., Presnell, K., Brown, A., & O'Boyle, M. (2009). An adolescent weight-loss program integrating family variables reduces energy intake. *Journal of the American Dietetic Association, 109,* 491–496.

Lebow, J., & Stroud, C. B. (2012). Assessment of effective couple and family functioning: Prevailing models and instruments. In F. Walsh (Ed.), *Normal family processes: Growing diversity and complexity* (4th ed.) pp. 501–528). New York, NY: Guilford.

Lee, C. (1988). Theories of family adaptability: Toward a synthesis of Olson's circumplex and the Beavers systems models. *Family Process, 27,* 73–85.

Lee, R. E., Jager, K. B., Whiting, J. B., & Kwantes, C. T. (2000) The factor structure of the beavers interactional scales. *Contemporary Family Therapy, 22*(1), 81–90.

Liddle, H., Dakof, G., Parker, K., Diamond, G., Barrett, K., & Tejeda, M. (2001). Multidimensional family therapy for adolescent drug abuse: Results of a randomized clinical trial. *American Journal of Drug and Alcohol Abuse, 27,* 651–688.

Kolevzon, M. S., Green, R. G., Fortune, A. E., & Vosler, N. R. (1988). Evaluating family therapy: Divergent methods, divergent findings. *Journal of Marital and Family Therapy, 14*(3), 277–286.

Mansfield, A., Keitner, G., & Dealy, J. (2015). The family assessment device: An update. *Family Process, 54,* 82–93.

Miller, I. W., Kabacoff, R. I., Epstein, N. B., Bishop, D. S., Keitner, G. I., Baldwin, L. M., & van der Spuy, H. I. J. (1994). The development of a clinical rating scale for the McMaster Model of Family Functioning. *Family Process, 33,* 53–69.

Miller, I. W., Ryan, C. E., Keitner, G. I., Bishop, D. S., & Epstein, N. B. (2000). The McMaster approach to families: Theory, assessment, treatment, research. *Journal of Family Therapy, 22,* 168–189.

Motarella, K. E., Philpot, C. I., & Fritzsche, B. A. (2001). Don't take out this appendix! Generalizability of the global assessment of relational functioning scale. *The American Journal of Family Therapy, 29,* 271–278.

Olson, D. H., & Gorall, D. M. (2003). Circumplex model of marital and family systems. In F. Walsh (Ed.), *Normal family processes* (3rd ed., pp. 514–548). New York, NY: Guilford Press.

Olson, D. H., Gorall, D. M., & Tiesel, J. W. (2006). *FACES IV package.* Minneapolis, MN: Life Innovations.

Pinsof, W., Zinbarg, R., & Knobloch-Fedders, L. (2008). Factorial and construct validity of the revised short form integrative psychotherapy alliance scale for couple, family, and individual therapy. *Family Process, 47,* 281–301.

Ross, N. M., & Doherty, W. J. (2001). Validity of the global assessment of relational functioning (GARF) when used by community-based therapists. *The American Journal of Family Therapy, 29,* 239–253.

Sanderson, J., Kosutic, I., Garcie, M., Melendez, T., Donoghue, J., & Perumbilly, S. (2009). The measurement of outcome variables in couple and family therapy research. *American Journal of Family Therapy, 37,* 239–257.

Thomas, V., & Olson, D. H. (1993). Problem families and the circumplex model: Observational assessment using the clinical rating scale. *Journal of Marital and Family Therapy, 19*, 159–175.

Yingling, L. C., Miller, W. E., McDonald, A. L., & Galewater, S. T. (1998). *GARF assessment sourcebook: Using the DSM-IV global assessment of relational functioning. Handbook.* New York, NY: Brunner/Mazel.

Zayas, V., Mischel, W., Shoda, Y., & Aber, J. L. (2010). Roots of adult attachment: Maternal caregiving at 18 months predicts adult peer and partner attachment. *Social Psychological and Personality Science, 2*(3), 289–297. doi:10.1177/1948550610389822

6

ONGOING ASSESSMENT WITH COUPLES AND FAMILIES

Len Sperry

The practice of behavioral health at the onset of the 21st century is increasingly different from practice during most of the 20th century. This is largely due to the paradigm shift in behavioral health practice that has been under way since the late 1980s. This shift involves every facet of behavioral health practice, including the role of the clinician and the nature of the relationship between clinician and client, and especially clinical practice patterns. This shift has already resulted in the demystification of some basic tenets and "sacred cows" of clinical lore.

Central to this paradigm shift is the increasing emphasis on quality and accountability of clinical services provided. Accordingly, quality indicators and cost effectiveness have become primary considerations in behavioral health. Not surprisingly, clinical outcomes data, a key marker of quality and of accountability, became the norm for the provision of behavioral health services for the past decade. Today, ongoing assessment of couples and families has reached a new plateau in the scientific literature with the publication of the book *Routine Outcome Monitoring in Couple and Family Therapy: The Empirically Informed Therapist* by Tilden and Wampold (2017). It joins an increasing number of articles, research studies, and book chapters on the topic.

A recent study (Hamilton & Carr, 2016) reveals the importance of the specialized ongoing couple and family assessment measures in comparison with commonly used self-report family assessment measures. A systematic review of eight common family assessment measures was conducted with regard to their psychometric properties, clinical utility, and theoretical underpinnings. They were: the McMaster Family Assessment Device (FAD), Circumplex Model Family Adaptability and Cohesion Evaluation

Scales (FACES), Beavers Systems Model Self-Report Family Inventory (SFI), Family Assessment Measure III (FAM III), Family Environment Scale (FES), Family Relations Scale (FRS), the Systemic Clinical Outcome Routine Evaluation (SCORE), and Systemic Therapy Inventory of Change (STIC). Results indicated that six family assessment measures are suitable for clinical use (FAD, FACES IV, SFI, FAM III, SCORE, and STIC), but two were not (FES, FRS). Of the six measures deemed clinically useful, three are ongoing assessment measures highlighted in this chapter—SFI, SCORE, and STIC. If the Hamilton and Carr review had been undertaken a decade ago, only one ongoing measure, the SFI would have been included, since the other two had not yet be validated and available. The take away point is that although ongoing assessment measures are relatively new, they have become essential to clinical practice today.

This chapter introduces the concept of *clinical outcomes assessment* with couples and families. It begins with a description of the emergence of the concept of *accountability* and the so-called outcomes revolution and its impact on clinical practice. It then has a description of the various types and levels of outcomes assessment and its clinical implications, particularly the practice of couples and family therapy. *Therapeutic effectiveness, efficacy,* and *efficiency* are defined, and the point is made that outcomes monitoring fosters the most important of the three concepts: therapeutic efficacy. Next is a discussion of recent developments in outcomes measurement and monitoring with couples and families and then a description of the use of seven specific measurement tools. Of these, three are primarily used with couples, while four are used primarily with families. Finally, a protocol for utilizing these tools in measuring and monitoring outcomes with couples and families is provided and illustrated with a couple therapy case example.

Clinicians, Family Therapy, and Outcomes Measurement

Clinical outcomes data and the associated outcomes revolution (Sperry, 1997) reflect a norm radically different from that in which most clinicians were trained. In the past, clinical practice was characterized by independence of clinical judgment, practice constraints, emphasis on therapeutic process, and subjective assessment of clinical progress. The recent shift in focus to an emphasis on accountability, that is, outcomes instead of process and objective assessment of clinical progress, has resulted in many clinicians' confusion and concern about the meaning and implications of this paradigm shift imposed on the profession. Some view this emphasis on accountability and quality as an intrusion into their practice style or as actually or potentially unethical. Some have embraced this norm wholeheartedly, while others have come to accept it as inevitable (Sperry, Brill,

Grisson, & Marion, 1997). Whatever their perspective, clinicians must contend with the reality that therapeutic accountability and clinical outcomes assessment in particular have become a core feature of clinical practice today and will be in the future.

In short, clinical outcomes assessment has been regarded as a necessary but unwelcome task by clinicians, particularly those conducting family therapy who are process oriented. "A focus on results rather than process has been anathema to family therapists" (Yingling, Miller, McDonald, & Galwaler, 1998, p. 49). Can this process versus outcome dilemma be resolved? Wynne (1988) suggested a potential solution, which is to "recommend that two primary baselines be given priority in family therapy research: (a) the multiple versions of the family members' 'initial' presenting problem and (b) the problem identified by consensus of family and therapist" (p. 253). Yingling and colleagues (1998) contend that using data from self-report measures of family members along with data from therapist ratings or observations (i.e., the Global Assessment of Relational Functioning [GARF]) can provide data relevant to process and outcome assessment. They also note that "discussing GARF parameters and charting progress with the client can enhance the therapeutic process … [and] the GARF can also be used as a process research tool when combined with case notes that include therapeutic interventions and reflections" (Yingling et al., 1998, p. 49).

Recent Developments in Ongoing Assessment of Couples and Families

Since the publication of the first edition of this book, there have been a few noteworthy developments in clinical outcomes assessment in general and with couples in particular. Most obvious is that clinical outcomes assessment has become increasingly mainstream. This reflects the "culture of accountability" in which we live and the expectation that clinicians will utilize evidence-based treatment and demonstrate the effectiveness of the therapy they provide. A related development is that a number of new instruments and assessment devices have become available and are increasingly being utilized not only to address specific assessment questions but also to monitor progress and evaluation treatment outcomes. It is noteworthy that clinicians and researchers are effectively responding to the phenomenon of high rates of premature termination (40–70%) by advocating the use of measuring and monitoring key therapeutic factors with brief assessment instruments (Lambert, 2010).

Particularly notable are the following developments. First is the introduction of shorter and *ultra-brief* instruments (often 3 or 4 items) taking only 1–2 min to complete. This contrasts with the 150 items of the Marital Satisfaction Inventory, Revised (MSI-R), which takes about 25–30 min to complete.

Second, because of the limited administration time, such as for the Outcome Rating Scale, it is possible and preferable to monitor client or family progress at each session. This contrasts with the necessity to limit monitoring of progress to every fourth session or so or, more commonly, before the first and after the last treatment sessions (the pre–post model of evaluation). Third, because of increasing use of these brief instruments (completed immediately before a session begins), it is now possible for client ratings to be discussed in that session. This "continuous progress feedback" strategy (Miller, Duncan, Brown, Sorrell, & Chalk, 2006) provides immediate client feedback, which facilitates the modification of the treatment process. This feedback process has been shown not only to increase treatment outcomes appreciably but also to reduce the likelihood of premature termination (Lambert, 2010).

Types of Outcomes Systems and Their Clinical Value

Most clinicians are likely to have had some experience with at least one type of outcomes system. The most common, and often the only, assessment of treatment outcomes that may be required is a simple measure of client satisfaction. Usually, client satisfaction is assessed by a short paper-and-pencil questionnaire that includes such items as how well the client thought he was treated by the therapist and how much he thought he improved during therapy. Although client satisfaction is important, it has not been shown to be an accurate assessment of treatment outcomes; in fact, it is actually a poor measure of clinical improvement. For example, Atkisson and Zwick (1982) showed that symptom improvement explains only 10% of the variance in client satisfaction, while the relationship between clinical improvement and reported satisfaction is not statistically significant for clients still in treatment or for those who have completed treatment.

On the other hand, other outcomes measures have shown clinical utility and value. Outcomes measures and outcomes measurement systems can yield three types of benefits, one of which is its capacity to identify effective treatments. This requires pre-treatment and post-treatment assessment of a client's status to determine changes that occurred as a result of treatment. Aggregation of these data across all clients who received a specific treatment is the basis for this first benefit. A second benefit is immediate feedback to clinicians and case managers. This feedback will enable clinicians to identify clients who are improving adequately, those who have improved to a point at which treatment may no longer be necessary, and those whose lack of progress or determination suggests that their treatment should be changed. The third benefit is the ability to identify the specific changes most likely to move the unimproved client onto a more positive growth path—that is, to determine whether involvement of a spouse or family in treatment, transfer to a different therapist and different type of therapy, referral for a medication evaluation, or some other alteration in treatment is most likely to get the client well.

By incorporating feedback from an outcomes system into ongoing clinical cases, clinicians effectively supplement or support a clinician's intuition about treatment decisions. Serial data on changes in symptoms and functioning can be utilized in modifying the course and duration of treatment in terms of focus, modality, and intervention strategies with individuals, couples, or families.

Essentially, three levels of outcomes assessment exist (Sperry, 1997):

Outcomes measurement—quantification or measurement of clinical and functional outcomes during a specific time period. Outcomes measures have traditionally been collected at the beginning and end of treatment. However, serial or concurrent assessment is becoming more common. Measures often include change in symptoms, well-being, functioning, and even patient satisfaction.

Outcomes monitoring—serial or concurrent use of outcomes measures during the course of treatment. The goal of outcomes monitoring is comparison against a standard of expected results to monitor progress or lack of progress over the course of treatment. Monitoring can be done after each session, every third session, or on some other scheduled basis. The data are then used to alter treatment when it is off course or stagnating. They can also be used to follow progress in a single case or summed and adjusted for risk to compare several patients or programs. Outcomes monitoring can only be accomplished with repeated or concurrent measures, and the information must be available during the treatment.

Outcomes management—ultimate utilization of monitored data in a way that allows individuals and health care systems to learn from experience. Usually, this results in reshaping or improving the overall administrative and clinical processes of services provided. Patient profiling, provider profiling, and site profiling are three common aspects of an outcomes management system.

In a sense, these three levels are developmental levels or stages, with each level being a prerequisite for the next. Currently, the majority of outcomes assessment activity is occurring at the outcomes measurement and the outcomes monitoring levels. It is useful to distinguish therapeutic effectiveness and efficacy from therapeutic efficiency. *Therapeutic effectiveness* is the determination that a treatment has a beneficial effect and is the expected outcome for a typical client treated in common practice settings by a typical clinician. On the other hand, *therapeutic efficacy* is the expected outcome for clients treated under optimal conditions by highly qualified clinicians. In short, efficacy defines optimal clinical practice, while effectiveness compares actual with optimal practice (Sperry, Brill, Howard, & Grissom, 1996).

In contrast, *therapeutic efficiency* refers to highly beneficial treatment tailored to the unique needs of a specific client (individual, couple, or family) as they are noted—or measured—over the course of treatment. Therapeutic effectiveness and efficacy answer the question, which treatment or approach is better or best? Therapeutic efficiency answers the question, which is the best treatment for this client and how can it be optimally provided? Accordingly, ongoing monitoring of clinical treatment outcomes fosters therapeutic efficiency (Sperry, et al, 1996).

Clinical Outcomes with Individuals, Couples, and Families

The earliest outcomes measurement efforts were primarily focused on psychotherapy with individuals, largely because a principal focus of psychotherapy research was on treatment outcomes. In the late 1980s, two instruments for outcomes assessment with individuals, COMPASS-OP and the Outcomes Questionnaire 45.2 (OQ-45), were widely utilized in clinical practice to measure pre–post-treatment outcomes, rather than monitor clinical outcomes on an ongoing basis. It is true that the Dyadic Adjustment Scale (DAS) was utilized as a pre–post-treatment measure of therapeutic effectiveness in a handful of research studies over the years.

However, only recently has the use of such inventories and scales as the DAS and the MSI-R been advocated for monitoring clinical outcomes of couples therapy (Jacobson, 1984; Jacobson & Follette, 1985; Latham, 1990; Prouty, Markowski, & Barnes, 2000; Snyder & Aikman, 1999).

In terms of treatment outcome measures with families, the SFI, GARF Scale, and the Systematic Assessment of Family Environment (SAFE) Scale have all been utilized as pre–post-treatment measures in clinical research studies (Hampson & Beavers, 1996a; Hampson, Prince, & Beavers, 1999; Yingling, 1996; Yingling, Miller, McDonald, & Galwaler, 1994a). As clinicians become more familiar with the GARF Scale, it has tremendous potential for monitoring clinical outcomes on a session-by-session basis with families (Yingling et al., 1998).

The next section of this chapter is a description of the use of five inventories and scales for clinical outcomes measurement and for the ongoing monitoring of clinical outcomes with couples and families: GARF, SFI, SAFE, DAS, and MSI-R.

Outcome Measures Primarily for Families

This section includes three well-regarded instruments with considerable potential in clinical outcomes measurement and monitoring: the GARF, the SAFE, the SFI, as well as a new and promising instrument, the Systemic Clinical Outcomes and Routine Evaluation.

Global Assessment of Relational Functioning (GARF)

Brief description of the GARF. The GARF is a therapist-rated device for indicating functioning or a family or other ongoing relationship on a continuum ranging from a low of 1 to a high of 100. The continuum is divided into five categories: 1–20 = chaotic, 21–40 = rarely satisfactory, 41–60 = predominantly unsatisfactory, 61–80 = somewhat unsatisfactory, and 81–100 = satisfactory. It is the only family-oriented measure included in the pages of the DSM-IV/DSM-IV-TR and is located in Appendix B (American Psychiatric Association, 2000). GARF is analogous to Global Assessment of Functioning (GAF) Scale, which is a measure of individual symptomatic distress and functioning; both are coded on Axis V. It should be noted that although the GARF is no longer included in DSM-5 (American Psychiatric Association, 2013), it remains a viable and clinically valuable assessment device with families.

When assessing or rating a relationship, the clinician is asked to consider three dimensions of relational functioning: problem-solving, organization, and emotional climate. Recent reliability and validly data on the GARF support it as a reliable and valid measure of relational functioning whose ratings can be made quickly and reliably, particularly among clinicians and supervisors with clinical experience, and are related to depression (Denton, Nakonezny, & Burwell, 2010).

Yingling and colleagues (1998) have slightly modified the dimensions Interactional, Problem-Solving, Organization, and Emotional Climate, making them subscales that are scored separately, along with an overall GARF score. The psychometric properties and additional information about GARF are discussed in Chapter 6.

The GARF as an outcomes measure. Considerable published research and clinical reports are available in which GARF is utilized as an outcomes measure. Most of these reports involve GARF in pre-treatment and post-treatment measurement (Hampson & Beavers, 1996b; Ross & Doherty, 2001; Yingling et al., 1994a, 1994b, 1998). With regard to ongoing assessment of outcomes, Yingling and colleagues (1998) discuss five case examples of the use of GARF as a treatment outcomes monitoring measure. These couple and family cases provide session-by-session ratings of overall GARF scores and subscale ratings for therapy lasting from 7 to 10 sessions. These case discussions are particularly valuable because data from the ongoing monitoring are utilized by the therapists to modify treatment focus and interventions.

GARF as an outcomes measure. In the past, relatively limited psychometric data has been reported on the GARF. However, a recent study provides important reliability and validity data on this instrument (Denton et al., 2010). The GARF scale was evaluated in consenting participants presenting to a family therapy training clinic. The purpose of this study was to

(a) assess whether the GARF could be administered quickly in a marriage and family therapy training clinic, (b) assess the interrater and internal reliability of GARF ratings of intake sessions, (c) examine the relationship of GARF ratings to established measures of relationship functioning, and (d) compare GARF ratings to a measure of depressive symptoms. Study participants completed the General Functioning Subscale of the Family Assessment Device (GFS/FAD), the Quality of Marriage Index (QMI), and the Center for Epidemiologic Studies-Depression Scale (CES-D). After intake sessions were conducted with study participants, GARF ratings were made by supervisors and observers who had observed the session from behind a one-way mirror. Cronbach's coefficient alphas and the average intraclass correlation coefficients were both .82 when ratings of the supervisor and two observers were compared and .78 and .79, respectively. Concurrent validity was established with regard to GARF ratings made by the supervisor and therapist and scores on the GFS/FAD, QMI, and CES-D (Denton et al., 2010).

Systematic Assessment of Family Environment (SAFE)

Brief description of the SAFE. The SAFE was developed by Yingling in 1991 along with field testing of the GARF (cf. Chapter 8 for an extended discussion of this instrument). It is a 21-item global assessment instrument for measuring three relational subsystem levels of the family system using two functioning factors for each subsystem level. The three subsystems are dyadic marital–executive subsystem, parent–child subsystem, and extended family subsystem. Organizational Structure and Interactional Processes are the two factors assessed for each subsystem. Scoring yields ranges for four family types: competent, discordant, disoriented, or chaotic (Yingling, 1996). SAFE is user friendly and available in a Spanish version as well as a cartoon version for use with children under the age of ten (Yingling et al., 1998). Validity is reported as .74 and .82 (Yingling et al., 1998).

SAFE as an outcomes measure. The SAFE provides information that can easily be incorporated into a treatment plan. Relatively little has been published about using SAFE for pre–post-treatment evaluation of change or ongoing monitoring of family therapy. Nevertheless, Yingling and colleagues (1998) report collecting serial data on GARF and SAFE for monitoring treatment outcomes. The ease of administration makes this instrument a valuable outcomes measure with families.

Self-Report Family Inventory (SFI)

Brief description of the SFI. The SFI is a 36-item self-report family instrument developed by Beavers and Hampson (1990) and is based on the Beavers

Systems Model of Family Functioning. It measures five family domains: health and competence, conflict resolution, cohesion, leadership, and emotional expressiveness. The SFI correlates highly with two well-regarded therapist observational rating scales: the Beavers Interactional Competence Scale and the Beavers Interactional Styles Scale. Spanish and Chinese versions are also available. The psychometric properties and additional information about SFI are discussed in Chapter 5.

SFI as an outcomes measure. Some research in which the SFI has been utilized as an outcomes measure has been published. These reports involve the SFI in pre-treatment and post-treatment measurement (Hampson & Beavers, 1996a, 1996b; Hampson et al., 1999). Apparently, no research or other published reports describe the use of the SFI as an ongoing measure of clinical outcomes; however, the ease of administration and brevity of the instrument (only 36 items) make it particularly valuable for monitoring session-by-session outcomes.

Systemic Clinical Outcome Routine Evaluation-15 (SCORE-15)

Brief description of SCORE 15. SCORE 15 is a self-report outcome measure that evolved from the original SCORE, a 40-item self-rating instrument (Stratton, Bland, Janes, & Lask, 2010). To make it more user friendly, it was reduced to 15 items, and factor analysis provided the basis for specifying three subscales: strengths and adaptability, overwhelmed by difficulties, and disrupted communication.

Score 15 was intended to be sensitive to the kinds of changes in family relationships that systemic family and couple therapists consider to be useful indications of therapeutic change. It was designed to be a brief measure that would be clinically useful across the full range of presenting problems, clientele, and treatment modalities: individual, couple, family and multi-family groups (Stratton et al., 2014). It consists of 19 questions (15 scale items plus four self-description items) which take only a few minutes for family members to complete (Carr & Stratton, 2017).

SCORE 15 as an outcomes measure. The SCORE 15 has these reported psychometric properties: Cronbach's alpha .89, split-half correlation .81; Guttman split-half coefficient .89. The extent to which the 15 items represent the original SCORE 40 items provided a multiple regression coefficient of .975. Data are reported from 584 participants aged above 11 years, representing 239 families. All couples and families had been referred for systemic couples and family therapy, completing the form at start of the first session and close to the fourth. The SCORE 15 is shown to be acceptable with strong consistency and reliability. Change over only three sessions was highly statistically significant. Further validation is provided by improvements in quantified scores correlating significantly with

independent measures provided by family members and by their therapists (Stratton et al., 2014).

The instrument is currently available free at the website of the Association
for Family Therapy copy of instrument and administration and scoring plus
a children's version (ages 8–11) https://www.corc.uk.net/media/1249/score_
userguide.pdf. It is in English, and it is reported that translation is underway
in 12 European languages (Stratton et al., 2010).

Outcome Measures Primarily for Couples

This section includes two well-regarded instruments with considerable potential in clinical outcomes measurement and monitoring: the DAS and
the MSI-R, as well as a new and promising instrument, the Intersession
Report.

Dyadic Adjustment Scale (DAS)

Brief description of the DAS. The DAS is a 34-item self-report instrument
for assessing dyadic or relationship adjustment. This instrument was developed by Spanier (1976) to measure the quality of adjustment of couples and
other dyads. The DAS comprises four scales: Dyadic Satisfaction, Dyadic
Cohesion, Dyadic Consensus, and Affectional Expression. It is one of the
first and most extensively utilized relational instruments in clinical practice. A shorter, 14-item version is also available. The psychometric properties and additional information about DAS are discussed in Chapter 7.
Spanier developed the instrument on the assumption that the quality of
relational adjustment was the key indicator of the viability of a relationship. He defined marital quality as "how the marriage functions during its
existence and how partners feel about and are influenced by such functioning" (Spanier, 1979, p. 290). The DAS has consistently distinguished
couples with better adjustment from those who are more dissatisfied with
their relationship, including couples with a greater likelihood of divorce
(Prouty et al., 2000). Well over 1,000 research studies have been published
involving the DAS. Although the instrument has evolved over the years, it
remains one of the most commonly used measures of couple adjustment by
researchers and clinicians.

DAS as an outcomes measure. The DAS has a long history of use as an
outcomes measure. Considerable research has been reported on its use
as a pre–post-treatment assessment tool in studies of therapeutic efficacy
and effectiveness with couples (Adam & Gingras, 1982; Brock & Joanning,
1983; Jacobson, 1984; Jacobson & Follette, 1985; Latham, 1990; Prouty
et al., 2000). Even though neither this research nor other published reports
describe the DAS as used as an ongoing measure of clinical outcomes, the

brevity of the instrument—particularly the 14-item version—makes it an attractive choice for monitoring session-by-session outcomes.

Marital Satisfaction Inventory, Revised (MSI-R)

Brief description of the MSI-R. MSI-R is a 150-item self-report instrument developed by Snyder (1997). The earlier version, MSI (Snyder, 1981), was well regarded and one of the most often used relational inventories in research and clinical practice. The MSI-R has 13 scales:

- Global Distress
- Affective Communication
- Problem-Solving Communication
- Aggression
- Time Together
- Disagreement About Finances
- Sexual Dissatisfaction
- Role Orientation
- Family History of Distress
- Dissatisfaction with Children
- Conflict Over Child Rearing
- Inconsistency (validity scale)
- Conventionalization (validity scale)

The MSI-R is useful as a diagnostic and a therapeutic tool, as well as a screening instrument. Psychometric properties of and additional information about MSI-R are discussed in Chapter 7.

MSI-R as an outcomes measure. The MSI-R is typically used in the initial phase of therapy in discussing the couple's presenting concerns and in formulating treatment goals. However, it can also be utilized before and after therapy, in a pre–post-treatment fashion, to evaluate overall treatment outcomes (Frank, Dixon, & Grosz, 1993; Iverson & Baucom, 1988; Snyder & Berg, 1983; Snyder, Mangrum, & Wills, 1993; Snyder, Wills, & Grady-Fletcher, 1991). Snyder and Aikman (1999) also note the value of using MSI-R serially throughout the course of treatment in the evaluation of change and for revising treatment goals and interventions. The instrument

Can be readministered at multiple points during treatment to evaluate and consolidate gains that the couple has made and to identify residual areas of distress for further work. This idiographic approach to outcome evaluation emphasizes within partner change across time.

(Snyder & Aikman, 1999, p. 1198)

Systemic Therapy Inventory of Change (STIC)

Brief description of the STIC. The STIC Feedback System includes two client-report measures which clients complete online: "STIC Initial" and the "STIC Intersession," which is a longer version of the STIC Initial (Pinsof et al., 2009; Pinsof & Chambers, 2010). It also includes an online Feedback Report which provides therapists feedback about their client systems and current status on its scales. STIC includes system scales that measure adult, child/adolescent, family, and couple functioning, as well as three scales for measuring the alliance in family, couple, and individual therapy (Pinsof, Goldsmith, & Latta, 2012). While initially developed for monitoring couples therapy, STIC can also be used to assess progress in individual and family therapy.

Before therapy begins, clients complete the STIC Initial which takes about 45 min. Subsequently, the STIC Intersession is completed before each therapy session which takes 2–3 min. It provides therapists with a brief, reliable snapshot of client functioning over the course of treatment. Clients over the age of 12 may complete the STIC, and each partner or family member completes the instrument separately.

STIC as an outcomes measure. STIC provides useful ongoing feedback to the therapists for defining problems, tracking change, and assessing outcomes. It can aid clinicians in making informed decisions about assessment, treatment planning, progress evaluation, and termination. Reportedly, its session-to-session use provides feedback that can decrease attrition and improve supervision (Johnson, Ketring, & Anderson, 2010; Pinsof, 2017).

Reliability is reported to be .74–.90 (Cronbach's alpha) depending on the scale (Pinsof et al., 2009; Pinsof et al., 2012). Research supports the convergent and discriminant validity of the STIC Initial (Zinbarg et al., 2018). The STIC Feedback System is available from Northwestern University Family Institute for a nominal fee.

Strategy for Ongoing Assessment

The following six-step protocol can be useful in utilizing the GARF, SFI, SAFE, DAS, MSI-R, SCORE, or STIC when measuring and monitoring clinical outcomes with couples and families.

1. Initially interview the couple or family.
2. Choose and administer specific inventories.
3. Collect collateral data (relevant work, school, medical records, etc.) and other interview data.

4. Review assessment data and plan treatment.
5. Monitor ongoing clinical outcomes and modify treatment accordingly.
6. Evaluate pre-treatment and post-treatment outcomes, if feasible.

Well-executed interviews of the couple and family (Step 1 and Step 3) are essential in providing sufficient data and background information to develop and implement an effective treatment plan and intervention strategies. At the present time, the decision of which inventories and rating scales (Step 2) to use to measure and/or monitor clinical outcomes is much less complex than the protocols suggested by Bagarozzi (Chapter 6) or Yingling (Chapter 8). For example, Bagarozzi advocates a four-step funneling or filtering process that progresses from choosing global measures to focused measures. Because of the limited number of suitable potential inventories and scales (i.e., ease of administration and reasonable cost), the clinician might decide to utilize the SFI and GARF or the SAFE and GARF with families and use the GARF and DAS or MSI-R with couples.

Step 5 reflects the basic reason for monitoring outcomes, for example, session by session, every third session, and so forth. In this step, outcomes data transform into valuable feedback information that the clinician can utilize to modify the course and duration of treatment in terms of focus, modality, and intervention strategies. As a result of this feedback and subsequent treatment "course correction," couple or family therapy becomes more closely tailored to couple or family need and circumstance. Presumably, this should lead to more effective and efficient treatment. Finally, the clinical value of outcomes measurement can be evaluated in Step 6 by examining overall pre–post-treatment effects on the given outcome measures, inventories, and/or scales.

Case Study

Jack and Nancy, both aged 33, were referred to couples therapy by Nancy's gynecologist. During their first conjoint session (Step 1), the therapist learned that the couple had been married for seven years and had a 2½-year-old daughter, Sybil. Sybil was their "wonder" child because she had been born after several years of unsuccessful efforts to conceive, including two years of painful fertility treatment. Jack had been an accountant at a low-tech manufacturing corporation until he was laid off some three months previously; Nancy had worked

(Continued)

as a nurse at a local hospital for 3 or 4 years before she married Jack. Both had known each other since college but had never really seriously dated until after graduation.

The couple presented with increased argumentativeness, social and emotional withdrawal, and decreased sexual intimacy. These issues were relatively new in their relationship, apparently beginning soon after Sybil's birth. Nancy had been concerned about Jack's rigidity and seeming lack of emotional expressiveness since they had married and on more than one occasion had indicated her desire for them to seek couples therapy, but Jack was not interested in talking to anyone about himself or his marriage. In the time since he had been laid off, Jack had become increasingly sullen and emotionally distant; Nancy, who had been working part time at the hospital, now felt "forced" to go full time to cover their bills. She was particularly distraught about this because it meant she had less time to care for her daughter. During a recent appointment with her gynecologist, Nancy had begun sobbing when asked how she was doing. It was at this point that the gynecologist referred Nancy for conjoint couples therapy. Both partners acknowledged a moderate level of commitment to their marriage and an even deeper commitment to Sybil, who had become, for all practical purposes, the center of their lives.

The plan was to administer the MSI-R to the couple at the end of the first conjoint session and to interview Nancy and Jack individually in the following week. Then, during their second conjoint session, extensive feedback would be provided incorporating MSI-R, GARF, and interview material to formulate a tailored treatment plan collaboratively with the couple. GARF would be evaluated at each conjoint session, and the MSI-R was to be administered after every third session and after the last session (Step 2).

Individual interviewing provided a fuller understanding of each partner, their attraction to one another, and the nature of their marital relationship. Nancy's description of her family of origin suggested that she had experienced a warm and secure attachment style and that her early life experiences with parents, siblings, and peers were wholesome and supportive. Her parents were described as encouraging and believed in expressing affection openly. She was the oldest of three siblings and enjoyed helping her mother raise her younger sister and brother. Nancy was a very good student and a leader among her peers. Although Nancy's depression did not meet criteria for a major depressive episode, a diagnosis of adjustment disorder with depressed mood was noted. Although her current GAF was 54, her highest level of function in the past 12 months was judged to be about 85.

On the other hand, Jack's family of origin was less warm and less secure. His mother was described as emotionally unavailable, and his father was often critical and demanding. He was a second child and, although he was a competent student, he was no match for his older brother, who was an honor student and top athlete. Needless to say, his brother was his father's favorite child. Jack's fearful attachment style seemed to reflect a sense of personal unworthiness along with an expectation that others would be rejecting and untrustworthy. Jack's current GAF was 62, although his highest level in the past year, when he was still working and quite content with his professional and family life, was probably about 72.

Not surprisingly, Jack had been wary of intimacy and tended to be socially distant and even awkward. However, he felt and acted differently when he first met Nancy. Her energetic presence seemed to make him come alive and feel hopeful about himself and the future. For her part, Nancy was attracted to Jack's quiet, patient gentleness as well as his ruggedly handsome features. Nancy described Jack as a caring father who adored Sybil. She noted that he was certainly more patient as a parent than she and that she had no qualms about his ability to care for their daughter while she was working. Nevertheless, she was angry that she had to work full time and so could not spend much time nurturing her growing daughter. It appeared that this reasonably healthy couple's GARF might have been in the mid-70s during the best period of their relationship but had slipped considerably in the past several months (Step 3).

An initial MSI-R profile was derived. It was noteworthy that raw scores on Global Distress (GDS) and Affective Communication (AFC) and Problem-Solving Communication (PSC) were extremely high for Jack and Nancy (see CS-1 in **Table 6.1**). In line with interview data, Jack and Nancy reported considerable marital distress in their relationship (GDS) and acknowledged a high degree of dissatisfaction with the extent of affection shown each other (AFC). This was particularly evident for Nancy, which reflected Jack's emotional distancing and lack of warmth. Similarly, the profile for both suggested their difficulty in intimate sharing, which most likely was exacerbated by their difficulty in resolving problems and conflict (PSC).

(Continued)

Table 6.1 MSI-R Subscale Score Monitoring per Specified Conjoint Session (CS) for Female (F) and Male (M) Partners

Subscale	Gender	CS-1	CS-3	CS-6	CS-9
Global Distress (GDS)	F	13	11	7	2
	M	12	9	6	3
Affective Communication (AFC)	F	12	8	5	2
	M	13	10	4	0
Problem-Solving Communication (PSC)	F	13	13	6	3
	M	12	11	5	2
Aggression (AGG)	F	2	1	0	0
	M	1	0	0	0
Time Together (TTO)	F	5	4	3	1
	M	4	4	3	2
Disagreement About Finances (FIN)	F	0	0	0	0
	M	0	0	0	0
Sexual Dissatisfaction (SEX)	F	7	7	5	2
	M	13	13	10	9
Role Orientation (ROR)	F	10	10	10	10
	M	10	10	10	10
Family History of Distress (FAM)	F	1	1	1	1
	M	4	4	5	5
Dissatisfaction With Children (DSC)	F	0	0	0	0
	M	0	0	0	0
Conflict Over Child Rearing (CCR)	F	0	0	0	0
	M	0	0	0	0

A GARF score of 52 was assessed, using Yingling's profiling system for the GARF (1998). Subscores on Interactional (46), Organizational (56), and Emotional Climate (42), as well as an overall score of 52 were recorded (see **Table 6.2**). Similar to the MSI-R, their GARF profile suggested that communication was frequently inhibited by unresolved conflict, that ineffective anger and emotional deadness interfered with their relationship, and that their decision making was intermittently effective at best. In short, ineffective communication was inhibiting intimacy, problem resolution, and decision-making processes.

Based on these clinical data, a treatment focus, goals, and intervention strategies were planned and implemented. Because this was a reasonably

Table 6.2 GARF Scores and Subscore Monitoring per Conjoint Session (CS)

Subscale/ global	CS-1	CS-2	CS-3	CS-4	CS-5	CS-6	CS-7	CS-8	CS-9
Interactional	46	46	62	66	70	71	78	80	83
Organizational	56	56	62	65	65	75	78	81	86
Emotional Climate	42	45	51	55	60	60	65	70	80
Global Therapist GARF	52	52	58	63	68	70	75	80	83

healthy and functional couple facing a major stressor (i.e., job loss and its relational sequelae) and the couple appeared to have some relational skill deficits, skill-focused couples therapy seemed indicated. It is also noteworthy that this couple brought some important strengths to therapy: a relatively conflict-free seven-year marriage, their positive experience as parents, and Nancy's early secure attachment style, which implies that she possesses considerable emotional resilience. Accordingly, the goals of treatment were to increase communication and foster emotional intimacy and effective problem resolution and decision making (Step 4).

The first and second sessions initiated this emphasis on communication by focusing on increasing listening skills and learning to use the language of affect. Little change was noticed on GARF subscales after session two or on GDS, AFC, and PSC scores of the MSI-R. Accordingly, the treatment focus shifted in subsequent sessions to assertive communication and conflict resolution. For the next four sessions, the couple worked in sessions and between sessions on skill learning and practice in these two areas. Not surprisingly, Interactional, Organizational, and Emotional Climate subscales of the GARF improved (see **Table 6.2**), as did the AFC and PSC subscales of the MSI-R when they were assessed at the sixth session. Because overall marital distress and dissatisfaction with this couple seemed to be linked intimately to affective communication and problem-solving communication, the GDS was significantly lowered by the sixth session (see **Table 6.1**). Subsequent sessions—sixth through the ninth—focused even more on emotional intimacy as well as problem-solving involving specific issues such as jobs and careers. Relationally, things had improved considerably, so treatment would terminate with the ninth session.

(Continued)

In session eight, Jack announced he had just been offered the position of comptroller for a mid-size service corporation. Although this was the next step in a senior accountant's career path, it was a step that Jack had avoided for the past few years, even though others had noted that he possessed the requisite skills and experience. Although he admitted to some feelings of uncertainty about whether he could handle the kinds of responsibilities associated with that position, he felt that with the recent upsurge in Nancy's support and encouragement, he would succeed (Step 5).

Pre–post-treatment outcomes reflected the significant degree of change and growth in this marital relationship. On the MSI-R, major pre–post-treatment changes were noted on the three subscales directly related to the couple's main concerns. On the GDS, the changes went from a 13 to a 2 for Nancy and a 12 to a 3 for Jack; with AFC, changes went from 12 to 2 for Nancy and 13 to 0 for Jack; and with PSC, changes went from 13 to 3 for Nancy and 12 to 2 for Jack. On these subscales, changes went from the highest or most problematic to the lowest or least problematic range (see **Table 6.1**). On the GARF, a noticeable shift in relational functioning was from occasionally unsatisfactory to highly satisfactory. More specifically, the following subscale changes were noted: Interactional subscale from 46 to 83, Organizational subscale from 56 to 86, Emotional Climate subscale from 42 to 80, and overall GARF from 52 to 83. In other words, now a greater degree of shared understanding and agreement about roles, tasks, and decision making; better problem-solving communication and negotiation; and a general atmosphere of warmth, caring, and sharing were present (Step 6; see **Table 6.2**).

Concluding Comments

Because the concepts covered in this chapter have only recently become a part of the conversation of assessment with couples and families, they are seldom discussed in texts on family therapy, much less books on family and couple assessment. Nevertheless, the paradigm shift in accountability in clinical practice has propelled clinical outcomes assessment to center stage. This chapter highlighted six measures that have been shown to have some clinical utility in measuring and monitoring outcomes in couples and family therapy. In short, the future of ongoing assessment is bright with the promise of additional instruments. **Table 6.3** summarizes these measures.

Table 6.3 Matrix: Reference Guide to Clinical Outcomes Assessment Instruments with Families and Couples

Assessment Instrument	Type/Use	Cultural/ Language	Administration: Time and Items	Computerized: a = Scoring; b = Report	Reliability (R); Validity (V)	Availability
GARF	Therapist Rating/Couples and Families		5–10 min for Inquiry/ scoring	None	R = 82 Alpha V = Concurrent	Appendix B of DSM-IV-TR
SFI	Self-report/ Families	Spanish; Chinese	Easy to Administer, 5–15 min; 36 items	None	R = Test–retest .30–.87; V = Criterion	Journal Article
SAFE	Self-report/ Families	Spanish	21 items	a = yes	V = .74 and .82	Yingling et al. (1998)
MSI-R	Self-report/ Couples	Spanish	25 min to Administer and Score; 150 items	a = yes; b = interpretive report	Factor Analysis	Western Psychological Services, Inc.
DAS	Self-report/ Couples	French; Chinese	5–10 min; 34 items (also 14-item version)	a = yes	R = .86–.96; V = .86–.88	Journal Article; Multi-Health Systems, Inc.
SCORE 15	Self-report/ Couples	12 European Languages	2–5 min Administer and Score 15 items	a = yes;	R = .89 Alpha .88 Split-Half	Journal Article; Website
STIC: Initial & Intersession	Self-report/ Couples		45 min for Initial; 2–3 min for Intersession	a = yes; b = interpretive report	R = .74–.90; V = Convergent & Discriminant	Northwestern University Family Institute

References

Adam, D., & Gingras, M. (1982). Short- and long-term effects of a marriage enrichment program upon couple functioning. *Journal of Sex and Marital Therapy, 8*, 97–118.

American Psychiatric Association. (2000). *Diagnostic and statistical manual of mental disorders* (4th ed., text revision [DSM-IV-TR]). Washington, DC: Author.

American Psychiatric Association. (2013). *Diagnostic and statistical manual of mental disorders* (5th ed., DSM-5). Alexandria, VA: Author.

Atkisson, C., & Zwick, R. (1982). The clients' satisfaction questionnaire: Psychometric properties and correlations with service utilization. *Evaluation and Program Planning, 5*, 233–237.

Beavers, W. R., & Hampson, R. B. (1990). *Successful families: Assessment and intervention.* New York, NY: Norton.

Brock, G., & Joanning, H. (1983). A comparison of the relationship enhancement program and the Minnesota couples communication program. *Journal of Marital and Family Therapy, 9*, 295–305.

Carr, A., & Stratton, P. (2017). The SCORE family assessment questionnaire: A decade of progress. *Family Process, 56*(2), 285–301.

Denton, W., Nakonezny, P., & Burwell, S. (2010). Reliability and validity of the global assessment of relational functioning (GARF) in a psychiatric family therapy clinic. *Journal of Marital and Family Therapy, 36*, 376–387.

Frank, B., Dixon, D., & Grosz, H. (1993). Conjoint monitoring of symptoms of premenstrual syndrome: Impact on marital satisfaction. *Journal of Counseling Psychology, 40*, 109–114.

Hamilton, E., & Carr, A. (2016). Systematic review of self-report family assessment measures. *Family Process, 55*(1), 16–30.

Hampson, R., & Beavers, W. (1996a). Family therapy and outcome: Relationships between therapist and family styles. *Contemporary Family Therapy, 13*(3), 345–370.

Hampson, R., & Beavers, W. (1996b). Measuring family therapy outcome in a clinical setting: Families that do better or do worse in therapy. *Family Process, 35*, 347–361.

Hampson, R., Prince, C., & Beavers, W. (1999). Marital therapy: Qualities of couples who fare better or worse in treatment. *Journal of Marital and Family Therapy, 25*(4), 411–424.

Iverson, A., & Baucom, D. (1988). Behavioral marital therapy outcomes: Alternative interpretation of the data. *Behavior Therapy, 21*, 129–138.

Jacobson, N. (1984). A component analysis of behavioral marital therapy: The relative effectiveness of behavior exchange and communication/problem-solving training. *Journal of Consulting and Clinical Psychology, 52*, 295–305.

Jacobson, N., & Follette, W. (1985). Clinical significance of improvement resulting from two behavioral marital therapy components. *Behavior Therapy, 16*, 249–264.

Johnson, L., Ketring, S., & Anderson, S. (2010). The intersession report: Development of a short questionnaire for couples therapy. *American Journal of Family Therapy, 38*, 266–276.

Lambert, M. (2010). *Prevention of treatment failure: The use of measuring, monitoring, and feedback in clinical practice.* Washington, DC: American Psychological Association.

Latham, J. (1990). Family-of-origin intervention: An intergenerational approach to enhancing marital adjustment. *Journal of Contemporary Psychotherapy, 20*, 211–222.

Miller, S., Duncan, B., Brown, J., Sorrell, R., & Chalk, M. (2006). Using outcome to inform and improved treatment outcomes: Making ongoing, real-time assessment feasible. *Journal of Brief Therapy, 5*, 5–23.

Pinsof, W. M. (2017). The Systemic Therapy Inventory of Change—STIC: A multi-systemic and multi-dimensional system to integrate science into psychotherapeutic practice. In T. Tilden & B. E. Wampold (Eds.), *Routine outcome monitoring in couple and family therapy: The empirically informed therapist* (pp. 85–101). New York, NY: Springer.

Pinsof, W., & Chambers, A. (2010). Empirically informed systemic psychotherapy: Tracking client change and therapist behavior during therapy. In J. Bray & M. Stanton (Eds.), *The Wiley-Blackwell handbook of family psychology* (pp. 431–446). Oxford, UK: Blackwell.

Pinsof, W. M., Goldsmith, J. Z., & Latta, T. A. (2012). Information technology and feedback research can bridge the scientist–practitioner gap: A couple therapy example. *Couple and Family Psychology: Research and Practice, 1*(4), 253–273.

Pinsof, W., Zinbarg, R., Lebow, J., Knobloch-Fedders, L., Durbin, E., Chambers, A., Latta, T., Karam, E., Goldsmith, J., & Friedman, G. (2009). Laying the foundation for progress research in family, couple, and individual therapy: The development and psychometric features of the initial systemic therapy inventory of change. *Psychotherapy Research, 19*, 143–156.

Prouty, H., Markowski, E., & Barnes, H. (2000). Using the DAS in marital therapy: An exploratory study. *Family Journal: Therapy for Couples and Families, 8*(3), 250–257.

Ross, N., & Doherty, W. (2001). Validity of Global Assessment of Relational Functioning (GARF) when used by community-based therapists. *American Journal of Family Therapy, 29*, 239–253.

Snyder, D. (1981). *Marital Satisfaction Inventory (MSI) manual.* Los Angeles, CA: Western Psychological Services.

Snyder, D. (1997). *Marital Satisfaction Inventory, revised (MSI-I) manual.* Los Angeles, CA: Western Psychological Services.

Snyder, D., & Aikman, G. (1999). Marital Satisfaction Inventory, revised. In M. Maruish (Ed.), *Use of psychological testing for treatment planning and outcome assessment* (2nd ed., pp. 1173–1210). Hillsdale, NJ: Erlbaum.

Snyder, D., & Berg, P. (1983). Predicting couples' response to brief directive sex therapy. *Journal of Sex and Marital Therapy, 9*, 114–120.

Snyder, D., Mangrum, L., & Wills, R. (1993). Predicting couples' response to marital therapy: A comparison of short- and long-term predictors. *Journal of Consulting and Clinical Psychology, 61*, 61–69.

Snyder, D., Wills, R., & Grady-Fletcher, A. (1991). Long-term effectiveness of behavioral versus insight-oriented marital therapy. *Journal of Consulting and Clinical Psychology, 59*, 138–141.

Spanier, G. (1976). Measuring dyadic adjustment: New scales for assessing the quality of marriage and similar dyads. *Journal of Marriage and the Family, 38*, 15–28.

Spanier, G. (1979). The measurement of marital quality. *Journal of Sex and Marital Therapy, 5*, 288–300.

Sperry, L. (1997). Treatment outcomes: An overview. *Psychiatric Annals, 27*(2), 95–99.

Sperry, L., Brill, P., Howard, K., & Grissom, G. (1996). *Treatment outcomes in psychotherapy and psychiatric interventions.* New York, NY: Brunner/Mazel.

Sperry, L., Grissom, G., Brill, P., & Marion, D. (1997). Changing clinicians' practice patterns and managed care culture with outcomes systems. *Psychiatric Annals, 27*(2), 127–132.

Stratton, P., Bland, J., Janes, E., & Lask, J. (2010). Developing an indicator of family function and a practicable outcome measure for systemic family and couple therapy: The SCORE. *Journal of Family Therapy, 32*, 232–258.

Stratton, P., Lask, J., Bland, J., Nowotny, E., Evans, C., Singh, R., ... Peppiatt, A. (2014). Detecting therapeutic improvement early in therapy: Validation of the SCORE-15 index of family functioning and change. *Journal of Family Therapy, 36*(1), 3–19.

Tilden, T., & Wampold, B. E. (Eds.). (2017). *Routine outcome monitoring in couple and family therapy: The empirically informed therapist.* New York, NY: Springer.

Wynne, L. (1988). *The state of the art of family therapy research: Controversies and recommendations.* New York, NY: Family Process Press.

Yingling, L. (1996). *A manual for the use of the Systematic Assessment of the Family Environment (SAFE): A self-report instrument for assessing multi-level family system functioning.* Rockwell, TX: J & L Human Systems Development.

Yingling, L., Miller, W., McDonald, A., & Galwaler, S. (1994a). *Verifying outcome: Paradigm for the therapist-researcher.* Paper presented at the meeting of the Texas Association for Marriage and Family Therapy, January, San Antonio, TX.

Yingling, L., Miller, W., McDonald, A., & Galwaler, S. (1994b). *Verifying outcome: Paradigm for the therapist-researcher.* Paper presented at the meeting of the American Association for Marriage and Family Therapy, November, Chicago, IL.

Yingling, L., Miller, W., McDonald, A., & Galwaler, S. (1998). *GARF assessment sourcebook: Using the DSM-IV global assessment of relational functioning.* Washington, DC: Brunner/Mazel.

Zinbarg, R. E., Pinsof, W., Quirk, K., Kendall, A., Goldsmith, J., Hardy, N., ... Latta, T. (2018). Testing the convergent and discriminant validity of the systemic therapy inventory of change initial scales. *Psychotherapy Research, 28*(5), 734–749.

7

COUPLE ASSESSMENT STRATEGY AND INVENTORIES

Dennis A. Bagarozzi and Len Sperry

Couple therapy has changed rather dramatically in the past few years in how it is perceived and how it is learned and practiced. It was quite unexpected that a survey (Norcross, Pfund, & Prochaska, 2013) of experts' predictions about the future practice of all psychotherapy modalities would find that couples therapy was the modality most likely to experience the greatest growth in the ensuing decade (Gurman, 2015). Increasing demand for training in couples work is reflected in participants' preference for workshop and seminar training and requests for coursework and supervision in couples therapy in Dr. Sperry's department. Furthermore, it was quite remarkable that couples therapy presenters at the 2016 Evolution of Psychotherapy Conference were drawing ten times the number of participants than most individual therapy presenters.

Another change involves the shift in expectations for intimate relationships that is occurring today. While it is no surprise that the "traditional marriage" gave way to the "companionate marriage" in past decades, the "all-or-nothing marriage" is in vogue today. In this new form of relationship, convincing data show that wives and husbands are expecting their partners to spur them on to become their best selves (Finkel, 2017). This means that intimacy, mutuality, and marital satisfaction, and their measurement, remain more important than ever (Singer, Labunko, Alea, & Baddeley, 2015).

At the same time, expectations for the use of empirically sound measures to assess and document the clinical outcomes of therapy with couples has also increased. This is consistent with the mandate for the development of instruments that can be used to address societal shifts. For example, as the middle class continues to shrink (Pew Research Center, 2018a), the importance of measures to assess the needs of couples of lower socioeconomic standing becomes further pronounced. In addition, as economic well-being of rural families increases, the need for assessment of these populations (USDA Economic Research Services, 2018) is likewise warranted.

Furthermore, chronic disease is a leading cause of death and disability in the United States (Centers for Disease Control, 2018). The demand for a brief instrument to evaluate levels of coping in couples facing such crises is critical. Of particular interest is the phenomenon of illness self-concealment, as it is associated with decreased trust, stability, and relational satisfaction (Wertheim et al., 2016).

Finally, Pew Research Center (2018b) data suggests that stigma regarding online dating continues to dwindle, as the rate of usage of online dating services continues to grow. As a result of the increased levels of anonymity that internet communications afford, levels of accountability that would occur in traditional face-to-face encounters is diminished significantly. Accordingly, high rates of deception and cyber abuse occur. The prevalence of such deception and abuse is seen especially among younger adults. Therefore, new measures have been developed to investigate this phenomenon (Hamby, 2013).

In response to the above concerns, some new instruments that are in the experimental stages of development are discussed here. This chapter, a revision and update of Bagarozzi and Sperry (2012), is intended for therapists who wish to incorporate empirically based assessment aids as part of their clinical work with distressed marriages and dyadic relationships. The self-report measures of dyadic functioning reviewed below are predominantly problem/issue focused. Some instruments, however, such as the Family Adaptability and Cohesion Scales and the Spousal Inventory of Desired Changes and Relationship Barriers (SIDCARB) are theoretically anchored in that they were developed to operationalize key constructs derived from accepted theories of marital/dyadic relationship structure, functioning and process.

A minimalistic approach to judging the success of marital therapy would be to ask spouses to answer the following two Likert-type scale questions: "In general, how satisfied are you with your spouse?" and "In general how satisfied are you with your marriage?" Bagarozzi (1983) found that these two seven-point Likert-type questions correlated with the Locke-Wallace Short Marital Adjustment Test (Lock & Wallace, 1959), .71 for spousal satisfaction and .73 for marital satisfaction. However, these questions do not identify specific areas of concern. The Locke-Wallace Marital Adjustment Test, on the other hand, does provide such information. Because of the history of this measure and its widespread use since it first appeared in 1959, it can be considered a benchmark standard for assessing marital adjustment and satisfaction. For this reason, the Locke-Wallace Marital Adjustment Test is included in this review.

The following section includes this and other instruments currently used with couples. Then, newly developed instruments are described. This is followed by a protocol for utilizing such instruments in clinical practice. Finally a detailed case example that illustrates the protocol is included.

Current Instruments

Locke-Wallace Marital Adjustment Test

Type of instrument. The Locke-Wallace Marital Adjustment Test was developed in 1959 to provide a reliable and valid measure of marital adjustment. Using selected, non-duplicated, and statistically significant items from a variety of previously developed measures with high item discrimination, Harvey Locke and Carl Wallace (1959) composed a 15-item marital adjustment scale. Marital adjustment is defined by Locke and Wallace as an "accommodation of partners to each other at a given time."

Use and target audience. The purpose of this brief instrument is to assess relational adjustment. The Locke-Wallace Marital Adjustment Test is used with married or cohabitating couples in clinical and in research settings.

Multicultural. This instrument is available in English.

Ease and time of administration. The Locke-Wallace Marital Adjustment Test is a self-report instrument that is easy to administer and takes approximately five minutes to complete. It is in a paper-and-pencil format.

Scoring procedure. This instrument can be hand scored in five minutes or less. No automated scoring system or computer-generated report is available.

Reliability. Reliability studies were initially conducted by Locke and Wallace (1959). Internal consistency was estimated by the Spearman-Brown formula and found to be .90 (Cross & Sharpley, 1981). Data on test–retest reliability are not available.

Validity. Known-groups validity of this instrument is high, with scores discriminating between adjusted and maladjusted couples. Hunt (1978) found the correlation between the Lock-Wallace Marital Adjustment Test and the Dyadic Adjustment Scale (DAS) to be .93 for husbands and for wives. Discrimination, item, and factor analyses have been conducted by Cross and Sharpley (1981).

Availability and source. The scale is available in the original journal article (Locke & Wallace, 1959) and online.

Comment. The Locke-Wallace Marital Adjustment Test has been used extensively since it first appeared in 1959. When it was introduced, it was one of the first short measures of marital adjustment, and it remains so today.

Dyadic Adjustment Scale (DAS)

Type of instrument. Like the Locke-Wallace Marital Adjustment Test, the Dyadic Adjustment Scale (DAS) had its origins in family sociology. Developed by Graham Spanier (1976), the DAS is a 32-item questionnaire that utilizes a Likert-type format. Because 11 of these items were taken directly from the Locke-Wallace Marital Adjustment Test, it is not surprising to find that the DAS correlates .86 with the Locke-Wallace Marital Adjustment Test.

Use and target audience. This instrument is designed to assess relational quality as perceived by couples. It has been used as a general measure of marital satisfaction by using total scores, or its subscales can be utilized to measure cohesion, consensus, satisfaction, and expression of affection.

Multicultural. This instrument is available in English, French-Canadian, and Chinese.

Ease and time of administration. This 32-item self-report instrument can be completed in five to ten minutes. A briefer, 14-item version is available (Busby, Christiansen, Crane, & Larson, 1995; Crane, Middleton, & Bean, 2000).

Scoring procedure. The instrument can be hand scored in five minutes or less.

Reliability. Cronbach's alpha for the overall scale is reported to be .96; for the Dyadic Consensus, Dyadic Satisfaction, Dyadic Cohesion, and Affectional Expression scales, the Cronbach's alpha scores are .90, .94, .86 and .73, respectively (Spanier & Thompson, 1982).

Validity. Criterion-related validity was established by comparing the responses of married and divorced individuals for each of the 32 items. The divorced sample differed significantly from the married sample at the $p < .001$ level for each item. T tests were used for making these comparisons. The mean total score for married individuals was 114.8; the mean score for divorced individuals was 70.7. Concurrent validity is evidenced by high correlations (.86) with the Locke-Wallace Marital Adjustment Test.

Availability and source. The scale is available in the original journal article (Spanier, 1976). The English language version is available for purchase at:
Multi-Health Systems, Inc.
http://www.mhs.com/product.aspx?gr=cli&prod=das&id=overview#scales

Comment: The DAS is one of the most extensively used relational instruments in clinical practice today. Besides its value in clinical practice, the DAS continues to be used by researchers throughout the world. Because of its favorable psychometrics and ease of administration, it is commonly utilized in thesis and dissertation research.

Spousal Inventory of Desired Changes and Relationship Barriers (SIDCARB)

Type of instrument. Although the Locke-Wallace Marital Adjustment Test and the DAS have been used to represent marital satisfaction, neither actually asked respondents to rate satisfaction with their spouse or their marriage.

Essentially, adjustment has been equated with satisfaction. However, stable marriages are not necessarily satisfying marriages, and spouses dissatisfied with their mates may simply have "adjusted" to their conjugal situation and lot in life. To assess the dynamics of marital satisfaction and its relationship to marital stability, Bagarozzi (1983) developed the SIDCARB, based upon the major principles of social exchange theory as applied to marriages.

Use and target audience. This instrument is useful in assessing marital satisfaction and stability in couples undergoing couple therapy and in couples' workshops.

Multicultural. This instrument is available in English.

Ease and time of administration. SIDCARB is a 26-item self-report questionnaire that takes approximately five minutes to complete. It is in a paper-and-pencil format.

Scoring procedure. The questionnaire is hand scored, and it takes approximately seven minutes to score each partner's questionnaire. No computer scoring or computer-generated report is available.

Reliability. Cronbach's alpha of reliability was computed for each subscale; the reliabilities were found to be .86, .74 and .80 for Factors I, II and III respectively.

Validity. Factor analysis revealed significant loadings on three factors: I = Dissatisfaction and Desire for Change in Spouse's Behavior; II = Willingness to Separate and Divorce, and Internal Psychological Barriers to Relationship Termination; and III = External Circumstantial Barriers to Relationship Termination (Bagarozzi & Pollane, 1983).

Availability and source. SIDCARB and scoring guidelines are reprinted in Appendix A of Bagarozzi (2001).

Comment. When the Locke-Wallace Marital Adjustment Test, DAS and SIDCARB are used in concert, the therapist can gain a better understanding of the interplay among several factors that will have a bearing on therapeutic outcome, for example, Satisfaction, Adjustment, Stability, Level of Commitment, and Barriers to Separation and Divorce.

Another important dimension to consider in marital assessment is the degree of emotional attachment that exists between the spouses. The presence of a positive emotional attachment (feelings of love, caring, closeness and affection) between the partners often portends a successful therapeutic outcome. Conversely, the more distant, removed, estranged, and apathetic the spouses are, the less successful the therapy is likely to be. Therefore, a measure of positive emotional attachment can be a very helpful diagnostic tool.

Marital Disaffection Scale (MDS)

Type of instrument. In 1993, Karen Kayser published the MDS (Kayser, 1993). She defined *disaffection* as the gradual loss of positive emotions—love, caring, affection, and closeness—that occurs between spouses over time, as dissatisfactions accumulate. Disaffection does not necessarily lead to relationship dissolution because a number of internal and external barriers may cause a couple to remain together in what appears to be a stable marriage, even when the emotional relationship is dead. The theoretical model of the disaffection process is based on the work of Snyder and Regts (1982) and Duck (1982).

Use and target audience. This instrument is a measure of the level of disaffection or loss of positive emotions toward one's spouse. Although it was designed primarily for use in couples therapy, it has been used in research studies with couples in clinical and nonclinical settings.

Multicultural. This instrument is available in English.

Ease and time of administration. The MDS is a 21-item self-report inventory that takes approximately three to five minutes to complete. Currently, this inventory is available in a paper version only.

Scoring procedure. The range of scores for the MDS is 21–84. This instrument can be hand scored in three to five minutes. No automated scoring or computer-generated report is currently available.

Reliability. Using Cronbach's alpha, internal consistency of the instrument is reported as .93 (Kayser, 1993). Kayser (1996) also presents data on interitem reliability.

Validity. To determine construct validity, factor analysis was performed. Although three factors—Attachment, Emotional Estrangement, and Emotional Support—could be discerned, many of the items were found to cross load so that clear and distinct independent factors did not emerge. Therefore, Kayser (1993) considers the MDS to be unidimensional, suggesting that only the total, full scale score be used when measuring disaffection. Kayser's criterion-referenced study offered additional support for the scale's validity. A comparison of recently divorced individuals with a random sample of married individuals from the general population showed means for these two groups were 70.8 and 33.7, respectively. Kayser (1996) presented additional data on criterion-related validity and discriminant validity.

Availability and source. The instrument and scoring instructions are included in *When Love Dies: The Process of Marital Disaffection* (Kayser, 1993).

Comment. Interestingly, scores on the MDS showed significant positive relationship (.36) with a spouse's problem drinking behavior and (.48) with workaholic behavior of a spouse. These results support the use of the MDS as a measure of emotional estrangement in marriage (Flowers, Robinson, & Carroll, 2000). Besides possessing good psychometric properties, this scale can serve as a good indication of a partner's motivation for therapy (Bagarozzi, 2013), i.e., the higher the disaffection score, the less motivated a partner will tend to be.

The Locke-Wallace Marital Adjustment Test, the DAS, the SIDCARB and the MDS all focus on global aspects of relationship dissatisfaction. The therapist who uses these assessment tools is responsible for helping partners identify specific issues of concern within each problem area so that targeted intervention can take place. Therapists who would like to get a much broader and behaviorally focused overview of marital conflicts and relationship problems may wish to employ the Areas of Change Questionnaire (Weiss, Hops, & Patterson, 1973).

Areas of Change Questionnaire

Type of Instrument. Behaviorists at the Oregon Research Institute developed the Areas of Change Questionnaire as part of their research into marital conflict (Weiss et al., 1973). This instrument targets 29 critical areas of behavior exchange and is divided into two sections. In the first section, respondents are asked to rate 34 behaviorally worded Likert-type items in terms of whether they would like their partners to increase the frequency of a desired (rewarding) behavior, decrease the frequency of an undesirable (punishing) behavior, or to maintain the current frequency level of enactment for the particular behavior in question. The second section of the questionnaire addresses what each respondent thinks his/her partner would like more of, less of, or not to change at all, i.e., is satisfied with the status quo. Thus this inventory lends itself to the calculation of a number of scores: desired change, perceived change, perceptual accuracy, and total change. Another version of this instrument, the Comprehensive Areas of Change Questionnaire, is briefly described in the *Comments* section.

Use and target audience. The Areas of Change Questionnaire is a 34-item self-report inventory designed to assess the amount of change couples desire in 13 domains of marital relations.

Multicultural. This instrument is available in English.

Ease and time of administration. The Areas of Change Questionnaire consists of 34 items with a seven-point Likert-scale format. This inventory is in a paper-and-pencil format. Contact the authors for further information. It takes between 10 and 20 minutes to complete this inventory.

Scoring procedure. Hand scoring of this inventory is initially cumbersome because the responses of both partners, on two separate scoring sheets, must be compared at the same time. The amount of scoring time depends on the number of items scored and the scorer's facility with the scoring process.

Reliability. Split-half reliability has been found to be .80; Cronbach's alpha is between .84 and .89; the test–retest reliabilities for husbands and wives are reported to be .96 and .74, respectively (Mead & Vatcher, 1985).

Validity. Discriminant validity has been demonstrated between distressed and non-distressed couples (Birchler & Webb, 1977). Pre-treatment and post-treatment sensitivity to change also has been reported (Baucom, 1982).

Availability and source. This instrument is available in the *Handbook of Family Measurement Techniques* (Perlmutter, Touliatos, & Holden, 2001).

Comment. Although the Areas of Change Questionnaire offers a global indexing of marital complaints, Mead and Vatcher (1985) found that only 13 of a possible 29 domains of marital relationship (identified in a national survey of practicing therapists) were covered by this instrument. Therefore Mead and Vatcher (1985) set out to develop a more comprehensive measure. As a result, the number of items included in the revised version was considerably increased. Psychometric properties of this revised version, the Comprehensive Areas of Change Questionnaire, equal or exceed the reliability and validity of the original version (Roberts, 1988; Vatcher, 1988). The revised questionnaire increases the number of items to 82, making the use of this revised questionnaire problematic for some therapists.

Refining the Process

The instruments reviewed thus far are all wide ranging in scope and are best used to help couples pinpoint problem areas in their relationship when no specific issue or complex of issues is clearly identified by either partner. Frequently, however, couples identify *communication* as their presenting problem, but when they are asked to discuss their communication difficulties in the presence of the therapist, it becomes evident that they are struggling with very specific long-standing relationship problems in addition to their communication difficulties.

Diagnostically it is important for the therapist to determine whether the problem issues that surface during such discussions truly are the source of the couple's distress or whether the couple is locked in a deadly power struggle for which their presenting problems are merely symptomatic. When power struggles are determined not to be the underlying dynamic, in depth exploration of the problem or problems complex is appropriate.

In many cases when couples identify *communication* as the presenting problem, they are really talking about intimacy. Two instruments: the Family Adaptability and Cohesion Scale: FACES IV, Couple Version (Olson, 2011; Olson, Sprinkle, & Russell, 1979) and the Intimacy Needs Survey (INS) (Bagarozzi, 1990, 2001) can be used to explore this critical area.

Family Adaptability and Cohesion Scales IV (FACES IV)

Type of instrument. FACES IV, made available in 2011, is the latest version of a self-report instrument designed to assess two central dimensions of the

Circumplex model of Marital and Family Systems. More than 1,200 published articles and dissertations have used the various versions of this instrument since it was first developed. The Circumplex model is comprised of three key constructs for understanding and measuring marital/family functioning. These three constructs translate into three fairly independent factor scales: (a) Cohesion, interpersonal closeness or intimacy, (b) Flexibility of relationship structure, and (c) Communication functionality. The main hypothesis of the Circumplex model (which is based on family systems theory) is that balanced levels of cohesion and flexibility are most conducive to healthy marital and family functioning, and unbalanced levels of cohesion and flexibility are associated with problematic functioning.

Use and target audience. FACES IV can be used throughout the entire treatment process (i.e., pre-treatment assessment, intersession monitoring, post-treatment evaluation, and follow-up investigations) and is appropriate for use with couples as well as entire family systems.

Multicultural. This version of FACES is available in multiple languages.

Ease and time of administration. This 42-item self-report measure can be completed in less than five minutes.

Scoring procedure. Each spouse's perception of his or her marriage or family system can be plotted on a 5x5 grid. Twenty-five combinations of cohesion and flexibility are possible. There are nine balanced types, which are located in the central area of the grid. Twelve mid-range types of relationships reflect imbalance in either cohesion or flexibility. The remaining four types of relationships are considered to be unbalanced. These reflect extreme scores for both cohesion and flexibility. A simple mathematical formula is used to calculate balanced and unbalanced scores for each dimension. These scores are then used to plot a spouse or family member's location on the Circumplex model.

Reliability. An alpha reliability analysis was used to examine internal consistency of the six factor analytically divined scales. These reliabilities are as follows: Enmeshed = .77, Disengages = .87, Balanced Cohesion = .89, Chaotic = .86, Balanced Flexibility = .84, and Rigid = .82.

Validity. Factor validity, concurrent validity, and discriminant validity have been reported for FACES IV (Olson, 2011).

Availability and source. Contact Life Innovations at: https://www.prepare-enrich.com

Comment. FACES has gone through a number of modifications since its introduction in 1979. It is one of the few theory-based and empirically validated measures available for both clinical and research purposes. Not only does it provide accurate pre-treatment assessments, but also it is very useful in helping couples and families formulate realistic treatment goals (e.g., to develop more or less structure in their relationship and to increase or decrease the degree of connectedness between spouses and family members who are involved in either disengaged or enmeshed relationships), monitor progress toward these objectives, and evaluate therapeutic progress and outcome.

Intimacy Needs Survey (INS)

Type of instrument. Bagarozzi (1990) developed the INS to help couples conceptualize their need for interpersonal closeness in a way that would make sense to them. This survey is a clinical tool that allows partners to explore whether their needs for intimacy are being met in nine specific areas: Emotional, Psychological, Intellectual, Sexual, Physical (Non-sexual), Spiritual, Aesthetic, Social and Recreational, and Temporal. Intimacy is conceptualized as a basic human need that has its origins in, and develops out of, the more fundamental survival need for attachment. Intimacy differs from individual to individual, and the nine components of this more general need also vary in strength from person to person.

Use and target audience. The INS is designed to assess couples' perceptions of their need for, and type of, intimacy. It allows the therapist to assess whether each partner's intimacy needs are being met satisfactorily by the other. In addition to use in couples therapy, it can be used in couples enrichment workshops.

Multicultural. This instrument is available in English.

Scoring Procedure. This instrument is hand scored in approximately 15 minutes. For the first eight subcomponent needs, numerical scores are calculated. The ninth dimension, Temporal, is viewed qualitatively and is considered separately. Three scores are computed for each of the eight component needs examined in the questionnaire: component needs strength, receptivity satisfaction, and reciprocity satisfaction. A total intimacy needs strength score is calculated simply by summing all eight component needs strength scores. No computer scoring, or computer-generated report is currently available.

Reliability. The INS is still in its experimental stages of development. Reliability has yet to be established.

Validity. The survey is still in its experimental stages of development. Validity has yet to be established. Nevertheless, four interrelated factors are evaluated: Overall Intimacy Need Strengths, Component Needs Strengths, Receptivity Satisfaction, and Reciprocity Satisfaction.

Availability and source. The INS is reprinted in Bagarozzi (2001).

Comment. This instrument assesses several components of intimacy that are not considered in other instruments. Among these are Spiritual Intimacy, Aesthetic Intimacy, and Temporal Intimacy. Because it is common for couples to complain that they have *intimacy problems,* it is valuable to distinguish these various components to determine which areas are problematic.

Significant differences in the need strength for sexual intimacy can be a cause of great concern for some couples, and it behooves the therapist to investigate the possible reasons for such differences. Desire discrepancy is a common problem presented to sex therapists who routinely conduct personal sex histories. Such histories allow the therapist to determine whether an individual's low level of desire is a reflection of an underlying constitutional factor (i.e., a low need for sexual intimacy), changes in hormonal levels due to aging or illness, the side effects of medication, substance abuse, etc. However, low sexual desire can also be symptomatic of depression that may be related to the couple's relationship difficulties. The Sexual Desire Inventory (Spector, 1992) used in conjunction with the MDS (Kayser, 1993) can be very helpful in making this determination, especially when detailed histories are impractical.

Sexual Desire Inventory

Type of instrument. The Sexual Desire Inventory was initially developed by Spector (1992) and further refined by colleagues (Spector, Carey, & Steinberg, 1996). Items included in the scale were selected based on models of sexual desire and the researchers' clinical experience in assessing sexual desire disorders. The inventory consists of two factors: Dyadic Sexual Desire (interest in having sexual relations with a partner, not necessarily one's partner) and Solitary Sexual Desire (interest in behaving sexually by oneself.)

Use and target audience. The Inventory allows the therapist to assess whether each partner's sexual needs are being met satisfactorily.

Multicultural. The Inventory is available in multiple languages.

Ease and time of administration. This self-report instrument consists of 14 items and is easy to administer. It takes less than five minutes to complete.

Scoring procedure. The instrument is hand scored in five minutes or less.

Reliability. Samples used to assess psychometric properties of the scale include college students (N = 380), geriatric adults (N = 40), and couples (N = 40). Internal consistency using Cronbach's alpha coefficient was .86 for the Dyadic Sexual Desire subscale and r = .96 for the Solitary Sexual Desire subscale. Test–retest reliability is reported to be r = .76 over a one-month period.

Validity. Factor validity as well as concurrent and discriminant validity are reported by Spector (1992). For females, Dyadic Sexual Desire was shown to be positively correlated with relationship adjustment, as measured by the DAS (Spanier, 1976); with sexual satisfaction, as measured by the Index of Sexual Satisfaction (Hudson, 1992); and with sexual arousal, as measured by the Sexual Arousal Inventory (Hoon, Hoon, & Wincze, 1976). For males, only Dyadic Sexual Desire was found to correlate with sexual satisfaction. Gender differences in responding to this scale have also been found; males were found to have significantly higher levels of dyadic and solitary desire than were females.

Availability and source. The Sexual Desire Inventory and scoring instructions are available online.

Comment. The Sexual Desire Inventory is a self-report instrument that is quick and easy to administer and score. In addition to having credible psychometric properties, it has remarkable clinical utility. More specifically, discussing the results of the inventory offers therapists and couples an occasion for discussing the matter of dyadic as well as personal sexual desire as these affect couples' overall intimacy satisfaction.

It is reasonable to assume that when couples enter treatment trust between the partners has been compromised to some degree. The extent to which trust has deteriorated will have a direct bearing upon the willingness of the partners to engage faithfully in the therapeutic process and will ultimately affect therapeutic outcome. The violation of un-verbalized and consciously unacknowledged rules and contracts that govern a couple's relationship is often at the heart of mistrust. Unearthing these relationship governing rules and non-verbalized contracts and how they have been violated is often a critical component of couples' therapy (Bagarozzi, 2013). This process can be facilitated by having couples complete the Trust Scale (TS) (Rempel, Holmes, & Zanna, 2001) at the outset of treatment.

Trust Scale (TS)

Type of instrument. The TS (Rempel et al., 2001) measures three components of trust in marriage: Predictability, Dependability, and Faith. It is a 17-item questionnaire. The respondent is asked to circle one of seven possible responses ranging from Strongly Disagree −3 to Strongly Agree +3. A Neutral option, 0, serves as a median between the negative and positive poles.

Use and target audience. The TS is designed to measure three dimensions of trust in marriage and intimate relationships. It can be used to assess all aspects of the clinical process, that is, pre-treatment, therapeutic progress, post-treatment, and follow-up evaluations.

Multicultural. This instrument is available in English.

Ease and time of administration. This measure can be completed in two or three minutes.

Reliability. Item-total correlations for each subscale were found to range from .43 to .60 for Faith, .35 to .59 for Dependability, and .33 to .58 for Predictability in a number of studies.

Validity. Validity was assessed through an exploratory factor analysis. Initially, the questionnaire contained 26 items. Ten items were constructed to measure Faith, nine items were devised to measure Dependability, and seven items were designed to measure Predictability. The final three-factor subscales showed significant loadings for seven items on the Faith factor, five items for the Dependability factor, and five items for the Predictability factor. Factor loadings using an oblique rotation ranged from .43 to .84.

Availability and source. The TS is available in the Handbook of Family Measurement Techniques (Perlmutter et al., 2001).

Comments. Even though the TS has been available for almost two decades, it has not been utilized by marital and couples therapists or clinical researchers. Its primary application has been the field of social psychology. It is our hope that as more integrative approaches to marital and family treatment are put forth that reliable and valid assessment measures developed in other disciplines will be adopted for use by clinicians when they are deemed to be relevant and appropriate.

Couples Illness Self-Concealment (CISC) Questionnaire

Type of instrument. The CISC Questionnaire was developed to evaluate self-concealment in couples coping with chronic illness (Wertheim et al., 2016). *Self-concealment* is defined as "a predisposition to actively conceal from others personal thoughts, feelings, actions, and events that one perceives as negative". Self-concealment has been linked to negative psychological and physiological outcomes, such as anxiety and somatic conditions. The CISC is a 13-item, seven-point Likert-style self-report measure.

Use and target audience. The purpose of the CISC Questionnaire is to measure levels of self-concealment in couples when one member is suffering from a chronic illness. The CISC is administered to the client suffering from the chronic illness.

Multicultural. This measure is available in English and Hebrew.

Ease and time of administration. This instrument can be hand scored in five minutes or less. Both a total scale score and mean total scale score can be calculated for interpretive purposes.

Reliability. Wertheim et al. (2016) report internal consistency to be .86.

Validity. Convergent validity was established by comparing the CISC to four related measures. Validity coefficients ranged from .45 to .46.

Availability and source. See Wertheim et al. (2016).

Comment. The validation sample was small, all subjects were cancer patients; N = 56.

Marital Engagement–Type of Union Scale (ME to US)

Type of instrument. The ME to US is a self-report measure developed by Singer and Labunko Messier (2005) to assess perceived mutuality. The ME to US measures the perception of "we-ness" with a 10-item, seven-point Likert-type scale.

Use and target audience. To assess the perception of relational mutuality in married couples.

Multicultural. This measure is available in English.

Scoring procedure. This paper-and-pencil instrument can be hand scored in less than five minutes. Both a total scale score and mean total scale score can be calculated for interpretive purposes.

Reliability. The ME to US demonstrates high internal consistency across genders, with Cronbach's Alpha at .86 for males and .91 for females (Singer et al., 2015). Additional reliability testing reflected similar outcomes for each gender in couples with children, with Cronbach's Alpha at .83 for males and .92 for females, and for childless couples, Cronbach's Alpha were .86 and .76 for males and females, respectively (Singer et al., 2015).

Validity. Convergent validity with a variety of satisfaction measures ranged from .19 to .72 (Singer et al., 2015).

Availability and source. See Singer et al. (2015).

Comment. The ME to US measures perceptions of marital mutuality.

More Recent Instruments

Controlling and Abusive Tactics (CAT-2) Questionnaire

Type of instrument. The CAT-2 Questionnaire was developed by Hamel, Jones, Dutton, and Graham-Kevan (2015) to assess emotional abuse and control by women and men arrested for domestic violence.

Use and target audience. This measure is designed to identify patterns of emotional and physical abuse. A 37-item gender-inclusive combined couples version of the CAT-2 is available, as well as a 35-item gender specific version. All three use a four-point Likert-style scale to measure: Derogation and Control, Jealous Hypervigilance, and Threats/Control of Space.

Multicultural. This measure is available in English.

Scoring procedure. Both total and mean scores are calculated. Scoring can be completed in approximately 10–15 minutes.

Reliability. Cronbach's Alpha for the male version range from .65 to .72 and for the female version .51–.73.

Validity. Concurrent validity with relevant measures ranged from .27 to .93.

Availability and source. This is a paper-and-pencil instrument. See Hamel et al. (2015).

Comment. In validating the CAT-2, both a clinical and a nonclinical sample was used.

Psychological Dating Violence Questionnaire (PDV-Q)

Type of instrument. The PDV-Q (Urena, Romera, Casas, Viejo, & Ortega-Ruiz, 2015) was developed to evaluate subtle and overt psychological abuse among dating couples. The PDV-Q (Urena et al., 2015) is made up of 13 Likert-type scale items.

Use and target audience. This brief measure is appropriate for use with intimate couples.

Multicultural. This measure is available in English and Spanish.

Scoring procedure. Scoring can be completed in 10–15 minutes. Both raw total scale scores and mean total scores can be calculated for the participant's rating of self and partner. The higher the score the higher the experienced violence.

Reliability. Internal consistency was established for the total scale, with a Cronbach's Alpha of .92. Reliability ratings for the two subscales, Victimization and Aggression, were .88 and .85, respectively.

Validity. Convergent validity with relevant measures ranged from .42 to .51.

Availability and source. This is a paper-and-pencil instrument. See Urena et al. (2015).

Comment. The PDV-Q is intended for use with young and dating couples.

The Partner Cyber Abuse Questionnaire (PCAQ)

Type of instrument. Hamby (2013) developed the PCAQ to measure *partner cyber abuse*. *Partner cyber abuse* is defined as "harassing, threatening, monitoring, impersonating, humiliating, or verbally abusing one's partner through the use of technology..."

Use and target audience. The purpose of this nine-item measure is to evaluate the presence, type, and frequency of cyber abuse perpetrated by an individual's intimate partner.

Multicultural. This measure is available in English.

Scoring procedure. Scoring can be completed in less than five minutes and involves tallying all items. The highest possible score is 9. The lowest possible score is 1.

Reliability. Internal consistency as reflected by Cronbach's Alpha is reported to be .71.

Validity. Convergent validity was established by correlating relevant measures. Scores ranged from .13 to .45.

Availability and source. This is a paper-and-pencil instrument. See Wolford-Clevenger et al., 2016).

Comment. The Partner Cyber Abuse Questionnaire takes only a few minutes to administer and score.

The Intersession Report

Type of Instrument. The Intersession Report is a short, nine-item questionnaire that clients complete at the beginning of each therapy session, allowing clinicians and researchers to assess clients' perceptions of improvement from session to session. The first seven Likert-type questions measure clients' subjective feelings about their personal and interpersonal functioning and progress toward therapeutic goals. The last two questions ask clients to rate their relationship with the therapist. Only the therapist's supervisor is privy to these responses.

Use and target audience. The Intersession Report has two general purposes, that is, to provide the clinician with periodic feedback about client progress and to offer supervisors clients' critical appraisal of the therapeutic relationship that supervisees have with individuals, couples and families whom they are treating.

Scoring procedure. No scoring procedures are available at this time.

Reliability. For the three factor analytically derived subscales, Cronbach's alpha estimates ranged from .74 to .86 for Functioning, .77 to .90 for Symptoms, and .86 to .90 for Alliance.

Validity. A three-factor solution was used to establish validity. Factor I-Functioning was found to represent 31% of the variance. Factor II-Symptoms was found to represent 18% of the variance, and Factor III-Alliance made up 16.9% of the variance. These three factors explained 66.3% of the total variance. Both convergent validity and discriminant validity are also reported.

Availability and source. The Intersession Report appears in Johnson, Kettering, and Anderson, (2010).

Comments. The Intersession Report can be a valuable tool for therapists and supervisors. It allows clinicians to monitor clinical progress and offers clinical trainers valuable insights into the therapeutic relationship/alliance. However, the effect of having clients rate the effectiveness of their therapy, on an ongoing basis, cannot be overlooked. Researchers have understood experimenter effects for decades. One should not lose sight of the fact that having clients evaluate their treatment is treatment. Similarly, having clients evaluate their therapists sets up a meta-therapeutic relationship between clients and supervisors. The possibility of client–supervisor–therapist triangulation becomes a reality that cannot be overlooked. Any research done with the Intersession Report in the future must address these issues.

Strategy for Selecting and Utilizing Assessment Instruments

The following process for selecting assessment instruments is offered for consideration.

1. Assess relationship/marital quality

    Overall relationship quality and global satisfaction should be assessed at the outset of treatment. Such evaluation serves as a baseline against which treatment success can be evaluated at the end of intervention and evaluated later during follow-up investigations.

2. Conduct comprehensive assessment

    In this initial stage of assessment, an instrument that can be used to canvas all major domains of marital/couples' functioning, possible conflicts, problem areas, etc. is administered.

3. Categorize areas of conflict and disagreement

   Once all areas of conflict, issues of disagreement, problems etc. have been identified, they are categorized so that they can be dealt with more effectively as a group of interrelated conflicts and issues. For example, conflict with in-laws, friends, former spouses, etc. may be symptomatic of a couple's failure to establish and maintain defined systems boundaries— boundary definition and/or maintenance then becomes the overarching category.

4. Refine instrument selection

   Once problem issues have been categorized, instruments are selected for use that makes it possible for the couple to deal with the problem in a systematic and targeted manner.

Case Example

Robert and Jessica had been married for only nine months when they sought marital counseling. Robert was a 33-year-old divorced father of two. Jessica had just celebrated her 22nd birthday. Her marriage to her high school sweetheart had ended shortly before she met Robert. The presenting problem from Robert's perspective was recurrent arguments and conflicts that never seemed to get resolved satisfactorily. He characterized Jessica as unpredictable and self-centered. Jessica complained that Robert was controlling, bossy, traditional, and old fashioned.

Assessment Overview

All couples accepted for therapy are first seen for an initial interview. During this interview, the couple is asked to identify the presenting problem and to agree on a desired therapeutic outcome. The couple's ability to communicate functionally and resolve conflicts is also assessed. A treatment contract is then negotiated. Each spouse is seen for two separate, individual interviews during which personal histories and relationship histories are gathered. These interviews are also used to make individual diagnoses.

Self-report instruments are determined by the nature of the presenting problem. The following measures were chosen for this couple:

1. SIDCARB
2. TS
3. MDS

(*Continued*)

4.   INS
5.   CAT-2
6.   ME to US

Assessment Findings and Interpretations.
SIDCARB

	Robert	Jessica
Factor I	62	69
Factor II	62	50
Factor III	68	53

The first factor is a measure of each spouse's perception of fairness and reciprocity in ten key areas of marital exchange. Each factor score has a mean of 50 and a standard deviation of 10. The higher the score, on this factor, the more inequitable and dissatisfying the exchange process is perceived to be and the greater the desire for change in one's spouse's behavior. Factor I scores for both Robert and Jessica are two standard deviations above the mean. Such scores are indicative of considerable dissatisfaction and desire for change.

Factor II measures each spouse's commitment to the relationship and the psychological and social barriers that would prevent that spouse from terminating the marriage. Here again, the higher the score, the higher the perceived barrier to separation/divorce.

Factor III assesses the barrier strengths of critical circumstances and conditions that would prevent a spouse from ending a dissatisfying marriage. For both Factors II and III, Robert's perception of prohibiting barriers is much stronger than Jessica's. This perception of low barrier strength gives Jessica more power and leverage in the marriage and often acts as a disincentive to therapy.

Trust and Disaffection

For all three subscale factors assessed by the TS (i.e., Faith, Dependability, and Predictability), both spouses' perceptions of each other's trustworthiness were considerably low. Surprisingly, however, Disaffection scores for both Jessica and Robert were also very low, indicating that each partner was still very positively and affectively involved with the other.

INS

Total Intimacy Need Strength scores for both spouses were in the average range. Only two subcomponent areas of intimacy were perceived as problematic for Robert: Recreational and Temporal (i.e., time spent together). For Jessica, three subcomponent areas were perceived as falling below acceptable levels of satisfaction: Psychological, Aesthetic, and Physical–Non-Sexual intimacy.

CAT-2

Both spouses indicated that there were significant difficulties in the way that they handled conflict by their responses to the CAT-2. All three subscale categories were identified as being problematic: Derogation and Control, Jealous Hypervigilance, and Threats/Control of Space. Numerous items were endorsed as consequential in all category areas by each partner.

ME to US

For the final measure administered—the ME to US—there were considerable differences in perceptions of couple unity and mutuality. The couple disagreed on 8 of the 10 relationship domains tapped by this instrument. The two areas of agreement were the decision to postpone having children and the division of domestic chores and responsibilities.

The Treatment Paradigm

The clinical model used with this couple is an integrative systems approach. Treatment is conducted systemically and systematically and begins with a skill training cognitive behavioral approach to treating the presenting problem or problems. If couples are resistant to using the communication and conflict negotiation skills taught to them at the outset of treatment to resolve their differences, strategic interventions are employed. These interventions are especially useful when couples are locked in escalating symmetrical power struggles or frozen in rigid complementary deadlocks. If these measures are successful in overcoming couples' collusive resistances (Bagarozzi, 2013), a return

(Continued)

to skills-based cognitive behavioral intervention is in order. Sometimes, however, strategic maneuvers prove to be ineffective. When this occurs, psychodynamic/object relations approaches may be used to overcome resistances. Whatever strategy is used to resolve resistance, the therapist always returns to the cognitive behavioral skills-based approach to dealing with the couple's problems once resistances have been successfully dealt with.

Application

Robert and Jessica were able to learn functional communication skills and conflict negotiation practices, and they were able to employ them successfully in the therapist's office but were unable to use them outside the treatment setting. Conflicts escalated and resistance to treatment was evidenced by the couple rescheduling sessions, arriving late for appointments, cancelling sessions, frequently requesting time changes, etc. On several occasions, only one partner would keep a scheduled appointment.

For the ninth session, Robert came in alone. Jessica had moved out of their home and was now living with her mother. This arrangement was not considered to be a permanent one but was indefinite. Robert's interpretation of events was insightful. He said that he probably had been treating Jessica more like his child than as his wife and that she, on several occasions, reminded him that he was not her "father" (her father had divorced her mother when Jessica was three years of age). He also said that Jessica's mother had been married four times and did not put much faith in the institution of marriage. The session ended on that note.

Concluding Comments

Although one can never predict therapeutic outcomes, assessment findings for Robert and Jessica did not portend well for the future of the couple's relationship. Transferential considerations aside, too many factors (e.g., differences in expectations, trust, disagreements about critical issues, perceptions of marriage, and low barriers to relationship termination) and the failure to utilize the relationship-enhancing skills taught to them by the therapist all made therapeutic success problematic. However, as this chapter was being written, the couple called to schedule another appointment (**Table 7.1**).

Table 7.1 Matrix: Self-Rating Scales for Couples

Assessment Instrument	Specific Couple Applications	Cultural/ Language	Instructions/Use: T = Time to Take S = Time to Score I = Items (# of)	Computerized: a = Scoring b = Report	Reliability (R) Validity (V)	Availability
Locke-Wallace Marital Adjustment Test	Assesses relationship adjustment, conflict resolution, cohesion communication	English	T = 3–5 minutes S = 5 I = 15	a = No b = No	R = α = .90 V = .63	Journal Article; Available online
DAS	Assesses relationship adjustment, couple satisfaction	English; French/ Canadian; Chinese	T = 5–15 minutes S = 5 minutes I = 34 (14 items)	a = Yes b = No	R = α = .86–.96 V = .86–.88	Journal Article; Multi-Health Systems, Inc.
SIDCARB	Assesses marital satisfaction & stability in couples	English	T = 5 minutes S = 10 minutes I = 26	a = No b = No	R = α = .74–.76 V = Factor	In: *Enhancing Intimacy in Marriage: A Clinician's Guide* (2001) Appendix A
MDS	Assesses level of disaffection or loss of positive emotions toward spouse	English	T = 3–5 minutes S = 3–5 minutes I = 21	a = No b = No	R = α = .93 V = Discriminant and criterion related	In: *When Love Dies: The Process of Marital Disaffection* (1993)
Areas of Change Questionnaire	Assesses the amount of change desired in relationship	English	T = 5 minutes S = 5 minutes I = 15	a = No b = No	R = α = .90 V = .63	In: *Handbook of Family Measurement Techniques V.3* (2001)

(Continued)

Assessment Instrument	Specific Couple Applications	Cultural/ Language	Instructions/Use: T = Time to Take S = Time to Score I = Items (# of)	Computerized: a = Scoring b = Report	Reliability (R) Validity (V)	Availability
FACES IV	Assesses adaptability & cohesion in marriage & family relationships	Multiple languages	T = 4–5 minutes S = 4–5 minutes I = 42	a = Yes b = Yes	R = α = .74–.90 V = Factor	Life Innovations www.prepare-enrich.com
INS	Assesses couples' perceptions of type & need of intimacy	English	T = 10 minutes S = 15 minutes I = 44	a = No b = No	R = No data V = No data	In: *Enhancing Intimacy in Marriage: A Clinician's Guide* (2001)
Sexual Desire Inventory	Assesses sexual desire (dyadic & solitary) in couples	Multiple languages	T = 5 minutes S = 5 minutes I = 14	a = No b = No	R = α = .76–.96 V = Factor analysis	Available online
TS	Assesses trust in marital relationships	English	T = 2–3 minutes S = 2–3 minutes I = 17	a = No b = No	R = α = .35–.60 V = Factor analysis	In: *Handbook of Family Measurement Techniques V.3* (2001)
Intersession Report	Assessment of client improvement and satisfaction with the therapist	English	T = 1–3 minutes S = N/A I = 9	a = N/A b = N/A	R = α = .74–.90 V = Factor analysis	Journal Article

Name	Description	Language	Administration	Cost	Reliability/Validity	Source
ME to US	Assesses social cognitive aspects of close relationships, namely, mutuality in married couples	English	T = 5 minutes S = 5 minutes I = 10	a = No b = No	R = α = .86 (males); .91 (females) V = .32–.72 (Convergent)	In: Couple Resilience (2015)
CISC	Assesses self-concealment behavior amongst couples Hebrew dealing with chronic illness	English	T = 5 minutes S = 5 minutes I = 13	a = No b = No	R = α = .86 V = .45–.46 (Content, Expert)	Journal Article
CAT-2	Assesses patterns of emotional abuse in both male and female partners in dyads	English	T = 15 minutes S = 10–15 minutes I = 35–37	a = No b = No	R = α = .89 (males) .84 (females) V = .27–.93 (Concurrent; incremental)	Journal Article
PDV-Q	Evaluates "subtle and overt psychological abuse among dating couples"	English; Spanish	T = 10–15 minutes S = 10–15 minutes I = 13	a = No b = No	R = α = .92 V = .42–.51 (external)	Journal Article
PCAQ	Evaluates the nature and prevalence of cyber abuse perpetrated by one's partner	English	T = 5 minutes S = <5 minutes I = 9	a = No b = No	R = α = .71 V = .13–.45 (Convergent)	Journal Article

References

Bagarozzi, D. A. (1983). Methodological developments in measuring social exchange perceptions in marital dyads (SIDCARB): A new tool for clinical intervention. In D. A. Bagarozzi, A. P. Jurich, & R. W. Jackson (Eds.), *New perspectives in marital and family therapy: Issues in theory, research and practice* (pp. 79–104). New York, NY: Human Sciences Press.

Bagarozzi, D. A. (1990). *Intimacy needs questionnaire* (Unpublished instrument). Human Resources Consultants, Atlanta, GA.

Bagarozzi, D. A. (2001). *Enhancing intimacy in marriage: A clinician's guide.* New York, NY: Brunner-Routledge.

Bagarozzi, D. A. (2013). *Couples in collusion: Short term assessment-based strategies for helping couples disarm their defenses.* New York, NY: Routledge.

Bagarozzi, D. A., & Pollane, L. (1983). A replication and validation of the Spousal Inventory of Desired Changes and Relationship Barriers (SIDCARB): Elaborations on diagnostic and clinical utilization. *Journal of Sex and Marital Therapy, 9*, 303–315.

Bagarozzi, D. A., & Sperry, L. (2012). Couples assessment strategy and inventories. In L. Sperry (Ed.), *Family assessment: Contemporary and cutting-edge strategies* (2nd ed., pp. 137–162). New York, NY: Routledge.

Baucom, D. H. (1982). A comparison of behavioral contracting and problem solving/communications training in behavioral marital therapy. *Behavior Therapy, 13*, 162–174.

Birchler, G. R., & Webb, L. J. (1977). Discriminating interaction behaviors in happy and unhappy marriages. *Journal of Consulting and Clinical Psychology, 45*, 494–495.

Busby, D. M., Christensen, C., Crane, D. R., & Larson, J. H. (1995). A revision of the dyadic adjustment scale for use with distressed and non-distressed couples: Construct hierarchy and multidimensional scales. *Journal of Marital and Family Therapy, 21*, 289–308.

Centers for Disease Control. (2018). *Chronic diseases: The leading causes of death and disability in the United States.* Retrieved from April 18, 2018 at: https://www.cdc.gov/chronicdisease/overview/index.htm

Crane, D. R., Middleton, K. C., & Bean, R. A. (2000). Establishing criterion scores for the Kansas marital satisfaction scale and the revised dyadic adjustment scale. *American Journal of Family Therapy, 28*, 53–60.

Cross, D. G., & Sharpley, C. F. (1981). The Locke-Wallace Marital Adjustment Test reconsidered: Some psychometric findings as regards its reliability and factorial validity. *Education and Psychological Measurements, 41*, 1303–1306.

Duck, S. (1982). A topography of relationship disengagement and dissolution. In S. Duck (Ed.), *Personal relationships IV; dissolving personal relationships* (pp. 1–30). London, UK: Academic Press.

Finkel, E. (2017). *The all-or-nothing marriage: How the best marriages work.* New York, NY: Dutton.

Flowers, C., Robinson, B., & Carroll, J. ((2000). Criterion-related validity of the marital disaffection scale as a measure of marital estrangement. *Psychological Reports, 86*, 1101–1104.

Gurman, A. S. (2015). The theory and practice of couple therapy. In A. Gurman, J. Lebow, & D. Snyder (Eds.), *Clinical handbook of couple therapy* (5th ed., pp. 1–18). New York, NY: Guilford.

Hamby, S. (2013, March). *The partner cyber abuse questionnaire: Preliminary psychometrics of technology-based intimate partner violence.* Paper presented at the annual convention of the Southeastern Psychological Association; Atlanta, GA.

Hamel, J., Jones, D. N., Dutton, D. G., & Graham-Kevan, N. (2015). The CAT: A gender-inclusive measure of controlling and abusive tactics. *Violence and Victims, 30*(4), 547.

Hoon, E. F., Hoon, P. W., & Wincze, J. P. (1976). The SAI: An inventory for the measurement of female sexual arousability. *Archives of Sexual Behavior, 5*, 291–300.

Hudson, W. (1992). *The WALMYR assessment scales scoring manual.* Tempe, AZ: WALMYR Publishers.

Hunt, R. A. (1978). The effect of item weighting on the Locke-Wallace Marital Adjustment Scale. *Journal of Marriage and the Family, 41*, 651–661.

Johnson, L. N., Ketring, S. A., & Anderson, S. R. (2010). The intersession report: Development of a short questionnaire for couple therapy. *American Journal of Family Therapy, 38*, 266–276.

Kayser, K. (1993). *When love dies: The process of marital disaffection.* New York, NY: Guilford Press.

Kayser, K. (1996). The marital disaffection scale: An inventory for assessing emotional estrangement in marriage. *American Journal of Family Therapy, 24*, 83–86.

Locke, H. J., & Wallace, K. M. (1959). Short marital-adjustment and prediction tests: Their reliability and validity. *Marriage and Family Living, 21*, 251–255.

Mead, D. E., & Vatcher, G. (1985). An empirical study of the range of marital complaints found in the Areas of Change Questionnaire. *Journal of Marital and Family Therapy, 11*, 421–422.

Norcross, J. C., Pfund, R. A., & Prochaska, J. O. (2013). Psychotherapy in 2022: a Delphi poll on its future. *Professional Psychology: Research and Practice, 44*(5), 363–370.

Olson, D. H. (2011). FACES IV and the circumplex model: Validation study. *Journal of Marital and Family Therapy, 37*, 51–80.

Olson, D. H., Sprenkle, D. H., & Russell, C. (1979). Circumplex model of marital and family systems: I. Cohesion and adaptability dimensions, family types and clinical applications. *Family Process, 18*, 3–28.

Perlmutter, B. F., Touliatos, J., & Holden, G. W. (Eds.). (2001). *Handbook of family measurement techniques: Instruments and index* (vol. 3). Thousand Oaks, CA: Sage.

Pew Research Center. (2018a). *5 facts about online dating.* Retrieved from April 18, 2018 at: http://www.pewresearch.org/fact-tank/2016/02/29/5-facts-about-online-dating/

Pew Research Center. (2018b). *America's shrinking middle class: A close look at changes within metropolitan areas.* Retrieved from April 18, 2018 at: http://www.pewsocialtrends.org/2016/05/11/ americas-shrinking-middle-class-a-close-look-at-changes-within-metropolitan-areas/

Rempel, J. K., Holmes, J. G., & Zanna, M. P. (2001). The Trust Scale. In B. F. Perlmutter, J. Touliatos, & G. W. Holden (Eds.), *Handbook of family measurement techniques: Instruments and index* (vol. 3, p. 111). Thousand Oaks, CA: Sage.

Roberts, S. (1988). *Test-retest reliability of the comprehensive areas of change questionnaire* (Unpublished master's thesis). Brigham Young University, Provo, UT.

Singer, J. A., & Labunko Messier, B. (2005). *Marital engagement-type of union scale.* New London, CT: Department of Psychology, Connecticut College.

Singer, J. A., Labunko, B., Alea, N., & Baddeley, J. L. (2015). Mutuality and the marital engagement–type of union scale [me (to us)]: Empirical support for a clinical instrument in couples therapy. In *Couple resilience* (pp. 123–137). Springer, Dordrecht.

Snyder, D. K., & Regts, J. M. (1982). Factor scales for assessing marital disharmony and disaffection. *Journal of Consulting and Clinical Psychology, 50*, 736–743.

Spanier, G. (1976). Measuring dyadic adjustment: New scales for assessing the quality of marriage and similar dyads. *Journal of Consulting and Clinical Psychology, 50*, 736–743.

Spanier, G. B., & Thompson, L. (1982). A confirmatory analysis of the dyadic adjustment scale. *Journal of Marriage and the Family, 44,* 731–738.

Spector, I. P. (1992). *Development and psychometric evaluation of a measure of sexual desire* (Unpublished doctoral dissertation). Syracuse University, New York, NY.

Spector, I., Carey, M., & Steinberg, L. (1996). The sexual desire inventory: Development, factor structure, and evidence of reliability. *Journal of Sex and Marital Therapy, 22,* 175–190.

United States Department of Agriculture Economic Research Services. (2018). *Rural poverty and well-being.* Retrieved from April 18, 2018 at: https://www.ers.usda.gov/topics/rural-economy-population/rural-poverty-well-being/

Ureña, J., Romera, E. M., Casas, J. A., Viejo, C., & Ortega-Ruiz, R. (2015). Psichometrics properties of psychological dating violence questionnaire: A study with young couples. *International Journal of Clinical and Health Psychology, 15*(1), 52–60.

Vatcher, G. (1988). *An empirical study of the comprehensive areas of change questionnaire* (Unpublished doctoral dissertation). Brigham Young University, Provo, UT.

Weiss, R. L., Hops, H., & Patterson, G. R. (1973). A framework for conceptualizing marital conflict, a technology for altering it, some data for evaluating it. In F. W. Clark & L. A. Hamerlynck (Eds.), *Critical issues in research and practice: Proceedings of the 4th Banff International conference on Behavior Modification* (pp. 309–342). Champaign, IL: Research Press.

Wertheim, R., Hasson-Ohayon, I., Mashiach-Eizenberg, M., Pizem, N., Shacham-Shmueli, E., & Goldzweig, G. (2016). Self-concealment among couples who cope with chronic illness: Development and preliminary validation of the Couples Illness Self-Concealment (CISC) questionnaire. *Supportive Care in Cancer, 24*(12), 4951–4959.

Wolford-Clevenger, C., Zapor, H., Brasfield, H., Febres, J., Elmquist, J., Brem, M., … Stuart, G. L. (2016). An examination of the partner cyber abuse questionnaire in a college student sample. *Psychology of Violence, 6*(1), 156.

8

CHILD AND ADOLESCENT ASSESSMENT STRATEGY AND INVENTORIES

Ali Cunningham Abbott

O ther chapters in this book address specific family dynamics (couples' conflict, divorce, separation, parenting, family violence) that influence couples and families. In contrast, this chapter addresses various child and adolescent conditions that can greatly influence family dynamics. Not surprisingly, these conditions can and do impact family functioning and well-being. This chapter will review the most common childhood and adolescent conditions that impact family functioning and gold-standard assessment inventories and strategies.

Across the fields of medical and behavioral health, increased efforts have been made to appropriately diagnose and treat children with behaviors that disrupt home and school life. The National Institute on Mental Health (NIMH) and the Centers for Disease Control (CDC) survey children across the country and report that for those between the ages of 8 and 18 years old, between 13% and 20% have a diagnosable mental disorder (NIMH & CDC, 2013) Based on these rates, it is clear that children with mental health conditions, and sometimes severe disorders, require effective treatment in order to be more successful in their environments. Included in these disorders are the most prevalent diagnoses that will be discussed in this chapter: attention deficit and hyperactivity disorder (ADHD), depression and mood disorders, autism spectrum disorder (ASD), obsessive-compulsive disorder (OCD) and learning disorders.

Differentiating among these diagnoses can prove difficult as many symptoms overlap and evolve over time creating confusion about how to best assess and treat these children. The educational system has done a lot of work to include these children at school, both academically and socially with legislation through the Individuals with Disabilities Education Act. Mental health professionals are an integral part in facilitating this inclusion through effective assessments and proper treatment planning. This will be a comprehensive description of assessments that are being used as best practice, open-access tools when providing services to children with the aforementioned diagnoses.

Our focus is to present clinicians with the most accessible and evidence-based assessment tools available for the most common conditions addressed. All of the instruments presented are authorized for use by a level C clinician to assist with assessment, diagnosis and treatment planning. Before presenting the recommended the assessment tools, a general understanding of the definitions of these diagnoses will be reviewed.

Conditions

ADHD

ADHD is the most prevalent diagnoses for children between the ages of 2 and 17, with an estimated 9.4% ever having been diagnosed in the United States (CDC, 2016). Children who present with this diagnosis exhibit characteristics of inattentive to details, easily distractible, fidgety and impulsive. When a child is considered "disruptive" in school or at home, an assessment for ADHD is common in order to distinguish whether symptoms are clinically significant enough to warrant a diagnosis.

ADHD by nature and clinical description is a diagnosis that provides caregivers and professionals with many externalized behaviors that are easily identifiable through observation. Children and adolescents exhibiting such observable behaviors must be doing so for a period of six months or longer at a level that is inappropriate to their developmental level. Diagnosticians are asked to focus on three categories of behaviors, (IA), hyperactivity-impulsivity (HI), marked by examples of behaviors such as forgetfulness, excessive talking and trouble waiting for one's turn.

Criteria within the diagnosis of ADHD provide clear examples, and therefore assessment tools have been created that parents, teachers and caregivers can easily relate to and clearly identify with children. Although this diagnosis seems clearly delineated through external behavioral examples, there is a good deal of clinical judgment used in determining levels of disturbance and inappropriateness for developmental level (APA, 2000). Clinicians need to utilize assessments tools to help them make the distinction between typical child's IA, activity level and impulsivity before diagnosing and treating especially because many children who receive the diagnosis of ADHD utilize both psychotherapy and medication interventions (APA, 2000). It is appropriate, if not strongly recommended, for clinicians to provide information and referrals to professionals such as psychiatrists or neurologists who can consult on the issues of medication management for children and adolescents with ADHD.

Depression and Mood Disorders

In the United States, approximately 2.1% of children and adolescents experience symptoms of depression (CDC, 2016). Unlike the externalized behaviors observable in ADHD, children with mood disorders such as major depressive disorder often demonstrate internalized symptoms that are more difficult to identify. Some of the red flags to be aware of when assessing for depression with a child are refusal to participate in daily activities like school or play, clinging to a caregiver, getting into trouble and a negative or irritable attitude. It is important not to overlook some of these symptoms as research shows us that childhood depression can be a predictor of more severe illnesses in the future (Weissman et al., 1999).

Interestingly, many children who suffer from depression go untreated because their behaviors are better attributed to the move through different developmental stages. Before the age of 15, or puberty, the prevalence of depression in males and females is matched, but after this critical developmental stage, girls are twice as likely to be diagnosed with a major depressive episode. In working to help treat children and adolescents with depression, a combination of psychotherapy and medication has proven to have the most effective outcomes (March et al., 2004). Educating families about this is important, and appropriate referrals and consultation with a physician is important.

Changes to *Diagnostic and Statistical Manual of Mental Disorders Fifth Edition* (DSM-5) resulted in a newly identified mood disorder in children entitled disruptive mood dysregulation disorder (DMDD) (APA, 2013). Prior to this diagnostic change, children who demonstrated criteria for this disorder may have been diagnosed with early onset bipolar disorder. In fact, in the previous version of this manual, the DSM-IV-TR, the only mention of childhood mood disorder beyond depression indicated that between 10 and 15% of adolescents with major depressive episodes will develop bipolar disorder (APA, 2000). Children who were diagnosed with DMDD earlier appear to be have more severe symptoms than when the criteria present later in life during older adolescence or adulthood. This is typically marked with more frequent mood swings, somatic symptoms and manifestations of both manic and depressive (mixed) episodes (Birmaher et al., 2006).

One of the most dangerous aspects of DMDD in children and teens is the increased risk of suicide ideation and attempts among these youth (Klein, Dougherty, & Olino, 2005). Therefore, it is important to utilize best practices in assessment and treatment when working with this population in childhood, adolescence and adulthood because treatment for this condition can be chronic requiring lifelong management of symptoms and mood stabilization. Currently, there is a significant amount of research being done to provide more information on the effectiveness of treatment through medication management and talk therapy (Roy, Lopes, & Klein, 2014).

ASD

Among all of the developmental disabilities, ASD is the most common world-wide affecting 1–2% of the population. ASD is being diagnosed at a rate of 1 in 59 children (CDC, 2018). The category of developmental disabilities is where ASD typically falls in describing common childhood conditions. In previous diagnostic guides, autism was considered a pervasive developmental disorder that included myriad other labels including Asperger syndrome, pervasive developmental disorder not otherwise specified (PDD-NOS), Rett syndrome and childhood disintegrative disorder (CDD). It is important to be aware of such pre-existing diagnostic categorizations since many in the community still refer to this language.

Like other disorders, autism is presented with mild, moderate and severe symptoms. Those who are diagnosed as severe typically demonstrate present with a speech delay or limited verbal abilities beginning in early childhood, repetitive behaviors that can sometimes be harmful or a detriment to the self or others, inability to achieve independence or master daily living activities and, in some cases, co-occur with cognitive impairments. Children with moderate to severe presentations of ASD are usually identified during early childhood, between 18 and 36 months old, when caregivers notice a child has not developed speech or has lost communication skills, lacks eye contact and moves their fingers or hands close to their eyes with little to no purpose (Filipek et al., 1999). Because their impairments are more significantly marked, these individuals will likely benefit from early intervention therapies in order to build their skills. Mild forms of autism can present differently. In most cases, these children do not demonstrate deficits or delays in communication or behaviors but instead have stereotypic or odd ways of developing in these areas. Children diagnosed with a milder presentation of ASD typically receive a diagnosis several years later than their moderate to severe counterparts, mostly due to the fact that the red flags involved in one are not present in another (Fitzgerald & Corvin, 2001).

Individuals with ASD demonstrate clinically significant impairment in the areas of social communication and repetitive behaviors or restricted interests. Within these two categories of deficit, there are different challenges. For example, in the area of social communication one individual diagnosed with ASD might have issues with communicating verbally at all and engages in self-injurious behaviors hundreds of times a day while another has an advanced vocabulary with a focus on teaching his classmates about every detail of the local transportation system. These two presentations are vastly different in their subjective experiences yet share the common thread of categorical deficits in those two areas. The message is clear that children with ASD can present quite distinctly from one another, and therefore effective assessment strategies and inventories need to be applied for the best, most accurate results and treatment plans.

Children and adolescents who are diagnosed with ASD benefit from treatment that includes medical, behavioral and social interventions. Depending on the severity of symptoms and the existence of co-occurring diagnoses, which happens in approximately 70% of cases, treatment will have to be tailored individually (Merikangas et al., 2010). Ideally a mental health practitioner will have access to neurodevelopmental reporting and releases to consult with psychiatrists or other physicians involved in the treatment of the child. Working to integrate the parents into therapy is a crucial piece to achieving long-lasting progress for children and adolescents with ASD. After understanding the medical needs and family dynamics, best practices in counseling autistic youth include applied behavior analysis (ABA) and cognitive behavioral therapies (CBT) (Ozonoff & Solomon, 2005). Social skills treatment is also an evidence-based practice that is best applied in group format and with the inclusion of caregivers (Frankel et al., 2010). With early intervention and comprehensive treatments highlighted above, children and adolescents with ASD can reach their potential.

OCD and Anxiety Disorders

OCD occurs in about one of every 200 children and adolescents and between 1 and 3% across pediatric and adult populations (Kessler et al., 2005). Symptomology of OCD with children and adolescents can present in many ways but is marked by recurrent intense behaviors and compulsions that interfere with daily life. Examples of common obsessions and compulsions include unrealistic and irrational beliefs that are persistent, ritualistic behaviors like hoarding or hand washing and internal behaviors such as counting or checking.

The onset of OCD can start at the earliest in preschool, but generally appears at first between the ages of 10 and 12 years old (March & Benton, 2007). Additionally, a significant percentage of children and adolescents diagnosed with OCD have a first-degree relative also diagnosed with OCD, indicating that childhood OCD has a strong genetic component (APA, 2013). Children and teens with OCD usually present with observable behaviors, which helps caregivers and professionals during initial assessment and screening. These behaviors include disrupted routines such as missing school due to needing to perform compulsive rituals, physical complaints, problems with social relationships and self-esteem and some anger management issues.

Children and teens commonly exhibit symptoms of anxiety disorders, a category of conditions under which OCD had been previously categorized and are considered closely related. The most common anxiety disorders among youth are generalized anxiety, panic, separation, social disorders, selective mutism and specific phobias (Our World Data, 2018).

Most research bears out that cognitive-behavioral therapy is the most effective treatment when working with children and teens diagnosed with

OCD and anxiety disorders. In cases where moderate to severe symptoms are present, medication should be considered as a supported recommendation of the American Academy of Child and Adolescent Psychiatry for physicians with expertise treating these conditions (POTS, 2004). Therefore a combination of effective psychotherapy from a cognitive-behavioral approach and expert medical intervention often yields positive results and symptom relief.

Specific Learning Disorders

Learning disorders are common in children. In schools, children with specific learning disabilities constitute the largest single category of special needs children. Children with learning disabilities make up over half of all children with an exceptional student education eligibility. Under federal special education terminology, the category is referred to as Specific Learning Disability (SLD). The DSM-5 identifies three such categories of learning disorder impairments in reading, mathematics and written expression. Each of these categories includes subcategories detailing the specific impairment one might exhibit, for example accuracy or fluency. While organizations use different terms for these disorders (i.e., dyslexia for a reading disability and dyscalculia for a math disability), the trend has been to use either the more descriptive DSM terms for a subject-specific disorder or to refer to significant academic challenges without co-occurring weaknesses in intellectual quotient (IQ).

Mental health professionals will recognize that an accompanying shift has taken place in how a child is formally assessed. In the past, when considering specific learning disabilities the discrepancy model was commonly used. Here, a child was given an assessment of intellectual functioning and assessed across a number of academic skill areas. The presumption was that a child with normal intelligence would achieve at normal levels in academic skills. However, a significant discrepancy between intelligence and achievement could then be seen as the basis for SLD eligibility. This model rested on the assumption that the causes of academic failure rested within the child and merely needed to be confirmed. The new experimental model relying on response to intervention (RTI) and similar active and sensitive remedial strategies looks for the cause as a mismatch in the learner's needs and the way the child is taught.

The clinicians' task is rather straightforward under this model. Assessment for learning disorders usually involves a series of steps. The first step is to obtain a valid IQ score and second to administer a standardized assessment of academic achievement. Then it is necessary to calculate the discrepancy between achievement and IQ. School and licensed psychologists are trained and authorized to conduct this testing; other mental health professionals are not able to administer or interpret these psychological evaluations.

Therefore, the information pertaining to IQ assessment measures and tools will not be included in this chapter.

As a next step, academic skills are considered separately or even further segmented (i.e., reading divided into reading recognition and reading comprehension). A mental health professional may be asked to conduct an evaluation to provide a clinical perspective for a family which has obtained a school district-provided evaluation, or the child may attend a school that does not routinely provide special education services. But, increasingly, the mental health professional will wish to understand the nature of the child's overall learning challenges and the instructional and environmental accommodations and modifications that may be used to address these challenges. Additional assessment tools and information collected from interview and observation can be used to capture the needs of the child and further parse out what the specific learning disorder may be.

After the specific learning disorder is identified, the counselor may wish to help the family and the child explore how the child learns best. Assessment at a young age and early intervention (EI) are the best practices in identifying learning disorders. This can be done during early childhood education opportunities. Once a specific learning disorder is identified, a broad array of accommodations are available for implementation at school and in the home. Typically, accommodations refer to ways to allow the student to work in ways that help them succeed in the area where they have a disorder but perhaps with modified timing or method of completing a task. The goal is to achieve the same degree of proficiency on a subject like their non-SLD peers. The family can be helped to monitor the levels of support and accommodation their child is receiving and to carefully review the child's progress.

Instruments

The instruments in this chapter have been selected for the purposes of offering counselors and other mental health professionals options that are both open access, free resources and evidence-based, best practice recommendations that are available at cost. Assessment tools that have restrictions on their use for licensed and school psychologists will not be reviewed simply because they are outside of the scope of use for Level-C clinicians.

ADHD

ADHD Rating Scale-5

Instrument name. The ADHD Rating Scale-5 was published in 2016 and is utilized for diagnosing and assessing treatment for children and adolescents. There are two questionnaires within the scale, a home version and school version.

Type of instrument. This rating scale is an 18-item questionnaire with questions linked directly to DSM-5 diagnostic criteria for ADHD. Questions ask the respondent to choose the best description of the child over the past six months in areas that specifically address hyperactivity-impulsivity HI and IA.

Use-target audience. The questionnaire is for parents/family members and teachers of children between the ages of 5 and 17 years old to assess behaviors in both the home and school environments. Once the screening tool is completed, it needs to be scored and interpreted by a c-level healthcare provider.

Multicultural. The home version of screening tool is available in both English and Spanish and uses language that can be easily understood by individuals of diverse backgrounds. The school version is available in English only. In its 5th edition, the instrument is also sensitive to gender with separate boy and girl versions.

Ease and time of administration. Participants answering the questionnaire typically complete it within 10–15 min (5 five minutes per scale). Once complete, the participants, ideally both caregivers at home and at school, submit them to be scored.

Scoring procedure. The respondent is requested to answer each question based on a four-point Likert scale. The responses correspond with the frequency of behaviors, "Never or Rarely" is zero, "Sometimes" is one, "Often" is two and "Very Often" is three. Raw scores are tallied and corresponding percentile scores assigned in the two categories of HI and IA and then are totaled for final measurement. The scoring sheet reflects results for boys and girls between 5 and 17 years old. The scoring tables provide guidelines for placing the child into percentiles within a two-year age range.

Reliability. Reliability for the questionnaire has been measured for internal consistency and test-retest reliability. Internal consistency for the screening tool yields a Cronbach's alpha between 0.89 and 0.96. The test-retest reliability scores range on the home and school versions from country to country with a range from 0.60 to 0.93 (DuPaul, Power, Anastapoulos, & Reid, 2016).

Validity. Strong support in the research to verify confirmatory factor analyses, concurrent validity and predictive validity for the assessment.

Availability and source. The manual can be purchased through Guilford Press at www.guilford.com. Purchasers of the packet (clinical manual and instrument) are deemed permission to copy the instrument which allows for a low-cost option. The questionnaire alone is available for free online through multiple sources.

Comment. The scale is designed to be completed independently by the child's parent/family member and teacher. If more than three of the questions are not rated by the respondent, the questionnaire should not be scored or interpreted.

Vanderbilt ADHD Diagnostic Rating Scales

Instrument name. The Vanderbilt ADHD Diagnostic Teacher Rating Scale (VADTRS) was developed in 1998, and soon thereafter the Vanderbilt ADHD Parent Rating Scale (VADPRS) became available in 2003.

Type of instrument. The VADTRS is a 43-item questionnaire, and the VADPRS is a 55-item questionnaire. The questionnaires ask respondents to rate the child according to age appropriateness. In both versions, there are two sections, the first specific questions about observable behaviors and the second about performance academically and behaviorally in the classroom.

Use-target audience. The tool is designed for an audience who has a reading level slightly below third grade for parents and teachers of children between 6 and 12 years old. Parents or family members should complete the VADPRS while teachers or school personnel should complete the VADTRS.

Multicultural. This rating scale performs well in large, ethnically diverse populations and is available in English, Spanish and German (Dulcan, 2009).

Ease and time of administration. The questionnaire takes approximately 20 min to complete and score. Its availability as a free resource and its ease of administering make it a useful tool for assessing the age group. Respondents are asked to respond to questions by rating their responses on four-point (first section) and five-point (second section) Likert scales.

Scoring procedure. The first section is scored with frequency measurements, in which zero through four are assigned values from "Never" to "Very Often." The second section is scored from one to five, where one through two is "Problematic", three is "Average" and four through five is "Above Average." Several different outcomes will be measured by scoring the scales, including identification of subtypes (inattentive, hyperactive/impulsive, combined) and screenings for comorbidities including Oppositional-Defiant/Conduct Disorder and Anxiety/Depression.

Reliability. Internal consistency is reported at 0.93 in both parent and teacher versions. Inter-rater reliability has also been reported as adequate.

Validity. Concurrent validity is high at 0.79 for both versions (Wolriach et al., 2003).

Availability and source. Free resource, available at http://www.nichq.org/adhd_tools.html.

Comment. There is a resource toolkit available in order to assist in explaining diagnosis to families and teachers, follow-up tools to assess treatment and resources.

Swanson, Nolan and Pelham Rating Scale-Revised (SNAP-IV)

Instrument name. The Swanson, Nolan and Pelham Rating Scale Revised (SNAP-IV) was revised in 1992 and 2003 from its original version in 1982 in order to be consistent with current DSM-5 diagnostic criteria for ADHD.

Type of instrument. The SNAP-IV is an 18-item or 90-item questionnaire that asks respondents, teachers and parents specifically, to check one of four columns that best describe the child.

Use-target audience. The scale is designed to assess children between ages of 6 and 18 from parent and teacher responses to the questionnaire.

Multicultural. The questionnaire requires that respondents have at least a high school reading level. The tool is available in English.

Ease and time of administration. The questionnaire takes ten minutes to complete and should be scored after receipt of both teacher and parent responses.

Scoring procedure. Respondents are asked to score questions on a four-point Likert scale from "Not At All" to "Very Often" (0–4). The scores are obtained by adding up the scores for each question and dividing the sum by the number of items in that subset. The subsets measure IA, HI and Combined types of ADHD. Scores in the top 5% are considered significant. The website indicates that software for electronic administration and scoring is coming soon.

Reliability. Both test-retest and internal consistency reliability measurements are adequate with a range between 0.76 and 0.97, while interrater reliability is weaker between 0.43 and 0.49 (Collett, Ohan, & Myers, 2003).

Validity. Predictive validity measurements have been made for the rating scale which indicate adequacy for parent respondents but poorer for teachers.

Availability and source. Free resource, available at www.adhd.net.

Comment: Questions asked and language used in this rating scale might be a barrier for less educated and culturally diverse populations. The tool also screens for comorbid diagnoses including oppositional defiant disorder, depression and conduct disorder.

Depression and Mood Disorders

Center for Epidemiological Studies-Depression Scale Modified for Children (CES-DC)

Instrument name. The CES-DC was developed in 1980 from the original adult scale by the same name. The inventory is designed to indicate levels of depressive symptoms in children and adolescents between the ages of 6 and 17 years old.

Type of instrument. The CES-DC is a 20-item self-report inventory of how an individual has felt or acted during the past week.

Use-target audience. As a self-report inventory, this tool is designed to be answered directly by children and adolescents between the ages of 6 and 17 years old.

Multicultural. The CES-DC is available in English, Spanish and Japanese.

Ease and time of administration. The self-report inventory takes five minutes to complete and asks respondents to rate how often they have felt during the past week from "Not At All," "A Little," "Some" or "A Lot," The tool uses child friendly language at a sixth-grade reading level.

Scoring procedure. It takes an estimated ten minutes to score the CES-DC with possible scores ranging from 0–60. Most questions are scored between 0 and 3, from "Not At All" to "A Lot," with the exception of some positively phrased questions, which are scored oppositely. A score over 15 is indicative of significant levels of depression (Weissman et al., 1999).

Reliability. The internal consistency coefficient alpha for the CES-DC is measured at 0.84 and the reported test-retest reliability is weaker at 0.51.

Validity. The reported concurrent validity for the CES-DC is moderate at 0.44 when measured against the Children's Depression Inventory (Weissman et al., 1999).

Availability and source. Free resource, available at www.brightfutures.org/mentalhealth/pdf/tools.html.

Comment. The CES-DC is designed to be a preliminary screening tool and should be followed up by more thorough assessment before diagnosis. The tool includes a comment indicating that more evaluating is required for individuals who screen positively on the CES-DC.

Kiddie Schedule for Affective Disorders and Schizophrenia in School-Age Children (K-SADS-PL)

Instrument name. The K-SADS-PL was developed in 1996 and updated in 2016 to assess the severity of symptoms of psychiatric disorders including major depression, dysthymia, mania, hypomania, cyclothymia, dysregulation disorder and many more.

Type of instrument. The K-SADS-PL is a semi-structured interview that encourages the administrator to utilize language appropriate to the educational level of the parent, child, teacher and others.

Use-target audience. The interview should be administered to the parents, child or adolescent and others, such as teachers, relevant to a child between 6 and 18 years old who are suspected of having psychiatric disorders in the categories of affective disorders, psychotic disorders, anxiety disorders, behavioral disorders and substance abuse and eating and tic disorders.

Multicultural. The screening tool is in 19 different languages, and each is available through different sources internationally (Edelbrock & Bohnert, 2000; Hersen, Hilsenroth, & Segal, 2004).

Ease and time of administration. Administration of the K-SADS-PL takes between 90 and 120 min and consists of six sections: (1) Introductory Interview, (2) Diagnostic Screening Interview, (3) Supplemental Completion

Checklist, (4) Diagnostic Supplements, (5) Summary Lifetime Diagnostic Checklist and (6) Children's Global Assessment Scale (C-GAS). The respondents are interviewed individually using sections 1–4. Sections 5 and 6 are a synthesis of all the data to be completed by the clinician after conducting the interviews. Each section has a detailed explanation of purpose, ranging from rapport building to symptom rating scales. When assessing pre-adolescents, it is recommended to conduct the parent interview first. When assessing adolescents, interview them first.

Scoring procedure. Each section is scored differently, and the manual provides a detailed description of scoring instructions. When discrepancies exist among respondents, the clinician is urged to use their best judgment in making a final selection. Discrepancies often exist in less observable behaviors such as experiencing feelings of guilt, hopelessness, interrupted sleep, hallucinations and suicidal ideation.

Reliability. Interrater and test-retest reliabilities have been measured for the K-SADS-PL and demonstrate a range for different diagnoses. For example, attention deficit yields a 0.55 reliability score while major depression yields a 1.00 reliability score, which is why this tool is used primarily to diagnose depression (Sorenson, Thomsen, & Bilenberg, 2007).

Validity. The K-SADS is reported to have adequate construct validity but weak predictive validity when compared with other diagnostic tools (Sorenson et al., 2007).

Availability and source. Free resource, available at https://www.kennedy krieger.org/sites/default/files/community_files/ksads-dsm-5-screener.pdf.

Comment. Questions do not have to be recited verbatim. The interviewer is encouraged to adapt language to the developmental level of the child.

General Behavior Inventory (GBI)

Instrument name. The GBI was created in 1981 in order to help identify individuals who are at risk for bipolar disorder.

Type of instrument. The GBI is a 73-item, self-report instrument to describe mood and behavior of a child or adolescent on a four-point scale.

Use-target audience. The assessment tool is completed by children or adolescents as young as 11 years old. An adapted screening tool exists—the Parent Version, General Behavior Inventory (P-GBI)—which asks parents to rate children and adolescents between the ages of 5 and 17 years old.

Multicultural. The GBI and P-GBI are available in English.

Ease and time of administration. Children and adolescents respond to the 73 questions based on a four-point scale on how frequently the experience behaviors, from "Never or Hardly Ever" to "Very Often or Almost Constantly." There is no information reported on how long it takes respondents to complete this self-report instrument.

Scoring procedure. The scoring consists of tabulating the dimensions of dysthymia, hypomania and biphasic. Individuals are identified as Dysthymic if the score sum is above the 95th percentile and Hypomanic if the score sum is above the 85th percentile.

Reliability. This rating scale has good reliability with an alpha coefficient 0.90 for its hypomanic and depression scales (Danielson, Youngstrom, Findling, & Calabrese, 2003; Youngstrom et al., 2004).

Validity. The GBI is reported to have strong criterion and excellent discriminative validity (Danielson et al., 2003; Youngstrom et al., 2004).

Availability and source. The GBI is a free resource, available at www.bipolar child.com/survey/gbi.html/. The P-GBI can be obtained by contacting the author, Eric Youngstrom, but has been more commonly used in research and not in clinical use.

Mood and Feelings Questionnaire Child & Parent Versions (MFQ-C & MFQ-P)

Instrument name. The MFQ-C & MFQ-P were created in 1987 in order to quickly and effectively evaluate core symptoms of depression.

Type of instrument. The MFQ is a self-report inventory designed for children, adolescents and their parents with a 33-item version and short 13-item version.

Use-target audience. The child version of the MFQ is designed for children and adolescents ages 8–18 years old. The parent version of the MFQ asks the same questions to the parent about their child's or adolescent's behavior.

Multicultural. The inventory is currently available in English.

Ease and time of administration. The MFQ is administered between 5 and 10 min between the long and short versions. The short version was designed to be the most efficient depression rating scale. The tool asks respondents to answer questions based on how the child has felt over the last two weeks, among "Not True," "Sometimes" or "True."

Scoring procedure. A clinician can score this assessment in approximately ten minutes.

Reliability. Both the child and parent versions of the inventory yield high alpha rates of internal consistency, 0.95 for the MFQ-C and 0.96 for the MFQ-P (Wood, Kroll, Moore, & Harrington, 1995).

Validity. The MFQ was measured against other depression inventories and yielded moderate to high criterion validity (Daviss et al., 2006).

Availability and source. Free resource available at devepi.duhs.duke.edu/ mfq.html.

Comment. For clinical efficiency and initial screening, the short version of the MFQ is recommended in practice.

Young Mania Rating Scale (YMRS)

Instrument name. The YMRS was developed in 1978 from a revision of the original tool used for adults with bipolar disorder. Consequently the Parent Version of the YMRS (P-YMRS) was created as a supplement to the YMRS.

Type of instrument. The YMRS and P-YMRS are 11-item clinician-administered interviews designed for children and adolescents and their parents or caregivers to assess the severity of manic symptoms.

Use-target audience. The rating scale is for children and adolescents between the ages of 5 and 17 years old.

Multicultural. The YMRS has been translated into Spanish and Turkish, although these versions are not as readily available as the English version (Gracious et al., 2002).

Ease and time of administration. The YMRS and P-YMRS can be administered within 10–20 min and ask respondents to report symptoms over the previous 48 hours. In addition to client response, the clinician is encouraged to make clinical judgments based on observation during the interview.

Scoring procedure. The score of the interview is determined by adding up the highest number circled on each question. Scores range between 0 and 60, and a score of 20 or above is indicative of manic or hypomanic symptoms. Individuals with Bipolar diagnoses scored at 25 qualifying for mania (Bipolar I) and 20 for hypomania (Bipolar II, Bipolar NOS and Cyclothymia) (Gracious et al., 2002).

Reliability. The English version of the YMRS shows a good internal consistency reliability of 0.91. The reports on both the Spanish and Turkish versions also indicate reliability and validity measures for the YMRS (Frazier et al., 2007; Serrano, Ezpeleta, Alda, Matali, & San, 2011).

Validity. The YMRS has an excellent diagnostic efficiency rating of 0.97 (Frazier et al., 2007).

Availability and source. Free resources, the YMRS is available at louisville.edu/depression/clinicials-corner/Young%20Mania%20Rating%20Scale-Measure.pdf and the P-YMRS is available at www.healthyplace.com/images/stories/bipolar/p-ymrs.pdf.

Comment. On their own, the YMRS and P-YMRS are not intended to diagnose bipolar disorder in children.

ASD

Autism Diagnostic Observation Scale (ADOS-2)

Instrument name. The Autism Diagnostic Observation Scale, 2nd edition (ADOS-2 is the gold standard in diagnosis of ASDs.

Type of instrument. The ADOS is a semi-structured standardized behavioral observation and coding instrument that is conducted through various social and communication interactions with the subject.

Use-target audience. The instrument can be conducted with any individual from toddlerhood to adulthood. Instrument modules are designed to fit the subject's communicative abilities and are not distributed by specific ages.

Multicultural. The ADOS is available in English and Spanish.

Ease and time of administration. The behavioral observation takes approximately 30–45 min to complete and involves different activities based on the Module appropriate for the subject. The appropriate Module is chosen by the clinician based on the subject's linguistic skills and chronological age. Modules 1 and 2 involve moving around the observation room with play while Modules 3 and 4 are conversation based and can be administered at a table. As the clinician administers different activities from the module, observations are recorded and later coded to identify a diagnosis.

Scoring Procedure. After administration of the ADOS, the clinician codes behavioral observations based on cut-offs and adds the scores to provide accurate diagnoses within the spectrum of autism (Wing, Gould, & Gillberg, 2011).

Reliability. This is not available.

Validity. This is not available.

Availability and source. The ADOS is available for purchase through Western Psychological Services, www.wpspublish.com.

Comments. The ADOS is a diagnostic tool that can be utilized by practitioners who attend a two-day clinical training workshop or purchase and watch the training DVD.

Autism Spectrum Quotient, Child & Adolescent Versions (AQ)

Instrument name. The AQ was developed by Baron-Cohen et al. (2006) (adolescent version); Auyeung, Baron-Cohen, Wheelwright, and Allison (2008) (child version).

Type of instrument. The AQ is a 50-item questionnaire that asks parents and/or professionals to measure the degree to which an individual child or adolescent possesses symptoms typical from the autistic spectrum (Auyeung, Baron-Cohen, Wheelwright, and Allison (2008)).

Use-target audience. The questionnaire was designed for parents, medical professionals and researchers treating children between the ages of 4 and 11 years old as well as adolescents 12–16 years old.

Multicultural. The AQ is available in English.

Ease and time of administration. The checklist takes approximately 10–15 min to complete and can be easily done electronically on the website below.

Scoring Procedure. Scoring of the AQ is done quickly through the electronic scoring system in place online.

Reliability. The AQ has a high internal consistency reliability rating of 0.94.

Validity. Current studies are being conducted and prepared for publication on the validity of the AQ.

Availability and source. The AQ is available at the free source of: https://www.autismresearchcentre.com/arc_tests.

Comments. Cut-off score of a 76 indicates a positive screen for Autism.

Modified Checklist for Autism in Toddlers, Revised with Follow-up (M-CHAT-R/F)

Instrument name. The M-CHAT-R/F was originally developed in 1999 for clinical, research and educational purposes. The revision with follow-up was published in 2009 (Robins & Dumont-Mathieu, 2006).

Type of instrument. The M-CHAT is a 23-item clinician-administered or self-report questionnaire in which parents are asked to respond "yes" or "no" questions about "how your child usually is."

Use-target audience. This screening tool is validated for use with toddlers between the ages of 16–30 months.

Multicultural. The M-CHAT is available in approximately 27 languages, with more translations being currently developed. In some languages, for example Spanish and Portuguese, there are distinct versions for Europe and South America demonstrating a high level of cultural sensitivity.

Ease and time of administration. The M-CHAT can be administered between 5 and 10 min, depending on method of administration and parent's need for clarification.

Scoring procedure. The screening tool can be scored in less than two minutes, either by hand or using the available electronic scoring system. A child who fails three or more of the questions in total or two of the critical items (indicated in the scoring instructions) should be referred for a comprehensive medical and psychological evaluation.

Reliability. The M-CHAT-R/F demonstrates adequate internal reliability and is found to be adequate, with a Cronbach's alpha ranging between 0.63 and 0.79 (Robins & Dumont-Mathieu, 2006).

Validity. Current cross-validation studies are being conducted in increase rates of sensitivity and specificity as well as decrease number of false positives generated by the M-CHAT.

Availability and source. The M-CHAT is a free resource, available at www.m-chat.org.

Comments. In 2008, the authors created the M-CHAT Follow-up Interview in order to reduce the rate of false positives and therefore unnecessary referrals for further evaluation.

Social Responsiveness Scale-2, School Aged (SRS-2)

Instrument name. The SRS-2, created by John N. Constantino, MD in 2012. The second edition of this test has the screener and power of a diagnostic tool.

Type of instrument. The SRS-2 is a 65-item yes/no questionnaire that is to be completed by a parent or caregiver of the identified subject who has at least one-month knowledge of the individual.

Use-target audience. The questionnaire can be administered to anyone over the age of 2.5 years old, with a cognitive age of at least two years old.

Multicultural. The SRS-2 is available in English and Spanish.

Ease and time of administration. The questionnaires are administrated by a parent or teacher. There are different forms for age ranges, 2.5–4.5 years old, 4–18 years old and 19+. The administration is completed in 15–20 min.

Scoring procedure. The SRS-2 can be hand scored or software scored.

Reliability. The SRS-2 reports having reliability measures of 0.94–0.96 for Cronbach's alpha and 0.88–0.95 for test-retest.

Validity. Current studies are being conducted and prepared for publication on the validity of the AQ.

Availability and source. The SRS-2 is available for purchase through Western Psychological Services, www.wpspublish.com.

Comments. Results are reported as a quantitative score for autistic social impairment. SRS-2 makes a unique contribution toward a comprehensive assessment of ASD, because it focuses specifically on aspects of social reciprocity and social communication (Bruni, 2014). This instrument can be used as one component in a more comprehensive examination of the individual.

OCD & Anxiety Disorder

Spence Children's Anxiety Scale (SCAS)

Instrument name. The SCAS was developed in 1997 by four clinicians specializing in anxiety disorders.

Type of instrument. The scale consists of 44 items, reflecting 38 of the symptoms of anxiety with six fillers to reduce negative response bias. Children are asked to rate how often these things happen to you on a four-point scale.

Use-target audience. This instrument is designed for children between the ages of 7 and 14. It can be used to identify diagnostic symptoms as well as a good evaluation tool for treatment effectiveness.

Multicultural. The SCAS is available in English, Spanish and 12 other languages.

Ease and time of administration. This scale can be administered in 5–10 min and scored in the same amount of time.

Scoring procedure. The instrument results and scoring can be calculated in two ways, one that yields a total score and an alternate calculation involving its subscales. Questions on the scale are divided into six subscales identified in the categories of different anxiety disorders, one of the subscales being obsessive compulsive. Instructions for scoring using electronic forms distinguished by age range and gender are provided on the website, www.scaswebsite.com.

Reliability. The SCAS has internal consistency reliability measurements between 0.60 and 0.92 and test-retest reliability between 0.45 and 0.60.

Validity. This is not available.

Availability and source. Free resource, available at www.scaswebsite.com.

Comment. Aside from its use in assessing clients and assisting with diagnosis and treatment planning, the SCAS is also used for community screening and prevention in order to monitor the outcome of interventions used to mitigate symptoms of anxiety.

Children's Yale-Brown Obsessive-Compulsive Scale (CY-BOCS)

Instrument name. The Yale-Brown Obsessive-Compulsive Rating Scale-Second Edition (Y-BOCS-II) was developed in 2006 as a revision of the original developed in 1989. The CY-BOCS was adapted from the Y-BOCS and published in 1997. The scales were developed as a method of distinguishing symptoms of OCD from depression or other anxiety disorders.

Type of instrument. The Y-BOCS II and CY-BOCS are two-part instruments consisting of a self-report checklist and clinician-administered scaling instruments. The CY-BOCS is available in at least five different versions.

Use-target audience. The Y-BOCS-II is used for adolescents older than 14 years of age and designed to measure symptom severity. The CY-BOCS is used with children and adolescents between the ages of 6 and 14 years old.

Multicultural. This tool is currently available in English only.

Ease and time of administration. The versions of Y-BOCS-II keep to 10 items and take 5–10 min to complete. The CY-BOCS is estimated at taking 40 min to complete, but with several different versions available, with different numbers of questions, the time to administer the scales differs.

Scoring procedure. Scoring of the Y-BOCS-II is done on a five-point scale, among "extreme symptoms" and "no symptoms." The clinician then totals the items and places the respondent among five categories, subclinical, mild, moderate, severe or extreme. The versions of CY-BOCS also require the totaling of symptoms in order to indicate clinical significance of symptoms present.

Reliability. The Y-BOCS-II yields a range of reliability rates for each of its subscales as follows, internal consistency reliability 0.63–0.91, inter-rater reliability 0.83–0.98 and test-retest reliability 0.75–0.90. The CY-BOCS reports having an internal consistency measurement of 0.87.

Validity. The Y-BOCS-II is moderately to strongly correlated in both convergent and discriminant validity measures. The CY-BOCS has a high correlation of 0.62.

Availability and source. The versions of the CY-BOCS are available by contacting Lawrence Scahill, MSN, Ph.D. lawrence.scahill@yale.edu Child Study Center, 230 South Frontage Road, P.O. Box 207900, New Haven, CT

06520–7900. The Y-BOCS-II may be obtained by contacting the first, third, fourth, or final author by contacting via email at estroch@health.usf.edu, phone at (727) 767–8293 or by mail at the Department of Pediatrics, University of South Florida, 800 6th Street South Box 7523, St. Petersburg, FL 33701.

Comment. The tools have been widely used in research and measurement of treatment effectiveness.

Specific Learning Disorders

Early Learning Observation & Rating Scale (ELORS)

Instrument name. ELORS is designed to gather and share information about the child with specific intention to characteristics that may show signs of early learning disabilities. This instrument was created by Gillis, West, & Coleman (2009).

Type of instrument. The ELORS is a 70-item assessment tool.

Use-target audience. Children aged 3–4 years old in the year before kindergarten.

Multicultural. Available in English.

Ease and time of administration. The test takes approximately 10–30 min to complete. The scoring is completed in 15–20 min. There are three ELORS forms: Whole-Class, Teacher–Individual Child, and Parent–Individual Child.

Scoring procedure. The scoring is completed manually.

Reliability. Current studies are being conducted and prepared for publication on the reliability of the ELORS.

Validity. Current studies are being conducted and prepared for publication on the validity of the ELORS.

Availability and source. This test allows parents and teachers to understand if the child would value from additional support. The free source for this test is at: http://www.getreadytoread.org/screening-tools/early-learning-observation-rating-scale.

Comments. This tool is utilized as an early intervention (EI) tool that should not be utilized on its own as a diagnostic assessment. The National Center for Learning Disabilities recommends clear steps for assessment and evaluation across early childhood through adulthood. Interview recommendations for each age range are provided through the LD Navigator at http://ldnavigator.ncld.org.

Peabody Individual Achievement Test-Revised (PIAT-R/NU)

Instrument name. PIAT-R/NU.

Type of instrument. Individualized, standardized test of academic achievement with subtests for general information, reading recognition, readings comprehension, written expression, mathematics and spelling.

Use-target audience. The assessment is designed for children between the ages of 5 and 22 years old or in grades K–12.

Multicultural. The child must be proficient in English. Administrators are cautioned that this test may not be appropriate for children with limited English proficiency.

Ease and time of administration. It typically takes approximately one hour to complete the test. Except for the subtest, written expression, all subtests are untimed.

Scoring procedure. A scoring key is provided, and most subtests have correct answers included on the scoring sheet. The format varies by subtest. After determining a ceiling level, the child is asked questions to which they offer a verbal reply. For some subtests they see the stimulus item and point to one of four choices. Basal is reached by the highest five consecutive correct answers. This procedure limits the number of out of range questions that the child confronts.

Reliability. The publishers provide split-half reliability for the total test of 0.98 (median of all grades). Kuder-Richardson Reliability Coefficients by grade range are from 0.98 to 0.99. Critics have noted that such high reliability measures would not have been obtained if all scores above the basal and below the ceiling had been considered during the norming process.

Validity. The publisher provides detailed information on both content and construct validity. Correlations between the Peabody Picture Vocabulary Test Revised and the PIAT-R are offered.

Availability and source. Pearson Clinical Assessment, Clinicalcustomer-support@pearson.com.

Comments. The PIAT-R/NU is a useful assessment that tends to be easily tolerated by children who have a history of academic challenge. Questions presented on an easel format with multiple pictorial representations for some subtests tend to reduce test anxiety.

See **Table 8.1** for a matrix outlining child assessment strategies and inventories.

Wide Range Achievement Test 4 (WRAT4)

Instrument name. WRAT4.

Type of instrument. An assessment of basic academic skills with subtests in sentence completion, reading, spelling and mathematical computation. This assessment is standardized and intended to be used individually but can also be used in groups of five or fewer.

Use-target audience. The WRAT4 is designed for persons between the ages of 5 and 94 years old.

Multicultural. The norms are based on a representative sample of over 3,000 individuals. According to the publisher, the normative sample was selected on a stratified national sample with proportionate representation controlled for age, gender, ethnicity, geographic region, and parental/obtained education as an index of socioeconomic status.

Ease and time of administration. The time varies with administration time for children 5–7 years of age of 15–25 min and for children over eight years being 30–45 min. The test is very easy to administer with most subtests

Table 8.1 Matrix: Child and Assessment Strategies and Inventories

Instrument	Specific family applications	Cultural/language	Instructions/use: T = time to take, S = time to score, I = items	Computerized a = scoring, b = report	Reliability (r)/ Validity(v)	Availability
ADHD						
ADHD Rating Scale-5	Children aged 5–17.	English and Spanish. Different scoring for boys and girls. (School version available only in English, home version available in both)	T = 5 min per scale S = n/a I = 18	a = No; b = No	R = Internal consistency: α = 89 to.96; test-retest range for both home and school versions: .62–.90. V = Strong confirmatory factor analyses, concurrent and predictive validity.	Available for purchase at www.guilford.com, as well as other online retailers. No copyright restrictions.
VADPRS VADTRS	Children aged 6–12.	English, German and Spanish	T = 10 min S = 10 min I = Parent: 55, Teacher: 43	a = No; b = No	R = .93 or higher internal consistency acceptable and consistent. V = concurrent .79	Free resource: www.nichq.org https://psychology-tools. com/vadrs-vanderbilt-adhd-diagnostic-rating-scale
SNAP-IV-R	Children aged 6–18.	English, Chinese, Portuguese (Brazil).	T = 5 min S = 10 min I = 18	a = No; b = No	R = Interrater .43–.49; Internal consistency: α = .76–96 V = Predictive validity strong for parent poorer for teacher.	Free resource: www.adhd.net

(Continued)

Instrument	Specific family applications	Cultural/language	Instructions/use: T = time to take, S = time to score, I = items	Computerized a = scoring, b = report	Reliability (r)/ Validity(v)	Availability
Depression & Mood Disorders						
CES-DC	Children 6–17.	English, Spanish, Japanese	T = 5 min; S = 10 min; I = 20	a = Yes; b = Yes	R = Test-retest .51; internal consistency: a = .84. V = concurrent validity moderate .44 between Children's Depression Inventory (CDI)	Free resource: Georgetown University http:// www.brightfutures.org/ mentalhealth/pdf/tools.html
GBI & P-GBI	GBI: Children 11 and older. P-GBI: Parents of children aged 5–17.	English	I = 73	a = No; b = No	R = alpha coefficient of .90 V = strong criterion validity & excellent discriminative validity	Free resources: Available by contacting Dr. Eric A. Youngstrom eay@cwru.edu
K-SADS-PL	Children aged 6–18. Parent and child interviews. Collect summary ratings from all sources (school, etc.).	English, Spanish, Israeli, Greek, Korean, Farsi	T = 90–120 min;	a = No; b = No	R = .63–.90 V = Predictive validity weak; construct adequate	Free resource: Kennedy Krieger https://www. kennedykrieger.org/sites/ default/files/community_files/ ksads-dsm-5-screener.pdf

Measure	Population	Languages	Time/Items	a/b	Reliability/Validity	Availability
Mood Feelings Questionnaire	Children aged 12–18.	English	T = 5–10 min; S = 10 min; Items = 33 (short version 13)	a = No; b = No	R = IC: α = .95 (child); .96 (parent) V = moderate to high criterion	Free resource: Duke University http://devepi.duhs. duke.edu/mfq.html
YMRS & P-YMRS	Children 5–17, clinician, parent and teacher reports.	English, Spanish and Turkish	T = 15–30 min (YMRS), 5 min (P-YMRS); S = 10 min (YMRS), 5 min (P-YMRS); I = 11	a = No; b = No	R = Internal consistency: α = .91 V = Diagnostic efficiency .97	Free resources: YMRS is available at louisville.edu/ depression/clinicials-corner/ Young%20Mania%20 Rating%20Scale- Measure. pdf, the P-YMRS is available at www.healthyplace.com/ images/stories/bipolar/p-ymrs.pdf.
ASD						
ADOS-2	12 months through adulthood.	English, Spanish, Czech, Danish, Dutch, Finnish, French, German, Italian, Norwegian, & Swedish	T = 40–60 min S = 10–30 min I = varies	a = Yes; b = No	R = Modules 1–3, internal consistency: α = .97–.92 Module 4, internal consistency .75; Social Communication domain, .85, .47 for the RRB domain. Test- Retest: .68–.92. V = improved in ADOS-2 with new algorithms	Available for purchase: Western Psychological Services www.wpspublish. com

(Continued)

Instrument	Specific family applications	Cultural/language	Instructions/use: T = time to take, S = time to score, I = items	Computerized a = scoring, b = report	Reliability (r)/ Validity(v)	Availability
ASD						
AQ	Children (4–11) and adolescents (12–16).	English	T = 10–15 min; S = less than 5 min; I = 50	a = Yes b = Yes	R = Internal consistency: α = .94	Free resource: https://www. autismresearchcentre.com/ arc_tests
M-CHAT-R/F	Children 16–30 months old.	Available in 27 languages.	T = 5–10 min; S = less than 2 min I = 23	a = Yes b = No	R: MCHAT R- Internal consistency: α = .63 MCHAT R/F Internal consistency: α = .79 V: Good convergent and divergent validity on specific domains	Free resource: www.m-chat.org
SRS-2	Individuals over the age of 2.5.	English, Spanish	T = 15–20 min; S = less than 5 min; I = 65	a = Yes b = Yes	R = IC: α = .94–.96 Test-retest. 88–.95	Available for purchase: Western Psychological Services https://www. wpspublish.com/ store/p/2994/srs-2-social-responsiveness-scale-second-edition

OCD & Anxiety Disorders

SCAS	Children aged 7–14.	English, Chinese, Swedish, Netherlands, Norwegian, Catalan, Czech, Portuguese, Italian, Arabic, Greek, German, Japanese, Spanish, Armenian, Bengali, Bulgarian, Hebrew, Polish, Ukrainian, Swedish, Turkish	T = 5–10 min; S = 10 min; I = 44	a = Yes; b = No	R = IC: α = .60–.92 TRT: .45–.60	Free Resource: Spence Children's Anxiety Scale www.scaswebsite.com
CY-BOCS and Y-BOCS-II	CY-BOCS: Children aged 6–14. Y-BOCS: adolescents older than 14.	English	Y-BOCS-II T = 5–10 min S = 5–10 min I = 10 CY-BOCS Various versions	Y-BOCS II a = Yes; b = Yes CY-BOCS a = No; b = No	Y-BOCS-II R: Internal consistency: α = .63–.91 Inter-rater reliability .83–.98 Test-retest: .75–.90 V: Convergent & discriminant moderately to strongly correlated CY-BOCS R: Internal consistency: α = .87, Intraclass correlations: .66–.91 V: High correlation: .62	CY-BOCS: Lawrence Scahill, MSN, Ph.D. lawrence.scahill@yale.edu Child Study Center, 230 South Frontage Road, P.O. Box 207900, New Haven, CT 06520–7900 Y-BOCS-II: Eric Stroch at email estroch@health.usf.edu, phone (727) 767–8293 or via mail at the Department of Pediatrics, University of South Florida, 800 6th Street South Box 7523, St. Petersburg, FL 33701

(Continued)

Instrument	Specific family applications	Cultural/language	Instructions/use: T = time to take, S = time to score, I = items	Computerized a = scoring, b = report	Reliability (r)/ Validity(v)	Availability
Specific Learning Disorders						
ELORS	Children aged 3–4.	English	T = 10–30 min; S = 15–20 min; I = 70	a = No b = No	N/A	Free resource: www.ncld.org
PIAT-R/NU	Children aged 5–18, adults 18–22 years old.	English, Spanish	T = 60 min; I = 500 (plus language subsets)	a = Yes b = Yes	R: 98–99 split-half reliability V: good content and construct validity	Available for purchase: Pearson Clinical Assessment, Clinicalcustomersupport@ pearson.com
WRAT4	Individuals between 5 and 94 years old.	English	T = 15–45 min (varies by age)	N/A	R: .78–.89 test–retest reliability IC: α = .87–.86 V: N/A	Available for purchase: Western Psychological Services www.wpspublish. com

resembling test formats children will be familiar with from regular classroom tests. Testing should be conducted in the following order: word reading, sentence comprehension, spelling and math computation.

Scoring procedure. The manual is very comprehensive, offering a full administration, scoring and interpretation information. The child typically generates correct answers on a response form. These are then scored with reference to the scoring key. A scoring key is provided.

Reliability. The publisher states that "alternate-form immediate retest reliability coefficients ranged from 0.78 to 0.89 for an age-based sample and from 0.86 to 0.90 for a grade-based sample." Median internal consistency reliability coefficients for subtests and the reading composite for an age-based sample range from 0.87 to 0.96.

Validity: The publisher provides a statement on how validity evidence is derived for the WRAT4 but does not provide on data in support of this statement.

Availability and source. The WRAT4 is available for purchase with Western Psychological Services www.wpspublish.com and Pearson Clinical Assessments https://www.pearsonclinical.com/education/products/100001722/wide-range-achievement-test-4--wrat4.html.

Comments. The WRAT4 is not intended to be used for formal identification of learning or cognitive disorders. Rather it is quick and simple assessment of basic academic skills. Two alternative forms of the WRAT4 are available. This may be useful for retesting a child who is receiving intensive instruction or other remediation.

Strategy for Utilizing Assessment Results

Case Example: Ramón

Background Information and Rationale for Assessment

Mark and Carolina have been married 14 years and have two children, Ramón 10 and Seth four years old. They have a healthy and stable marriage. Mark works as an accountant of the local power company, and Carolina is a testing supervisor for a juice company. Both sons are well cared for. Ramón attended preschool from the age of three, and Seth will begin preschool soon. Ramón was cared for at home by Carolina's mother during working hours until he began preschool.

Ramón has a number of problems at home and preschool. He prefers to play by himself. He was clearly interested in cars and trucks from an early age. His play was somewhat atypical however, in that he tended to not use the cars within the context of any imaginary play. Rather he focused on the car and especially the parts of the car or truck. He learned

(Continued)

academic content quickly and was an early reader. He loved to read about cars and trucks, and Carolina and Mark got him every early reader book they could find to encourage his early reading. He now reads at an above average level, which helps him across the board. Math is easy, and he can do most of the problems without writing out the steps.

The present issue relates to a classroom incident. Ramón's teacher announced that a fellow student would be absent for a few days because her mother had died from a brain hemorrhage. While the other children remained silent, Ramón said, "So, what?" and continued his work. The other children could not comprehend this response, and some began to call Ramón names until the teacher stopped them from doing so. Nevertheless, Ramón was confused and became upset. He then refused to go back to school for several days, and his parents have been keeping him home. Ramón understands his reason for staying home is because "the other kids are mean to me."

Testing Summary

Ramón was assessed using a number of instruments. First, he was administered the WRAT in which he scored at or above the normal range on word reading, sentence comprehension, spelling and math computation. Ramón scored almost 1.0 standard deviations below the mean on sentence comprehension. During a clinical interview, Ramón was asked if he liked to play with other children. He replied that he did not except when they played with cars and they did so, "the way he wanted them to play." Asked if he had any friends, he mentions only his mother, father and brother Seth. When asked what he liked to do for fun, he said, "play with cars."

When asked about the classroom incident, Ramón said the other children don't like him and that they, "Don't know how to do things right." As part of the interview, I asked Ramón to show how someone would look if they were sad. He replied that he was not sure. When asked how he could ask someone to stop something without using words, he pushed on an imaginary brake and pushed the horn button on a pretend steering wheel. He did this without eye contact.

In an initial interview, the parents were asked to describe their concerns about Ramón. They noted his intense focus on cars and trucks. They report that he would read about them and play with a collection of toy cars and trucks for hours each day. He was especially interested in the cars with hatchbacks and cars and trucks with doors or hoods that opened. He would operate these for long periods of time. When playing, he first had to "get them right" by which he meant lining them up and putting them in an order that only he knew. If his parents attempted to initiate play without Ramón setting his toys in the correct sequence, they reported that they could expect a tantrum. When he was younger, the parents reported not being concerned about his intense interest. They reported that as Ramón began preschool he would still play with cars and trucks but always alone. He resisted efforts to get him to play with other children. They had some brief success with facilitated play centered on cars and trucks with other boys, but as soon as an adult left the play setting, a problem would ensue. Eventually, Ramón was left to play alone most of the time. Prior to entering kindergarten, Ramón developed an interest in picture books and then reading, mostly about cars and trucks, and the parents reported that they hoped his social issues would become less prominent as he seemed to do well with learning tasks.

The parents were each asked to complete the Social Responsiveness Scale-Revised, a 60-item checklist. Both parents provided scores that indicated Ramón had mild impairments in social communication and restricted interests and repetitive behaviors (RRBIs) for males among school-aged children. Ramón's teacher was also asked to complete the instrument and resulted in moderate impairments in both diagnostic categories.

In addition to the parent and teacher report, the school psychologist and speech language pathologists were trained in using the ADOS-2 and administered this assessment. The professionals used Module 3 for verbally fluent children and adolescents. Results from the ADOS-2 indicate scores above the cut-off providing a third party clinical observation that is consistent with parent and teacher reporting.

Using the DSM-5 diagnostic criteria for ASD, mild (299.10), Ramón appears to meet the criteria. Ramón meets the following criteria for diagnosis: A1) difficulty with social and emotional reciprocity when presented with sad (death) or distressing (play) with others, A2) challenges in understanding relationships and the ability to adjust to social contexts at school with peers. B2) Ramon insists on sameness in routine and interests he engages in (vehicles) and B3) would engage in this interest with excessive attachment and time spent in the activity. C) Parent report reveals that these concerns have been present since about two years old but have worsened recently with additional social and behavioral demands. D-E) These challenges are causing problems for him at school (more so) and home (less so) and are not explained by an intellectual disability (performs above average cognitively).

(Continued)

Treatment Recommendations

In an effort to rule out any possible physical etiology, Ramón should receive a comprehensive medical and neurological examination. The parents should become knowledgeable about ASD by reading books and viewing videos on the disorder as well as registering with local state or privately funded ASD support agencies. The parents could seek Exceptional Student Educational (ESE) services from Ramón's current school beginning with an educational eligibility assessment. While specialized services may benefit Ramón, he is likely to remain in the same general education classroom with the provision of inclusion supports as needed. His teachers should understand that Ramón is not being intentionally rude or uncaring toward the other children. Rather, he is struggling with a disorder that impairs his social communication. The teachers can help by directly and clearly explaining social situations to Ramón and by informing him about the expected and successful social behaviors for various settings. This can be done with counselors, psychologists and other school-based therapists through pull out sessions at first and then refreshed with brief prompts and booster sessions once they have been learned.

In an effort to target Ramón's social communication impairments, he will benefit from weekly social skills instruction in a group format which can be conducted by a speech language pathologist or other clinical staff. The parents are urged to put supports in place that can aid a transition and shift in his restricted interest in cars. They can do this by reducing and then eliminating the number of toy cars that are for younger aged children and introduce more age specific car or transportation related toys and entertainment. In order to increase flexibility and new interests, it would be helpful to introduce books and other activities with different themes to expand his opportunities and interests. They are advised to broaden his interests while being respectful of it. Such broadening could include helping Ramón consider the places he can go in cars or the activities and people he can become involved with using a car or other vehicles and modes for transportation. Finally, it will be helpful to conduct weekly counseling session with Ramón. Here the focus can be on appreciating the perspectives of others, role-playing a variety of social situations and reviewing his weekly social successes and challenges. When he is slightly more mature, understanding that he has been diagnosed with ASD may be helpful in gaining insight and building self-awareness and advocacy skills so he can get his needs met in a variety of environments and relationships with others.

Concluding Comments

Assessing children for these conditions will continue to be an important element of practice for most mental health professionals. The etiological differences, environmental pressures on children and challenges some face without knowledge or education about these conditions will require that large numbers of children receive quality professional care. A few major areas of change are readily identifiable for growth and development. First, technology will broaden the access to assessment tools and information about childhood disorders. From improved assessment tools, procedures and resources to better training and information on these conditions with technological and clinical advancements, the prognosis for children and adolescents with these conditions has never had this level of potential in our history. Second, viewing a child's problems as existing solely within the child will yield with increasing speed to seeing the larger context in which the child lives. Change efforts become more system focused with both the family, educational system and the child needing to understand how they can call for supports.

Technology is making the dissemination of information about special needs and diagnoses even more accessible. While some smaller percentage of the population have little or no access to the internet, most families and certainly all professionals have easy access to the widest possible array of sources of information on any disorder or treatment. This certainly can add stress to the lives of families as they sometimes careen around the internet often with limited discernment and confront a host of unsupported claims for miracle therapies. But it does also allow them to also access sound information that will help them make good choices for their children. Professionals must be prepared to take advantage of these capabilities. Posting information of promising and sound treatments is one way; sharing training videos that will enable families to enhance their capacity is another. Due to the internet, professionals now have immediate access to an ever-widening assortment of free or low-cost assessment instruments. Consider the Autism Spectrum Quotient (free resource) or SRS-2 (at cost), mentioned in relation to ASD as one example. Fortunately, many assessment developers have discovered that they can benefit from their work through sales of support or value-added materials while freely giving away the assessment. Hopefully, this trend will continue. Cutting-edge technology with direct assessment of young children by analyzing eye movements in response to social stimuli (Klin, Jones, Schultz, Volkmar, & Cohen, 2002) or EEG measures that may provide information about subtle anomalies in the architecture of the young child's brain (Bosl, Tierney, Tager-Flusberg, & Nelson, 2011) may soon replace or at minimum supplement traditional assessment techniques in ASD and perhaps other disorders.

Perhaps the most important development is the accelerating trend away from seeing any learning or behavioral disorder in childhood as existing only within the child. This trend is clearly evident in public school and family counseling practice. Now, before most children with suspected learning disorders are considered for special education, they are provided active and evidence-based interventions within the context of their regular classroom. A process is instituted to ensure that they are receiving quality instruction and that different teaching techniques are implemented and carefully monitored, and changes are made, all in an effort to preclude the need for special education. This is also part of a larger trend toward early intervention and prevention of disorders through family education and comprehensive integrated behavioral care. Here, the role of the mental health professional will be enhanced as they have the opportunity to guide a problem-solving team to determine the optimal learning and social conditions for a child now facing challenges. This can occur in the home, at a medical office such as the pediatrician or in schools. Assessment in our current and future practice is a dynamic process rather than a static one based purely on examining the individual through testing. In this dynamic process, the clinician seeks to understand not just how the child scores on assessments but how the social, family and other contexts can be altered to promote optimal growth for the child.

References

American Psychiatric Association. (2000). *Diagnostic and statistical manual of mental disorders* (4th ed., Text Revision). Washington, DC: Author.

American Psychiatric Association. (2013). *Diagnostic and statistical manual of mental disorders* (5th ed.). Washington, DC: Author.

Auyeung, B., Baron-Cohen, S., Wheelwright, S., & Allison, C. (2008). The Autism Spectrum Quotient: Children's Version (AQ-Child). *Journal of Autism and Developmental Disorders, 38*(7), 1230–1240. doi:10.1007/s10803-007-0504-z

Baron-Cohen, S., Ring, H., Chitnis, X., Wheelwright, S., Gregory, L., Williams, S., Brammer, M., & Bullmore, E. (2006). fMRI of parents of children with Asperger Syndrome: A pilot study. *Brain and Cognition, 6*(1), 122–130. doi:10.1016/j.bandc.2005.12.011

Birmaher, B., Axelson, D., Strober, M., Gill, M. K., Valeri, S., Chiappetta, L., … Kellar, M. (2006). Clinical course of children and adolescents with bipolar spectrum disorders. *Archive of General Psychiatry, 63*(2), 175–183.

Bosl, W., Tierney, A., Tager-Flusberg, H., & Nelson, C. (2011). EEG complexity as a biomarker for autism spectrum disorder risk. *BMC Medicine, 9*, 18. doi:10.1186/1741-7015-9-18

Bruni, T. (2014). Test review: Constantino, J.N., & Gruber, C.P. (2012). Social responsiveness scale-second edition (SRS-2). *Journal of Psychoeducational Assessment, 32*, 365–369.

Centers for Disease Control. (2016). *Attention-deficit/hyperactivity disorder*. Retrieved from https://www.cdc.gov/ncbddd/adhd/data.html

Centers for Disease Control. (2018). *Autism spectrum disorder*. Retrieved from https://www.cdc.gov/ncbddd/autism/index.html

Collett, B. R., Ohan, J. L., & Myers, K. M. (2003). Ten-year review of rating scales. V: Scales assessing attention-deficit/hyperactivity disorder. *Journal of American Academy of Child & Adolescent Psychiatry, 42*(9), 1015–1037.

Danielson, C. K., Youngstrom, E. A., Findling, R. L., & Calabrese, J. R. (2003). Discriminative validity of the general behavior inventory using youth report. *Journal of Abnormal Child Psychology, 31,* 29–39.

Daviss, W. B., Birmaher, B., Melhem, N. A., Axelzon, D. A., Michaels, S. M., & Brent, D. A. (2006). Criterion validity of the mood and feelings questionnaire for depressive episodes in clinic and non-clinic subjects. *Journal of Child Psychology and Psychiatry, 47*(9), 927–934. doi:10.1111/j.1469-7610.2006.01646.x

Dulcan, M. K. (2009). *Dulcan's textbook of child and adolescent psychiatry.* American Psychiatric Publishing.

DuPaul, G. J., Power, T. J., Anastapoulos, A. D., & Reid, R. (2016). *ADHD Rating Scale-5 for children and adolescents: Checklists, norms and clinical interpretation.* New York, NY: Guilford Press.

Edelbrock, C., & Bohnert, A. (2000). *Handbook of psychological assessment* (3rd ed.). New York, NY: Pergamon.

Filipek, P. A., Accardo, P. J., Baranek, G. T., Cook Jr., E. H., Dawson, G., Gordon, B., ... Volkmar, F. R. (1999). The screening and diagnosis of autism spectrum disorders. *Journal of Autism and Developmental Disorders, 29*(2), 439–484.

Fitzgerald, M., & Corvin, A. (2001). Diagnosis and differential diagnosis of Asperger syndrome. *Advances in Psychiatric Treatment, 7,* 310–318.

Frankel, F., Myatt, R., Sugar, C., Whitham, C., Gorospe, C., & Laugeson, E. (2010). A randomized controlled study of parent-assisted Children's friendship training with children having autism spectrum disorders. *Journal of Autism & Developmental Disorders, 40*(7), 827–842. doi:10.1007/s10803-009-0932-z

Frazier, T. W., Demeter, C. A., Youngstrom, E. A., Calabrese, J. R., Stansbrey, R. J., McNamara, N. K., & Findling, R. L. (2007). Evaluation and comparison of psychometric instruments for pediatric bipolar spectrum disorders for four age groups. *Journal of Adolescent and Child Psychopharmacology, 17*(6), 853–867.

Gillis, M., West, T., & Coleman, M. R. (2009). *Early Learning Observation & Rating Scale (ELORS).* Retrieved from http://www.getreadytoread.org/screening-tools/early-learning-observation-rating-scale

Gracious, B. L., Youngstrom, E. A., Findling, R. L., & Calabrese, J. R. (2002). Discriminative validity of a parent version of the Young Mania Rating Scale. *Journal of the American Academy of Child & Adolescent Psychiatry, 41*(11), 1350–1359. doi:10.1097/00004583-200211000-00017

Hersen, M., Hilsenroth, M. J., & Segal, D. L. (2004). *Comprehensive handbook of psychological assessment.* Hoboken, NJ: John Wiley & Sons, Inc.

Kessler, R. C., Berglund, P., Demler, O., Jin, R., Merikangas, K. R., & Walters, E. E. (2005). Lifetime prevalence and age-of-onset distributions of DSM-IV disorders in the National Comorbidity Survey Replication. *Archives of General Psychiatry, 62*(6), 593–602.

Klein, D. N., Dougherty, L. R., & Olino, T. M. (2005). Toward guidelines for evidence-based assessment of depression in children and adolescents. *Journal of Clinical Child and Adolescent Psychology, 34*(3), 412–432.

Klin, A., Jones, W., Schultz, R., Volkmar, F., & Cohen, D. (2002). Visual fixation patterns during viewing of naturalistic social situations as predictors of social competence in individuals with autism. *Archives of General Psychiatry, 59,* 809–816.

March, J., & Benton, C. (2007). *Talking back to OCD.* New York, NY: The Guilford Press.

March, J., Silva, S., Petrycki, S., Curry, J., Wells, K., Fairbank, J., ... Severe, J. (2004). Fluoxetine, cognitive-behavioral therapy and their combination for adolescents with depression: Treatment for Adolescents with Depression Study (TADS) randomized controlled trial. *Journal of the American Medical Association, 292*(2), 1231–1242.

Merikangas, K. R., He, J., Burstein, M., Swanson, S. A., Avenevoli, S., Cui, L., … Swendsen, J. (2010). Lifetime prevalence of mental disorders in U.S. adolescents: Results from the National Comorbidity Study-Adolescent Supplement (NCS-A). *Journal of American Academy of Child and Adolescent Psychiatry, 49*(10), 980–989.

National Institutes on Mental Health & Centers for Disease Control. (2013). *Mental health surveillance among children 2005–2011*. Retrieved from https://www.cdc.gov/mmwr/preview/mmwrhtml/su6202a1.htm

Our World Data. (2018). *Mental health*. Retrieved from https://ourworldindata.org/mental-health#anxiety-disorders

Ozonoff, S., & Solomon, M. (2005). Evidence-based assessment of ASD in children and adolescents. *Journal of Child & Adolescent Psychology, 34*(3), 523–540. doi:10.1207/s15374424jccp3403_8

Pediatric OCD Treatment Study (POTS) Team. (2004). Cognitive-behavior therapy, sertraline, and their combination for children and adolescents with Obsessive-Compulsive Disorder: The Pediatric OCD Treatment Study (POTS) Randomized Controlled Trial. *Journal of the American Medical Academy, 292*(16), 1969–1976.

Robins, D. L., & Dumont-Mathieu, T. D. (2006). Early screening for autism spectrum disorders: Update on the Modified Checklist for Autism in Toddlers and other measures. *Developmental and Behavioral Pediatrics, 27*, 111–119. doi:0196-206X/06/2702-0111

Roy, A. K., Lopes, V., & Klein, R. G. (2014). Disruptive mood dysregulation disorder (DMDD): A new diagnostic approach to chronic irritability in youth. *The American Journal of Psychiatry, 171*(9), 918–924. doi:10.1176/appi.ajp.2014.13101301

Serrano, E., Ezpeleta, L., Alda, J. A., Matali, J. L., & San, L. (2011). Psychometric properties of the YMRS for the identification of mania symptoms in Spanish children and adolescents with attention deficit/hyperactivity disorder. *Psychopathology, 44*(2), 125–132. doi:10.1159/000320893

Sørensen, M. J., Thomsen, P. H., & Bilenberg, N. (2007). Parent and child acceptability and staff evaluation of K-SADS-PL, a pilot study. *European Child & Adolescent Psychiatry, 16*(5), 293–297.

Weissman, M. M., Wolk, S., Goldstein, R. B., Moreau, D., Adams, P., Greenwald, S., … Wichramaratne, P. (1999). Depressed adolescents grown up. *Journal of the American Medical Association, 281*(18), 1701–1713.

Wing, L., Gould, J., & Gillberg, C. (2011). Autism spectrum disorders in the DSM-5: Better or worse than the DSM-IV? *Research in Developmental Disabilities, 32*, 768–773.

Wolriach, M. L., Lambert, W., Doffing, M. A., Bickman, L., Simmons, T., & Worley, K. (2003). Psychometric properties of the Vanderbilt ADHD diagnostic parent rating scale in a referred population. *Journal of Pediatric Psychology, 28*(8), 559–568.

Wood, A., Kroll, L., Moore, A., & Harrington, R. (1995). Properties of the mood and feelings questionnaire in adolescent psychiatric outpatients: A research note. *Journal of Child Psychology and Psychiatry, 36*(2), 327–334.

Youngstrom, E. A, Findling, R. L, Calabrese, J. R., Gracious, B. L., Demeter, C., Bedoya, D. D., & Price, M. (2004). Comparing the diagnostic accuracy of six potential screening instruments for bipolar disorder in youths aged 5 to 17 years. *Journal of the American Academy of Child & Adolescent Psychiatry, 43*(7), 847–858. doi:10.1097/01.chi.0000125091.35109.1e

9

PARENT–CHILD ASSESSMENT STRATEGY AND INVENTORIES

Len Sperry

During the past decade, there has been considerable progress in developing new and more focused measures of parent–child relationships. Of particular note are developments in measures targeting underserved and underrepresented populations, family adjustment, parental distress, and trauma and posttraumatic stress in children.

The need for measures which are better targeted to underserved populations and cost effective has recently garnered attention. Unfortunately, available instruments are limited since few screen for psychiatric diagnoses and are not appropriate for children under five years of age. Also lacking are instruments that are brief and focus on competencies. Furthermore is the need for instruments that assess self-efficacy which is increasingly recognized as important in parent–child relationships (Morawska, Sanders, Haslam, Filus, & Fletcher, 2014).

A related development and trend is the increasing numbers of underrepresented of groups with issues of family adjustment and parental distress. The rate of poverty continues to rise in the United States with 14.5% living in poverty and 23.1% receiving welfare services with 32%–38% of children living in households receiving public assistance (Daire, Gonzalez, & O'Hare, 2017). Parents and families experiencing poverty are at greater risk of family fragmentation, parental distress, emotional problems and challenges in obtaining necessary resource parental distress and emotional problems.

Increasing recognition of trauma and posttraumatic stress in children is another trend. Youth who are exposed to family aggression are more likely to suffer from a wide range of emotional and behavioral difficulties, including posttraumatic stress, depression, anxiety, and conduct disorders (Cecil, McCrory, Viding, Holden, & Barker, 2016). The results of family aggression increase a child's risk for psychiatric and medical disorders later on in life. As such, family aggression is recognized as a major risk factor to be targeted for prevention and intervention efforts (Gilbert et al., 2009). The need for cost-effective, brief instruments have gained popularity. Unfortunately, most existing trauma measures do not distinguish between childhood maltreatment and exposure to intimate partner violence (IPV). Detection of posttraumatic stress disorder (PTSD) and its symptoms in children and adolescents is recommended as a first step to identify youth needing trauma-focused interventions (Cohen, Bulik, & Walter, 2010). Given that the diagnostic criteria of PTSD have been modified in DSM-5, existing trauma measures need to be updated. Since existing child trauma questionnaires are in the English language and based on the DSM-IV, creating an internationally validated instrument with appropriate developmental language for children is most needed.

Accordingly, this chapter includes a number of new instruments. These include the the Parental Stress and Coping Inventory (PSCI), Child Adjustment and Parent Efficacy Scale (CAPES), new edition of Behavior Assessment System for Children Parenting Relationship Questionnaire (BASC-3 PRQ), and the Family Aggression Screening Tool (FAST).

The following sections of this chapter will describe several family systems instruments and models available for assessing clients. The first section includes instruments for family members over the age of ten, while the next section includes instruments for those family members under the age of ten. Next, an assessment strategy for utilizing these instruments with parents and children is described. Finally, a detailed case example illustrates this strategy in clinical practice.

Self-Report Assessments for Family Members Age 10 and Older

Systemic Assessment of the Family Environment (SAFE)

Instrument name. The Systemic Assessment of the Family Environment is referred to as the SAFE. It was developed by Yingling, Miller, McDonald, & Galewaler (1998) to assess three generational subsystems of the family system using a single instrument for clinical and research purposes prompted the development of the SAFE.

Type of instrument. The SAFE is a self-report paper-and-pencil instrument for all family members age ten and older.

Variables measured. Organizational structure and interactional processes are measured. These variables were identified as global constructs in family systems theory, which was generally included in other family assessment instruments. At the same time that the SAFE was defined, the Global Assessment of Relational Functioning (GARF) (American Psychiatric Association, 1994) was defined by Lyman Wynne's *Diagnostic and Statistical Manual of Mental Disorders* (DSM) task force as an observational tool using very similar constructs. The two models were then used simultaneously in a doctoral clinic and later in a free-standing family therapy institute by Yingling.

Use and target audience. Scoring flexibility permits the SAFE to be used for families with or without children by separating the completion and scoring of relationship dynamics by family subsystems: A = parent/spouse/partner to parent/spouse/partner; B = parent to child; and C = parent/spouse/partner to grandparent. Directions are clear for couples who have not been married and for stepfamilies. The wording of items is adapted for each of three respondent formats: child, parent, and grandparent.

Multicultural. All three formats (child, parent, and grandparent) have been translated into Spanish by linguist Todd Smith. It has also been translated and published in French (Favez, 2010). The constructs are global enough to be useful in various cultural settings.

Ease and time of administration. The 21-item semantic differential one-page paper-and-pencil instrument requires approximately five minutes for most clients to complete, making it very user friendly as a clinic intake tool. Directions are self-explanatory, even for most children.

Scoring procedure. Weighted scores for each blank on the semantic differential line are provided on a separate sheet and can be copied onto a transparency overlay for quick scoring. A paper-and-pencil scoring grid on a separate page creates a plotted outcome for each of the three generational relationships (parent–parent, parent–child, and parent–grandparent), as well as the overall averaged family system. Outcomes fall within one of four quadrants based on the intersection of interactional and organizational scores: competent, discordant, disoriented, or chaotic. Recommended interventions based on family therapy theory are implied by the quadrant results according to subsystem. Competent families may need only an opportunity to tell their story to manage an unusually heavy outside stressor, discordant families need communication skills training, and disoriented families need structural interventions. Chaotic families may need strategic interventions to realign structure before learning to communicate so that they can sustain an effective structure and create a safe environment in which family members can grow.

Reliability. Clinical use of the SAFE indicates highly reliable results with moderate- to low-functioning families who have enough safety to be honest in reporting. Children in low-functioning families do not always have the necessary level of safety.

Validity. One dissertation study (Scoville, 1999) tested the construct validity using Pearson correlations of the SAFE subscales with other accepted subsystem instruments. The SAFE Parent–Child Nuclear Family subscale score had a negative correlation of $r = -.74$ when correlated with the Beavers SFI score (the SFI scoring has higher numbers for lower functioning). Correlation of the SAFE Marital subscale with the ENRICH Marital Satisfaction scores yielded a coefficient of .82. No correlation was evident between the SAFE Family-of-Origin scores and the Personal Authority in the Family System (PAFS) (Bray, Williamson, & Malone, 1984). Research on the SAFE is limited, although a variety of research projects around the world using the SAFE are in process.

Availability and source. The instrument and instructions are published in the *GARF Assessment Sourcebook* (Yingling et al., 1998). A more recent development of the stepfamily version is available at www.SystemsMediation.com under "Resources."

Comment. Through 20 years of use in private practice as well as in clinic settings, Yingling and several trainees have found the SAFE a valuable and efficient assessment tool to use with all clients. Some family mediators have found it especially helpful as a screening tool for planning mediation strategy. Initial concern about the need to reverse random items to increase reliability has not been confirmed by clinical observation. Despite the positive items loaded on the left side of the semantic differential scale, persons completing the questionnaire tend to spread out answers appropriately. Marking all responses on the same extreme rating is an immediate indication of untrue responses; the reason for this is then explored in therapy. The completed instrument is extremely efficient because it creates an immediate profile of three levels of the family system. The therapist does not need to score the instrument to see implications for therapeutic intervention. Immediate indications of power struggles in the marriage and contamination from extended family are especially helpful in determining effective therapeutic interventions.

Global Assessment of Relational Functioning (GARF) Self-Assessment for Families

Instrument name. The GARF Self-Assessment for Families was developed by Yingling based on the descriptors included in the GARF clinical rating observational scale in the DSM-IV Appendix (American Psychiatric Association, 1994; Group for the Advancement of Psychiatry Committee on the Family, 1996; Kaslow, 1996; Yingling et al., 1998). The GARF clinical rating scale was developed by a DSM-IV task force under the leadership of Dr. Lyman Wynne. A collaborative effort of family assessment researchers in the field produced the GARF, with possible results of calming the "range war" engaged in by the second generation of family therapists.

Type of instrument. This one-page, paper-and-pencil instrument lists all the descriptors included in the observational model of the GARF in the DSM-IV with a requested rating of 1–10 for each descriptor. The descriptors are grouped under the three variables with an "other" blank to allow family members to contribute their own thoughts to the family functioning concept. Self-scoring instructions are included on the single page.

Variables measured. The three variables measured by the GARF Self-Assessment are (a) problem-solving/interactional skills for making this family work well, (b) the way in which this family is organized and structured, and (c) how members of this family feel about being a part of the family.

Use and target audience. All family members with basic reading and simple math skills (generally age ten and above) can complete and score the instrument. It can be completed by any family subsystem members available, although more perspectives provide a more accurate picture of the family system. A primary use has been to train therapists in understanding and using the GARF clinical rating model. Dr. Dudley Chewning has developed a version of the GARF for assessing organizational team functioning (see www.SystemsMediation.com).

Multicultural. The instrument is available in English and Spanish at www. SystemsMediation.com, as translated by linguist Jordan Smith.

Ease and time of administration. Completing and scoring the instrument generally requires approximately five minutes. Therapist plotting of family scores on the profile chart generally requires less than five minutes.

Scoring procedure. Simple scoring procedures are included on the one-page instrument. Points under the three variables are totalled and averaged by the family member or the therapist/researcher. A GARF Profile Chart is included on a second page, which plots the averaged scores of each variable for each family member in a comparison chart. This chart is quickly completed by the therapist and shared with family members to evoke discussion of how various members perceive the strengths and weaknesses of family functioning.

Reliability. No published or reported reliability testing is available for the self-report instrument. For data on the GARF clinical rating model, see Chapter 6 of this book; Dausch, Miklowitz, and Richards (1996) and Yingling et al. (1998).

Validity. No published or reported validity testing is available for the self-report instrument. Personal use indicates moderate to high clinical utility and validity. For data on the GARF clinical rating model, see Chapter 5 of this book; Dausch et al. (1996), Denton, Nakonezny, and Burwell (2010), Wilkins and White (2001), Yingling et al. (1998).

Availability and source. The self-report is available at www.SystemsMediation.com.

Comment. This instrument works well for periodic assessment of family functioning by all family members to help set and measure change goals. Parenting coordinators and court-ordered family therapists find this instrument useful for assessing change in functioning. An unexpected use of the instrument has been to train therapists to become familiar with the GARF clinical rating model.

Beavers Self-Report Family Inventory (SFI)

Instrument name. The SFI was developed by Robert Beavers and Robert Hampson following extensive research with the Beavers Systems Model Clinical Rating Scale on which it is based (Beavers & Hampson, 1990). Intent was to allow clinical constructs to drive the self-report instrument development.

Type of instrument. The 36-item self-report questionnaire uses a Likert scale response from 1 (yes: Fits Our Family very Well) to 5 (No: Does Not Fit Our Family). Items 35 and 36 are global ratings of Competence and Style.

Variables measured. The two major constructs of the clinical model are Health/Competence and Style. Attempts at measuring style reliably in self-report format have not been very successful; the Cohesion scale is used as an estimate of style. Primary factors measured in the SFI are Health/Competence as a global score and Conflict, Leadership, and Emotional Expressiveness as sub scores.

Use and target audience. All family members age 11 and older complete the questionnaire.

Multicultural. Research using the clinical rating scale with Caucasian, African–American, and Mexican–American families indicates some style differences but no significant differences based on ethnicity (Hampson, Beavers, & Hulgus, 1990). The SFI is available in Spanish, Italian, German, Rumanian, San Carlos Spanish, Japanese, Chinese, Greek, Portuguese, and French, as well as English.

Ease and time of administration. Instructions are straightforward and require approximately 10–15 minutes to complete. An inexperienced rater will likely require 10–15 minutes for scoring each instrument.

Scoring procedure. Scoring is rather complex, with reversed numbers using mathematical formulas to obtain individualized item scores. A scoring grid is provided, along with a chart for equating the self-report score to the observational score. The score for Competence can then be plotted with the Style score on the "pair of pants" graph, which divides competence into a ten-point continuum with five categories: severely dysfunctional, borderline, midrange, adequate, and optimal.

Reliability. Reported Cronbach's alphas are between .84 and .93, with test–retest reliabilities of .85 or better.

Validity. Validity is supported by canonical correlations of .62 or better on the SFI and clinical rating of Competence (Hampson, Prince, & Beavers, 1999), as well as high correlations of .77–.92 with factors in the Family Assessment Device (FAD) and Family Adaptability and Cohesion Evaluation Scale III (FACES III) instruments.

Availability and source. The SFI is published in the book *Successful Families: Assessment and Intervention* (Beavers & Hampson, 1990) and is printed in Walsh (2003). The SFI manual and scales are available from Robert

B. Hampson, Ph.D., Psychology Department, P.O. Box 0442, Southern Methodist University, Dallas, TX 75275-0442; rhampson@smu.edu. Use of the SFI is available without charge in exchange for a copy of the final study results.

Comment. The clinically based foundation for the SFI has the advantage of leading directly to clinical interventions for the highly trained and experienced family therapist. However, the scoring and theoretical interpretations are challenging for inexperienced clinicians and require specialized training.

McMaster Family Assessment Device (FAD)

Instrument name. The FAD developed from ongoing work on the clinical McMaster Model of Family Functioning (Epstein, Bishop, & Levin, 1978) and was first published in its current form in 1983 (Epstein, Baldwin, & Bishop, 1983). Development of the model continued at McGill University for a decade before moving to McMaster University in the late 1970s; in the 1980s, it moved to the Brown University Family Research Program. Beginning with an all-inclusive approach to item development with elimination of what did not support psychometric properties, the lack of theoretical foundation and supporting research have been criticized (L'Abate & Bagarozzi, 1993). A 1990 updated research report (Kabacoff, Miller, Bishop, Epstein, & Keitner, 1990) addressed some of the criticisms by providing a comprehensive report of data. For more recent challenges to the validity of the instrument in measuring proposed constructs with the current scoring, see Ridenour, Daley, and Reich (1999, 2000), Miller, Ryan, Keitner, Bishop, and Epstein (2000).

Type of instrument. The 60-item paper-and-pencil questionnaire is to be completed by all family members aged 12 and above. Responses are on a four-point Likert scale from Strongly Agree, Agree, and Disagree to Strongly Disagree.

Variables measured. The FAD includes a general functioning scale for Overall Health Pathology and six dimensional scales: Problem Solving, Communication, Roles, Affective Responsiveness, Affective Involvement, and Behavior Control. The scales are detailed in Walsh (2003). Ridenour and colleagues' (2000) construct validity challenge proposes that the FAD actually measures two constructs: Collaboration and Commitment. These two constructs appear to be similar to the SAFE and GARF constructs of Interactional Processes and Organizational Structure.

Use and target audience. The FAD was designed as a clinical screening tool for family functioning. The intent was "to identify problem areas in the most simple and efficient fashion possible" (Epstein et al., 1983, p. 171).

Multicultural. The FAD has been used in many countries and has versions in at least 16 different languages, including Afrikaans, Chinese, Croatian, Danish, Dutch, French, Greek, Hebrew, Hungarian, Italian, Japanese, Portuguese, Russian, Swedish, and Spanish.

Ease and time of administration. The questionnaire takes approximately 15–20 minutes to complete. Scoring for each questionnaire requires approximately 15 minutes.

Scoring procedure. A separate two-page scoring sheet that converts negative items and groups responses into the seven scales is provided. Scales are first summed and then divided by the number of completed answers in that scale to obtain an averaged score for each scale. Computerized scoring is available.

Reliability. Six of the seven scales have reported internal reliability correlations above .70. The Roles scale has a reported alpha of .69 in psychiatric and medical samples but a lower .57 correlation in non-clinical samples. Consequently, use of the Roles scale in non-clinical samples is questionable (Kabacoff et al., 1990).

Validity. Factor analyses results seem comparable to other similar instruments in accounting for variance. The General Functioning scale was reported as highly correlated with other items, supporting it as a single index of family functioning (Kabacoff et al., 1990).

Availability and source. A detailed description of the model is published in Walsh (2003). Comprehensive information is available in *Evaluating and Treating Families: The McMaster Approach* (Ryan, Epstein, Keitner, Miller, & Bishop, 2005).

Comment. The McMaster model authors contend that two basic findings from the original 1969 study are still valid: (a) family functioning variables (organizational, structural, and transactional patterns) are more powerful than intrapsychic variables in determining family member behavior; and (b) emotional health of a child is closely related to the emotional relationship between the child's parents (Walsh, 2003). Keeping these two principles in mind will be helpful as family therapy professionals continue to evolve the self-report family assessment process into clinically useful resources, as well as reliable research instruments.

Family Aggression Screening Tool (FAST)

Instrument name. The Family Aggression Screening Tool (FAST) (Cecil et al., 2016) was developed to be a brief, self-report pictorial measure of caregiver aggression, including direct victimization and exposure to IPV. Improvements were made to the Children's Memories of Family Violence (CMFV) in order to construct the FAST.

Type of instrument. The FAST is a brief, self-report tool that makes use of pictorial representations to assess experiences of caregiver aggression, including direct victimization and exposure to IPV. It measures both experiences of direct victimization and exposure to IPV. Each pictorial representation depicts three characters, an adult male (father), an adult female (mother), and a child. Depending on the form of aggression measured, each representation also includes one of three symbols: (1) a broken heart, to depict emotional hurt (e.g., doing or saying mean things, hurt feelings); (2) a megaphone, to depict verbal aggression (e.g., shouting, threatening, swearing); and (3) a jagged arrow, to depict physical aggression (e.g., slapping, hitting or anything worse). The direction of the symbols indicates who the perpetrator is (i.e., adult male or female) and who the victim is (i.e., adult male or female or child). As a result, half of the 12 representations assess experience of direct victimization (i.e., emotional, verbal, or physical victimization from adult male to child or adult female to child), while the other six representations assess exposure to IPV (i.e., exposure to emotional, verbal, or physical IPV from adult male to adult female or from adult female to adult male).

Use and target audience. High-risk youth. Validity testing sample participants aged 16–24.

Multicultural. The FAST is available only in English.

Ease and time of administration. This simple, self-reporting pictorial tool can be administered in under five minutes.

Scoring procedure. The FAST consists of 12 pictorial representations. On seeing each representation, participants are asked three consecutive yes/no questions: (1) Did this ever happen? (2) Has it ended? And (3) How often did it happen? Scoring is based on a Likert scale: 0 = never, 5 = sometimes, and 10 = a lot. If participants answered "no" to the first question, they are automatically directed to the next representation. For victimization items, child (FAST subscale 1, 2, and 3), scores indicating aggression from adult male to the child and from adult female to the child were summed together to form three subscales (emotional, verbal, and physical victimization; range = 0–20). For the IPV exposure items (FAST subscale 4, 5, and 6), scores indicating aggression from adult male to adult female and from adult female to adult male were summed to form the other three subscales (exposure to emotional, verbal, and physical IPV; range = 0–20). Additionally, the six subscales were summed to create a FAST total score, to provide an indicator of overall caregiver aggression (range = 0–120). Scoring can be completed in five minutes.

Reliability. Internal Consistency: Internal consistency of the FAST was good ($\alpha = .82$).

Validity. Convergent and Discriminant Validity: The FAST total score was strongly correlated with the Childhood Trauma Questionnaire (CTQ) total score ($r = .70$). Zero-order bivariate Pearson correlations across the subscales ranged from low to strong ($r = .17–.64$), with the strongest correlations found between corresponding subscales.

Construct Validity: The FAST total score was moderately associated with both self-report ($r = .36$) and other-report ($r = .37$) total psychiatric symptomatology, supporting the construct validity of the FAST.

Availability and source. Freely available at Cecil et al. (2016). Initial validation of a brief pictorial measure of caregiver aggression: The Family Aggression Screening Tool (FAST) is available online using Psytools software (Delosis Limited).

Comment. The use of pictorial representations may also provide a means for clinicians to initiate a dialogue regarding the young person's history of exposure in a way that is potentially less invasive than verbal screening tools. As it is designed to minimize verbal demands, the FAST may also prove useful in facilitating assessment in hard-to-screen populations (e.g., youth with poor literacy, non-native English speakers, younger respondents)—although this has yet to be tested empirically. Constructed from a small sample size.

Parental Stress and Coping Inventory (PSCI)

Instrument name. The Parental Stress and Coping Inventory (PSCI) (Daire et al., 2017) was developed to measure stress and coping in low-income and low-resource parents.

Type of instrument. The PSCI was modified from the 30-item Family Adjustment Measure (FAM; Daire et al., 2017) by removing all terminology related to children with special needs so that the measure would be applicable for parents with typically developing children. Diare, Gonzalez, and O'Hare acknowledge that although family assessments exist to evaluate family adjustment, including FACES IV (Olson, 2011), Family Assessment Measure, and the Family Assessment Measure-III, cost, administration time, and user qualification level may preclude the use of many assessments in a public health setting (2017). More so, these and similar assessments were not developed or normed on a diverse population of low-income and low-resource individuals. As a response to the need, the PSCI was developed. It is an 18-item measure with three subscales: parental distress, social support, and family-based support self-reporting inventory using a Likert scale.

Use and target audience. The PSCI can be completed by low-income and low-resource parents who are 18 and older. Can be used in clinical practice for treatment conceptualizing and progress.

Multicultural. The PSCI is offered only in English.

Ease and time of administration. The Family member completion requires approximately 15 minutes. Administration of the measure is fast, and instructions are self-explanatory.

Scoring procedure. The 18 PSCI items are organized on a five-point Likert-type scale: 1 = never, 2 = rarely, 3 = sometimes, 4 = frequently, and 5 = almost always, marking the degree to which the participant connects with each item. The sum of each item for the particular subscale is calculated to determine level of coping: Parental Distress—Items 1, 5, 7, 9, 12, 16, and 18; Social Support—Items 3, 4, 6, 10, 14, 15, and 17; Family-Based Support—Items 2,

8, 11, and 13. Higher scores in either family-based support or social support do help clients and clinicians to identify areas of strengths that can be harnessed to assist in the lower scored area. Additionally, the lower scores family-based or social support does provide insight into areas of intervention and development.

Reliability. Internal Consistency: The alpha reliability for the Parental Distress, Social Support, and Family-Based Support subscales were .81, .84, and .69, respectively.

Validity. Concurrent Validity: The RAS correlated with the Parental Distress ($r = -.32$), Social Support ($r = .17$), and Family-Based Support ($r = .73$) scale.

Availability and source. The PSCI can be retrieved from Daire, Gonzalez, and O'Hare (2017). Parental Stress and Coping Inventory [Database record]. Retrieved from PsycTESTS. doi: http://dx.doi.org/10.1037/t66575-000. Although there is no fee for use, permission is necessary from the publisher.

Comment. The PSCI is found to be a beneficial tool to briefly and effectively evaluate family adjustment both as a screening tool and a tool to guide clinical interventions. The PSCI could be given periodically throughout treatment to determine progress in decreasing distress and increasing areas of support. Future research can further validate the PSCI, particularly with more heterogeneous samples. Authors indicate a lack of cutoff scores for the three scales in the PSCI.

Child Adjustment and Parent Efficacy Scale (CAPES)

Instrument name. The CAPES was developed by Morawska, Sanders, Haslam, Filus, and Fletcher in 2014.

Type of instrument. The CAPES is a 30-item measure paper-and-pencil parent reporting instrument of child behavioral and emotional adjustment and parental efficacy. The 30 items are rated using a scale with the following response options: 0 = "not true of my child at all," 1 = "true of my child a little, or some of the time," 2 = "true of my child quite a lot, or a good part of the time," and 3 = "true of my child very much, or most of the time." Twenty of the 30 items are also rated using a scale ranging from 1 = "certain I cannot do it" and 10 = "certain I can do it."

Use and target audience. This paper-and-pencil instrument can be completed by parents of children 2–12 years old. Parent age groups: adulthood (18 yrs. & older), young adulthood (18–29 yrs.), thirties (30–39 yrs.), and middle age (40–64 yrs.)

Multicultural. The instrument is available in English, Spanish (Mejia, Filus, Calam, Morawska, & Sanders, 2016), and Chinese (Guo, Morawska, & Filus, 2017).

Ease and time of administration. Family member completion requires approximately 15 minutes. Administration of the measure is fast, and instructions are self-explanatory.

Scoring procedure. CAPES is a 30-item measure of child behavioral and emotional adjustment and parental efficacy. Twenty of the items are two-part questions that assess both child characteristics and parent self-efficacy. The instrument consists of an Intensity scale (30 items) with two subscales. The Behavior subscale (26 items) measures child behavioral concerns and competencies, and the Emotional Maladjustment subscale (four items) measures child emotional adjustment. The instrument also contains a Self-Efficacy scale (20 items) that measures a parent's confidence in managing specific child problem behaviors. Some items are reverse scored. Items are summed to yield a total intensity score (CAPES intensity scale: range of 0–90), which is made up of a behavior score (range of 0–78) and an emotional maladjustment score (0–12) where high scores indicate higher levels of problems. The self-efficacy scale consists of 20 items and measures parents' level of self-efficacy in managing child emotional and behavioral problems. Items are rated on a ten-point scale, ranging from certain "I cannot do it" (1) to "certain I can do it" (10). A total efficacy score with a possible range of 20–200 is calculated by summing all efficacy items, with higher scores indicating a greater level of self-efficacy.

For the CAPES intensity, behavior subscale:

parcel 1: items 24, 1; parcel 2: items 2, 16; parcel 3: items 4, 14; parcel 4: items 5, 7; parcel 5: items 12, 28; parcel 6: items 9, 18; parcel 7: items 21, 13; parcel 8: items 15, 17; parcel 9: items 25, 26; parcel 10: items 22, 29; parcel 11: items 8, 20; parcel 12: items 6, 10; and parcel 13: items 23, 30. For the CAPES confidence: parcel 1: items 1 and 2; parcel 2: items 3 and 4; parcel 3: items 5 and 6; parcel 4: items 7 and 8; parcel 5: items 9 and 10; parcel 6: items 11 and 12; parcel 7: items 12 and 16; parcel 8: items 13 and 14; parcel 9: items 17 and 18; and parcel 10: items 19 and 20.

Reliability. For CAPES intensity, Cronbach's alphas were .90 (total scale score), .90 (behavior), and .74 (emotional maladjustment). The Cronbach's alpha for CAPES self-efficacy was .96. Thus, Cronbach's alphas were above the recommended cut-off value of .70 for good internal consistency of the measure.

Validity. Convergent Validity: The Intensity scale and the Self-Efficacy scale showed reasonable convergent validity as measured by average variance extracted estimates, the composite reliability estimates, and examination of factor loadings. Discriminant Validity: Intensity scale and the Self-Efficacy scale demonstrated discriminant validity.

Availability and source. Available in Morawska, Alina; Sanders, Matthew R; Haslam, Divna; Filus, Ania; Fletcher, Renee. Child Adjustment and Parent Efficacy Scale: Development and initial validation of a parent report measure. Australian Psychologist, Vol. 49(4), Aug 2014, 241–252. Appendix A, Page 251.

Comment. The validation also needs to be extended to more diverse samples in terms of sex, age, and ethnicity. Further, there is a need for evaluation of the validity of CAPES by investigating patterns of relationships between CAPES and other measures assessing similar and different constructs. Its strength lies in its brevity and assessment of both child behavior and parenting efficacy in a single measure, which has significant benefits in assessment in a clinical setting where a psychologist may need to assess a variety of areas to formulate and to offer a tailored intervention effectively.

Self-Report Assessments for Family Members Under Age 10

Self-report family assessment instruments provide family members a way to communicate how the family system is working for them when they may not be able to conceptualize and verbally communicate that information directly and quickly to the family therapist. Developing reliable and valid instruments is quite a challenge, as indicated from the development of the preceding instruments. However, those described instruments are designed for children approximately aged 10 and above. How does a therapist hear the voice of the child younger than age 10? The younger the child is, the more the child functions on an intuitive metaphorical level. Consequently, instruments for children must be based on their communication styles.

Systematic Assessment of Family Environment (SAFE) Cartoons

Instrument name. The SAFE Cartoons instrument was adapted from the SAFE, described earlier.

Type of instrument. This single-page set of four cartoons is flexibly used with verbal instructions to children.

Variables measured. The assessment tool uses four cartoon drawings of family interactions involving parents and children but omitting grandparents: (a) father, mother, brother, and sister all holding hands and smiling with the children connected between the parents; (b) father and mother fighting with brother and sister watching helplessly; (c) mother, father, sister, and brother smiling (sister and brother are much larger in size than mother and father); and (d) mother and father watching helplessly as brother and sister fight while standing in front of the parents. These four pictures equate to the competent, discordant, disoriented, and chaotic quadrants in the scoring grid of the SAFE instrument.

Use and target audience. The SAFE Cartoons were developed for use with children aged 10 and under to elicit communication about stressors in family functioning that are affecting the child.

Multicultural. The cartoons used are generic as to skin color, although specific racial characteristics have not been developed to relate to various cultures. Conversation with the child can be adjusted to account for cultural factors.

Ease and time of administration. This can be less than five minutes or expanded to the extent to which the child will continue to describe family functioning.

Scoring procedure. Children are handed a copy of the cartoon page and asked to tell the therapist which picture reminds them most of their family and why. If only one cartoon is selected, the therapist may ask if the family ever looks like any other of the cartoons and, if so, when. Comments from the child are recorded on the sheet by the therapist for the case file.

Reliability. This is not available.

Validity. This is not available.

Availability and source. The cartoon drawings are available in the *GARF Assessment Sourcebook* (Yingling et al., 1998) and www.SystemsMediation.com.

Comment. This tool has proven valuable in eliciting information about family functioning. Children will often comment that children are or are not bigger than the parents in this family (disoriented family). They will also talk about the parents fighting and how helpless they feel (discordant family). Insisting that the family is always the competent cartoon is a clue that something may be hidden in this family, resulting in the children feeling unsafe to be truthful.

Global Assessment of Relational Functioning Self-Report for Families

Instrument name. The GARF Self-Report for Families was developed by Dr. Alice McDonald.

Type of instrument. Selection of the most representative fairy tale provides a "quantitative" global rating similar to that of the GARF. However, the instrument is used primarily to elicit discussion about stressors and strengths in the family from the child's perspective.

Variables measured. Five brief descriptions of somewhat modified but familiar fairy tales are printed: (a) The Three Bears, (b) Little Red Riding Hood, (c) Cinderella, (d) Hansel and Gretel, and (e) The Ugly Duckling. Descriptions are written to parallel the descriptors of the five levels of the GARF.

Use and target audience. Children ages 8–12 make up the targeted group, depending on reading level.

Multicultural. The fairy tales used are rather universal, although the language available at this time is limited to English.

Ease and time of administration. Depending on the reading level, the child will likely take 10–15 minutes to read through the fairy tales. Discussion time with the therapist varies.

Scoring procedure. Directions are for children to read through each story and decide which fairy tale is most like the family they live in right now; the selected story equates to one of the five quintiles in the GARF. If children are too young to read, the story can be read to them. To gain more specific information from older children who read well, the therapist can ask children to underline any descriptors in any of the five stories that remind them of their family.

Reliability. This is not available.

Validity. This is not available.

Availability and source. The instrument is available in the *GARF Assessment Sourcebook* (Yingling et al., 1998) and at www.SystemsMediation.com.

Comment. The underlined characteristics provide a great opportunity to discuss with the therapist their family problems on a metaphorical fairy tale level which feels safer for the child.

Behavior Assessment System for Children, Third Edition, PRQ Child/Adolescent (BASC-3 PRQ)

Instrument name. The BASC-3 PRQ was published in 2015 by Cecil R. Reynolds and Randy W. Kamphaus to improve both psychometric properties of the scales and comprehensiveness of the construct associated with each scale. Items on the original version were developed based on a review of the literature and refined through several iterations of data collection. Some items from the original version were subsequently eliminated based on user feedback (Reynolds, Kamphaus, & Vannest, 2015).

Type of instrument. The BASC-3 PRQ is a norm-based, self-report measure designed to assess parent or caregiver perceptions of the parent–child relationship in several important areas. These areas include various indicators of the quality of the parenting relationship along with satisfaction with a school's efforts to meet a child's educational and emotional needs.

Use and target audience. The BASC-3 PRQ is designed for use with parents or caregivers of children ages 2 through 18 years. There are two versions of the test. The preschool version, the BASC-3 PRQ-P, is for use with parents or caregivers of children ages 2 through 5 and consists of 60 items. The child/adolescent version, the BASC-3 PRQ-CA, is for use with parents or caregivers of children and adolescents ages 6 through 18 and consists of 87 items. The test is designed for use in a variety of settings including clinical, pediatric, counseling, and school. Individuals must have a Level B qualification to purchase and use this product.

Multicultural. Available in English and Spanish. Experts in the field reviewed all items on the BASC-3 PRQ for potential gender or race bias.

Ease and time of administration. The test takes approximately 10–15 minutes to complete by paper and pencil or by computer.

Scoring procedure. The scoring software is available to make the computation and interpretation of scores much quicker. The computer-scored version generates an additional parent feedback report, and use of computer software also allows for comparison of mother and father ratings as well as for tracking progress over time with multiple administrations of the test. A sample Interpretive Summary Report is included. Hand scoring can be completed within 5–10 minutes in addition to administration time. Hand scoring is straightforward. Scores on each scale are converted to T scores and percentile ranks. A score classification system is provided for ease of interpretation and communication of test results to parents and caregivers.

Reliability. The BASC-3 PRQ shows strong reliability for a test of this nature. Alpha coefficients are provided for each norm group and range from .76 to .96. Internal reliability is generally in the high .80 and .90 range for all scales, with the exception of Discipline Practices. Test–retest reliability coefficients (corrected for restriction of range) for BASC-3 PRQ-P scales range from .73 for the Attachment scale to .89 for the Relational Frustration scale. For the BASC-3 PRQ-CA, corrected test–retest reliability coefficients range from .70 for Discipline Practices to .88 for Satisfaction with School. Separate test–retest reliability estimates are not provided for each age band on the BASC-3 PRQ-CA.

Validity. The test manual provides extensive evidence of validity for the BASC-3 PRQ. Correlations between scores on the BASC-3 PRQ and scores on the original version are consistently high for all scales, indicating continuity across versions of the test. The test manual also shows correlations of the BASC-3 PRQ with the Parenting Stress Index and the BASC-3 Self Report of Personality, with data overall supporting the validity of the BASC-3 PRQ. Of all scales, Discipline Practices generally demonstrated the lowest correlations, suggesting additional validation may be useful for this scale.

Availability and source. Available from Pearson Clinical; www.pearsonclinical.com/BASC3; telephone: (800) 627–7271; fax: (800) 232–1223; clinicalcustomersupport@pearson.com.

Comment. The test has the potential for use in a wide variety of settings and yields key information on the parent–child relationship that can potentially contribute to various types of evaluations and treatment planning. The intended use is not to evaluate pathology, rather provide valuable information regarding parent perceptions that may contribute to broader case conceptualization and treatment planning. Although it is offered in Spanish, the teacher forms are not available in Spanish.

Considerations in Utilizing Family Assessment Instruments

Psychotherapy incorporates a broad spectrum of theories from which to choose. Effective family assessment requires a full commitment to family systems theory and, even within this theory, many different viewpoints abound. Because theory is the continuing thread from assessment, hypothesis formulation, and revising intervention planning–implementation, a clear understanding of one's theoretical foundation is critical for good results. Instruments discussed in this chapter are based on family systems theories that generally include assumptions about functional family structure (parental hierarchy, egalitarian marital relationships, and differentiated adult–adult family-of-origin relationships); effective communication (honest and open disclosure, listening and understanding, and effective problem solving); and a general environment of safety and support, which nurtures individual development within the family.

The setting for therapy defines some parameters for family assessment. Operating in a clinic with plenty of waiting room and administrative staff allows for incorporating a wider array of assessment strategies; family members need private space to answer paper-and-pencil questionnaires honestly. Having a therapy team behind the mirror also expands opportunities for using clinical rating scales, perhaps reducing the number of self-report instruments needed. Working in a training facility is a "resort" setting that includes clinic space and administration, therapy teams, live and group supervision, and a research focus. Family assessment is and should be a major component of family therapy training facilities. The budget for operating a facility can limit the use of purchased instruments. However, all instruments discussed in this chapter are available at minimal or no cost except for duplication of materials and purchase of books or manuals to use in interpretation. Creating a computerized record-keeping system with research analysis of family assessment data is a great asset in improving services. However, a solo practitioner can benefit from incorporating at least some of the instruments and strategies discussed in this chapter as part of the intake process.

Confidentiality Complications for Release of Information

When a therapist is working with families involved in the court process, the therapist's clinical files sometimes become the target of subpoena. Without a release of information signed by all adult family members, the therapist must have a court order, statutory authorization, or threat of safety in compliance with state laws to release family information in the file. Protection of children's records is more unclear. Divorced parents have access to therapy records of their children unless prohibited by court order. Therapists can resist release of records, based on threat of harm, but the process is legally complicated. Collaborative work between family therapy and family law professional organizations is needed to clarify and protect family therapy files legally (including family assessment documents) while allowing disclosure when a threat of family (including spousal) violence exists. Greater understanding of Health Insurance Portability and Accountability Act (HIPAA) regulations will help clarify which documents are included in therapy records versus notes and which confidentiality procedures apply.

Strategy for Utilizing Family Self-Report Instruments

Requesting clients to complete assessment instruments without a clear use in therapy or specifically authorized research is unethical. Consequently, assessment instruments must be brief and clinically useful. In a training facility, assessment data are especially useful in supervision to connect the theoretical base in assessment and intervention. In independent practice, assessment data should be utilized in creating treatment plans and should be shared with family members.

A suggested protocol for utilizing family assessment in the course of therapy includes these steps:

1. The family therapist should plan an intake procedure that includes some standardized method of self-report family functioning, such as the SAFE, and an assessment of trauma or family violence, such as the FAST, as well as interview and clinical observation.
2. Clients must first provide the family therapist with a written informed consent before turning in any written family functioning assessments.
3. Assessment continues throughout therapy, with regular documentation of family functioning in the GARF completed by the therapist.
4. Dynamic assessment guides the therapy process by the therapist's using clinical observations, the family genogram, and children's instruments to plan interventions and share data for goal setting with the client family.

Case Example

The following family story illustrates how family assessment tools can guide the process of therapy to a successful improvement in family functioning. This family was referred to the author's office to help resolve parental access conflicts blocking the finalization of divorce, which had been ongoing for two years; this was the second time the parents had separated and filed for divorce. The mother was now requesting supervised access for the father to the seven-year-old son, with accusations of family violence. This was investigated and found to be unfounded during the second divorce filing; the father had no attorney on the first filing charges, and the mother obtained a protective order against him. She had set him up to violate the order and then charged him with violation, resulting in his being on probation.

During the first attempt at divorce, a social study had been conducted that recommended joint managing conservatorship (custody), with the father establishing primary residence because of the mother's history of psychological disturbance. The mother had revealed to the father that she was molested by her father but had never been in therapy to resolve the trauma. She was completing her Master's degree in counseling when ordered into the program. The father admitted that he had historically had a problem with alcohol and was currently living with his parents because of financial difficulties resulting from the alcohol problems. The social study on the second divorce filing was almost finished when they came into therapy.

Family Assessment Process

The SAFE and the CATS (see Chapter 11) were completed (Step 1) just prior to the first therapy session with the family. The parents signed the consent forms (Step 2). During the first session, the SAFE cartoons (Step 4) were discussed with the son in a private interview. The genogram (Step 4) was used during the first session with all three family members present. In addition to structural information, family-of-origin rules about divorce and conflict management were identified on the genogram. The son added his own family drawings on the bottom of the easel page, including parents, grandparents, and two of his mother's children from a prior marriage who did not have primary residence with her. At the conclusion of the session, the therapist assigned the GARF score on the GARF Profile Chart (Step 4). Observational data were revealed during the session and by outside faxes.

Assessment Results and Utility

Because of the history of domestic violence charges, screening for family violence was the first goal of assessment (Step 1). The CATS (see Chapter 11) scores from the caregivers showed consistent reporting from both parents. Interview revealed significant physical conflict had occurred during their living together, with each accusing the other of being the primary perpetrator; however, the physical assaults had stopped since the separation two years ago. CATS (see Chapter 11) scores on the child self-report and caregivers were all in the mild/moderate range. The SAFE final item under the marital relationship assessment provided more confidence in safety (Step 4). The father reported extreme control and submission in the relationship, but the mother reported a neutral response. If the accused abuser had reported "both work together equally" and the supposed victim had reported "one

(Continued)

controls and the other submits," the therapist would have been more inclined to investigate safety further.

Surprisingly, the mother scored the marital relationship midrange on all items of the semantic differential. The father scored the marital relationship on the low side, with one exception to the lowest score. Both scored the relationship between themselves and the son as somewhat positive but not perfect, although the mother indicated more power struggles than did the father. The father scored his relationship with his own parents as generally good; the mother scored her relationship with her parents as generally bad. It appeared that the mother perceived the relationship with the father as better than the relationship with her parents, despite how bad the marriage was. The son's first response to the SAFE cartoon was to select the competent family as his family. Later he reported that his parents did sometimes fight like the discordant family.

The genogram (Step 4) revealed that the mother had a prior marriage in which two children had chosen to live with their father and see her infrequently. Although molestation was not revealed in the joint session, the mother indicated that conflict was handled by her mother submitting to her father's controlling behavior. The father's family-of-origin family resolved conflicts by talking things through, although his father traveled extensively; his mother, the primary caretaker, did not work outside the home.

Clinical observation (Step 4) was very revealing in this family. The mother had said that she could not be in the same room with the father, but attorneys did not back that up. She seemed quite comfortable in the same room but insisted that she leave the office first and be given at least five minutes before the father left. This action appeared to be more of an attempt to convince the therapist of safety fears than actual fears for safety. Outside the sessions, the mother repeatedly faxed accusations of the father physically abusing the son and her calling Child Protective Services (i.e., the son had a bruise on his knee after spending the weekend with his father, or the son said he bumped the end of the bed when getting up to go to the bathroom, assuring his mother that his father was neglectful). The son's reaction with both parents in the room was obvious anxiety and no talking at all. After his private interview with the therapist, he was able to share openly with his parents that he needed for them to stop fighting, be best friends, give him sweet dreams, and not let him watch scary movies.

At the conclusion of each of the six sessions with this family, the therapist recorded the GARF scores (Step 4). Scores progressed as follows:

- Interactional changed from 20 at the first session and 25 at the third session a month later to 30 at the final session six weeks later.
- Organizational changed from 30 at the first session and 35 at the third session to 40 at the final session.
- Emotional Climate changed from 10 at the first session and 30 at the third session to 35 at the final session.
- The son's openness with the parents seemed to have a big impact on them. Although many contaminations kept the functioning level low, the emotional climate did seem to level out with the organization and interaction functioning.

Outcome for the Family

Although family functioning remained low, the parents were able to reach significant agreements in the later sessions, which relieved some of mother's anxiety regarding an abusive father. Guidelines for ensuring no drinking or illegal drugs when either parent was with the child were agreed to. Parenting guidelines regarding bedtime, parental exchange, and mutual support of the son's activities helped structure this family for more effective divorced co-parenting. Parents worked out a plan for the father to take possession of his personal property, which had been stored in the mother's house for two years and had possibly been stolen during a burglary. This concrete action seemed to free them up to move forward with the divorce. Further litigation was avoided, and both parents believed that their son could have "sweet dreams."

Concluding Comments

There is no question that formal measures of parent–child relationships have come into their own. What is particularly gratifying is that now there are a number of new instruments that address the issues pointed out in the beginning of this chapter: underserved groups, underrepresented groups, family adjustment, parental distress, and trauma and posttraumatic stress in children. These instruments not only improve the quality and accuracy of assessment, but also they are likely to improve therapeutic outcomes. Perhaps the real therapeutic benefit of using such instruments is in reframing parent–child relationships from linear to systemic thinking before therapy begins. **Table 9.1** summarizes the key features of the instruments reviewed in this chapter.

Table 9.1 Matrix: Parent-Child Assessment Strategies and Inventories

Assessment instrument	Specific couple and family applications	Cultural/ language	Instructions/use: T = time to take; S = time to score; I = items	Computerized: a = scoring; b = report	Reliability (R)/ validity (V)	Availability
SAFE	All family members ages ten and up; provides four typologies of systemic functioning: Competent, Discordant, Disoriented, Chaotic	English; Spanish	T = 5 minutes; S = 5 minutes or less; I = 21	NA	R = NA; V = .74 and .82	Yingling et al. (1998), GARF Assessment Sourcebook; www. SystemsMediation.com
GARF Self-Assessment for Families	All family members ages ten and up; provides scores in three variables: Organizational Structure, Interactional Processes, and Emotional Climate	English	T = 5 minutes; S = 5 minutes; I = 16	NA	R = NA; V = NA	www.SystemsMediation. com

FACES-III	All family members aged 12 and up; provides scores in two variables: Cohesion and Adaptability	English	T = 5 minutes; S = 5 minutes or less; I = 20	NA	R = α = .84 and .79; .83 and .93 test–retest; V = questioned	University of Minnesota, Family Social Science, 290 McNeal Hall, 1985 Buford Ave, St. Paul, MN, 55108, (612) 625–7250 or www.lifeinnovations.com
Beavers SFI	All family members aged 11 and up; provides scores in two variables: Health/Competence and Style	English	T = 10–15 minutes; S = 10–15 minutes; I = 36	NA	R = α = .84 and .93; .85 test–retest; V = .62	Family Studies Center, 6517 Hillcrest, STE 401, Dallas, TX, 75205 or www.familystudiescenter.org
McMaster FAD	All family members aged 12 and up; provides scores in seven variables: General Functioning, Problem-Solving, Communication, Roles, Affective Responsiveness, Affective Involvement, and Behavior Control	English; 15 other languages; others in process	T = 15–20 minutes; S = 15 minutes; I = 60	a = scoring available; b = printout of scores with subscales	R = α = .57–70 V = NA	Dr. Christine Ryan, Potter 3, Rhode Island Hospital, 593 Eddy St., Providence, RI, 02903; manual currently in publication process with Brunner-Routledge

(Continued)

Assessment instrument	Specific couple and family applications	Cultural/ language	Instructions/use: T = time to take; S = time to score; I = items	Computerized: a = scoring; b = report	Reliability (R)/ validity (V)	Availability
GARF Self-Report for Families	Children ages 8–12; if adequate reading level, provides a global rating in one of five functioning quintiles	English	T = 10–15 minutes; S = NA; I = 5	NA	NA	Yingling et al. (1998), GARF Assessment Sourcebook; www. SystemsMediation.com
SAFE Cartoons	Children ages 10 and under; provides a global rating in one of four typologies	Administer in any language	T = 5 minutes or less; S = NA; I = 4	NA	NA	Yingling et al. (1998), GARF Assessment Sourcebook; www. SystemsMediation.com
Family Genogram	All members; structural and interactional data	Administer in any language	T = 10–30 minutes; S = NA; I = NA	NA	NA	McGoldrick & Gerson (1985), Genograms in Family Assessment; DeMaria, Weeks, & Hof (1999), Focused Genograms
Kinetic Family Drawing (KFD)	Self-report/children; also adolescents and parents; to assess family relationships and interaction	Administer in any language	T = 20 minutes; S = variable time to score/interpret; I = NA	NA	R = .87–.95 interscorer agreement; V = not reported	Journal article; Western Psychological Services

PSCI	Low-income and low-resource parents or caregivers (18 yrs. & older)	English	T = 15 minutes. S = 15 minutes. I = 30	a = no a = no	R = Parental Distress (α = .81) Social Support (α = .84) Family-Based Support scales (α = .69) V = Strong validation criteria for Family-Based Support (r = .73) scale	Journal article
CAPES	Parents or caregivers (18 yrs. & older) of children ages 2–12	English, Spanish, and Chinese	T = 15 minutes. S = 15 minutes. I = 30	a = no b = no	R = n/a CAPES intensity: total α = .90; behavior α = .90; and emotional maladjustment α = .74 CAPES self-efficacy α = .96. V = reasonable convergent validity	Journal article

(Continued)

Assessment instrument	Specific couple and family applications	Cultural/ language	Instructions/use: T = time to take; S = time to score; I = items	Computerized: a = scoring; b = report	Reliability (R)/ validity (V)	Availability
Behavior Assessment System for Children, Third Edition, Parenting Relationship Questionnaire (BASC-3 PRQ	Parents or caregivers of children ages 2–18	English and Spanish	T = 10–15 minutes. S = hand score 5–10 minutes. Computer score immediate BASC-3 PRQP (ages 2–5) I = 60 BASC-3 PRQ-CA (ages 6–18) I = 87	a = yes b = yes	R = n/a A = .80–.90 Test-retest = α = .73–.89 V = consistently high for all scales	Available for purchase: www.pearsonclinical. com/BASC3; telephone: (800) 627–7271; clinicalcustomersupport@ pearson.com
FAST	High risk youth	English	T = 5 minutes. S = 5 minutes. I = 12	a = no b = no (pictures on computer using Psytools software)	R = α = .82 V = strong criterion (r = .70) -Moderately associated with self-report and other- report psych. symptomology	Journal article

Note: NA = not available.

References

American Psychiatric Association. (1994). *Diagnostic and statistical manual of mental disorders* (4th ed.). Washington, DC: Author.

Beavers, W. R., & Hampson, R. B. (1990). *Successful families: Assessment and intervention.* New York, NY: Norton.

Bray, J. H., Williamson, D. S., & Malone, P. E. (1984). Personal authority in the family system: Development of a questionnaire to measure personal authority in intergenerational family processes. *Journal of Marital and Family Therapy, 10*(2), 167–178.

Cecil, C. A. M., McCrory, E. J., Viding, E., Holden, G. W., & Barker, E. D. (2016). Initial validation of a brief pictorial measure of caregiver aggression: The Family Aggression Screening Tool (FAST). *Assessment, 23*(3), 307–320.

Cohen, A., Bulik, C. M., & Walter, H. (2010). Practice parameter for the assessment and treatment of children and adolescents with posttraumatic stress disorder. *Journal of the American Academy of Child & Adolescent Psychiatry, 49*, 414–430.

Daire, A. P., Gonzalez, J. E., & O'Hare, V. N. (2017). Parental stress and coping inventory. *Measurement and Evaluation in Counseling and Development, 50*(1–2), 18–26.

Dausch, B. M., Miklowitz, D. J., & Richards, J. A. (1996). Global assessment of relational functioning scale: II. Reliability and validity in a sample of families of bipolar patients. *Family Process, 35*, 175–189.

Denton, W. H., Nakonezny, P. A., & Burwell, S. R. (2010). Reliability and validity of the Global Assessment of Relational Functioning (GARF) in a psychiatric family therapy clinic. *Journal of Marital and Family Therapy, 36*(3), 376–387.

Epstein, N. B., Baldwin, L. M., & Bishop, D. S. (1983). The McMaster Family Assessment Device. *Journal of Marital and Family Therapy, 9*(2), 171–180.

Epstein, N. B., Bishop, D. S., & Levin, S. (1978). The McMaster Model of Family Functioning. *Journal of Marriage and Family Counseling, 4*, 19–31.

Favez, N. (2010). *L'examen clinique de la famille: Modèles et instruments d'évaluation* [Clinical examination of the family: Models and assessment tools]. Wavre: Editions Mardaga. Retrieved from www.mardaga.be

Franklin, C., Cody, P. A., & Jordan, C. (2003). Validity and reliability in family assessment. In A. Roberts & K. Yeager (Eds.), *Desk reference of evidence-based research in health care and human services.* New York, NY: Oxford University Press.

Gilbert, R., Widom, C. S., Browne, K., Fergusson, D., Webb, E., & Janson, S. (2009). Burden and consequences of child maltreatment in high-income countries. *Lancet, 373*, 68–81.

Group for the Advancement of Psychiatry Committee on the Family. (1996). Global assessment of relational functioning scale (GARF): I. Background and rationale. *Family Process, 35*, 155–172.

Guo, M., Morawska, A., & Filus, A. (2017). Validation of the parenting and family adjustment scales to measure parenting skills and family adjustment in Chinese parents. *Measurement and Evaluation in Counseling and Development, 50*(3), 139–154.

Hampson, R. B., Beavers, W. R., & Hulgus, Y. (1990). Cross-ethnic family differences: Interactional assessment of white, black, and Mexican–American families. *Journal of Marital and Family Therapy, 16*(3), 307–319.

Hampson, R. B., Prince, C. C., & Beavers, W. R. (1999). Marital therapy: Qualities of couples who fare better or worse in treatment. *Journal of Marital and Family Therapy, 254*, 411–424.

Kabacoff, R. I., Miller, I. W., Bishop, D. S., Epstein, N. B., & Keitner, G. I. (1990). A psychometric study of the McMaster Family Assessment Device in psychiatric, medical, and nonclinical samples. *Journal of Family Psychology, 3*, 431–439.

Kaslow, F. W. (Ed.). (1996). *Handbook of relational diagnosis and dysfunctional family patterns.* New York, NY: Wiley.

L'Abate, L., & Bagarozzi, D. A. (1993). *Sourcebook of marriage and family evaluation.* New York, NY: Brunner/Mazel.

McGoldrick, M., & Gerson, R. (1985). *Genograms in family assessment.* New York, NY: Norton.

Mejia, A., Filus, A., Calam, R., Morawska, A., & Sanders, M. R. (2016). Validation of the Spanish version of the CAPES: A brief instrument for assessing child psychological difficulties and parental self-efficacy. *International Journal of Behavioral Development, 40*(4), 359–372.

Miller, I. W., Ryan, C. E., Keitner, G. I., Bishop, D. S., & Epstein, N. A. (2000). Commentary: Factor analyses of the family assessment device by Ridenour, Daley, & Reich. *Family Process, 39,* 141–144.

Morawska, A., Sanders, M. R, Haslam, D., Filus, A., & Fletcher, R. (2014). Child adjustment and parent efficacy scale: Development and initial validation of a parent report measure. *Australian Psychologist, 49*(4), 241–25.

Olson, D. H. (2011). FACES IV and the Circumplex model: Validation study. *Journal of Marital and Family Therapy, 3*(1), 64–80.

Olson, D. H., Russell, C. S., & Sprenkle, D. H. (Eds.). (1989). *Circumplex model: Systemic assessment and treatment of families.* New York, NY: Haworth Press.

Reynolds, C. R., Kamphaus, R. W., & Vannest, K. J. (2015). *Behavior assessment system for children Third edition (BASC-3).* Toronto, ON: PscyhCorp.

Ridenour, R. A., Daley, J. G., & Reich, W. (1999). Factor analysis of the family assessment device. *Family Process, 38,* 497–510.

Ridenour, R. A., Daley, J. G., & Reich, W. (2000). Further evidence that the family assessment device should be reorganized: Response to Miller and colleagues. *Family Process, 39,* 375–380.

Ryan, C. D., Epstein, N. B., Keitner, G. I., Miller, I. W., & Bishop, D. S. (2005). *Evaluating and treating families: The McMaster approach.* Philadelphia, PA: Brunner-Routledge.

Scoville, A. F. (1999). *Obesity and family functioning patterns of the marital, nuclear, and extended family systems* (Unpublished doctoral dissertation). Texas A&M University, Commerce, TX.

Walsh, F. (2003). *Normal family processes* (3rd ed.). New York, NY: Guilford.

Wilkins, L. P., & White, M. B. (2001). Interrater reliability and concurrent validity of the Global Assessment of Relational Functioning (GARF) scale using a card sort method: A pilot study. *Family Therapy, 28*(3), 157–170.

Yingling, L. C., Miller, W. E., Jr., McDonald, A. L., & Galewaler, S. T. (1998). *GARFassessment sourcebook: Using the DSM-IV Global Assessment of Relational Functioning.* New York, NY: Brunner-Routledge.

10

CHILD CUSTODY AND DIVORCE ASSESSMENT STRATEGY AND INVENTORIES

Sloane E. Veshinski, Christine Sacco-Bene, and M. Sylvia Fernandez

Today's family courts, focusing on the welfare of minor children, are called to review increasingly complex family divorce and intimate partner separation cases and determine apposite guidelines for custody and child visitation in the best interest of the children. There are countless reasons people opt to separate or divorce. However, the dissolution of the family is not easy for any member who experiences this; and though there are resilient children who come through the process relatively unscathed, other children do not fare as well (Weaver & Schofield, 2015). Research suggests that high levels of parental conflict, domestic violence, parental mental health difficulties, changes in economic resources, and diminished parental competence in child management behaviors increase stress in children as well as internalize and externalize problems in children and adolescents and their adjustment to divorce (Bergman & Rejmer, 2017; Deutsch & Clyman, 2016; Gustavsen, Nayga Jr., & Wu, 2016; Lamela, Figueiredo, Bastos, & Feinberg, 2016). To facilitate reasonable outcomes, in addition to psychologists and social workers, mental health counselors and marriage and family therapists are often asked to assist the courts in making appropriate decisions. Child custody evaluations are necessary when one or both parents are unable or unwilling to work out the issue of custody between themselves or there is a high-conflict divorce. In the US, there is an increase of grandparents raising grandchildren and seeking custody from parents not competent to make suitable decisions about the welfare of their children (Meara, 2014). To this end, mental health professionals conduct assessments of the family, including administration of psychological tests; gather data about parent and child strengths and weaknesses and areas of conflict; and identify family support systems. In making recommendations, the well-being of the child(ren) is the priority. Mental health professionals seek to ensure that the child will be placed in an environment in which he or she is and feels safe, despite the fact that it may be considered different than what is best for the parent or others involved in the custody dispute (Rohrbaugh, 2008).

Today's family courts have the complex task of addressing the ways in which families are now defined and viewed. The varying constellations of families is attributed to a variety of reasons such as changing rates of marriage, choices of delaying marriage and opting for cohabitation, raising children as single parents, changes in States' laws regarding marriage for gay and lesbian couples, and even the current opioid crisis that necessitates grandparents to parent their grandchildren when their own children no longer can. The adult who has primary caregiving responsibility is shifting from biological parent to adoptive parent or grandparents for a variety of reasons in some households, thus changing definitions of parent. Caring for children after divorce or intimate partner separation involves multifaceted considerations, and disputes over how to best care for children are common in family law (McIntosh & Tan, 2017).

This chapter will focus on assessing the post-divorce/separation parental relationship, the child's or children's relationship with each parent, and overall post-divorce/separation family functioning. The outcome of testing and assessment will be to make recommendations for child custody and visitation, as well as to determine the parents' ability to work together in the best interest of the child(ren).

Issues and Challenges of Assessing Child Custody and Divorce

When a couple with a child or children decides to separate and/or divorce, subsequent decisions and arrangements have to be made with regard to custody and visitation, with the ultimate focus on the overall needs and welfare of the children involved (Simmons, 2010). In the event of a need to adjudicate these arrangements, mental health professionals must have requisite knowledge, skills, and training to assess the intrapsychic, interpersonal, and developmental characteristics of the parents and children (Ramage & Barnard, 2005). Multiple issues must be considered while attending to the presenting challenges when administering tests and conducting assessments to facilitate custody and visitation recommendations and decisions.

Evaluation of family members in regard to custody and visitation also requires understanding of family systems and cultural competence. The multiple issues to be considered comprise the family context, family relationships, family culture, and how the individual members identify racially, ethnically, and culturally. The family context includes family demographics (i.e., the current ages of the children involved), socioeconomic status, and living conditions such as each parent's ability to provide for the child(ren). Also, safe and appropriate living arrangements, educational level of parents, and family of origin issues, such as the involvement of grandparents in the child's or children's lives and available family support systems, need to be considered. Identifying family relationships refers to family status (i.e., blended, step, single parent-led, gay/lesbian, or grandparents functioning as parents). Delineating the family culture aids in ascertaining several features: individual members' perceptions of the family, identified parental systems (matriarchal or patriarchal), parental and gender roles, parenting styles (authoritative, authoritarian, permissive), and parenting skills. Systems considerations are necessary, but it is equally important to bear in mind the influence of each family member's racial, ethnic, and cultural background and how these factors are regarded in family courts. Integral to reducing bias and injustices in custody and visitation evaluations is the acknowledgment of racial, ethnic, and cultural difference (Maldonado, 2017).

Presenting challenges to testing and assessment may include:

- presence of domestic violence (physical, emotional, sexual, or economic) and who the perpetrator(s) and victim(s) might be,
- presence and type of substance abuse("recreational," daily, binge, or in recovery) and the type of substance abused (alcohol or other Central Nervous System depressants, stimulants, hallucinogens, or designer drugs),
- presence of any active court actions (restraining orders, dependency actions, or misdemeanor/felony charges),
- motivational issues (who is requesting the testing/assessment or the effects of assessment outcome on the family constellation) and the win-lose mentality toward the assessment process, and
- Parental Alienation Syndrome (PAS), estrangement, or other diagnosed pathologies of parents and/or child(ren).

Professional codes of ethics in mental health professions (e.g., AAMFT, ACA, NASW, and APA) address standards in providing testimony specifically related to custody of minor children; how to mitigate potentially conflicting roles; and how to take appropriate action to minimize conflicts of interest. The American Psychological Association (APA) published *Guidelines for Child Custody Evaluations in Family Law Proceedings* (1994, 2010) to exclusively focus on how psychologists must conduct evaluations in custody court cases. Many states' jurisdictions have since developed assessment guidelines for family court cases dealing with custody and visitation based on the APA's professional guidelines (Simmons, 2010). Additionally, professionals administering the psychological tests must also adhere to the guidelines for the test and must have the requisite training and skills to administer the test and interpret the results. It is incumbent upon the assessor/evaluator to practice ethically. If an assessment is required of a family in which physical, emotional, or sexual abuse may be present, compounded by substance abuse or mental illness, a general clinician is well advised to refer the family to someone who specializes in this area for this assessment. Finally, "social scientists and family court professionals whose work involves child custody issues should be on the alert for woozles by becoming familiar with the various woozling techniques [misusing or abusing of data] that too often lead us astray" (Nielsen, 2015, p. 626).

Instruments

The following review includes long-established instruments and new instruments that show promise in custody and visitation disputes in divorce and intimate partner separation court cases. The following assessment instruments are best used in combination with other sources of data and not as stand-alone instruments due to the limitations of what each is designed to measure. Multiple qualitative and quantitative data sources (i.e., observations, home visits, clinical interviews, review of documentation, and psychological testing) provide the best information to make appropriate recommendations. Therefore, mental health professionals conducting assessments in these cases must do so according to guidelines, regulations, and codes of ethics as set by state regulatory boards and professional codes of ethics (Rohrbaugh, 2008).

A Comprehensive Custody Evaluation Standard System (ACCESS)

Instrument name. ACCESS developed by Barry Bricklin and Gail Elliot was published in 2002.

Type of instrument. ACCESS, a sequenced evaluation system to assist family courts determine primary custodial parent, consists of questionnaires, structured interviews, an observation system, and standardized tests. Two basic measurements used by ACCESS are the Bricklin Perceptual Scales (BPS), published in 1990 as a projective test designed to assess children's perceptions or emotional comprehension on 32 activities related to parenting capacity in situations categorized as Competency, Supportiveness, Follow-up consistency, and Admirable character traits (Kramer & Conoley, 1992), and the Perception-of-Relationships Test (PORT), a seven-item projective test focused on drawings of self and family (Bricklin, 1990). Before making a final judgment and a custody plan, it is recommended that a Critical Target form be completed. This form is a subjective summary of 40 prescribed sources of information, which also provides data for the development of a custody plan. The Custody Evaluation Kit provides three parent self-reports, three structured child interviews, and five structured interviews to be used with teachers, physicians, mental health professionals, and any other interactions. The Family Interaction Observation system is used to determine parenting through using games and puzzles (Robert, 2001). While the BPS is designed for children six years and older, the PORT can be used with children three years and older to assess the child's perception of the nature of his/her relationship with his/her parents. The PORT allows for maximization of these relationships.

Multicultural. Not reported.

Ease and time of administration. The ACCESS is fairly complex and time consuming due to the use of multiple other instruments and a recommendation for cross-validation with additional measures. The BPS is administered verbally to children where the child rates each parent on 32 parenting functions in category specific situations. It takes about 40 minutes to complete. The PORT is administered individually and is well standardized and objectively scored and takes about 30 minutes to complete the projective test.

Scoring procedure. This is dependent on the combination of tests that are used. The BPS responses can be verbal and the nonverbal. In response to a question, the child is required to punch through a card through a line that reveals each parent's score on the four categories. Meanwhile, for the PORT, a Parent of Choice is determined from each drawing and the parent with the highest number of preferences is the identified Parent of Choice of the child. Scoring is subjective.

Reliability. Reliability has not been addressed adequately (Carlson, 1995).

Validity. Validity data are reported in terms of percentages of agreement between the BPS and an unpublished test that utilizes children's drawings (83%), children's and parent's questionnaires (70%), judgments based on clinical and historical information, and courtroom decisions on custody (94%) (Hagin, 1992). In addition, PORT data are also reported in terms of percent agreement ranging from 83% to 95% across six samples, comparing the PORT with other measures for determining Parent of Choice (e.g., judicial custody outcomes, BPS, and professional mental health assessments) (Roberts, 2001).

Availability and source. This system is available from Village Publishing.

Comment—using with families. This is a broad system for conducting child custody evaluations. It offers the evaluator a range of instruments that may be used in a variety of combinations. While the system is not psychometrically sound, it is a valuable tool for assessment (Roberts, 2001). Fundamental to the PORT is the conceptual measure significance of parental behaviors to the child and the impact these factors have on the child. Custody arrangements can then be made that provides the maximum benefits of these relationships (Bricklin & Elliot, 2009).

Ackerman-Schoendorf Scales for Parent Evaluation of Custody (ASPECT)

Instrument name. The ASPECT developed by Marc Ackerman and Kathleen Schoendorf was published in 1992.

Type of instrument. ASPECT is a self-report questionnaire used to evaluate parents' fitness for custody by quantifying characteristics pertinent to effective custodial parenting for the purpose of making custody recommendations (Ackerman, 2005). The ASPECT includes a Parent Questionnaire and unstructured interview to determine a Parental Custody Index (PCI). The assessor, using the ASPECT system, is required to make use of multiple methods of data gathering in order to answer 56 yes-or-no questions, based on information gathered (i.e., the ASPECT Parent Questionnaire, parent interview—with and without the child, and any test data obtained from other tests). The Questionnaire assesses the parent's psychological and family history; motivations for seeking custody; identification of strengths and weaknesses as a parent of self and the other parent; each parent's ideal custody and visitation arrangements; child-rearing philosophy, caregiving practices, and discipline techniques of each parent; current and future childcare arrangements; and sources of regular social contact available to the child. The unstructured interview provides observational data on parent's appearance, expressions of emotion, and allows for obtaining other information not provided on the questionnaire such as parent's understanding of the effect of divorce on the child, prior arrests or abuse (physical, sexual, or substance), or indicators of psychopathology. An unstructured interview is also conducted with the child (or children) to ascertain the child's feelings about each parent, the evaluation process, and potential outcomes of the custody dispute (Melton, 1995). There is also a 41-item Short Form available that may be administered by any mental health clinician. The ASPECT three scale scores Observational, Social, and Cognitive-Emotional are used to provide the basis for the Parental Custody Index, which is to indicate each parent's overall effectiveness and help guide custody decisions (Valerio & Beck, 2017).

Use–target audience. This instrument is designed for use with parents engaged in a child custody dispute and should be used as part of a battery of tests.

Multicultural. The normative sample is homogeneous and predominately Euro-American.

Ease and time of administration. Each parent is asked to individually complete a Parent Questionnaire and participate in an unstructured individual interview. Administration times vary.

Scoring procedure. The ASPECT-PCI yields three scores: Observational which assesses parent's self-presentation, Social which assesses suitability of the social environment provided by the parent, and Cognitive-Emotional which assesses the parent's cognitive and emotional capability to provide effective parenting.

Reliability. Reported internal consistency reliability is .76 (Cronbach's alpha), and interrater reliability on the PCI is .96. The interrater reliability coefficients on the Observational, Social, and Cognitive-Emotional scales range from .92 to .94.

Validity. Considered content and face valid because questions on the Parent Questionnaire resulted from extensive literature review of custody-related issues in families. A critique offered is the assessment's lack of internal validity. However, the author stresses that it is critical to use more than one instrument for overall validity for custody recommendations (Ackerman, 2005).

Availability and source. ASPECT may be obtained from Western Psychological Services and is available in two forms.

Comment—using with families. The ASPECT is an attempt to both quantify aspects of parental effectiveness and interpret test results. Used in concert with other tests and sources of information (psychological tests, home visits, court records), ASPECT is a clinical tool that provides multidimensional information to determining and making custody recommendations (Melton, 1995). The ASPECT has been criticized regarding the unclear administration and scoring guidelines, lack of normative data, and weak reliability and validity (Valeriao & Beck, 2017). This instrument is not intended for use with non-parent relatives, same-sex couples, cohabitating partners, or grandparents.

Behavior Assessment System for Children, Third Edition (BASC-3)

Instrument name. BASC-3 was developed by Cecil R. Reynolds and Randy W. Kamphaus in 1992, revised in 2004 and again in 2015.

Type of instrument. BASC-3 is a multi-method, multidimensional system designed to assess behaviors observed by others and self-perceptions of individuals aged 2–21. The BASC-3 consists of five subtests intended to gather information about children or adolescents from a variety of sources, such as Teacher Rating Scale (TRS), Parent Rating Scale (PRS), Student Observation System (SOS), Self-Report of Personality (SRP), and Structured Developmental History (SDH). In addition, the BASC-3 Parenting Relationship Questionnaire (BASC-3 PRQ), described below, is used to further assess parent or caregiver perceptions of the parent–child relationship. The TRS, PRS, and SRP have strong psychometric properties. The BASC-3 measures both positive/adaptive behaviors and negative/maladaptive behaviors (Konold, 2017; Medway, 2017).

Use–target audience. Those completing the instrument are asked to read each statement on the questionnaire and mark the response that best describes how the child has acted over the previous six months. This instrument is used to assess individuals between the ages of 2 and 21 for emotional and behavioral disorders and design treatment interventions.

Multicultural. The norming sample represented population of U.S. children and young adults aged 2 through 21 (and college students aged 18 through 25) as detailed in 2013 U.S. Census Bureau American Community Survey. BASC-3 PRS, SRP, and SDH are available in the United States in both English and Spanish.

Ease and time of administration. The BASC-3's five subtests may be used singly or in any combination. The instrument is designed for individual administration and each component takes about 10–30 minutes to complete.

Scoring procedure. The questionnaire has a built-in scoring system: the score is computed by summing up the number of circled items in each row. The total for each scale is found by summing the numbers in each column. The scores are Activities of daily living; Adaptability; Adaptive skills; Aggression; Anger control; Anxiety; Attention problems, Attitude to school; Attitude to teachers; Atypicality; Behavior symptoms index; Behavioral symptoms index; Bullying; Conduct problems; Depression; Developmental social disorders; Ego strength; Emotional self-control; Emotional symptoms index; Executive functioning; Externalizing problems; Functional communication; Hyperactivity; Inattention/hyperactivity attention problems; Inattention/hyperactivity; Internalizing problems; Interpersonal relations; Leadership; Learning problems; Locus of control; Mania; Negative emotionality; Personal adjustment; Relations with parents; Resiliency; School problems; Self-esteem; Self-reliance; Sensation seeking; Sense of inadequacy; Social skills; Social stress; Somatization; Study skills; Test anxiety; and Withdrawal. Computer scoring is also available. Although no specialized training is required for administration, individuals need to have at least a Master's degree to interpret the results of the questionnaire.

Reliability. Internal consistency ranges between .82 and .97. Test–retest reliability ranges from .76 to .93. Interrater reliability ranges from .62 to .82. These range reports are inclusive of all eight versions.

Validity. Correlation coefficients for the general combined norm samples were .80 and above in which BASC-3 scores were compared to BASC-2 scores. In addition, there is evidence of validity through correlations between the BASC-3 and other widely used behavior and autism spectrum rating scales, as well as the BASC-2 (Medway, 2017).

Availability and source. Pearson offers eleven versions of the instruments, each age specific.

Comment—using with families. The BASC-3 provides a multidimensional view of the child or adolescent from multiple informants using multiple methods. This instrument is most effective with children and adolescents when used as part of an assessment battery with preschool children. The derived information of personality and behavior can lead to educational and therapeutic interventions to facilitate coping with the divorce and/or for working with problems that have arisen as a result of the divorce (Konold, 2017; Medway, 2017).

BASC-3 PRQ

Instrument name. BASC-3 PRQ developed by Randy W. Kamphaus and Cecil R. Reynolds in 2006 and revised in 2015.

Type of instrument. BASC-3 PRQ is a paper-and-pencil questionnaire that captures each parent's perspective on the parent–child relationship. Separate forms are provided for age groups: preschool (ages 2–5: BASC-3 PRQ-P) and child and adolescent (ages 6–18: BASC-3 PRQ-CA). The instrument is norm-based, self-report measure designed to assess parent or caregiver perceptions of the parent–child relationship and can be used in school, clinical, pediatric, counseling, and other settings (Smith, 2017; Widaman, 2017).

Use–target audience. The BASC-3 PRQ was designed to provide information about the traditional parent–child dimensions such as attachment and involvement and provides information on parenting style, confidence, stress, and satisfaction with the child's school.

Multicultural. Normative samples, for both female and male raters, that are closely matched to 2013 U.S. Census population estimates.

Ease and time of administration. The BASC PRQ takes approximately 10–15 minutes to complete and can be scored by hand (5–10 minutes) or computer.

Scoring procedure. The BASC-3 PRQ-P is for use with parents or caregivers of children ages 2 through 5 and consists of 60 items, which can be scored by hand or via ASSIST Software. Scores are provided as T scores and percentiles based on a general population. The child/adolescent version, the BASC-3 PRQ-CA, is for use with parents or caregivers of children and adolescents ages 6 through 18 and consists of 87 items. Parents or caregivers rate frequency of occurrence of each item on a four-point scale, ranging from never to almost always. The preschool form (PRQ-P) assesses five dimensions: Attachment, Discipline Practices, Involvement, Parenting Confidence, and Relational Frustration. The child and adolescent form (PRQ-CA) assesses the same five dimensions as the PRQ-P with the addition of two other age appropriate dimensions: Communication and Satisfaction With School.

Reliability. Internal reliability ranges in the high .80 and .90 for all scales except for the BASC-3 PRQ-P Discipline Practices scale, ranging between .76 and .83. Test–retest reliability coefficients were reported both in raw form and corrected for sample variability relative to the population. Test–retest reliabilities range between .70 and .89.

Validity. Intercorrelations among the Attachment, Communication, Involvement, and Parenting Confidence scales ranged from .40 to .79. Discipline Practices and Relational Frustration scales were less highly correlated or correlated in negative manner (e.g., Relational Frustration with most other scales). Correlations of BASC-3 PRQ scale scores with the previous version of the PRQ were strong, with a median correlation coefficient of about .97.

Availability and source. The forms are available in both English and Spanish.

Comment—using with families. The BASC-3 PRQ has potential for use in a wide variety of settings and provides information on the parent–child relationship that can potentially contribute to various types of evaluations, including custody dispute cases and treatment planning. Reviewers caution, however, that this assessment should not be used to evaluate level of pathology in a child or adolescent (Smith, 2017; Widaman, 2017).

Burks' Behavior Rating Scales, Second Edition (BBRS-2)

Instrument name. BBRS-2, developed by Harold F. Burks in 1977 and revised in 2006 with Christian Gruber, is designed to measure behavior patterns in children and adolescents (Burks & Gruber, 2006).

Type of instrument. The BBRS-2 is a 100-item rating scale designed for use with children or adolescents from 4 to 18 years of age who have been referred for school behavior and adjustment problems. There is a Teacher form and a Parent form.

Use–target audience. A parent or teacher rates on a five-point Likert scale how often a behavior is seen in the child.

Multicultural. The normative sample was represented by gender, age, ethnicity, and region consistent with the 2005 U.S. Census.

Ease and time of administration. The instrument, written at the fifth-grade reading level, is completed in 10–15 minutes individually by raters, teachers, or parents, who have daily contact with the child. It is recommended that interpretations be made by or with a Master's-level clinician.

Scoring procedure. The hand or computer scored instrument yields seven scores: Disruptive behavior, Attention and impulse control problems, Emotional problems, Social withdrawal, Ability deficits, Physical deficits, and Weak self-confidence.

Reliability. Internal consistency reliability was reported to range from .84 to .89. Test–retest reliability ranged from .80 to .90. Interrater reliability ranged from .69 for parents and .62 for teachers.

Validity. Concurrent validity ranged from .42 to .78 with the Child Behavior Checklist/Teacher's report form, the Behavior Evaluation form, and the Conner's rating Scales-Revised.

Availability and source. The BBRS-2 forms are available from Western Psychological Services.

Comment—using with families. The BBRS-2 is a useful screening tool for rating behaviors and is age and developmentally specific. This instrument delineates problem behaviors and indicates special needs a child may have at home and/or school that, in turn, provide information for determining appropriate placement with parents(s) who can best meet the child-rearing demands (Suen, 2010).

Child's Risk Index for Divorced or Separated Families (CRI-DS)

Instrument name. The CRI-DS is a brief, 15-item, three-point Likert-style parent report measure intended to predict problem outcomes for children who have experienced familial separation or divorce (Tein, Sandler, Braver, & Wolchik, 2013).

Type of instrument. The item pool for the CRI-DS was inspired by means of a meta-analysis of the literature dedicated to risk and protective factors for children who have experienced divorce. This brief measure requires parent report of child behavior problems and family level risk and protective factors. The CRI-DS was designed as an initial screening tool to be followed by a more in-depth assessment of post-divorce family functioning.

Use–target audience. The CRI-DS screens for behavioral problems, protective factors, and familial levels of risk in an effort to predict child welfare following divorce. The CRI-DS is administered to parents in families facing dissolution.

Multicultural. This measure is available only in an English version.

Scoring procedure. Hand scoring takes approximately 5–10 minutes. Raw score tallies can be recorded for the total scale. Higher raw scores indicate increased levels of risk to child welfare. The cut-off point for indicating high risk is set at 6 (Tein et al., 2013).

Reliability. Not available.

Validity. A longitudinal study, including cross-validation, indicated that the CRI-DS predicted child behavior outcomes and substance abuse problems in children who faced divorce for up to six years following the event. Predictive validity across the three studies comprising the development and psychometric testing of the CRI-DS ranged from $r = .42–.89$ (Tein et al., 2013).

Availability and source. Paper-and-pencil self-report items, responses, and scoring instruction are available in Tien et al. (2013), "Development of a brief parent-report risk index for the children following parental divorce."

Comment—using with families. The promising predictive nature of the CRI-DS, as reported in the final cross-validation study associated with the development and assessment of the measure, lends credence to the scale's integrity as a screening tool for risk assessment. The CRI-DS's strength is in identifying the need for, but not nature of, supportive services for children in families facing divorce (Tien et al., 2013). Noncustodial fathers were not included in the participant samples used to assess this measure; hence, a certain level of exclusionary bias can be assumed. Pending further psychometric testing, the CRI-DS shows promise as a screening tool for identifying potential problem outcomes of children who have experienced parental divorce.

Contact Refusal Scale

Instrument name. The Contact Refusal Scale developed by Huff, Anderson, Adamsons, and Tambling in 2017, is a self-report inventory designed to better understand the complex relationships and actions that follow parental divorce or separation.

Type of instrument. The Contact Refusal Scale is ten-item, seven-point Likert-style self-report measure developed to assess contact refusal in children following the divorce of their parents.

Use–target audience. The Contact Refusal Scale is intended for older children and young adults whose parents are undergoing or have completed the process of separation and/or divorce. A third-grade reading level and communication skills are necessary to complete the scale. The Contact Refusal Scale is most-appropriately administered during the first year following parental separation (Huff et al., 2017). The scale requires that the child report variables of their relationship with each parent.

Multicultural. This measure is available only in an English version.

Scoring procedure. Hand scoring takes approximately 5–10 minutes. Both raw scores and mean score tallies can be recorded for the total scale. Higher raw and mean scores indicate increased levels of parental refusal (Huff et al., 2017).

Reliability. Internal consistency was exceptional in regard to the evaluation of a child's relationship with both their mother and father, with Cronbach's alpha reaching .95 and .96, respectively (Huff et al., 2017).

Validity. Contact refusal of fathers was positively correlated to father's alienating behaviors, with $r = .35$, $p < .001$. Contact refusal was negatively correlated with father's warmth, with $r = -.55$, $p < .001$. A similar pattern was revealed in regard to contact refusal of mothers, with mother's alienating behaviors positively correlated at $r = .46$, $p < .001$, and negatively correlated with mother's warmth at $r = -.49$, $p < .001$ (Huff et al., 2017).

Availability and source. Paper and pencil available in Huff et al. (2017). For the purposes of publication of the Contact Refusal Scale, permission must be obtained from the publishing company and/or the primary developer.

Comment—using with families. With exceptional psychometrics, this scale shows promise for application in family therapy settings and custody cases, as it provides insight into the unique relationships a child forms with each of their parents. However, because the convenience samples utilized in each study were skewed in regard to gender, further examination of differences between father and mothers must be assessed to capture the accurate nature of parent–child relationships and their inherent challenges in the face of divorce and/or separation.

Level of Conflict Assessment (LOCA)

Instrument name. The LOCA is a 25-item, self-report rating scale set on a four-point Likert-style scale developed by Mary R. Langenbrunner, Mary Ellen Cox, and Donna Cherry in 2013.

Type of instrument. The LOCA is a rating scale designed to assess for early identification of parental conflict of divorcing parents of minor children. Development of the LOCA was inspired by an exhaustive meta-analysis of literature pertaining to high-conflict divorce (Langenbrunner et al., 2013).

Multicultural. This measure is available only in an English version.

Scoring procedure. Total scale scores for the LOCA are computed in accordance to the following formula:

$$S = (M-1)(100)/K-1$$

where S = the scale score, M = the mean item score, and K = the largest possible value for an item response. Scoring for the LOCA may exceed 15 minutes.

Reliability. The internal consistency reliability of the scale was very high ($\alpha = .94$).

Validity. Content validity was established and found to be acceptable. Linear modeling regressions established scale validity.

Availability and source. Paper-and-pencil rating scale (Langenbrunner et al., 2013).

Comment—using with families. The LOCA is a broad-scoped instrument that assesses levels of parental conflict in accordance to the following domains: domestic violence, cooperation & communication, degree of perceived attachment with partner, importance of the other parent to child development and well-being, and willingness to receive help. A strength highlighted by the developers is that the LOCA can be a useful tool for facilitating discussion during parent education programs. The LOCA is meant to help in the divorce transition for children and their families.

Millon Pre-Adolescent Clinical Inventory (M-PACI)

Instrument name. The 97-item M-PACI, developed by Theodore Millon, Robert Tringone, Carrie Millon, and Seth Grossman and published in 2005, is a multidimensional self-report personality inventory designed to identify, predict, and understand a range of common psychological disorders found in 9–12 year old pre-adolescents.

Type of instrument. The M-PACI is used as an initial evaluation for troubled adolescents to confirm diagnostic hypotheses and in planning individualized treatment programs.

Use—target audience. The M-PACI is used for assessment of troubled pre-adolescents.

Multicultural. The representation in the normative samples reasonably approximate the U.S. population in gender and ethnicity.

Ease and time of administration. The true/false items, written at the third-grade level, take approximately 15–20 minutes to complete and can be administered individually or in a group in paper-and-pencil or online formats.

Scoring procedure. Three options are available for scoring are MICROTEST Q Assessment System software, mail-in scoring, and hand scoring. The 16 scales of the M-PACI are organized in three categories: (1) Emerging Personality Patterns: Confident, Outgoing, Conforming, Submissive, Inhibited, Unruly, and Unstable; (2) Current clinical signs: Anxiety/fears, Attention deficits, Obsessions/Compulsions, Conduct problems, Disruptive behaviors, Depressive moods; and Reality distortions; and (3) Response validity indicators: Invalidity and Response Negativity. Report formats in profile or interpretive are available (Geisinger, Spies, Carlson, & Plake, 2007).

Reliability. Cronbach's alpha reliabilities presented in the manual range from .63 to .84.

Validity. Concurrent validity coefficients range from .65 to .75 with the Behavior Assessment System for Children, Self-report of Personality, Children's Depression Inventory, and the Revised Children's Manifest Anxiety Scale.

Availability and source. The M-PACI is available in paper-and-pencil format or online from Pearson.

Comment—using with families. The M-PACI is most effective with adolescents experiencing a level of significant problems or concerns so as to determine treatment options. The mental health needs and self-perceptions of a troubled adolescent in the family raise co-parenting issues and the "role" the troubled adolescent plays in the functioning, or lack thereof, of the family (Atlas, 2007; Pfeiffer, 2007).

Millon Adolescent Clinical Inventory (MACI)

Instrument name. The 160-item MACI, developed by Theodore Millon, Carrie Millon, Roger Davis, and Seth Grossman and published in 1993, is a self-report personality inventory designed to assess adolescent personality characteristics, concerns, and clinical syndromes.

Type of instrument. The MACI is used as an initial evaluation of troubled adolescents to confirm diagnostic hypotheses, in planning individualized treatment programs and measuring treatment progress.

Use–target audience. The MACI is used for assessment specifically with "disturbed" adolescents, 13–19 years of age, in outpatient, inpatient, or residential treatment settings.

Multicultural. The minority representation in the normative samples ranged from 16% to 28%. The audio recorded version of the MACI is also available in Spanish (Stuart, 1995).

Ease and time of administration. Through a series of questions, the clinician assesses an adolescent's personality along with self-reported concerns. The true/false items are written at the sixth-grade level; it takes approximately 25–30 minutes to complete and can be administered individually or in a group.

Scoring procedure. Four options available for scoring are MICROTEST Q Assessment System software, mail-in scoring, hand scoring, and optical scan scoring ("Millon® Adolescent Clinical Inventory: Scoring and Reporting," n.d.). The MACI has 27 content scales and four response bias scales. The Content scales are 12 Personality Patterns scales (Introversive, Inhibited, Doleful, Submissive, Dramatizing, Egotistic, Unruly, Forceful, Conforming, Oppositional, Self-Demeaning, and Borderline Tendency), 8 Expressed Concerns scales (Identity Diffusion, Self-Devaluation, Body Disapproval, Sexual Discomfort, Peer Insecurity, Social Insensitivity, Family Discord, and Childhood Abuse), and 7 Clinical Syndromes scales (Eating Dysfunctions, Substance Abuse Proneness, Delinquent Predisposition, Impulsive Propensity, Anxious Feelings, Depressive Affect, and Suicidal Tendency). The Response Bias scales are four modifying indices (Reliability, Disclosure, Desirability, and Debasement) ("Millon® Adolescent Clinical Inventory: Scoring and Reporting," n.d.).

Reliability. Cronbach's alpha reliabilities range from .73 to .91, with most of the internal consistencies in the 0.80s (Retzlaff, Sheehan, & Lorr, 1990). Test–retest reliabilities range from .57 to .92.

Validity. Responses to the MACI were favorably intercorrelated with the Beck Depression Inventory, Beck Anxiety Inventory, and Eating Disorder Inventory.

Availability and source. The MACI is available in paper-and-pencil format or online from Pearson.

Comment—using with families. The MACI is most effective with adolescents experiencing a level of significant problems or concerns so as to determine treatment options and measuring treatment progress. The mental health needs of a troubled adolescent in the family raise co-parenting issues, contradictory hidden parental messages, issues of loyalty in the family system, and the "role" the troubled adolescent plays in the functioning, or lack thereof, of the family (Stuart, 1995).

Parent Awareness Skills Survey (PASS)

Instrument name. The PASS developed by Barry Bricklin, Ph.D., in 1990, and revised in 2002, identifies strengths and weaknesses of a parent's response to 18 typical childcare situations.

Type of instrument. The PASS is a semi-structured interview that presents parents with 18 childcare problems or dilemmas in six categories and asks how they would respond to each situation. The instrument reflects parent awareness skills of effective parenting regardless of the age of the children and specifics of their particular situation.

Use–target audience. This survey for parents of children aged 2 through 15 assesses parental awareness of adequate solutions in given situations, their communication methods with their child, and how attuned they are to their child's feelings and the unique manner in which their child is able to respond and profit from that communication.

Multicultural. The survey is easily understood by parents of varying educational levels and diverse cultural backgrounds.

Ease and time of administration. Individually and orally administered to each parent, it may take between 30 and 60 minutes depending on the experience of the clinician with the PASS. The parent is presented with 18 different situations and asked to tell what he or she would do in each situation. After responses are recorded, probing questions are asked to determine the issues the parents believe they should think about before and after their choice of response.

Scoring procedure. Scores reflect parents' responses at three levels: (a) spontaneous level is the unprompted and uninterrupted initial response; (b) Probe Level I asks two gentle, non-leading questions; and (c) Probe Level II asks two direct questions. Each level allows respondents to improve their score. PASS responses are scored with a 0 for no awareness, a 1 for minimal awareness, or a 2 for pronounced awareness in each of the six areas at each of the three levels. The six areas are Awareness of critical issues, Awareness of adequate solutions, Awareness of communicating in understandable terms, Awareness of acknowledging feelings, Awareness of the importance of relevant aspects of a child's past history, and Awareness of feedback data. The scoring is subjective to the clinician's skill and knowledge in psychology and child development (Bischoff, 1995; Cole, 1995).

Reliability. Not reported.

Validity. Not reported.

Availability and source. The PASS Comprehensive Starting Kit is available from Village Publishing.

Comment—using with families. The PASS provides information on the parent's awareness of child-related critical issues and adequate solutions or interventions to these issues. The PASS also provides information about the level of parent's awareness of his or her communications to the child in understandable terms to them, the importance of acknowledging the child's feelings, the relevance of the child's past history, and the need to attend to the child's feedback to the parents' response. Data are used to determine relative strengths and weaknesses of each parent, their conscious efforts for good parenting, and the influence of parental behavior on the child for making custody decisions. The basic assumption of the instrument is that parenting effectiveness is a function of parent's awareness of the appropriate skills. The PASS is a good screening tool and is best used in combination with other instruments (Bischoff, 1995; Cole, 1995).

Parent–Child Relationship Inventory (PCRI)

Instrument name. The PCRI developed by Gerard Anthony and published in 1994 provides a qualitative evaluation of parent–child interactions.

Type of instrument. The PCRI is a 78-item self-report questionnaire that measure parents' dispositions/attitudes and behaviors about parenting and their children. Items are clustered in Content scales: Parental Support, Satisfaction with Parenting, Involvement, Communication, Limit Setting, Autonomy, and Role Orientation.

Use–target audience. The PCRI is used in evaluating parents and their children (ages 3–15). Separate norms are provided for mothers and fathers.

Multicultural. It is reported that the normative sample was less diverse than the U.S. population.

Ease and time of administration. The PCRI, written at the fourth-grade level, can be administered individually or in a group and takes about 15 minutes to complete.

Scoring procedure. The PCRI may be hand scored, computer scored through purchase of software, or scored through a fax or mail-in service provided by Western Psychological Services.

Reliability. PCRI test–retest reliability for the seven scales range (Cronbach's alpha coefficient) from .70 to .88. The median value alpha on individual scales is .80. After a week, ranges were from .68 to .93; and at five months, test–retest reliability ranged from .44 to .71.

Validity. Inventory's author cites studies that support PCRI's predictive validity; the critique of this analysis, however, suggests findings from these studies seem somewhat overstated (Boothroyd, 1998). In fact, research examining the PCRI has found mixed validity results (Valeriao & Beck, 2017).

Availability and source. The PCRI is available from Western Psychological Services.

Comment—using with families. Gerard (1994) indicated that the PCRI was developed to assess parents' attitudes toward parenting as well as toward their children. The evaluation of parental attitudes and skills, family interaction, the presence of abuse, and the identification of areas of difficulty between parents and their children provides information about conscious parenting and competence and the quality of the familial relationship (Boothroyd, 1998; Marchant, 1998).

Parenting Stress Index, Fourth Edition (PSI-4)

Instrument name. The PSI, a 120-item instrument developed by Richard Abidin, Ph.D. in 1983 is in its fourth edition (2012).

Type of instrument. The PSI-4 is a parent inventory designed to evaluate stressful parent–child systems across three major domains of stress: child characteristics, parent characteristics, and situational/demographic life stress. The PSI-4, a screening tool for stress in the parent–child relationship, identifies dysfunctional parenting and predicts potential for parental behavior problems and child adjustment difficulties within the family system. It is used for early identification and prevention of family problems and helpful in planning intervention and treatment, assessing child abuse, and in evaluations for child custody.

Use–target audience. Although intended primarily for parents of the preschool child, the PSI can also be used with parents whose children are 12 years old or younger.

Multicultural. The fourth edition was revised to improve cultural sensitivity of language and to include fathers in the standardization sample. In addition, the normative pool was updated to match demographic composition of the 2007 U.S. Census (APA, n.d.).

Ease and time of administration. Parents complete 120 items on the self-report inventory, which is written at the fifth-grade reading level and can be administered in a group format (Carlson, Geisinger, & Jonson, 2014). It takes about 20–30 minutes to complete the paper-and-pencil PSI and takes approximately five minutes to score. There is also an online administration and scoring option via PARiConnect. The 36-item Short Form takes 10–15 minutes to complete.

Scoring procedure. A total stress score and two scale scores, Child Domain and Parent Domain, each of which identifies sources of stress within the family, are available for the standard form. The Short Form only provides a total stress score. Scoring time for this tool varies based on whether it is hand scored or if the PSI software is utilized.

Reliability. Test–retest reliability coefficients ranged from .55 to .82 for the Child Domain, from .69 to .91 for the Parent Domain, and from .65 to .96 for the Total Stress score. Reliability coefficients for the two domains and the Total Stress scale were .96 or greater (Abidin, 2012).

Validity. Validity is reported to be strong. In particular, construct and predictive validity is supported by various studies carried out in diverse locations and with diverse populations (Young, 2014).

Availability and source. Both forms can be administered in pencil-and-paper format or online using the PSI software System, which automatically scores item responses and generates a report available from Psychological Assessment Resources.

Comment—using with families. The PSI-4 identifies three major sources of stress: child characteristics, parent characteristics, and situational/demographic life stress. Child variables include Distractibility/Hyperactivity, Adaptability, Reinforces Parent, Demandingness, Mood, and Acceptability. Parent variables include Competence, Isolation, Attachment, Health, Role Restriction, Depression, and Spouse. Life stress factors include Interrupted Infantile Apnea, Spina Bifida, Craniofacial Birth Defects, Insulin-Dependent Diabetes, Divorce, Marriage, Pregnancy, Income Increased, Debt, Moves, Promotions, Alcohol or Drug Problem, Death of Close Family Friend, New

Job, School, Legal Problems, and others. The identification of the sources of conflict, parents' ability to cope with these, and child–parent adjustment will facilitate assessing placement of the child in the least stressful environment and with the more appropriate parent while making recommendations for counseling/therapy or stress management education (Young, 2014).

Parting Parental Concerns Inventory (PPCI)

Instrument name. The PPCI is a 28-item, five-point Likert-type self-inventory developed by Sanford and Rivers (2017).

Type of instrument. The PPCI was developed to examine the following six areas of concern related to post-divorce family adjustment: retaliatory malice, power, custody, child rejection, esteem, and finance.

Use–target audience. The PPCI assesses constructs that are germane to applied contexts, such as divorce mediation, child custody examinations (CCE), and in psychotherapeutic settings with individuals who are coping with the process and aftermath of divorce (Sanford & Rivers, 2017).

Multicultural. This measure is available only in an English version.

Ease and time of administration. Not reported.

Scoring procedure. Both raw scores and mean score tallies can be recorded for individual subscales and the total scale. Scores and reports digitally generated.

Reliability. Internal Consistency, as measured by Cronbach's alphas, as they pertain to subscales were as follows: .92 (malice), .89–.93 (power), .88–.91 (custody), .90–.92 (child rejection), .89–.92 (esteem), and .83 (finance) (Sanford & Rivers, 2017).

Validity. Construct validity indicated 25 convergent validity variables were significantly correlated. In regard to convergent validity, each concern subscale was supported. Finally, regarding discriminant validity, all inter-factor correlations fell below the cutoff of $r = .85$ (Sanford & Rivers, 2017).

Availability and source. A paper-and-pencil version of the PPCI is available in Sanford and Rivers (2017). A digital version may be obtained by contacting the primary developer.

Comment—using with families. The PPCI is a robust measure initially designed for the purposes of research, though it can be applied as a screening and assessment tool in clinical settings. Extensive psychometric testing, including confirmatory factor analysis (CFA) was conducted in efforts to confirm the fit of the six-factor structure. This recently developed instrument shows promise in generating useful results dedicated to the domains assessed. The PPCI is especially salient in regard to anticipating factors such as child outcomes following divorce, divorce settlement satisfaction, holistic parental well-being, and custody arrangements. A summary of the assessment instruments discussed with their applications and psychometric information can be found in **Table 10.1**.

Table 10.1 Matrix: Child Custody and Divorce Assessment Strategies and Inventories

Assessment/ Instrument	Specific Couple and Family Applications	Cultural/ Language	Instructions/Use: T = Time to Take S = Time to Score I = Items (#)	Computerized (a) Scoring (b) Report	Reliability (R) Validity (V)	Availability
ASPECT	Parents; evaluate parents' fitness for custody by quantifying characteristics for making custody recommendations	English	T = varies S = varies I = 56 (41 short form)	(a) no (b) no	R = α = .96 internal consistency reliability on PCI; interrater reliability coefficients on the Observational, Social, & Cognitive-Emotional Scales .92–.94. V = conflicting reports	Western Psychological Services
BASC-3	Children, parents, and parent surrogates; assess and identifies children and adolescents with emotional and behavioral disorders	English; Spanish (parent version & self-report)	T = 15–35 minutes for each scale S = 15–35 minutes (manually) I = 5 separate subtests; varying no. of items	(a) yes (b) yes	R = Internal consistency .82–.97; test–retest reliability .76–.93; interrater reliability .62–.82. V = Correlation coefficients .80 and above	Pearson Clinical
BASC-3 PRQ	Parents; captures each parent's perspective on the parent–child relationship	English; Spanish	T = 10–15 minutes S = 5–10 minutes (hand score) I = 60	(a) yes (b) yes	R = Internal reliability ranges in the high .80 and .90 for all scales except for the BASC-3 PRQ-P Discipline Practices scale; test–retest .70–.89. V = Intercorrelations among most scales ranged .40–.79	Pearson Clinical

Measure	Description	Language	Administration	Norms	Reliability/Validity	Source
BPS— component of ACCESS	Children; assess children's perceptions or emotional comprehension on 32 activities related to parenting capacity	English	T = varies S = varies I = 32 (64 cards; 32 about mom and 32 about dad)	(a) yes (b) yes	R = not available V = reported in terms of percentages of BPD agreement with unpublished children's drawings test (83%); children's and parent's questionnaires (70%); court custody decisions (94%)	Village Publishing
BBRS-2	Parents and teachers; identifies problem behavior patterns in children	English	T = 10–15 minutes S = 15–20 minutes (hand) I = 100	(a) yes (b) yes	R = Internal consistency reliability .84–.89; test–retest reliability .80–.90; interrater reliability ranged from .62 to .69 V = Concurrent validity ranged from .42 to .78	Western Psychological Services
CRI-DS	Risk assessment intended to predict outcomes for children who have experienced familial separation	English	T = 10 minutes S = 5–10 minutes I = 15	(a) no (b) no	R = data unavailable V = r = .42–.98 (predictive)	Journal Article
Contact Refusal Scale	Assess parental contact refusal in children during the first year following familial separation	English	T = 10 minutes S = 10 minutes I = 10	(a) no (b) no	R = α = .95 (mother); α = .96 (father) V = r = −.55 to .49	Journal Article

(*Continued*)

Assessment Instrument	Specific Couple and Family Applications	Cultural/ Language	Instructions/Use: T = Time to Take S = Time to Score I = Items (#)	Computerized (a) Scoring (b) Report	Reliability (R) Validity (V)	Availability
LOCA	Assesses perceived levels of conflict within divorcing/ separating couples	English	T = 10–15 minutes S = 15 minutes I = 25	(a) no (b) no	R = α = .94 V = Expert Panel, meta-analysis (content); Linear Regression (scale)	Journal Article
M-PACI	Psychological disorders in preadolescents (9–12 years old)	English	T = 15–20 minutes S = differs based on method I = 97	(a) yes (b) yes	R = α = .63–.84. V = Concurrent validity coefficients range from .65 to .75	Pearson Clinical
MACI	Disturbed adolescence: self-report personality inventory; assess adolescent personality characteristics and clinical syndromes	English; Spanish	T = 20–30 minutes S = 20–30 minutes manually I = 160	(a) yes (b) yes	R = .73–.91 internal consistency; .57–.92 test-retest V = favorably intercorrelated with Beck Inventory, Anxiety Inventory, and Eating Disorder Inventory	Pearson Education
PASS	Parents; reflects parents' awareness of effective parenting	English	T = 30–60 minutes/ questioning S = 30–60 minutes I = 18 situations	(a) no (b) no	R = not available V = not available	Village Publishing

Measure	Description	Language	Administration		Reliability/Validity	Source
PCRI	Parents; provides a qualitative evaluation of parent–child interactions	English	T = 15 minutes S = differs based on method (hand or digital) I = 78	(a) yes (b) yes	R = α = .70–.88; at one week .68–.93; five months .44–.71. V = mixed reports	Western Psychological Services
PSI-4	Parents; identifies stressful parent–child systems	English	T = 20–30 minutes (long form); 10–15 minutes (short form) S = 5 minutes standard form I = 120 (long form) 36 (short form)	(a) yes (b) yes	R = α = .55–.82 test–retest reliability for the Child Domain; .69–.91 for the Parent Domain; .65–.96 Total Stress score V = established validity	Psychological Assessment Resources
PPCI	Evaluates six areas of concern related to post-separation family adjustment	English	T = 15 minutes S = 5 minutes (digital); 10 minutes (hand) I = 28	(a) yes (b) yes	R = α = .83–.92 V = r = .85 (discriminant); significant (construct); supported (convergent)	Journal Article
PORT— component of ACCESS	Children; projective test is designed to measure the extent to which a child feels or seeks closeness with each parent and the impact of these relationships	English	T = 15–30 minutes S = 15–30 minutes I = 7 tasks	(a) no (b) yes	R = not available V = reported as percent agreement, ranging from 83% to 95% across six samples	Village Publishing

Strategy for Utilizing Assessment Results

The American Psychological Association (APA) in 1994 developed guidelines for child custody evaluations that stressed the need for multiple methods of data collection and cautious interpretation of assessment data (Ackerman & Ackerman, 1997). The 2010 updated guidelines further promote proficiency of custody evaluations when conducted by mental health professionals (APA, 2010). When assessments/evaluations are conducted, systematic orientation and procedure are important to ensure consistent, comprehensive, and accurate data gathering. The following steps identify the essential information needed and from whom, the qualitative and quantitative data desired and data gathering methods, and how and when this assessment plan will be operationalized. The subsequent case example illustrates the use of the identified procedure: (1) collect biopsychosocial data including client's perception of current legal situation; educational, medical (physical and emotional), criminal, and employment history; past and present substance use and/or abuse; family constellation; support systems; and religious/spiritual orientation; (2) review collateral data: divorce agreement, court orders, school records, and/or mediation agreements; (3) collect and/or review clinical data including prior and current individual, couples, and family counseling/therapy; (4) interview the whole family and individual members; (5) administer selected inventory/testing tools; (6) interpret the results of the inventory; (7) identify recommendations and interventions; (8) provide feedback to the couple and/or family as appropriate; and (9) provide report and/or recommendations to court.

Case Example

Background Information and Reason for Testing

Betty and Archie had been married for 12 years when Betty decided she no longer wanted to be married to Archie due to his reported drinking, neglect of their three (3) children, and his overall lack of family consideration. Further, they suffered financial struggles because of Archie's drinking and inability to hold stable and effective employment, which resulted in their home going into foreclosure and their car being repossessed. This instability is also purportedly the reason for Betty's depression and anxiety. They have three daughters (Tara age 10, Kelly age 8, and Quinn age 6). Betty and her three daughters currently reside in Betty's family home, with her father. Betty is seeking to be primary residential parent and have sole parental responsibility. She is currently denying Archie access time with the children due to his drinking and irresponsible behaviors. Archie is living with his parents. He denies his drinking is excessive and is seeking shared parental responsibility and an equal sharing of access time with his daughters.

Biopsychosocial Data Collection

In their initial interviews, both Betty and Archie were made aware that all information collected during the Court ordered assessment would be used for the purposes of their divorce and a child sharing determination; thus, all information would be made available to the Court. They both signed *Release of Information* forms for this purpose.

During the assessment interview, Betty indicated that she and Archie married 12 years ago; and, at that time, Archie asked her to stop working as he would provide for the family and she would stay home and raise any children that were born within the marriage. She stated that she has some college credits but never completed college and previously worked in a secretarial position. She reported that she is physically healthy but suffers from depression and anxiety, which she attributes to living with Archie, who she describes as an alcoholic. She denied any criminal history and does not use any substances (although her father has a history of alcohol dependence but is now sober). Betty indicated that she is currently living with her father in the family home she was raised, but most of her family lives out of state. Her mother is deceased. She stated that she has no religious affiliation although she was raised Jewish. Her children, on the other hand, were all baptized in the Catholic Church at the request of Archie and his family. She asserted that she has been the primary parent through her children's lives and that Archie only takes part in a yearly Father-Daughter dance each spring.

Archie, during his meeting for the assessment interview, indicated that he was a business owner when they married but that business failed; as a result, he has had a series of jobs over the last ten years that have provided for the family. Archie reported that he completed a few college courses but never completed his degree. At this point, he is in a blue-collar occupation and works up to 50 hours per week to support his family. He stated that he has some health issues that include high blood pressure and circulation issues. He disclosed that he drinks but explained that his drinking is moderate. He also admitted to one arrest for DUI (driving under the influence), which he stated was not fair as it was on a holiday and he was driving home. Archie indicated that his

(*Continued*)

entire family lives within three miles of each other. He reported that he is living with his parents who are loving and supportive of him and his three daughters. Archie identified as Catholic, although not practicing. Archie explained that he feels Betty wants full custody of the children, so she can relocate to be closer to her family and deny him the experiences of the children's upbringing. He stated that he is an active parent who loves his daughters and wants to be an active participant in their lives but added Betty has denied him this opportunity.

Collateral Data Review

The evaluator/assessor reviewed the initial divorce petition (No Fault), recent court orders for testing and assessment, the children's school records, and a tentative mediation agreement to guide the assessment process. The evaluator/assessor noted nothing was considered remarkable except for the children's academic records, which show some deficits in learning although no developmental delays were reported. Presently, there is a supervised visitation process in place for Archie to spend time with his daughters once a week for one hour with a Masters' level practitioner. Betty resides with the children and cares for the girls' daily needs while Archie provides appropriate child support, as ordered by the Court.

Clinical Data

Both parties deny any participation in couples or family therapy. Betty admits to attending individual counseling to address her depression and anxiety. She states that she is currently on antidepressant medications to assist her in mood stabilization, which she explains has been effective for her. In a telephone call (with the appropriate release), Betty's therapist reported that her client attends all scheduled sessions and has been compliant with treatment. The therapist also reported mood improvement since Archie is no longer living with her and their daughters. There has not yet been a report from the supervised visitation representative, although both parties anecdotally report that it is going well.

Family Interviews

Betty and Archie were interviewed separately. Contents of those interviews are included in earlier sections of this case study. In the interview, specifically addressing the family system, Betty contended that she has been the primary parent to her three daughters, and has been responsible for providing oversight of the girls' daily care, helping them with homework, taking them to their social and recreation activities, and paying for and ensuring they receive regular medical care. She explained that she gave birth to the second daughter and third daughter by herself because Archie did not come to the hospital for their births. However, he showed up after the birth with his family. She stated that, while she has not worked, she took oversight of the family finances after their home was foreclosed and the family car was repossessed. Betty reported that Archie, before he pays support for the children, takes approximately 20% of his weekly wages out for beer and his other expenses, despite the family needs. She informed the interviewer that she is currently looking for employment since their youngest has just entered first grade and her schedule is more open for a job. As part of her request to the Court, she is asking to care for the children on her own. According to Betty's report, the children "have no relationship" with their father. In fact, when they were all living together, she explained that Archie would stay away from the family, drinking in a separate part of the house when he came home from work. She stated that he can be verbally abusive and calls her and their daughters names when he is drinking but has never hit her or the children. She stressed that she no longer loves Archie and is seeking to end the marriage as well as to protect the children from his alcoholic behaviors. Because she was exposed to having an alcoholic parent as a child, she stated that she feels it has negatively affected her as an adult and does not want her girls to "go through the same thing." Betty shared that, when sober, Archie is a good father who loves his children; and she sees no reason he should not have time with the children if he amends his work schedule and is able to stay sober. Finally, she reported that they communicate well now that they are separated.

Archie shared his perspective of the family system and his role as father. He stated that he has worked hard to provide for his family and feels that taking money each week is "his due" since he is the only one working. He explained that he tries to be there for his children but can't be as available as he would like due to his work schedule, as well as tries to avert conflict by avoiding contact with Betty. He stated that he has a close relationship with his daughters and that they always appeared to be happy to see him when he returned from work when they were all together. He stated that he is unable to spend "real time" with them due to his increased work hours because he is the only form of financial support for the family. When asked about drinking, Archie indicated

(Continued)

that he drinks about 3–4 beers per evening and that he does not feel that this is excessive, nor does it cause him any behavioral changes—"I drink to relax and unwind after my day at work." While he stated that he is not at home a lot, he explained that he has always tried to spend time with the girls for special events, when he has time off. He disclosed that, while he still loves Betty, they are no longer able to communicate; so, he removed himself from the family. He reported that he knows that the divorce will one day be final and expressed sadness at no longer sharing time as a family. He stated that he and Betty communicate better now that they are separated; but he's stressed because they may move away.

The children were interviewed separately as the evaluator/assessor did not want one sister's comments to affect the others. Tara (10), the oldest of the three girls, expressed that she loves her father and her mother. She expressed sadness that her father is not in the house, as she "loves him a lot." She says that he works a lot and spends time alone "drinking beer." She says that he looks sad and that her mother is always frustrated and angry. She shared that she does not like school and has a hard time with reading and math. Tara is currently in fifth grade but will probably go back into fourth grade because she was not academically prepared to move to the higher-grade level. She explained that all the "stress in the house" has caused her to be unable to focus. She stated, since her father moved out, things are calmer, and her mother is happier; but she feels sad and misses her dad. She remarked that she looks forward to her visits with her father and that he brings her McDonald's to eat, which she "loves." Finally, Tara stated that she "gets into fights with Mommy because she is frustrated that Daddy isn't there."

Kelly (8), the middle child, indicated that she is "closer with Mommy because she always helps me." Kelly is academically doing well in school and stated that she "tries to get along with her sisters but they always touch her stuff." She explained that she rarely misses her father and would rather "play outside or read" than go to the supervised visits. She stated that she loves her father but likes to be with her mother because she does "crafts with us and takes us to the pool and does homework with us." Kelly was able to verbalize that she knows that Tara "misses Daddy a lot but [she] really [doesn't]." She also shared that "Mommy is a lot happier since Daddy moved in with my grandparents."

Quinn (6) was difficult to interview and redirect as she presented with increased energy. She was able, however, to share that her daddy now lives with "Grandmom and Grandpop in a big house." She stated that she is beginning first grade and is excited because she has a new teacher. Quinn shared that she likes to see Daddy because "he brings McDonald's that Mommy can't buy and it tastes good." She also shared that her daddy "makes her laugh when he does silly things." She stated that she loves her mommy and her daddy "a whole bunch."

Administration of Tests

The PORT was administered to all three girls to ascertain their own relationship with each parent. All three were able to draw the assigned pictures (themselves, their parents, their pet in the preferred parents' home, and the pet's dreams about its parents) and were able to work together to share crayons and colored pencils so that their pictures were done to their liking.

The BASC-3-PRQ-CA was administered to Betty and Archie to assess their perceptions of their relationship with their daughters as well as their parenting styles, confidence, stress about parenting, and satisfaction with the children's schools. The CA type was used due to the ages of the children (6–10).

The PCRI was administered to both parents to assess parental support, their satisfaction with parenting, their involvement with their children, effective communication, ability to set limits, autonomy, and their role in the children's life.

An *observational assessment*, a component of the ACCESS assessment, was also conducted with each parent and the children to better understand the strengths and weaknesses of the parent–child bond. This involved the parent and children identifying and playing a game together to observe interactions, fair play, conflict resolution, and time-sharing when all three girls were together with the individual parent. The results of the observation were used in addition to the aforementioned tests to better understand the family dynamics and interactions.

The parents indicated that they want what is best for their girls, despite not knowing how to achieve that result without the help of the Court. In addition, the parents are seeking guidance from the Court about Betty's desire to move closer to her extended family, in the future, so that she and the girls have a better opportunity for a comfortable, healthy, and happy life. As part of this arrangement, when he achieves sobriety for a period of no less than six (6) months as determined by an addiction counselor, Archie would have access time with the girls during holidays and summer/winter breaks.

(Continued)

Interpretation of Results

Each child was provided the PORT, and each completed the pictures in the time frame provided. Results indicated that Tara feels a closer connection to her father and is favorable toward him. Both Kelly and Quinn's tests indicated a closer relationship with their mother and did not show any connection to their father. In fact, the drawing of him was smaller and less prominent than their mother in pictures the girls drew.

The BASC-3-PQR-CA was provided to both parents individually. Each was able to complete the assessment in the time allotted. Results indicated that Betty was more attached to the children and felt more involved in their lives and with their education. It also indicated a lower, but still positively significant, score specific to parenting confidence and discipline practices. There was a high significant score specific to her overall relationship with her children as well as communication with her children. Archie's BASC-3-PRQ-CA results indicated that he had difficulties in several areas of the assessment including communication with the children, discipline, and overall involvement with the children and their schooling. He showed a higher score in parenting confidence, despite the other scores and scored in the mid-range specific to his relationship with his children.

Both parents also completed the PCRI. Scores on this assessment tool were similar to the BASC-3-PRQ-CA in that the mother appeared more involved and confident in her abilities as a parent and in her relationship with her children than did the father. Archie scored higher in limit setting and parental autonomy. Both appeared to have love and concern for their children, although Betty appeared to be the more involved parent of these three young children.

Results of the observational assessment were notable as each parent was given the opportunity to select and play a game with all three children. The purpose of the observation was to monitor interactions and ability to parent each child while involving the others simultaneously. These observations were made with the therapist behind a one-way mirror to avoid affecting the interactions. All parties were aware that they were being observed. Archie appeared to have a level of difficulty managing all three girls at once and helping them to pick a game they could all play. He was eventually able to manage them when Tara, the oldest, stepped in to decide for the group. He was able to balance his time once the game started. Although Tara showed an increased desire to sit next to her father, explain the game, and interpret the rules, Archie did not redirect any of her "bossy" behaviors and attributed it to her being the oldest. Archie and the girls all interacted appropriately.

Kelly was noticeably quieter than the other two, and Archie did not make any efforts to involve her in the game process. Quinn took attention when she wanted it and focused on the game when it was her turn. She was observed to "climb" on her father when she wanted attention, and he reciprocated. During the observational assessment with Betty, there appeared to be a calmer transition from deciding on a game to playing the game. She set the rules with the girls and determined an order of turns. She was both encouraging and interactive with all the girls and supported them equally throughout the process. There appeared to be a higher level of familiarity between Betty and her daughters, which allowed for a smoother game playing experience. No clear pathology or learning disabilities were noted.

Recommendations and Interventions

The following is recommended for this family:

1. Therapeutic supervised visits should take place with a focus on assisting Archie in his relationships with all his daughters as they appear to love him but do not feel wholly comfortable around him. This should take place weekly for no less than two months and no more than six months—unsupervised visits should be considered with progress in sessions.
2. Both parents should take a parenting class for divorcing couples to assist them in co-parenting and communication, in the best interests of their daughters. This can be done separately or alone.
3. Betty should continue with her individual therapy and work with her therapist to gain better control over her anxiety and depression as well as to gain necessary time management skills to assist in caring for all three children.
4. Archie should meet with an individual therapist, who holds credentials as an addiction professional, to assess his drinking behaviors and determine the degree to which it is problematic. If his drinking is negatively impacting his daily functioning, he should continue with individual therapy focusing on his sobriety. He should maintain sobriety and not attend any child-focused events under the influence of alcohol, which should be assessed by the visitation supervisor at all meetings. If alcohol is smelled on his breath or person, the session should be cancelled and rescheduled.
5. Betty and Archie should be referred to co-parenting counseling to assist them in developing healthier relationships with their children and better co-parenting strategies.

(Continued)

Provide Feedback to the Couple

Both Betty and Archie attended a feedback session with the evaluator/assessor to discuss the findings of the assessments. When presented, neither party appeared to be upset or shocked by the information and agreed that they would be able to meet with the appropriate individuals to enact the recommended interventions. They both indicated that the assessment process allowed them to think more about their own actions within the marriage and how they have affected their children. The evaluator/assessor reiterated that the findings and recommendations would be forwarded to the Court and both would receive a copy of the final report. While Betty indicated that she still wants to relocate, she now better understands how that may impact the girl's relationship with their father and stated she would wait until they were a bit older to revisit this plan.

Report

A formal report was submitted to the Court as required under the Court order for assessment.

Concluding Comments

This chapter has described the use of psychological assessment methods and clinical interviews to evaluate the post-divorce/intimate partner separation parental relationship, the child's or children's relationship with each parent, and overall post-divorce/intimate partner separation family functioning, as well as to determine the parents' ability to work together in the best interest of the child or children with the purpose of making recommendations for child custody and visitation. In this chapter, 15 instruments were discussed and a protocol for using these instruments in clinical practice was provided and illustrated by a case example.

References

Abidin, R. R. (2012). *Parenting stress index* (4th ed.). Lutz, FL: PAR.

Ackerman, M. J. (2005). The Ackerman-Shoendorf scales for parent evaluation of custody (ASPECT): A review of research and update. *Journal of Child Custody, 2*(1), 179–193. doi:10.1300/J190v02n01_10

Ackerman, M. J., & Ackerman, M. C. (1997). Child custody evaluation practices: A survey of experienced professionals (revisited). *Professional Psychology: Research and Practices, 28*(2), 137–145.

American Psychological Association. (1994). Guidelines for child custody evaluations in divorce proceedings. *American Psychologist, 49*, 677–680. doi:10.1037/0003-066X.49.7.677

American Psychological Association. (2010). Guidelines for child custody evaluations in family law proceedings. *American Psychologist, 65*(9), 863–867. Retrieved from http://www.apa.org/pubs/journals/features/child-custody.pdf

American Psychological Association (n.d.). *Parenting stress index.* Retrieved from http://www.apa.org/pi/about/publications/caregivers/practice-settings/assessment/tools/parenting-stress.aspx

Atlas, J. A. (2007). Test review of Millon Pre-Adolescent Clinical Inventory. In K. F. Geisinger, R. A. Spies, J. F. Carlson, & B. S. Plake (Eds.), *The seventeenth mental measurements yearbook.* Retrieved from https://web-a-ebscohost-com.ezproxy.barry.edu

Bergman, A., & Rejmer, A. (2017). Parents in child custody disputes: Why are they disputing? *Journal of Child Custody, 14*(2–3), 134–150. doi:10.1080/15379418.2017.1365320

Bischoff, L. (1995). Test review of Parent Awareness Skills Survey. In J. C. Conoley & J. C. Impara (Eds.), *The twelfth mental measurements yearbook.* Retrieved from https://web-a-ebscohost-com.ezproxy.barry.edu

Boothroyd, R. A. (1998). Test review of Parent Child Relationship Inventory. In J. C. Impara & B. S. Plake (Eds.), *The thirteenth mental measurements yearbook.* Lincoln, NE: Buros Center for Testing.

Bricklin, B. (1990). *Parent awareness skills survey.* Doylestown, PA: Village.

Bricklin, B., & Elliot, G. (2009). *What you should know about the Frye standard, the federal rules of evidence, and the Daubert criteria when you go to court: The admissability of expert testimony, including testimony on science, by mental health professionals.* Doylestown, PA: Village.

Burks, H. F., & Gruber, C. P. (2006). *Burks' behavior rating scales, second edition: Manual.* Los Angeles, CA: Western Psychological Services.

Carlson, J. F. (1995). Test review of Perceptions of Relationships Test. In J. C. Conoley & J. C. Impara (Eds.), *The twelfth mental measurements yearbook.* Retrieved from https://web-a-ebscohost-com.ezproxy.barry.edu

Carlson, J. F., Geisinger, K. F., & Jonson, J. L. (Eds.). (2014). *The nineteenth mental measurements yearbook.* Lincoln, NE: Buros Center for Testing.

Cole, D. (1995). Test review of Parent Awareness Skills Survey. In J. C. Conoley & J. C. Impara (Eds.), *The twelfth mental measurements yearbook.* Retrieved from https://web-a-ebscohost-com.ezproxy.barry.edu

Deutsch, R. M., & Clyman, J. (2016). Impact of mental illness on parenting capacity in a child custody matter. *Family Court Review, 54*(1), 29–38.

Geisinger, K. F., Spies, R. A., Carlson, J. F., & Plake, B. S. (Eds.). (2007). *The seventeenth mental measurements yearbook.* Lincoln, NE: Buros Center for Testing.

Gerard, A. (1994). *Parent–child relational inventory (PCRI).* Los Angeles, CA: Western Psychological Services.

Gustavsen, G., Nayga Jr., R., & Wu, X. (2016). Effects of parental divorce on teenage children's risk behaviors: Incidence and persistence. *Journal of Family and Economic Issues, 37,* 474–487. doi:10.1007/s10834-015-9460-5

Hagin, R. A. (1992). Test review of Bricklin Perceptual Scales. In J. J. Kramer & J. C. Conoley (Eds.), *The eleventh mental measurements yearbook.* Retrieved from https://web-a-ebscohost-com.ezproxy.barry.edu

Huff, S. C., Anderson, S. R., Adamsons, K. L., & Tambling, R. B. (2017). Development and validation of a scale to measure children's contact refusal of parents following divorce. *The American Journal of Family Therapy, 45*(1), 66–77.

Konold, T. R. (2017). Test review of behavior assessment system for children. In J. F. Carlson, K. F. Geisinger, & J. L. Jonson (Eds.), *The twentieth mental measurements yearbook* (3rd ed.). Retrieved from https://web-a-ebscohost-com.ezproxy.barry.edu

Kramer, J. J., & Conoley, J. C. (1992). (Eds.), *The eleventh mental measurements yearbook.* Lincoln, NE: Buros Center for Testing.

Lamela, D., Figueiredo, B., Bastos, A., & Feinberg, M. (2016). Typologies of post-divorce coparenting and parental well-being, parenting quality and children's psychological adjustment. *Child Psychiatry Human Development, 47,* 716–728.

Langenbrunner, M., Cox, M., & Cherry, D. (2013). Psychometrics of LOCA: Level of conflict assessment of divorcing couples. *Journal of Divorce & Remarriage, 54*(6), 439–457.

Maldonado, S. (2017). Bias in the family: Race, ethnicity, and culture in custody disputes. *Family Court Review, 55*(2), 213–242.

Marchant, G. J. (1998). Test review of parent-child relationship inventory. In J. C. Impara & B. S. Plake (Eds.), *The thirteenth mental measurements yearbook.* Retrieved from https://web-a-ebscohost-com.ezproxy.barry.edu

McIntosh, J. E., & Tan, E. S. (2017). Young children in divorce and separation: Pilot study of a mediation-based co-parenting intervention. *Family Court Review, 55*(3), 329–344.

Meara, K. (2014). What's in a name? Defining and granting a legal status to grandparents who are informal primary caregivers of their grandchildren. *Family Court Review, 52*(1), 128–141.

Medway, F. J. (2017). Test review of behavior assessment system for children. In J. F. Carlson, K. F. Geisinger, & J. L. Jonson (Eds.), *The twentieth mental measurements yearbook* (3rd ed.). Retrieved from https://web-a-ebscohost-com.ezproxy.barry.edu

Melton, G. (1995). Test review of Ackerman-Schoendorf scales for parent evaluation of custody. In J. C. Conoley & J. C. Impara (Eds.), *The twelfth mental measurements yearbook.* Lincoln, NE: Buros Center for Testing.

Millon® Adolescent Clinical Inventory: Scoring and reporting. (n.d.). Retrieved from https://www.pearsonclinical.com/psychology/products/100000667/millon-adolescent-clinical-inventory-maci.html#tab-scoring

Nielsen, L. (2015). Pop goes the woozle: Being misled by research on child custody and parenting plans. *Journal of Divorce & Remarriage, 56*(8), 595–633. doi:10.1080/10502 556.2015.1092349

Pfeiffer, S. I. (2007). Test review of Millon pre-adolescent clinical inventory. In K. F. Geisinger, R. A. Spies, J. F. Carlson, & B. S. Plake (Eds.), *The seventeenth mental measurements yearbook.* Retrieved from https://web-a-ebscohost-com.ezproxy.barry.edu

Ramage, F. A., & Barnard, C. P. (2005). Custody evaluations: Critical contextual and ethical considerations. *The American Journal of Family Therapy, 33,* 339–351. doi:10.1080/01926180500274500

Retzlaff, P., Sheehan, E., & Lorr, M. (1990). MCMI-II scoring: Weighted and unweighted algorithms. *Journal of Personality Assessment, 55,* 219–223.

Reynolds, C. R., & Kamphaus, R. W. (1992). *Behavior assessment system for children: Manual.* Circle Pines, MN: American Guidance.

Roberts, M. (2001). Test review of a comprehensive custody evaluation standard system. In S. Plake & J. C. Impara (Eds.), *The fourteenth mental measurements yearbook.* Retrieved from https://web-a-ebscohost-com.ezproxy.barry.edu

Rohrbaugh, J. B. (2008). *A comprehensive guide to child custody evaluations: Mental health and legal perspectives.* New York, NY: Springer.

Sanford, K. & Rivers, A. S. (2017). The parting parent concerns inventory: Parent's appraisals correlate with divorced family functioning. *The Journal of Family Psychology, 37*(7), 867–877.

Simmons, D. K. (2010). A review of the practice and science of child custody and access assessment in the United States and Canada. *Professional Psychology: Research and Practice, 41*(3), 267–273.

Smith, J. V. (2017). Test review of behavior assessment system for children parenting relationship questionnaire. In J. F. Carlson, K. F. Geisinger, & J. L. Jonson (Eds.), *The twentieth mental measurements yearbook*. Retrieved from https://web-a-ebscohost-com.ezproxy.barry.edu

Stuart, R. B. (1995). Test review of Millon adolescent clinical inventory. In J. C. Conoley & J. C. Impara (Eds.), *The twelfth mental measurements yearbook*. Retrieved from https://web-a-ebscohost-com.ezproxy.barry.edu

Suen, H. K. (2010). Test review of Burks' behavior rating scales. In R. A. Spies, J. F. Carlson, & K. F. Geisinger (Eds.), *The eighteenth mental measurements yearbook* (2nd ed.). Retrieved from https://web-a-ebscohost-com.ezproxy.barry.edu

Tien, J. Y., Sandler, I. N., Braver, S.L., & Wolchik, S. A. (2013). Development of a brief parent-report risk index for children following parental divorce. *Journal of Family Psychology, 27*(6), 925–936.

Valeriao, C., & Beck, C. J. (2017). Testing in child custody evaluation: An overview of issues and uses. *Journal of Child Custody, 14*(4), 260–280.

Weaver, J. M., & Schofield, T. J. (2015). Mediation and moderation of divorce effects on children's behavior problems. *Journal of Family Psychology, 29*(1), 39–48.

Widaman, K. F. (2017). Test review of behavior assessment system for children parenting relationship questionnaire. In J. F. Carlson, K. F. Geisinger, & J. L. Jonson (Eds.), *The twentieth mental measurements yearbook*. Retrieved from https://web-a-ebscohost-com.ezproxy.barry.edu

Young, S. (2014). Test review of parent stress index. In J. F. Carlson, K. F. Geisinger, & J. L. Jonson (Eds.), *The nineteenth mental measurements yearbook*. Retrieved from https://web-a-ebscohost-com.ezproxy.barry.edu

11

CHILD ABUSE ASSESSMENT STRATEGY AND INVENTORIES

Vassilia Binensztok and Tiffany E. Vastardis[1]

In the past several years, the issue of psychological abuse has begun to take the forefront, in terms of both assessment and research. From this trend, a myriad of complications arise, most specifically the subjective nature of the conceptualization of such offenses, a lack of robust assessment tools to effectively capture such experiences for the purposes of screening, reporting, and intervention, and the omission of formal diagnoses which adequately illustrate the consequences born from such experiences. However, with the widely utilized Adverse Childhood Experiences (ACE) questionnaire's (Felitti et al., 1998) revolutionary turn toward a focus on issues of emotional neglect and abuse, the National Child Traumatic Stress Network's (NCTSN) operationalization of the definition of interpersonally based *complex trauma* (NCTSN, n.d.), and the proposal of diagnoses to support such experiences (van der Kolk et al., 2009), it is likely that the body of assessment tools and literature are likely to continue to expand as we engender a deeper understanding of the nature and impact of these occurrences.

In gathering information for child maltreatment evaluations, it has become increasingly evident that deficiency and inconsistency abound, serving detrimental to the outcome of decisions made in critical circumstances. While it was once the case that parents were the primary informants in such cases, a significant body of research indicated that their accounts are often highly unreliable (Stockhammer, Salzinger, Feldman, & Mojica, 2001). While improvements in accuracy can be gleaned from also gathering information from children (Jent et al., 2009), their lack of comprehension of what constitutes inappropriate treatment can limit the magnitude of their contribution. Furthermore, though reports constructed by Child Protective Service (CPS) agencies are often considered to be the most objective, it should be noted that a great deal of the information that they gather comes through third party channels and often lacks details pertaining to less overt forms of abuse (Kobulsky, Kepple, & Jedwab, 2018). Hence, a movement toward collecting information from a more holistic informant base is becoming the new standard in maltreatment investigations.

Finally, cultural and societal factors pertaining to perceptions and acts of child maltreatment take the stage in this update, as the breadth of research on child maltreatment originates in Western countries. Subsequently, norms of behavior subscribe to theories based on related philosophy; however, the demographic portrait of society continues to diversify at an increasing rate, and such standards are no longer representative of the population at large. Perspectives of what constitutes maltreatment varies across cultures (Raman & Hodes, 2011) and of increasing importance becomes the various means to define such acts in a culturally sensitive manner. Furthermore, with current unrest abound in the global sociopolitical climate, issues such as immigration-related child abuse and trauma have surfaced in the assessment and research literature across both legal and human services fields (Allen, Cisneros, & Tellez, 2015; de Arellano et al., 2018). Further complicating the assessment of childhood maltreatment is the phenomenon of transgenerational trauma, wherein the vestiges of psychological injury are inherited by means of generational exposure to collective traumatic events. A burgeoning body of research suggests that these intergenerational traumas can lend to unresolved internalizing factors and epigenetic changes in affected families (Durham & Webb, 2014) and further manifest as various forms of maladaptive externalizing behaviors and other forms of psychopathology (Osher et al., 2011).

In sum, the deliberate assessment cases of child maltreatment must be assumed through a broad-scoped lens, inclusive of considerate of factors both overt and explicit, as well as covert and implicit. In terms of the latter, the available body of research and assessment tools, remains limited. Yet, it is imperative that concerned parties take into account variables that extend beyond personal values and norms, while making certain to adhere to principles of evidence-based practice.

With this update comes the addition of new instruments supporting to the assessment and diagnosis of Post-Traumatic Stress Disorder (PTSD), Post-Traumatic Stress Syndrome (PTSS), and Developmental Traumatic Disorder (DTD) across various sociocultural contexts, including the well-known and widely utilized ACE questionnaire. As multidimensionality is integral to contemporary child abuse investigations, a measure assessing attitudes towards sexual abuse amongst community members and service providers is integrated into this chapter's supportive case examination protocol.

Assessment Complexities

Acts versus Diagnoses

All forms of child maltreatment, including physical abuse, sexual abuse, psychological abuse, neglect, and exposure to family violence are events rather than diagnoses, in and of themselves (Olafson & Connelly, 2012). Therefore, the psychological symptoms that arise as consequences to these events must be assessed in terms of diagnostic criteria (Babiker & Herbert, 1996). Many victims and perpetrators, however, may not display symptoms (Olafson & Connelly, 2012). Additionally, the definitions of abusive acts and the level of harm caused can vary greatly between individuals, families, and cultures. Certain parental discipline methods, including yelling and threatening, can be observed in many families, without necessarily being labeled as abusive (Arruabarrena, De Paul, Indias, & Ullate, 2013). For this reason, psychological abuse can be particularly difficult to assess and substantiate (Arruabarrena et al., 2013). Finally, longer-term effects of child maltreatment can overlap with signs that abuse is currently taking place and clinicians must be careful to differentiate past and current abuse.

Informants

Acquiring accurate and adequate information is critical in child maltreatment evaluations. Unfortunately, use of collateral information is often neglected in child abuse assessment. A review of evaluations completed by the Florida Child Protection Team found that only a small number of evaluations included information from multiple sources such as relatives, teachers, and doctors (Jent et al., 2009). Accuracy can be improved by evaluating both children and parents (Gilbert et al., 2009), although studies have identified numerous constraints to both child and parental reports (Stockhammer et al., 2001). Conte, Berliner, and Schuerman (1986 assessed 369 sexually abused children using the Child Behaviour Profile for parents and the Symptom Checklist for social workers. They found that parents and social workers presented largely different reports of the children's functioning and hypothesized that social workers were more likely to focus on behavioral disturbance. Parents were found to be highly unreliable reporters of child maltreatment. They found husbands and wives often reported domestic violence differently and were likely to underestimate the effects of intimate partner violence on children (Stockhammer et al., 2001). Distraught and hostile mothers were found to be more likely to evaluate their children more severely, and abusive parents were more likely to ascribe unfavorable motives to their children's behavior (Stockhammer et al., 2001).

Consequently, reports from Child Protective Services (CPS) may be more reliable because they report specific dates and details of alleged abuse events.

Still, CPS reports can be inadequate, based on hearsay and vary from worker to worker. CPS reports have been found to lack a full range of the abuse details, have low agreement with self-reports of abuse, and are more likely to detect seriously injurious incidents rather than less severe abuse and emotional abuse (Kobulsky et al., 2018).

Children, themselves, can also be poor sources of information for assessment of sexual abuse as they may be afraid or reluctant to report information or may be confused about the nature of the abuse because of a lack of sexual knowledge. The use of multiple sources of information (i.e., children, parents, non-offending relatives, teachers) is recommended for a thorough evaluation of maltreatment.

Symptomology and Diagnosis

Symptomology

Symptoms resulting from child maltreatment can be difficult to assess as their patterns and manifestations can change as children mature. Additionally, clinicians should be aware of a "sleeper effect" (Olafson & Connelly, 2012, p. 267), as some children may appear asymptomatic after experiencing abuse, and their symptoms only become apparent much later. Often, those children that show the fewest initial symptoms have poorer prognoses over time (Olafson & Connelly, 2012). Common long-term psychological effects of maltreatment include decreased self-esteem and altered self-other schemas which may not be apparent during initial assessment but affect future mental health, employment, and relationship outcomes.

Resiliency, understanding and meaning-making, and cultural influences can affect a child's presentation during assessment, making it more difficult to evaluate maltreatment (Maitra, 1996). "Dimensions of abuse" (Stockhammer et al., 2001, p. 322) including the type of abuse, severity, frequency and duration, the child's developmental period, and separation from caregivers can all compound the complexity of symptom assessment. Symptoms can be moderated by child factors like temperament or environmental factors like social support so that maltreated children may present with symptoms that do not adequately reflect their experiences (Arruabarrena et al., 2013).

Diagnostic Criteria

The *Diagnostic and Statistical Manual of Mental Disorders* (DSM) diagnosis for PTSD was created based on the symptomatic presentation of Vietnam war veterans (Olafson & Connelly, 2012). Although abused children frequently develop PTSD, they may not meet the DSM criteria on paper (Landauer, 2012). In some cases, a designation of PTSS may be indicated. However, in others, the disconnect between traumatic experiences and presentations can be attributed to the difference between Type I and Type II traumas. While Type I traumas include single events, Type II or *complex traumas* involve repeated exposure to traumatic events over time. More specifically, the NCTSN (n.d.) has defined *complex trauma* as "a series of traumatic experiences that are usually interpersonal in nature and lead to numerous long-term adverse effects on health and well-being," (Hudspeth, 2015, p. 195). When such inter-relational traumas are present, it is more than likely that they will be evidenced not only in the presentation of the affected child, but also in interruptions in the functioning of the dynamics of the entire family or household unit (Kira, 2001).

The DSM diagnosis of PTSD refers to Type I traumas and therefore does not account for the more complex presentation of Type II trauma. Furthermore, children are affected by trauma differently than adults and these experiences can alter the developmental course of their personalities, cognitive abilities, attachment, and emotional regulation. Type II traumas can have the most detrimental effects on children younger than seven (Olafson & Connelly, 2012). A survey of 1,699 children receiving trauma-focused therapy through the NCTSN (2005) revealed that 78% of those children had experienced Type II traumas yet fewer than a quarter qualified for the diagnosis of PTSD (van der Kolk et al., 2009). For these reasons, clinicians and researchers have proposed new diagnoses for Complex PTSD (cPTSD) in adults, and DTD in children. While neither cPTSD nor DTD were integrated into the DSM, Fifth Edition (APA, 2013), both are being proposed for inclusion into the next iteration of the World Health Organization's International Classification of Diseases.

Limits of Instrumentation

We do not have instruments to assess some of the most damaging sequelae of childhood maltreatment. Attachment is studied formally in laboratory settings using the Strange Situation but less formally in clinical settings, and observations comprise the most useful data points for children (Friedrich, 2002). Research continues on an adult measure, the Adult Attachment Interview (Bakermans-Kranenburg & van IJzendoorn, 2009). Self-report measures for youth have also been developed but do not yet have full reliability and validity data available (www.nctsn.org). Many psychological batteries depend heavily on patient self-report inventories that contain validity scales to assess reporting attitudes. Individual, ethnic, cultural, developmental, and gendered reporting styles influence parent and child reports. When abuse and trauma are at issue, validity is especially challenging to assess. For example, children, especially those traumatized children whose post-traumatic symptoms include numbing and avoidance, are often poor reporters of their own internal states and symptoms (Friedrich, 2002; Olafson, 1999). Parent reports tend to focus on children's externalizing symptoms while under-reporting children's internalizing symptoms such as anxiety and depression (Stover & Berkowitz, 2005). Even non-traumatized children minimize undesirable response patterns such as anger. Traumatized adults who have PTSD or dissociative symptoms may appear to be "faking bad" on standard measures, or their test results may erroneously indicate that they suffer from thought disorders (Briere, 1997; Carlson, 1997). Adults with PTSD symptoms may over-report their children's PTSD symptoms (Laor, Wolmer, & Cohen, 2001). Secondary motives may also affect reporting accuracy, as when clients are suing in civil court for damages, or when custody and visitation are at stake (Olafson & Connelly, 2012).

Misdiagnosis and Comorbidity

Child maltreatment can be misdiagnosed for many reasons, one of which is false reporting. Children can be coerced into making false claims or can be swayed by leading questions. On the other hand, therapists' fears of implanting false memories can sway them from evaluating suspicions of sexual abuse, leading them not to diagnose actual events (Babiker & Herbert, 1998). The comorbidity of different types of maltreatment can also lead to misdiagnosis. Neglect and psychological abuse often co-occur with and worsen the effects of physical abuse. Comorbidity makes it difficult to assess the nature of maltreatment and the qualities of the families in which these events take place (Stockhammer et al., 2001). While psychological abuse can have the most damaging effects, and often co-occurs with other forms of maltreatment, it can also be the most difficult to assess (Arruabarrena et al., 2013).

Children can present with other mental health problems, often precipitated by maltreatment, that can obscure the presence of a maltreatment history (Gilbert et al., 2009). For example, rates of ADHD symptoms were 20% more likely in sexually abused girls than in girls with no abuse history. Symptoms of maltreatment like impulse control problems, hypersexuality, and emotional dysregulation can look like Bipolar symptoms (Olafson & Connelly, 2012). Many maltreated children can develop depression, anxiety, and behavior problems (Landauer, 2012), self-harming behaviors, suicidality (Wilson, Hansen, & Li, 2011) as well as aggression, poor peer relationships, and decreased academic performance (Stockhammer et al., 2001) leading clinicians to underestimate the effects of trauma. Children in the juvenile delinquency system are often misdiagnosed as well as the focus tends to be on their behaviors. One review revealed that up to 90% of children in legal custody had experienced some form of maltreatment, and sexual abuse was specifically prevalent in offending girls (Gilbert et al., 2009). Subsequent to child maltreatment, changes in the hypothalamic-pituitary-adrenal axis may lead to symptoms that point to other disorders, leaving a trauma history unrecognized (Wilson et al., 2011).

Cultural and Societal Factors

Cultural Factors

Clinicians must consider cultural factors when assessing child maltreatment, particularly in non-Western individuals. Scholars describe cultural identity as encompassing multiple 'selves' that are formed through acculturation (an individual's socialization into a second culture) and enculturation (an individual's socialization into their culture of origin). Most research on child maltreatment originates in Western countries, and views of what is considered normal based on Western standards can affect both assessment and treatment (Maitra, 1996). Definitions of maltreatment vary across cultures, and promoting one's own cultural values on assessment does not reflect ethical practice and can lead to false assumptions (Raman & Hodes, 2011).

Questions arise as to how to define maltreatment in a culturally sensitive way. For example, clinicians may struggle with defining neglect in cultures where resources are severely lacking (Maitra, 1996). Numerous studies show variation in cultural definitions of behavior. A study by Hackett and Hackett found the families of Gujarati Indian boys had expectations of behavior and views on conflict resolution that differed drastically from their English peers (Raman & Hodes, 2011). Similarly, Segal (1992) found that health and social workers in India did not find physical abuse to be as serious as American workers did, yet they rated a greater number of adult sexual behaviors as harmful to children.

Researchers recommend basing assessment decisions on morbidity yet caution clinicians to consider who set the standards for what is harmful and what is acceptable. For example, scarification is typically not considered as harmful as clitoridectomies (Maitra, 1996). Caution must be taken not to excuse maltreatment based on cultural norms in the case of acts like honor killings and female genital mutilation. Yet, these issues may lead Western therapists to reconsider their values by re-examining culturally acceptable Western traditions like circumcision (Raman & Hodes, 2011).

Several models promote culturally competent decision making. The Kamoa model suggests a continuum of child-rearing practices that range from beneficial to harmful. The Korbin model suggests clinicians acknowledge cultural differences, understand that abusive acts can be viewed as those that deviate from a specific culture's norms, and increase knowledge of greater environmental factors like poverty (Raman & Hodes, 2011). While these models provide a framework for understanding, neither fully addresses the complexities of culturally competent assessment.

Societal Factors

Factors like socioeconomic status, access to resources and education, and residence in disordered or unsafe neighborhoods have long been known to negatively impact children, often leading to long-term consequences (Zuberi &

Teixeira, 2017). Changing political landscapes and policies in the United States are now highlighting factors associated to immigration, leading to further complications in assessment of child maltreatment. Over 200,000 individuals were deported from the United States in 2015 (Immigration and Customs Enforcement, 2015). Children in families who have been separated during the immigration or deportation process are at risk of trauma and the inconsistency with which they are evaluated and treated at medical or mental health centers creates a barrier to assessment (Knopf, 2017). Furthermore, a study on the impact of parental deportation found that children with a deported parent were more likely to display both internalizing and externalizing problem behaviors than children without a deported parent (Allen et al., 2015).

Transgenerational Trauma

Considering the effects of transgenerational trauma is essential to assessing and understanding non-European-American clients. Transgenerational trauma, also referred to as historical trauma, multigenerational trauma, collective trauma, historic grief, etc., refers to the inherited effects of psychological injuries sustained by generations as a result of collective exposure to traumatic events and abuses such as genocides, slavery, and internment. Transgenerational trauma can lead to unresolved historical grief, chronic feelings of disenfranchisement, internalized oppression, and epigenetic changes (Durham & Webb, 2014). These experiences can manifest through oppositional or destructive behaviors, difficulty processing internal states, depression, anxiety, and other mental health symptoms (Osher et al., 2011), further complicating the assessment of symptoms in children potentially exposed to child abuse.

Assessment Limitations

This chapter does not address the neuropsychological symptoms suffered by many child maltreatment victims. If a batterer has beaten a pregnant woman's abdomen, shaken her or her child, or beaten the mother or child on the face or head, a complete neuropsychological assessment referral for these victims is recommended (Valera & Barenbaum, 2003). In many cases, impulsive and aggressive males and females would benefit from neuropsychological assessments to determine if targeted psychopharmacological interventions might be of assistance to counter the effects of possible brain damage from child abuse or adult affrays (Olafson & Connelly, 2012).

Adaptations of standard psychological inventories for adults that include the Minnesota Multiphasic Personality Inventory, revised version (MMPI-2), Millon Clinical Multiaxial Inventory, third edition (MCMI-III), Rorschach (Exner System), Weschler Intelligence Scale for Children III, and Wechsler Adult Intelligence Scale III (WAIS III) are not addressed in this chapter. Instruments that assess adult post-traumatic symptoms, such as the Trauma

Symptom Inventory (TSI), are also not included, although evaluation of parents may be essential for treatment success. (Readers are referred to Briere, 1997; Foa, Keane, & Friedman, 2009; Friedrich, 2002; Olafson, 1999; Wilson & Keane, 1997.) Every competent evaluator should become aware of the limitations and the distorted diagnostic picture that may emerge when only standard instruments are applied to trauma survivors such as combat veterans and child sexual abuse victims (Olafson & Connelly, 2012).

Selection of Instruments

Many instruments used to assess children are based on adult PTSD symptoms, viewing children through an "adult-based lens" (Olafson & Connelly, 2012, p. 267). There are no instruments to assess some of the most detrimental consequences of child maltreatment (i.e., attachment, holistic socioemotional trauma), and most instruments are used primarily in research settings (Gilbert et al., 2009). Not only do children have difficulty reporting internal states, but also cultural and developmental factors can influence reporting. Standardized assessment is difficult to achieve, because instruments may need to be administered differently, based on children's reading abilities and needs. Furthermore, no full reliability and validity data exists for self-report instruments (Olafson & Connelly, 2012).

Assessment Instruments

Parent, Caregiver, and Teacher Report Measures

Child Behavior Checklist (CBCL) PTSD Subscale
Child Sexual Behavior Inventory (CSBI)
Child Dissociative Checklist (CDC)
Pediatric Emotional Distress Scale (PEDS)
Child Abuse Potential Inventory (CAPI)
Parent–Child Conflict Tactics Scale (CTSPC)
The Child Sexual Abuse Attitudes Measure

Child Self-Report Measures

ACE Questionnaire

Trauma Symptom Checklist for Young Children (TSCYC)
The Child and Adolescent Trauma Screen (CATS)
Impact of Events Scale (IES)
Adolescent Dissociative Experiences Scale (A-DES)
Children's PTSD-Reaction Index (CPTS-RI)
The Child Victimization Trauma Assessment

Parent, Caregiver, and Teacher Report Measures
Child Behavior Checklist (CBCL) PTSD Subscale

The full CBCL is covered elsewhere in this edited volume (Chapter 10). The family of CBCL-related instruments is informative and useful in studies of traumatized and maltreated children. There have been two attempts to develop PTSD-related subscales from the CBCL (Levendosky, Huth-Bocks, Semel, & Shapiro, 2002; Wolfe, Gentile, Michienzi, Sas, & Wolfe, 1991). Levendosky and colleagues (2002) found no correlations between their version of the scale and a standard PTSD scale. However, Dehon and Scheeringa (2006) modified the subscale for preschoolers and studied 62 traumatized children aged 23 months through six years of age. Mothers were interviewed about the child's PTSD symptoms and then filled out the CBCL. The PTSD subscale correlated highly ($r = .66$) with the number of PTSD symptoms described during interviews, with a cutoff score of nine having the best sensitivity and specificity for classifying children who met diagnostic criteria for PTSD (Dehon & Scheeringa, 2006).

Parental rejection of the child will be reflected in CBCL results. For example, elevated CBCL scores by parents, relative to teachers, are closely related to parental endorsement of such items as "My child knows how to bug me," and "I will feel better when this child is out of the room" (Friedrich, Lysne, Sim, & Shamos, 2004).

Child Sexual Behavior Inventory (CSBI)

Instrument name. The CSBI was developed by William N. Friedrich, Ph.D., with the assistance of numerous colleagues (Friedrich, 1997). This measure has been used in an increasing number of studies examining normative and disturbed sexual behavior in children.

Type of instrument. The CSBI is a 38-item measure developed for use with 2- to 12-year-old children. Either parent can complete it although the norms are based on maternal report. An additional four items designed to assess more aggressive and intrusive sexual behavior are described elsewhere (Friedrich, 2002). Clinical use with teachers, day care providers, and other relatives has also been reported in the literature. Training is required for administration and scoring.

Use and target audience. CSBI is intended for children living in a home setting, aged 2–12 years, and assesses a variety of sexual behaviors exhibited over the past six months falling into such face-valid factors as boundary problems, self-stimulation, gender-related behaviors, sexual intrusiveness, and sexual knowledge.

Multicultural. The CSBI has been translated into several Western European languages and has also been used in epidemiological studies of sexual behavior in several Eastern European countries, including Latvia, Moldova, Macedonia, and Lithuania (Sebre et al., 2004).

Ease and time of administration. The CSBI requires from 5 to 10 minutes to complete; parents should have the opportunity for clarification of individual items.

Scoring procedure. CSBI is hand-scored and provides three summary scores, including total sexual behavior, developmentally related sexual behavior, and sexual abuse specific items. Developmentally related sexual behaviors are those behaviors that are reported by at least 20% of the normative sample for that age and gender. Sexual abuse specific items are those behaviors that significantly discriminated abused from non-abused children for specific age and gender subgroups after controlling for age, gender, maternal education, and family income. A number of very unusual behaviors, which typically are exhibited primarily by sexually abused children, are not included in the CBSI because of their rarity but, when present, certainly raise concern.

Reliability, validity, availability, and source. The CSBI has very adequate test–retest reliability, and parents typically correlate with each other. It has demonstrated utility in identifying sexually abused children. Studies of normative sexual behavior in Sweden, the Netherlands, and the United States show considerable similarities among the more unusual behaviors. The CSBI is available from Psychological Assessment Resources, Odessa, Florida.

Comment. The CSBI is the only normed, validated, and published measure of sexual behavior in children. Parents of sexually abused children tend to either minimize or maximize their child's sexual behavior more so than do parents of non-abused children, and reviewing each behavior with parents can be useful to determine the validity of their reports. Although high scores raise concern about possible sexual abuse, they may also reflect response bias, exposure to pornography or overt family sexuality, or some mixture of externalizing behavior problems with sexual provocativeness.

Child Dissociative Checklist (CDC)

Instrument name. The CDC was developed by Frank W. Putnam, M.D., and his associates in the 1980s (Putnam, Helmers, & Trickettt, 1993; Putnam & Peterson, 1994). Over the course of its development, the CDC has progressed through three major versions. The current version (v3.0-2/90) is a 20-item instrument. It is designed to be both a clinical screening tool and a research tool for dissociative disorders but is not intended for use as a diagnostic instrument.

Type of instrument. The CDC is a 20-item parent/adult report measure using a three-point scale response format (i.e., 2 = very True, 1 = Somewhat or Sometimes True, and 0 = Not True). The CDC lists behaviors that describe children, and reporters are asked to circle the corresponding number (i.e., 2, 1, or 0) for each item that describes their child "now" or "within the past 12 months." However, clinicians are free to specify another time frame, when, for example, the instrument is administered periodically to assess treatment progress.

Use and target audience. The CDC is designed for children aged 5–14. The CDC should be completed by a parent, caretaker, teacher, therapist, or inpatient staff member who is very familiar with the child's behavior and is in frequent contact with the child.

Multicultural. Putnam (1997) reports, "We know less about the effects of gender and culture on CDC scores. I am certain that these factors influence reported scores in some cases, and probably more so for children than for adults" (p. 252). The CDC has been translated into Spanish and Italian. Translations are available by request at http://www.ohiocando4kids. org/Dissociation.

Ease and time of administration. The CDC is a brief, 20-item observer report measure that takes 5–10 minutes to administer and score.

Scoring procedure. The CDC score is the sum of all of the item scores and can range from 0 to 40 on version 3.0. Developmental, cultural, and individual variables must be taken into account when interpreting a CDC score. CDC scores tend to decrease with age, suggesting that young children experience slightly more dissociation than do older children. However, in the most extreme cases of dissociation, maturation does not affect scores. Generally, a score of 12 or higher is considered an indication of pathological dissociation warranting further evaluation. Children who do not have a trauma or maltreatment history generally have very low scores on the CDC, just above a score of 2. Maltreated children have higher scores, a mean of 6.0. The mean for children with dissociative disorders is about 20.

Reliability. The CDC has been shown to be a reliable instrument in several studies. The CDC shows moderate to good one-year test–retest stability ($r = .65$) and internal consistency (Cronbach's alpha = .86).

Validity. The validity of the CDC has primarily been assessed on its ability to discriminate among groups. Several studies have found that sexually abused children score significantly higher on the CDC than non-abused comparison children, and the CDC is generally able to discriminate between children with pathological dissociation and those without. In one study of four test samples, the CDC discriminated between normal control girls, sexually abused girls, children with Dissociative Disorder NOS, and children with Dissociative Identity Disorder (Putnam et al., 1993). Good convergent and discriminant validity have been indicated. The more serious the abuse history (e.g., combined physical and sexual abuse, multiple perpetrators), the higher the CDC score (Putnam, Helmers, Horowitz, & Trickett, 1994).

Availability and source. The CDC is a public domain document freely available for reproduction, distribution, and use. Readers who wish to make changes to it are asked to change the name to reduce confusion. The CDC is available by request at http://www.ohiocando4kids.org/Dissociation and in the appendices of Putnam (1997).

Comment. The complex disorders associated with severe and prolonged childhood trauma and maltreatment include pathological dissociation; indeed, dissociative disorders are rarely seen among those who have no victimization histories (Putnam, 1997). This easily administered, freely available, valid, and reliable instrument fills a need for screening children as young as five years old for the presence of pathological dissociation. High scores alert clinicians and evaluators to undertake structured clinical interviews for formal diagnosis. Many CDC items can be confounded with attention deficit disorders, so that interviews with parents are necessary to determine if endorsed items are suggestive of dissociation or are related to ADHD (Friedrich, 2002). The two diagnoses are not mutually exclusive. The CDC's sensitivity to dose exposure adds to its usefulness with children. Because the CDC is freely available and easily administered, it is widely used in clinical and research settings.

Pediatric Emotional Distress Scale (PEDS)

Instrument name. The PEDS was published in 1999 by Conway Saylor, Ph.D., and colleagues. It is not a measure of PTSD as defined in the DSM, Fourth Edition (DSM-IV), a diagnosis derived from work with traumatized adults and then adapted for use with children. Instead, the items on this scale were chosen based on behaviors that have been identified as occurring to young children who have experienced or are experiencing trauma.

Type of instrument. The PEDS consists of 21 items (17 general behavior and four event-specific) rated by the parent or guardian to measure the behavioral problems of children aged 2 through 10 years old after trauma. The scale consists of three subscales: Anxious/Withdrawn, Fearful, and Acting Out. In addition, there are items that ask about post-traumatic behaviors by children such as games, stories, and play about the trauma.

Use and target audience. Children 2 through 10 years old who have been traumatized by homelessness, sexual abuse, natural disasters, and other negative experiences.

Multicultural. The PEDS is among the few instruments in which psychometric properties have been examined for homeless children. As a recently developed instrument, the PEDS has not been tested widely among diverse cultural groups. The PEDS is not intended for use alone as a diagnostic or forensic instrument but as a screening measure that forms part of a more complete assessment.

Ease and time of administration. The PEDS takes 5–10 minutes to administer and score. The PEDS appears to be a sensitive measure of stress in children, and its brevity provides an advantage in assessments during high-stress situations.

Scoring procedure. The higher the scores are, the greater the child's distress is.

Reliability. The overall alpha coefficient for the first 17 items was .85. Test–retest reliability at six weeks ranged from .55 to .61. Interrater reliability between fathers and mothers ranged from .65 for the PEDS total and ranged from .47 to .64 for subscales.

Validity. Parental evaluations correlated with total scores. Further work on discriminant validity is needed. The scale shows good sensitivity and specificity for traumatized children compared with non-clinical samples of non-traumatized children. The scale shows good sensitivity to the stressors experienced by homeless children, for example. Although the PEDS assesses behavior problems that are common among traumatized children, many of these same behaviors also occur among clinical samples of children who have not been traumatized, and further studies are needed to assess the discriminant validity of this measure on traumatized versus non-traumatized clinical samples (Ohan, Myers, & Collett, 2002). Years of education affected maternal scores, with less educated mothers endorsing fewer items at a high level.

Availability and source. A copy of this brief scale is printed in Saylor, Swenson, Reynolds, & Taylor (1999). The Pediatric Emotional Distress Scale: A brief screening measure for young children exposed to traumatic events. *Journal of Clinical Child Psychology, 28,* 70–81. Before using the scale, contact Conway Saylor for consent and further clinical information.

Comment. This brief and promising instrument fills a need by screening the responses of preschool children to trauma, but it is still in the early stages of development and validation, and further work on discriminant validity is expected. This instrument has the advantage of not trying to fit stressed and traumatized children's symptom patterns into diagnostic categories developed during research with adults. The scale was constructed in consultation with investigators who had studied the effects of disasters on children, and then the scale was reviewed by doctoral-level clinical psychologists for appropriateness. Because the symptoms of fearfulness, anxiety, withdrawal, and acting out observed in traumatized children are also commonly seen in non-traumatized clinical samples, discriminant validity studies may not usefully separate these two populations. Nevertheless, anxiety or acting out associated with abuse and trauma histories in children will require different treatment approaches than non-trauma-based anxiety or acting out in children. Complete abuse and trauma histories should always be obtained as part of differential diagnostic work for these presenting symptoms in young children.

Parenting Stress Index (PSI)

The PSI is covered in Chapter 10 of this volume and is widely used in trauma and maltreatment assessments.

Child Abuse Potential Inventory (CAPI)

Instrument name. The CAPI was developed by Joel Milner (Milner, 1986).

Type of instrument. The CAPI was developed with the goal that it could be employed by protective services workers to screen for physical child abuse. Because of its use in the field, another goal was that it be relatively simple. The initial item pool represented the existing empirical and theoretical literature on maltreatment.

Use and target audience. The CAPI is intended to be used primarily as a screening tool for the detection of physical child abuse. Although specifically designed to be employed by protective services workers, it is also used as a psychological test.

Multicultural. The CAPI has norms not only for the United States but also for Spain. It has been translated into a number of other languages, and research in other cultures has indicated that the underlying constructs of the CAPI are present in other cultures. However, this is an under-researched area of the CAPI.

Ease and time of administration. There is no time limit for completing the test, and given the circumstances of its use, some parents approach this task in a very deliberate manner. Typically, it takes from 12 to 20 minutes to complete.

Scoring procedures. These scales can be hand scored or computer scored. The primary clinical scale is a 77-item physical child abuse scale. This abuse scale can be divided into six factor scales: Distress, Rigidity, Unhappiness, Problems With Child and Self, Problems With Family, and Problems With Others. In addition, the CAPI contains three validity scales: lie scale, random response scale, and inconsistency scale. The validity scales are used in various combinations to produce three response distortion indices: faking good index, faking bad index, and random response index.

Reliability, validity, availability, and source. The CAPI manual (Milner, 1986) reports an impressive body of research supporting the internal consistency and temporal stability of the CAPI. In addition, the CAPI correlates with the PSI ($r = .62$) as well as relevant personality factors derived from the Edwards Personal Preference Schedule, the 16 personality factor questionnaire, and the MMPI. CAPI abuse classification rates in the literature are typically in the range of 80% to 90% when severe abuse parents are compared to non-abusing parents. The measure, manual, and scoring information are available from PSYTEC, Inc., DeKalb, Illinois.

Comment. Both the PSI and the CAPI assess relevant and similar dimensions of the parent–child relationship. The advantage of the CAPI is that it also assesses for physical abuse potential. Consequently, if physical abuse is ever an issue, it is preferable to administer the CAPI rather than the PSI. Otherwise for treatment purposes, the PSI-Short Form (PSI-SF) is usually sufficient to determine the degree to which parents are in need of support and how accurately they view their child. Because of its general nature, the CAPI cannot be used to differentiate between neglect and abuse.

Parent–Child Conflict Tactic Scale (CTSPC)

Instrument name. The CTSPC was developed by Murray Straus Hamby, Finkelhor, Moore, and Runyan (1998), many of them at the Family Research Laboratory at the University of New Hampshire. This scale is one of several conflict tactic scales (CTS) developed by Straus and colleagues.

Type of instrument. The CTSPC is a brief measure that is practical for epidemiological research on child maltreatment and for clinical screening by professionals. It contains 22 items that assess nonviolent discipline, psychological aggression, and physical assault. In addition, five neglect items can also be included as well as supplemental questions regarding weekly discipline and sexual maltreatment experienced by the parent.

Use and target audience. The CTSPC is intended for the parents of children living in their home, typically aged 6–17, although the authors report that the prevalence and chronicity of corporal punishment decline rapidly from about the age of five on, and consequently using it with younger children is appropriate.

Multicultural. The CTSPC research reveals no clear differences between Euro-American and either African-American or Hispanic-American parents, although research on severe assaults has typically found higher rates for the two minority groups.

Ease and time of administration. The CTSPC requires 6–8 minutes to complete, and parents should have the opportunity for clarification of items.

Scoring procedure. The three core CTSPC scales contain 22 items. Fourteen supplemental questions that assess neglect, weekly discipline, and sexual maltreatment of the parent and the child can be added to the CTSPC core scales. The standard instructions for the CTSPC ask the parent to describe what happened in the previous year although this time period can be altered depending on the individual. The parent is asked to describe his or her practices with a specific child and can rate the frequency of discipline strategies on a six-point scale, with additional information on whether or not the parent has used this strategy, has used this strategy in the past but not in the past year, or has never used this strategy. The CTSPC subscales include nonviolent discipline, psychological aggression, minor assault (corporal punishment), severe assault (physical maltreatment), and very severe assault (severe physical maltreatment).

Reliability, validity, availability, and source. The internal consistency of the CTSPC varies widely depending on the frequency of item endorsement, with very low coefficients for neglect and severe physical assault but acceptable coefficients for the other subscales. Given the recency of its development, research is only now developing regarding its discriminant and construct validity. A measure is available either from the Family Research Laboratory or from Straus et al. (1998). The CTSPC is a good companion to either the PSI-SF or the CAPI in that it allows the parent to more specifically indicate discipline strategies. Parents presenting to a clinical program vary in terms of their defensiveness on all self-report measures, and given the face validity of the items, outright denial is certainly likely. However, when used in the context of a clinical interview, or as part of an ongoing therapy process, the openness of the parent is usually appropriate and can help make them aware of the need for changes.

The Child Sexual Abuse Attitudes Measure

Type of instrument. The Child Sexual Abuse Attitudes Measure (Bailey, Mace, & Powell, 2016) is a ten-item measure set on a ten-point visual analogue scale that ranges from "strongly agree" to "strongly disagree." The Child Sexual Abuse Attitudes Measure was developed to assess the attitudes of community members and service providers, as they pertain to child sexual abuse, in accordance to four factors: Personal understanding and knowledge, Entrenched issues, Communication between community and government, and Community action (Bailey et al., 2016).

Use and target audience. The Child Sexual Abuse Attitudes Measure (Bailey et al., 2016) was designed as an adult self-report measure to be administered to community-based service providers, such as day care staff, and community members, in efforts to assess perceived levels of knowledge and awareness germane to the phenomena of child sexual abuse. Furthermore, this measure aims to assess the means by and extent to which the topic of sexual abuse is addressed within an individual's community.

Multicultural. This measure is available only in an English version.

Ease and time of administration. There is no time limit for the administration of this test, though it should take less than ten minutes.

Scoring procedure. Raw scores tallies can be recorded for the total scale, by means of manually adding up points recorded. Scoring should take roughly five minutes. A digital version is also available, which tabulates scores recorded on the digital analogue template and generates reports upon completion of the measure.

Reliability. Internal Consistency, as measured by Cronbach's alphas recorded for the total scale and across factors ranged from medium to low. Internal Consistency for the total scale was .53. Cronbach's alpha scores for the four factors as demonstrated by the final factor analysis were: Personal Understanding and Knowledge = .82, Entrenched Issues = .67, Communication between Community and Government = .63, and Community Action = .34 (Bailey et al., 2016).

Validity. One-way ANOVAs for community member and service provider groups by the four factors were run to determine discriminant validity for this new measure, revealing significant differences between groups for Entrenched Issues and Communication between Community and Government. Only Factor Communication between Community and Government was found to be significantly different between groups based on socioeconomic membership status.

Availability and source. Paper and Pencil. In: Bailey, C., Mace, G., Powell, M. (2016). Measuring community and service provider attitudes to child sexual abuse in remote indigenous communities in Western Australia. *Psychiatry, Psychology and Law*, 23(3), 435–445. doi: 10.1080/13218719.2015.1080147.

Permission for use must be obtained by contacting the publisher or corresponding author.

A Digital version of the scale may be obtained by means of contacting the corresponding author at: Powell, Martine: Deakin University, School of Psychology, 221 Burwood Hwy, Burwood, Victoria, Australia, 3125, martine.powell@deakin.edu.au.

Comment. The Child Sexual Abuse Attitudes Measure was designed to address attitudes toward sexual abuse in rural, indigenous populations in Western Australia, for legal and forensic purposes; however, the universality of the item pool deems it reasonably applicable across various contexts. The items are straightforward, and the measure easy to score and administer. While there are no fees, permissions must be obtained prior to usage.

The integrity of this brief assessment was investigated by means of a variety of psychometric applications, and though internal consistency is relatively inconsistent across factors, such for the total scale is satisfactory. Furthermore, a factor analysis of the final scale indicated a four-factor solution explaining a total of 65.5% of the variance, suggesting a factor structure in the minimally acceptable range.

Child Self-Report Measures

ACE Questionnaire

Name and type of instrument. The ACE questionnaire was developed by Felitti et al. (1998) to examine the relationship between the experience of child abuse and disease risk factors and incidence, quality of life, health care utilization, and mortality in adulthood. The ACE questionnaire is a ten-item forced-choice (yes/no) instrument, which assesses for experiences falling within the following domains: psychological, physical or sexual abuse; violence against mother; living with household members who were substance abusers, mentally ill and/or suicidal, or who were ever imprisoned during one's childhood. The latter domains were included to capture the phenomenon of neglect, both physical and psychological, making the ACE the first of its kind to assess for such experiences. ACE questionnaire finds its origins in a study conducted at Kaiser Permanente's Health Appraisal Clinic in San Diego, CA, where over 9,000 individuals who were receiving basic services were sent a paper-and-pencil version of the survey, in efforts to link adult health outcomes to adverse early experiences (Felitti et al., 1998).

Use and target audience. This brief measure is appropriate for administration to any individual over the age of 18, though it is often administered to younger individuals. ACE questionnaire is appropriate to all clinical settings for the purposes of screening, case conceptualization, and intervention design. In addition, as ACE questionnaire was designed to investigate "[t]he relationship of health risk behavior and disease in adulthood to the breadth of exposure to childhood emotional, physical, or sexual abuse, and household dysfunction during childhood..." (Felitti et al., 1998, p. 245), it is also applicable for the purposes of outcome and correlational research.

Multicultural. This measure is available in an English version, as well as a more recently developed International version.

Ease and time of administration. There is no time limit for the administration of this test, though it should take no more than ten minutes.

Scoring procedure. Scoring of the ACE survey takes less than five minutes, as all that it necessitates is a simple tally of the number of questions answered "Yes." As the number of ACEs increases, so does the risk for outcomes, such as risky health behaviors, low life potential, and early death. Those scoring 1-3/10 are considered to be at low risk for such outcomes, with those scoring 4-6/10 considered to be at moderate risk for such outcomes, while those scoring 7-10/10 are considered to be at high risk for such outcomes.

Reliability. Kappa coefficients (Dube, Williamson, Thompson, Felitti, & Anda, 2004) were yielded to determine the test–retest reliability of 658 participants' responses to the ACE questionnaire. For both individual component questions as well as each category of childhood abuse and household dysfunction, the kappa coefficients (K = .41–.86) yielded demonstrated moderate to substantial agreement (Dube et al., 2004). In regard to the total scale, the ACE score, "has repeatedly shown a strong graded relationship to the risk of numerous behavioral and health outcomes" (Dube et al., 2004, p. 735) with K = .64.

In addition, in subsequent analyses, interrater reliability analyses demonstrated high reliability of clinician rating scores generated independently on the same sample of children (Bethell et al., 2017).

Validity. According to a meta-analysis of related studies using the original ten-item version of ACE questionnaire "showed efficiency and confirmatory factor analysis as well as latent class analysis supported a cumulative risk scoring method. Formative, as well as reflective measurement models further support cumulative risk scoring and provide evidence of predictive validity" (Bethell et al., 2017, S51).

Availability and source. Paper and Pencil. In: Felitti, V. J., Anda, R.F., Nordenberg, D., Williamson, D.F, Spitz, A.M., Edwards, V., Koss, Marks, J.S. (1998). Relationship of childhood abuse and household dysfunction to many of the leading causes of death in adults: The ACES study. *American Journal of Preventive Medicine, 14(4),* 245–258. doi:http://dx.doi.org.ezproxy.fau.edu/10.1016/S0749-3797(98)00017-8.

Online PDF. At: https://www.ncjfcj.org/sites/default/files/Finding%20 Your%20ACE%20Score.pdf.

Digital. National Public Radio. (2015, March 2). Take the ACE quiz—And learn what it does and doesn't mean. Retrieved from https://www.npr.org/ sections/health-shots/2015/03/02/387007941/take-the-ace-quiz-and-learn-what-it-does-and-doesnt-mean.

Comment. With its ease in regard to both administration and scoring, the ACE questionnaire is a valuable and accessible tool. As the first measure psychometric test to retroactively assess for covert forms of abuse and neglect, ACE questionnaire aims to shed light on phenomenology underlying adverse physical and behavioral manifestations in adulthood. More specifically, the ACE questionnaire retroactively surveys for experiences of psychological abuse, physical abuse, and contact sexual abuse. It also measures four categories of exposure to household dysfunction during childhood: substance abuse, mental illness, violent treatment of mother or stepmother, and criminal behavior. In sum, these areas of assessment are clustered under three domains: Abuse, Neglect, and Household Dysfunction.

While ACE questionnaire was designed and initially utilized roughly 20 years ago and has been applied across numerous contexts, data reports of reliability and validity are relatively scarce. The items included in the ACE scale are formulated to capture experiences of abuse and dysfunction within traditional household structures, only, making it exclusive to those of whom hail from less conventional backgrounds. Finally, a recent body of literature has called for revisions to this widely utilized measure.

Trauma Symptom Checklist for Young Children (TSCYC)

Instrument name. The TSCYC was developed and initially tested by John N. Briere and colleagues (Briere et al., 2001) as a caregiver or parent-report measure to supplement Briere's earlier Trauma Symptom Checklist for Children (TSCC) (1996). The TSCYC assesses the same broad range of trauma-related symptoms as the TSCC but for a different age range (3–12 rather than 8–16). For children aged 8–12, administration of both scales allows comparison of caregiver and child responses and may yield more useful clinical information than the use of either instrument alone (Lanktree et al., 2008).

Type of instrument. The TSCYC is a 90-item, caregiver report measure intended to assess both acute and chronic posttraumatic symptoms in children aged 3–12. As with the TSCC, items are answered on a four-point response format: Never, Sometimes, Lots of Times, and Almost All of the Time. An abbreviated version is available. No training is required for administration, but the TSCYC must be interpreted by professionals trained in psychometrics.

Use and target audience. The TSCYC is intended for parent/caregiver report of children aged 3–12 to assess a range of trauma-related symptoms. Unlike many caregiver measures, it contains two reporter validity scales for under-reporting and over-reporting (Response Level and Atypical Response) as well as an item that assesses average waking hours per week the reporting caregiver spends with the child on a scale from 1 (0–1 hours) to 7 (over 60 hours). The TSCYC contains eight clinical scales: Posttraumatic Stress Intrusion (PPS-I), Posttraumatic Stress Avoidance (PTS-AV), Posttraumatic Stress Arousal (PTS-A), Sexual Concerns (SC), Dissociation (DIS), Anxiety (ANX), Depression (DEP), and Anger/Aggression (ANG). There is also a summary score for Posttraumatic Stress Total (TOT).

Multicultural. The TSCYC has been translated into a number of languages. Translations are available at www.parinc.com.

Ease and time of administration. The TSCYC can be administered in 15–20 minutes.

Scoring procedure. The TSCYC can be easily hand scored, but a computer program is also available. There are separate norms for males and females and for children in three age groups (3–4, 5–9, and 10–12).

Reliability and validity. Validity and reliability were studied in a multi-site sample of 219 children who had been sexually abused, physically abused, or exposed to domestic violence (Briere et al., 2001). The individual clinical scales showed good to excellent reliability, with *Alpha* internal consistency ranging from .81 for SC to .93 for PTSD-Total. The average *alpha* was .87. As for construct validity, Briere and colleagues (2001) write, "The TSCYC scales most associated with different types of childhood abuse were those measuring posttraumatic stress, followed by sexual concerns and dissociation," but there was an unexpected lack of association between anxiety, depression, and anger and abuse history even though these scales had good face validity (p. 1009). The authors suggest that dysphoric mood may broadly discriminate between abused and non-abused children without varying as a function of type of abuse, a hypothesis to be tested in future analyses of the TSCYC in a sample that contains both abused and non-abused children. *Availability.* The TSCYC is available from Psychological Assessment Resources, Odessa, FL at (800)-331-TEST, or www.parinc.com.

Comment. The advantage of the TSCYC is that it assesses not only single incident traumas using the formal PTSD construct, but also a number of symptom domains more consistent with the emerging proposed diagnosis for chronically maltreated children, Developmental Trauma Disorder. As a caregiver report measure, the TSCYC enables assessment of these pervasive maltreatment responses for children as young as three. In addition, caregiver reports for children aged 8–12 may well serve as a corrective to the under-reporting characteristic of many children on self-report measures. Because of the ease with which it can be administered and the gaps it fills among existing instrumentation, the TSCYC is widely used by NCTSN centers and by many clinicians throughout the United States, and further work on its validity and multicultural applications is under way.

The Child and Adolescent Trauma Screen (CATS)

Name and type of instrument. The CATS (Sachser et al., 2017) is a 20-item self-report measure set on a four-point Likert-type scale. CATS is designed to screen for exposure to traumatizing events that meet criteria as perpetuants underlying a diagnosis of PTSD in children and adolescents, as per the *Diagnostic and Statistical Manual for Mental Disorders, Fifth Edition* (DSM-5) (APA, 2013). CATS was also designed as a screening tool for post-traumatic symptoms in children and adolescents.

Use and target audience. CATS (Sachser et al., 2017) was designed as self-report measure for children and adolescents, aged 3–17 years, to screen for post-traumatic events (PTEs) and PTSD in children and adolescents. It also includes an auxiliary caregiver-report measure, which includes questions parallel to the child and adolescent self-report measure.

Multicultural. This measure is available in an English, German, Norwegian, and Spanish version.

Ease and time of administration. There is no time limit for the administration of this measure, which should take no more than ten minutes for both the child and caretaker.

Scoring procedure. Raw scores tallies can be recorded for the total scale, by means of manually adding up points recorded for each individual item. No subscales are included. Scoring should take roughly 5–10 minutes.

Reliability. Internal Consistency, across all various language versions was good to excellent for both the child self-report and caregiver versions, with Cronbach's Alphas ranging from .88 to .94 (Sachser et al., 2017).

Validity. In terms of convergent and discriminant validity, medium to strong correlations were indicated when administered with measures of depression ($r = .62–.82$) and anxiety ($r = .40–.77$). However, low to medium correlations were indicated when administered with measures of externalizing symptoms ($r = -.15–.43$). These results were stable across all language versions (Sachser, et al., 2017).

Availability and source. Paper and Pencil. In: Sachser, C., Berliner, L., Holt, T., Jensen, T. K., Jungbluth, N., Risch, E., Rosner, R., Goldbeck, L. (2017).

International development and psychometric properties of the Child and Adolescent Trauma Screen (CATS). *Journal of Affective Disorders, 210*, 189–195. http://dx.doi.org.ezproxy.fau.edu/10.1016/j.jad.2016.12.040.

Permission for use outside of educational or research contests must be obtained by contacting authors.

Comment. CATS is a robust new measure that was tested on an international version to better establish external validity. It is both easy to score and administer and includes both a child self-report scale and a caregiver report scale, further lending to the credibility of scores obtained. Further supporting the psychometric integrity of CATS is the execution of a Confirmatory Factor Analysis (CFA), undertaken by the developers, which indicated a factor structure with four symptom clusters supporting a PTSD diagnosis, as per DSM-5 (APA, 2013): Re-experiencing, Avoidance, Negative alterations in mood and cognitions, and Hyperarousal. While at present permission must be obtained for application of this measure outside of academic contexts, it shows promise as a reliable and effective screening tool in clinical practice.

Impact of Events Scale (IES)

Instrument name. The IES was published in 1979 by Mardi Horowitz, Nancy Wilner, and William Alvarez. It was designed to measure the psychological impact of trauma or stress on adults. It has since been used with children and adolescents as young as eight years old. The IES was created prior to the inclusion of PTSD in the American Psychiatric Association's diagnostic manuals: PTSD first appeared in DSM-III in 1980.

Type of instrument. The IES is a 15-item, self-report measure. Seven of the items measure intrusion, eight measure avoidance, and when combined, they provide a total subjective stress score. Respondents are asked to rank each item on a four-point scale according to how often each has occurred in the past seven days. The scale assesses the frequency with which experiences of "intrusions," "avoidance," and emotional numbing related to traumatic/stressful events were experienced in the last week.

Use and target audience. The scale can be used with adults and with children and adolescents 8–18 years old. Because of its brevity, it can easily be administered in the immediate aftermath of mass catastrophes as well as individual traumas. However, like many PTSD measures developed on adults and adapted for children, the IES has not undergone adequate developmental modification. Questions are merely reworded, rather than changed, to reflect child-specific post-traumatic symptoms and behaviors.

Multicultural. The IES has been translated into many languages and has been applied to adolescents from various cultures. The IES has helped to demonstrate that reactions to trauma are consistent across cultures. It has discriminated between traumatized and non-traumatized youth in Britain, Cambodia, among refugee populations in Asia and in the West, and among French children exposed to disasters. It has been translated into many languages.

Ease and time of administration. The IES takes ten minutes to administer and score.

Scoring procedure. A total score is calculated by summing all 15 item responses.

Reliability. Both the intrusion and avoidance scales have displayed acceptable reliability (alpha of .79 and .82, respectively) and a split-half reliability for the whole scale of .86 (Horowitz, Wilner, & Alvarez, 1979). The factor structure is not clear, and one possible subscale, Numbing, has only two items. There is no normative base available.

Validity. The IES has also displayed the ability to discriminate a variety of traumatized groups from non-traumatized groups (see Briere, 1997 for review) including Britain, Cambodia, the United States, and France. The IES can be used for repeated measurement over time, and its sensitivity to change allows for monitoring clients' progress in therapy.

Availability and source. Horowitz, M., Milner, M., & Alvarez, W. (1979). Impact of Events Scale: A measure of subjective stress. *Psychosomatic Medicine, 41,* 209–218.

Comment. As one of the earliest trauma-specific measures developed, the IES has been useful, especially as a quick and dirty screening measure that can be administered even during the chaotic days following mass disasters. It has been very widely translated and used since its first appearance a generation ago, and in its original form, is better used as a screening device than as a full PTSD assessment tool. A recent revision, the IES-R (Weiss, 2002; Weiss & Marmar, 1997), has been developed for adults, but normative data for children are not yet available.

The IES was developed as an instrument before PTSD had been constructed and does not reflect full PTSD criteria (Horowitz et al., 1979). Designed to measure the impact of a single trauma rather than the chronic severe trauma and maltreatment experienced by many children being assessed, it has nevertheless been very widely used with children and adults in the generation since its creation and widely translated. It has been moderately good at distinguishing traumatized from non-traumatized people in a variety of cultures. The lack of developmental adaptation limits its applicability to children and adolescents.

Adolescent Dissociative Experiences Scale (A-DES)

Instrument name. When compared to parents of younger children, parents of teenagers are less familiar with the details of their children's lives. Because of this, and because adolescents are better self-reporters of behavior than younger children, the utility of the CDC during adolescence is limited. The A-DES was the product of a collaborative effort among a number of individuals organized by Judith Armstrong, Eve Bernstein Carlson, and Frank Putnam to come up with a self-report scale for teenagers to screen for pathological dissociation (Armstrong, Carlson, Libero, & Smith, 1997).

Type of instrument. The A-DES is a 30-item self-report screening tool for serious dissociative and post-traumatic disorders. Items are neutrally worded and are generally worded in the present tense. The questions ask about different kinds of experiences that happen to people. The answer response format is a 0–10 scale, anchored at the ends with Never (0) and Always (10). Adolescents circle the corresponding number based on how often the experiences happen to them when they have not had drugs or alcohol.

Use and target audience. The A-DES is a self-report measure for adolescents ages 11–20.

Multicultural. The A-DES has been translated into many languages, and they are available by request at http://www.ohiocando4kids.org/Dissociation.

Ease and time of administration. The A-DES is a brief 30-item adolescent self-report measure. It takes about ten minutes to administer and score.

Scoring procedure. The A-DES is scored by summing item scores and dividing by 30 (number of items). The overall score ranges from 0 to 10. A mean score of four or above signifies pathological dissociation. As a rule of thumb, the A-DES score is approximately the Dissociative Experiences Scale (DES), an adult measure of dissociation (Putnam, 1997), score divided by ten. The A-DES-T is a taxometric subscale of the A-DES measuring pathological dissociation. It is scored by adding item scores and dividing by eight (number of items). Scores of 4 or higher are considered indicative of significant dissociation deserving further clinical evaluation. The A-DES-T may also be used as a shortened version of the A-DES.

Reliability. Psychometric data on the A-DES indicate excellent reliability (Cronbach's alpha = .93; split-half = .92).

Validity. The A-DES differentiated abused and non-abused psychiatric patients, and dissociative adolescents who were diagnosed independently of the A-DES scored significantly higher on the A-DES than other inpatients.

Availability and source. The A-DES is a public domain document freely available for reproduction, distribution, and use. (Readers who wish to make changes to it are asked to change the name to reduce confusion.) The complete 30-item A-DES is available by request at http://www.ohiocando4kids.org/Dissociation and in the appendix of Putnam, F. W. (1997). *Dissociation in children and adolescents: A developmental perspective.* New York: Guilford Press.

Comment. Because of its face validity, the A-DES depends on the willingness of youth to report unusual feelings and internal states. It is not to be used for diagnosis but as a screening measure to be followed by a full clinical interview to assess the presence or absence of dissociation. However, adolescents who engage in daydreaming or fantasy games such as Dungeons and Dragons may score high on this scale. In addition, as an adaptation of an adult interview, some of its components are not appropriate for adolescents. However, despite these caveats, the A-DES is a useful instrument to screen for dissociation among adolescents (Ohan et al., 2002).

Children's PTSD-Reaction Index (CPTS-RI)

Instrument name. The CPTS-RI was developed by Robert Pynoos and his associates at UCLA in 1987 and has been widely used in the United States, Europe, and Asia. It has been selected as one of the instruments by which the federally funded NCTSN collects data on traumatized youth among its 35 centers.

Type of instrument. The CPTS-RI is a clinician-administered scale, but it can also be used as a self-report measure. Training is required for administration and scoring.

Use and target audience. It is intended for children aged 7–18 to assess symptoms following exposure to trauma. The Child version is worded for ages 7–12; the Parent version mirrors the Child version for ages 7–12; and the Adolescent version contains minor changes in wording from the Child version designed for youth aged 13–18.

Multicultural. The PTSD-Reaction Index has been translated into several languages and has been used in Armenia, Kuwait, Cambodia, and the United States.

Ease and time of administration. All three instruments are designed as self-report measures, which makes them easier to administer than other children's PTSD measures such as the Children's PTSD Inventory, the CPTSDI (Saigh, 2002) or the Clinician-Administered PTSD Scale for Children, the CAPS-C (Nader et al., 2002). All three versions of the CPTS-RI contain 27 questions in the traumatic exposure section. For PTSD symptoms, the Child version contains 20 questions, the Parent version 21, and the Adolescent version 22 questions. The instruments can also be administered verbally to individuals or groups.

Scoring procedure. Scores are hand tallied. Scores of 12–24 = mild PTSD, 25–39 = moderate, 40–59 = severe, and higher than 60 very severe PTSD.

Reliability. Internal consistency for the child version is .69–.80, interrater reliability for the adolescent version .88; and test–retest reliability for adolescents over one week .93.

Validity. Children with greater exposure to traumas had higher scores (Thaber & Vostanis, 1999). Both sensitivity and specificity for PTSD diagnosis are moderate or good. The CPTS-RI factors overlap with but do not exactly measure PTSD symptoms as constructed in the DSM-IV. However, because PTSD in children differs from the DSM-IV's largely adult-based construct (AACAP, 1998), these differences may not signal diminished validity.

Availability and source. The CPTS-RI is not commercially available, but it may be obtained from Robert Pynoos, M.D., at UCLA or Kathleen Nader, DSW, in Cedar Park, Texas. A recently released administration and scoring CD for use by NCTSN sites and others (2003) is available through Robert Pynoos, M.D., Trauma Psychiatry Service, UCLA, 300 UCLA Medical Plaza, Los Angeles, CA 90024-6968.

Comment. Among the new instruments designed to measure PTSD symptoms in children, the CPTS-RI has several advantages. More extensively researched than some of the other new child instruments, it does not require clinician administration. It has been shown to be suitable for children with different kinds of trauma, of different ages, and from varied cultures. It is among the best studied of contemporary instruments for post-traumatic stress disorder as defined in the DSM-5. As the regional centers of the NCTSN apply this instrument to collect their data on a variety of traumatized youth, from domestically violent homes to homeless shelters to residential treatment homes, its utility may increase. One disadvantage is that this instrument is not designed to measure complex PTSD, that is, the pervasive effects of long-term exposure to severe trauma and abuse that many children experience in their homes, schools, and neighborhoods (Herman, 1992; Pelcovitz et al., 1997). In addition, like other PTSD child measures, the CPTS-RI assesses traumatized children using a construct first identified in adults and then adapted for children, rather than building the construct afresh by studying traumatized children (AACAP, 1998).

The Child Victimization Trauma Assessment

Name and type of instrument. The Child Victimization Trauma Assessment is a modified measure that was developed to screen for experiences of immigration trauma among Hispanic youth (de Arellano et al., 2018). The inventory is set to a semi-structured interview format and includes 42 items capturing experiences of sexual abuse, physical abuse, other physical assaults, witnessing domestic violence, witnessing community violence, and non-assault traumas.

Use and target audience. The Child Victimization Trauma Assessment is geared towards Hispanic immigrant youth, aged 9–17 years. It is designed to assess exposure to traumatic events which occurred during the process of immigration (de Arellano et al., 2018).

Multicultural. This measure is available in an English and Spanish version.

Ease and time of administration. There is no time limit for the administration of this measure. Administration should take roughly 30 minutes, in the absence of a language divide.

Scoring procedure. Scoring is tabulated in accordance to the number of items answered "Yes"/"Si" versus "No"/"No." All items included in the interview measure are closed-ended. A raw score can be tabulated by tallying the number of items answered "Yes"/"Si." Scoring should take less than ten minutes.

Reliability. Internal Consistency for this measure was good, with Cronbach's Alpha reaching .70 (de Arellano et al., 2018).

Validity. No validity estimates were reported for this measure (de Arellano et al., 2018).

Availability and source. Paper-and-Pencil. In de Arellano, M. A., Andrews, A. R. III, Reid-Quiñones, K., Vasquez, D., Doherty, L. S., Danielson, C. K., & Rheingold, A. (2018). Immigration trauma among Hispanic youth: Missed by trauma assessments and predictive of depression and PTSD symptoms. *Journal of Latina/o Psychology, 6(3),* 159–174. http://dx.doi.org.ezproxy.fau.edu/10.1037/lat0000090.

Comment. Taking into account the current sociopolitical climate, the Child Victimization Trauma Assessment is a very salient measure, which includes questions modified from the National Survey of Adolescents (NSA) Trauma Assessment Interview (Kilpatrick et al., 2000). As awareness of immigration-related traumas is beginning to surface both in the helping field literature and popular media, it is predicted that the use of measures such as these will be on the rise.

Because the Child Victimization Trauma Assessment is formatted as a structured interview, its administration is rather timely, as compared to self-report measures. However, inherent in the same reality is that confounds, such as a lacking of accountability in item response is less likely to limit the results yielded from its administration. Further studies must be undertaken to support the psychometric integrity of this measure. Permission for use outside of educational or research contexts must be obtained by contacting authors.

Depression Measures

Children and adults who have been victimized by abuse and violence are far more likely than non-victims to suffer from major depression or dysthymia (Kolko & Swenson, 2002; Putnam, 2003). A history of child physical or sexual abuse appears also to alter major depression's clinical presentation and be associated with earlier onset and less responsiveness to standard depression treatments with Selective Serotonin Reuptake Inhibitors, but depressive symptoms linked to a history of child abuse do respond to cognitive-behavioral therapies (Putnam, 2003). When boys are sexually abused, their symptom presentation during childhood and into adulthood is more severe than that of sexually abused girls (Gold, Lucenko, Elhai, Swingle, & Sellers, 1999). The Beck Depression Inventory and the Children's Depression Inventory (CDI) are covered elsewhere in this volume.

Anxiety Measures

The Multidimensional Anxiety Scale for Children (MASC) is an appropriate ancillary measure to the TSCC, which also assesses anxiety, although the anxiety scale from the TSCC is not as inclusive. Affective distress is common in maltreated children, and the MASC provides a much more detailed assessment of anxiety, should there be any indication of this disorder based on the CBCL or the TSCC. The MASC is fully covered elsewhere in this volume.

Strategy for Utilizing Childhood Abuse and Trauma Instruments

Because trauma, maltreatment, and abuse vary greatly in their content and their effects, no single protocol is recommended. This chapter has given information about 15 instruments without covering all that are available in this rapidly developing and exciting field of inquiry. To complete an assessment, select the tests based on the assessment question—for example, is trauma suspected? If so, was the trauma a one-time event or repeated over time? Were there multiple traumas and stressors? Are there concerns about anxiety or depression? Was the child maltreated by a family member or by a stranger? Was there sexual assault, so that possible sexualized behaviors need to be assessed? The following are general guidelines that are then applied to a single case for illustrative purposes.

Select psychological tests appropriate to this child. Include self-report measures, if the child is old enough, and parent or caretaker report measures, as well as teacher report measures if possible and appropriate.

Depending on the circumstances for this evaluation, review confidentiality and privilege parameters with the child, caretakers, and others, if applicable.

Administer and score the tests.

Collect additional information on the child's history, circumstances, and family situation through interview, observation, clinical records, court or social workers or victim advocates if applicable.

Review and share the findings and your report with the child and with the child's caretakers.

Make recommendations for the family or other interested parties as indicated by your test findings and your interviewers.

Table 11.1 outlines child abuse and family assessment strategies and inventories.

Table 11.1 Matrix: Child Abuse and Family Assessment Strategies and Inventories

Assessment instrument	Specific applications	Cultural/ language	Instructions/use: T = time to take; S = time to score; I = items	Computerized a = scoring; b = report	Reliability (R); validity (V)	Availability
CBCL	For children living in the home, aged 18 months to 18 years; to assess a broad range of internalizing and externalizing symptoms	Translated into over 30 languages, including several versions of Spanish; used throughout the world	T = 10–20 min; S = +1 min; I = 100 or 118	a = yes; b = yes	R = excellent test–retest = .75–.97; good interparent agreement V = very good construct	Dr. Achenbach, Center for Children, Youth and Families, University of Vermont in Burlington, 05401 www.aseba.org
CSBI	For children aged 2–12; assesses sexual behaviors exhibited over preceding six months	Spanish; German; French; Dutch	T = 5–10 min; S = 5 min; I = 38	a = no; b = no	R = excellent test–retest = .85; α = .72–.92; V = good convergent and divergent	PAR, Odessa, FL: (800) 331-TEST or www. parinc.com
CDC	A dissociation screening measure for children aged 5–14	Spanish and other languages	T = 5–10 min; S = 5–10 min; I = 20	a = no; b = no	R = moderate to good one-year test–retest stability (r = .65); α = .86; V = good convergent and divergent	Public domain— freely available for reproducing, distribution, use; available in appendix Putnam (1997)

(Continued)

Assessment instrument	Specific applications	Cultural/ language	Instructions/use: T = time to take; S = time to score; I = items	Computerized a = scoring; b = report	Reliability (R); validity (V)	Availability
PEDS	2–10 year olds traumatized by homelessness, sexual abuse, natural disasters, and other negative experiences	Has been examined for homeless children; not yet tested on wide variety of cultural groups	T = 5–10 min; S = 5–10 min; I = 21	a = no; b = no	R = α = .85 total; IR: .65 total; TR: .56 total	Journal article
Milner CAPI (3rd ed.)	Intended to be used as a screening tool for detection of physical child abuse; also used as psychological test	Norms for U.S. and Spain; translated into other languages; research finds constructs present in other cultures	T = 12–20 min; S = 20 min; I = 77	a = yes; b = no	R = split-half: .96; alpha = .93; test-retest = .71–92; V = excellent divergent and construct	Available from PSYTEC, Inc., PO Box 564, DeKalb, IL, 60115
CTSPC	For parents of children living in the home, aged 6–17; assesses nonviolent discipline, psychological aggression, and physical assault	English	T = 6–8 min; S = 8 min; I = 22–36	a = no; b = no	R = α = .58–.68; test-retest = .80; V = moderate to excellent construct validity	Family Research Laboratory, University of New Hampshire

Measure	Description	Languages/Availability	Time	a/b	Reliability/Validity	Source
The Child Sexual Abuse Attitudes Measure	Developed to assess the attitudes of community members and service providers regarding sexual abuse	English	T = 5–10 min; S = 5–10 min; I = 10	a = yes b = yes	R = α = .34–.82; V = ANOVA reported; significant differences between groups (discriminant)	Journal Article; martine.powell@ deakin.edu.au
ACE ACE Questionnaire	Developed to investigate the relationship between child abuse and early household dysfunction and risk factors in adulthood	English; International	T = 5 min; S = 5 min; I = 10	a = yes b = yes	R = K = .41–.86; V = CFA; cumulative risk scoring (predictive)	Journal Article; various websites
TSCYC	Children aged 3–12; caretaker report	Used in many countries and available in many languages	T = 15 min; S = 8 min; I = 54	a = yes; b = yes	R = Excellent IC with α = .81 for SC SC; .93 for PTSD total; α = .87 average across all measures V = moderate (convergent; discriminant)	Psychological Assessment Resources, Odessa, FL, (800) 331-TEST or www.parinc. com
CATS	Designed to assess for PTEs and PTSD in children and adolescents; caretaker report	English; German; Norwegian; Spanish	T = 5–10 min S = 5–10 min I = 20	a = no; b = no	R = α = .88–.94 V = r = .15–.92 (convergent; discriminant)	Journal Article

(Continued)

Assessment instrument	Specific applications	Cultural/language	Instructions/use: T = time to take; S = time to score; I = items	Computerized a = scoring; b = report	Reliability (R); validity (V)	Availability
A-DES	Ages 11–20; screening tool for serious dissociative and post-traumatic disorders	Translated into more than 15 Asian and European languages	T = 10–15 min; S = 5 min; I = 30	a = no; b = no	R = α = .93; split-half = .92; V = face validity	Public domain document freely available for reproducing distribution and use, available by request at http://www. ohiocando4kids.org/ Dissociation
CPTS-RI	Children aged 7–18; to assess symptoms following exposure to trauma	Translated into several languages; has been used in Armenia, Kuwait, Cambodia, and U.S.	T = 20–45 min; S = 20–45 min; I = 27—traumatic exposure section: 20 (child); 21 (parent); 22 (adolescent); PTSD symptoms section	a = no; b = no	R = α = .69–80; IR: .88 total; TR: .93 over one week; V = conv .29–.91	Not commercially available, but may be obtained from Trauma Psychiatry Service, UCLA
The Childhood Victimization Trauma Assessment	Developed to screen for experiences of immigration trauma in Hispanic youth	English; Spanish	T = 30 min; S ≥ 10 min I = 42	a = no; b = no	R = α = .70 V = none reported	Journal Article

Case Example

Abby is a ten-year-old girl who was referred because she sexually touched Calvin, a four-year-old boy, in a day care setting. In her three months in this day care, she had inserted herself into a parental role and frequently helped out with serving snacks, getting children packed up when parents arrived, and helping two younger children with toileting. One of these was Calvin, the four-year-old boy who reported being sexually touched during toileting.

Abby was adopted at the age of four. She lived with her adoptive parents and had a 17-year-old sister, the biological daughter of her parents. Her post-adoption adjustment was characterized as uneventful, and she had never been identified as having behavioral problems. For example, her grades in school were typically above average. Her pre-adoptive experiences included neglect and physical abuse; sexual abuse has never been confirmed although it has been expected, given her rearing circumstances.

Betsy, the adoptive mother, was interviewed, and she reported that Abby had exhibited a 9- to 12-month history of greater sexual interest and genital touching after the adoption, but this had faded before she entered kindergarten. More recently, she had started talking about boyfriends, and Betsy felt that Abby had a longstanding problem of being overly friendly with adult males. However, this has never presented itself as a problem. She also wondered if the interest in boyfriends paralleled her 17-year-old daughter's having a boyfriend.

Betsy also reported that she and her husband were in marital therapy and most likely would be separating. Her return to full-time employment was in response to this likelihood and was why Abby was now in after school day care. She agreed that Abby had a very helpful side to her and thought this varied directly with her anxiety.

Betsy wondered whether Abby was adversely affected by the upsurge in family tension over the previous six months. She also was concerned about Calvin, the four-year-old boy, whom she knew from having observed him at the day care. Betsy described a number of incidents suggesting that he was an aggressive and provocative child. It was her opinion that Abby was in a vulnerable position with him and regretted that the two had been together unsupervised in the bathroom.

At the end of this first meeting, Betsy completed the CBCL, the PSI-SF, the CSBI, and the CTSPC. She signed a release form to have Abby's teacher complete a Teacher Report form, which was modified to include three additional sexual items: plays with sex parts in

(Continued)

public, sex play with peers, and sex problems (Friedrich, 1997). Betsy also agreed to ask the day care provider to complete a CBCL and CSBI on Abby.

Abby was very subdued on my first meeting her and exhibited some separation anxiety in the waiting area, which persisted into the first few minutes of the interview. She had little recollection of her pre-adoptive life although she had been told that she was hospitalized once as a baby for not gaining weight. She said she likes school and wants to be a teacher when she grows up. She identified her best friend as a seven-year-old girl in the neighborhood.

She was highly uncomfortable speaking about the incident with Calvin and flushed and squirmed in the chair during this portion of the interview. She agreed that she had touched Calvin's penis three times and volunteered that he had asked her to touch him the first time and that his penis "grew bigger when I touched it." He asked to see her "privates," but she only showed them to him "once." She felt "funny" when this happened but was able to elaborate after looking over a feelings poster that she had felt "scared," "excited," "ashamed," and "anxious." She knew it was "wrong" and assured the interviewer that it would never happen again because "Calvin can use the bathroom himself." She completed the MASC, CDI, and TSCC after having agreed to my request that she read each item carefully and answer "honestly."

Parent and Caregiver Reports

Betsy's responses to the CBCL suggested social competence scores within normal limits, including Social, a subscale measuring relationships with friends. Two clinical elevations were noted, one on Anxious/Depression (T = 66) and also on Withdrawal (T = 65). She endorsed such items as "cries," "nervous," "fearful," "guilty," and "self-conscious" for Anxious/Depressed and "secretive," "shy," and "withdrawn" for Withdrawal. She endorsed four items on the CSBI. These were "stands too close to others," "overly friendly with men they don't know well," "touches another child's sex parts," and "interested in the opposite sex." This translated into T scores of 67 on total sexual behavior, 71 on developmentally related sexual behavior, and 60 on sexual abuse specific items. On the PSI-SF, she answered validly and nondefensively, with her defensive responding score at the 45th percentile. Scores range from 15% on Parental Distress, 51% on Parent–Child Dysfunctional Interaction, and 44% on Difficult Child. This results in a total Stress

Score at the 40th percentile. Finally, she not only reported primarily positive parenting strategies on the CTS, for example, use of time out, positive reinforcement, but also admitted to occasional shouting and slapping on the hand.

Further support for the accuracy of Betsy's perceptions of Abby comes from the Achenbach Teacher Report Form completed by Abby's fifth-grade teacher. Adaptive Functioning scores were in the normal range. Clinical scales were also in the normal range with the exception of a mild elevation on Withdrawn (T = 63). The teacher did not endorse any of the three sexual behavior items.

The day care provider had only known Abby for three months. Consequently, she was less sure of many items on Social Competence. However, she did not report any clinical problems. On the CSBI, she endorsed two of the four items Betsy had, that is, "stands too close to others" and "touches another child's sexual parts." This translated into a Total Sexual Behavior of T = 52, T = 45 for Developmentally Related Sexual Behavior, and T = 45 for Sexual Abuse Specific Items. At the bottom of the measure, she wrote that had she rated Calvin, she would have endorsed 15–20 items. This comment suggested that Calvin was far more sexually focused than was Abby. Finally, Both Abby's adoptive mother and day care worker were administered the Child Sexual Abuse Attitudes Measure. Both scored within the normal range, indicating a willingness to report any indicated or suspected child sexual abuse.

Child Report

Abby did report a clinically significant elevation (T = 67) on Social Anxiety from the MASC, with a secondary elevation on Humiliation/Rejection, a subscale from that domain. A sample item from Humiliation/Rejection is "I'm afraid other people will think I'm stupid." However, she did not report significant level of Physical Symptoms or Harm Avoidance, and her MASC total score was T = 57.

On the CDI, she was clinically elevated on Negative Self-Esteem (T = 68; e.g., "I do not like myself") and Interpersonal Problems (T = 67; e.g., "I am bad many times"). On the TSCC, she answered validly, and most T scores were in the 52–58 range with the exception of SC (T = 72) and the related subscale, Sexual Distress (T = 87). In addition, Abby was administered the CATS for children aged 7–17, on which she scored 25, indicating the expression of event-related PTSS, which, if not monitored, may evolve into PTSD.

Summary

In summary, parent and caregiver ratings of Abby's general behavior suggests a girl who feels less sure with peers and responds with some withdrawal. She also tends to be more anxious and emotional than average. Some of her sexual behaviors are more specific to the incident with Calvin, but others suggest a needy girl whose interpersonal boundaries need shoring up. Her adoptive mother does not report Abby to be overly challenging to parent; she describes her in a generally positive tone, and she generally employs very appropriate discipline techniques and an understanding of and willingness to report acts of sexual abuse.

It is not very common, but always heartening, to see overlap between parent and child reports. Abby reported a significant level of peer insecurity and feelings of badness. When questioned, the Negative Self-Esteem items from the CDI were related to her behavior with Calvin and suggest some elevation in shame. In addition, her report of elevated SC and CATS score is appropriate to the situation and reflects a girl who is not denying her vulnerability in this domain. The fact that other trauma-related scales from the TSCC were not elevated is also a positive and in keeping with her report that she remembers very little of her life prior to her adoption.

Recommendations

The test data allow us to suggest that Abby's preference for caretaking and befriending younger children put her in a vulnerable situation with a provocative and sexualized boy. Her adoptive parents' potential separation and divorce most likely add to her behavioral reactivity. Treatment suggestions include a greater focus on developing peer relations via play dates (Frankel & Wetmore, 1996), helping Abby see herself more accurately and with less shame, and increasing overall positive parent–child interactions (Hembree-Kigin & McNeil, 1995). In addition, Betsy and her husband were requested to work even harder on providing reassurances to Abby about her continued well-being despite their problems.

Concluding Comments

The evaluation of traumatized or maltreated children is made complex by several factors. First, these evaluations often have forensic implications. Second, the evaluation target can be very elusive, not only because of "sleeper effects" but also because there is no one psychological diagnosis or syndrome type associated with trauma, adversity, and maltreatment. Third, maltreated children being evaluated are often quite guarded about what they reveal and frequently are less capable of accurately talking about their feelings than children from non-abusive households. Fourth, maltreatment often occurs in deleterious contexts that have their own pernicious effects on the developing child. For example, it is very difficult to sort out the effects of poverty versus the effects of physical abuse, and to attempt to do so is contraindicated. Rather, the evaluator needs to know the child's context and spell it out clearly as part of the evaluation. Fifth, psychologists trained in traditional assessment need to learn an entirely new set of assessment strategies for abused or traumatized children than are typically taught in graduate school and used in clinical practice. Finally, evaluators need to know how PTSD may superficially overlap with many other diagnoses that can be less precise in describing the child's functioning, such as attention, mood, or anxiety disorders (Olafson & Connelly, 2012).

The assessment of the abused child should include objective measures that assess the more common symptoms associated with maltreatment. In addition, maltreatment occurs in a context, and the assessment of the parent's potential for further abuse (if the parent was the abuser), or parental perceptions of the child, is as important as the input parents provide on behavior rating scales. This chapter has compiled some of the most commonly used and valid tools in this area (Olafson & Connelly, 2012).

It is also very important to remember that psychological assessment in abuse and trauma cases may be initiated as a clinical activity but that legal issues are also operative, and the evaluator may need to testify, even when the case did not start out as a forensic case (Olafson & Connelly, 2012).

The Use and Misuse of Tests in Child Custody Evaluations

This is one arena where maltreatment allegations are often raised. Psychologists asked to conduct these evaluations need to keep in mind that these evaluations can be profoundly difficult to accomplish. Prejudices about the psychological features of parents involved in custody disputes need to be set aside, and any competent assessment must include testing on both parents. The overwhelming majority (85%–90%) of divorcing parents with minor children settle custody without a dispute that requires professional evaluation. Custody disputes indicate that there is something wrong, and it is simplistic to reflexively believe that both parents have character disorders and are simply using the children as bargaining chips (Olafson & Connelly, 2012).

There is research indicating that in many custody disputes, one parent may be concerned about the safety and well-being of children in the other household (Brown, Frederico, Hewitt, & Sheehan, 2000). Throughout the marriage, the protective parent may have buffered the children from intermittent psychotic episodes, drinking binges, battering, emotional abuse, or child physical or sexual abuse by the other parent. When this parent finally gives up on the marriage, he or she may well learn that the courts do not buffer the children as this parent once did (Olafson & Connelly, 2012).

Physical abuse, partner battering, and child sexual abuse are crimes to be investigated and adjudicated rather than evaluated and mediated in domestic relations courts. Psychologists are not detectives; they must be aware of their roles and the limitations of their scope of practice when these issues arise (Olafson & Connelly, 2012)

Cautions against Overly Simplistic Interpretation

Psychological tests cannot be used to definitively determine (a) if a child has been abused, (b) if a parent will abuse again, (c) if abuse is the sole cause of the child's symptoms, or (d) if a parent is a batterer or a sexual perpetrator. Many abused children are asymptomatic, and the impacts can be extremely variable. Many batterers and sexual abusers appear psychologically normal when evaluated (Olafson & Connelly, 2012).

Group data are used to establish norms for the measures that are suggested in this chapter, but each case must be interpreted in the context of the child's history and culture. For example, an abused child who scores low on a test of sexual behavior may or may not have a sexual abuse history. The same is true if a child scores high on this same measure. In addition, the child who scores low may score low for a number of reasons. For example, the child (a) may truly not have sexual behavior problems, (b) may have sexual behavior problems but has a parent who does not report them because this parent is protective of a spouse, (c) may have sexual behavior problems but has a parent who does not report them because this parent is a poor observer, or (4) may have sexual behavior problems that are more subtle and likely to cause future problems but do not show up in terms of current overt behaviour (Olafson & Connelly, 2012).

Similar problems occur with PTSD. Follow-up interviewing as well as an appreciation of the child's context is critical to determining if a child has PTSD after scoring either low or high on a structured PTSD protocol. Some children deny some PTSD symptoms simply because they are so bothered by any reminders that they deny all symptoms related to the event in question (Olafson, & Connelly, 2012).

Parent–Child Relationship

The parent–child relationship is critical to the child's short- and long-term adjustment. Our assessment framework does not specifically assess parent–child attachment because measures to do so still lack convincing normative data. However, the Parent-Child Conflict Tactics Scale (CTSCP) and the PSI can be used to evaluate the strength and quality of a parent's relationship with a child and thus indirectly speak to the security of attachment (Olafson & Connelly, 2012).

Reports of overly harsh parenting, whether emotional or physical, certainly imply insecure attachment, because attachment is compromised in over 95% of cases where maltreatment is present (Cicchetti & Toth, 1995).

Assessment and Treatment Planning

Assessment results must be relevant to therapy to justify the use of screening measures and tests. The first step is to view assessment and treatment as seamlessly connected. Assessment measures should prepare the child for therapy by outlining which issues are important. These same measures can be transported into therapy and used as a basis for early sessions, at least with some children. For example, cognitive distortions expressed on the CATS can lead to CBT-based interventions such as Trauma-Focused Cognitive Behavioral Therapy (TF-CBT; Cohen, Mannarino, & Deblinger, 2006).

Therapists can also benefit from input from the evaluator regarding the child's ability to be open and nondefensive. Severe abuse that is not accompanied by the child reporting distress on at least some of the TSCC subscales, for example, raises concerns about the child's perceptions of how safe it is to be open about emotions. There can be other reasons for a child's lack of self-disclosure, such as cultural constraints or dissociation, but lack of permission to talk about the abuse is one strong possibility that needs to be clarified early in the treatment process.

Finally, the field of therapy for maltreated children moves forward if we learn what works. As therapists implement the most strongly evidence-based therapy for traumatized children and their caregivers, Parent–Child Interaction Therapy (PCIT; McNeil & Hembree-Kigin, 2010), we strongly encourage therapists to readminister measures at intervals throughout therapy, at the conclusion of therapy, and after time has elapsed after treatment, in order to learn which children seem to get better and which do not and in this way inform their practice.

Note

1 We wish to acknowledge the contributions of the three authors of previous editions of this chapter, William M. Fredrich, Lisa Connelly, and Erna Olafson. William and Lisa have since passed away. Although Erna Olafson has retired, she has graciously provided valuable feedback to the authors of this edition.

References

Allen, B., Cisneros, E. M., & Tellez, A. (2015). The children left behind: The impact of parental deportation on mental health. *Journal of Child and Family Studies, 24*, 386–392.

American Academy of Child and Adolescent Psychiatry. (1998). Practice parameters for the assessment of children and adolescents with posttraumatic stress disorder. *Journal of the American Academy of Child and Adolescent Psychiatry, 37* (Supplement 10), 4–26.

American Psychiatric Association. (2013). *The diagnostic and statistical manual of mental disorders* (5th ed.). Alexandria, VA: Author.

Armstrong, J. G., Putnam, F. W., Carlson, E. B., Libero, D. Z., & Smith, S. R. (1997). Development and validation of a measure of adolescent dissociation: The adolescent dissociative experiences scale. *Journal of Nervous Mental Disorders, 185*, 491–497.

Arruabarrena, I., De Paul, J., Indias, S., & Ullate, M. (2013). Psychologists and child psychological maltreatment severity assessment. *Psicothema, 25*(4), 482–487.

Babiker, G., & Herbert, M. (1996). The role of psychological instruments in the assessment of child sexual abuse. *Child Abuse Review, 5*, 239–251.

Babiker, G., & Herbert, M. (1998). Critical issues in the assessment of child sexual abuse. *Clinical Child and Family Psychology Review, 1*(4), 231–252.

Bailey, C., Mace, G., & Powell, M. (2016). Measuring community and service provider attitudes to child sexual abuse in remote indigenous communities in Western Australia. *Psychiatry, Psychology and Law, 23*(3), 435–445. doi:10.1080/13218719.2015.1080147

Bakermans-Kranenburg, M., & van IJzendoorn, M. H. (2009). No reliable gender differences in attachment across the life-span. *Behavioral and Brain Sciences, 32*, 22–23.

Bethell, C. D., Carle, A., Hudziak, J., Gombojav, N., Powers, K., Wade, R., & Braverman, P. (2017). Methods to assess adverse childhood experiences of children and families: Toward approaches to promote child well-being in policy and practice. *AcademicPediatrics, 17*(7), S51–S69.

Briere, J. (1996). *Trauma Symptom Checklist for Children (TSCC), professional manual.* Odessa, FL: Psychological Assessment Resources.

Briere, J. (1997). *Psychological assessment of adult posttraumatic states.* Washington, DC:American Psychological Association.

Briere, J., Johnson, K., Bissada, A., Damon, L., Crouch, J., Gil, E., … Ernst, V. (2001). The Trauma Symptom Checklist for young Children (TSCYC): Reliability and association with abuse exposure in a multi-site study. *Child Abuse & Neglect, 25*, 1001–1014.

Brown, T., Frederico, M., Hewitt, L., & Sheehan, R. (2000). Revealing the existence of child abuse in the context of marital breakdown and custody and access disputes. *Child Abuse & Neglect, 246*, 849–859.

Carlson, E. B. (1997). *Trauma assessments: A clinician's guide.* New York, NY: Guilford Press.

Cicchetti, D., & Toth, S. L. (1995). Child maltreatment and attachment organization: Implications for intervention. In S. Goldberg, R. Muir, & J. Kerr (Eds.), *Attachment theory: Social, developmental, and clinical perspectives* (pp. 279–308). Hillsdale, NJ: Analytic Press.

Cohen, J. A., Mannarino, A. P., & Deblinger, E. (2006). *Treating trauma and traumatic grief in children and adolescents.* New York, NY: Guilford Press.

Conte, J., Berliner, L., & Schuerman, J. (1986). The impact of sexual abuse on children (Final Report No. MH 37133). Rockville, MD: National Institute of Mental Health.

de Arellano, M. A., Andrews, A. R. III, Reid-Quiñones, K., Vasquez, D., Doherty, L. S., Danielson, C.K., & Rheingold, A. (2018). Immigration trauma among Hispanic youth: Missed by trauma assessments and predictive of depression and PTSD symptoms. *Journal of Latina/o Psychology, 6*(3), 159–174. doi:10.1037/lat0000090.

Dehon, C., & Scheeringa, M. (2006). Screening for preschool PTSD with the child behavior checklist. *Journal of Pediatric Psychology, 31*, 431–435.

Dube, S. R., Williamson, D. F., Thompson, T., Felitti, V. J., & Anda, R. F. (2004). Brief communication: Assessing the reliability of retrospective reports of adverse childhood experiences among adult HMO members attending a primary care clinic. *Child Abuse & Neglect, 28*(7), 729–737. doi:10.1016/j.chiabu.2003.08.009

Durham, M., & Webb, S. S. (2014, October). Historical trauma: A panoramic perspective. *The Brown University Child and Adolescent Behavior Letter, 30*(10), 1–3.

Felitti, V. J., Anda, R.F., Nordenberg, D., Williamson, D.F, Spitz, A.M., Edwards, V., … Marks, J. S. (1998). Relationship of childhood abuse and household dysfunction to many of the leading causes of death in adults: The ACES study. *American Journal of Preventive Medicine, 14*(4), 245–258. doi:10.1016/S0749-3797(98)00017-8

Foa, E. B., Keane, T. M., & Friedman, M. J. (2009). *Effective treatments for PTSD: Practice guidelines from the International Society for Traumatic Stress Studies.* New York, NY: Guilford Press.

Frankel, F., & Wetmore, B. (1996). *Good friends are hard to find: Helping your child find, make, and keep friends.* London, UK: Perspective Publishing.

Friedrich, W. N. (1997). *Child sexual behavior inventory.* Odessa, FL: Psychological Assessment Resources.

Friedrich, W. N. (2002). *Psychological assessment of sexually abused children and their families.* Thousand Oaks, CA: Sage.

Friedrich, W. N., Lysne, M., Sim, L., & Shamos, S. (2004). Assessing sexual abuse in high-risk adolescents with the Adolescent Clinical Sexual Behavior Inventory (ACSBI).*Child Maltreatment, 9*(3), 239–250.

Gilbert, R., Kemp, A., Thoburn, J., Sidebotham, P., Radford, L., Glaser, D., & MacMillan, H. L. (2009, January 10). Recognising and responding to child maltreatment. *The Lancet, 373,* 167–180.

Gold, S., Lucenko, B., Elhai, J., Swingle, J., & Sellers, A. (1999). A comparison of psychological/psychiatric symptomatology of women and men sexually abused as children. *Child Abuse & Neglect, 23,* 683–692.

Hembree-Kigin, T. L., & McNeil, C. B. (1995). *Parent-child interaction therapy.* New York, NY: Plenum.

Herman, J. L. (1992). Trauma and recovery: The aftermath of violence—From domestic violence to political terror. New York, NY: Basic Books.

Horowitz, M. J., Wilner, N., & Alvarez, W. (1979). Impact of event scale: A measure of subjective stress. *Psychosomatic Medicine, 41,* 209–218.

Hudspeth, E. F. (2015). Children with special needs and circumstances: Conceptualization through a complex trauma lens. *The Professional Counselor, 5*(2), 195.

Immigration and Customs Enforcement. (2015). *Immigration and removal statistics.* Retrieved from https://www.ice.gov/removal-statistics/2015#wcm-survey-target-id

Jent, J. F., Merrick, M. T., Dandes, S. K., Lambert, W. F., Haney, M. L., & Cano, N. M.(2009). Multidisciplinary assessment of child maltreatment: A multi-site pilot descriptive analysis of the Florida Child Protection Team model. *Children and Youth Services Review, 31,* 896–902.

Kilpatrick, D. G., Acierno, R., Saunders, B., Resnick, H. S., Best, C. L., & Schnurr, P. P. (2000). Risk factors for adolescent substance abuse and dependence: Data from a national sample. *Journal of Consulting and Clinical Psychology, 68*(1), 19.

Kira, I. A. (2001). Taxonomy of trauma and trauma assessment. *Traumatology, 7*(2), 73–86.

Knopf, A. (2017, October). Immigration policy: Separating children from parents unnecessary and costly trauma. *The Brown University Child and Adolescent Behavior Letter, 33*(10), 4.

Kobulsky, J. M., Kepple, N. J., & Jedwab, M. (2018). Abuse characteristics and the concordance of child protective service determinations and adolescent self-reports of abuse. *Child Maltreatment, 23*(3), 269–280.

Kolko, D. J., & Swenson, C. C. (2002). *Assessing and treating physically abused children and their families: A cognitive-behavioral approach.* Thousand Oaks, CA: Sage.

Landauer, R. J. (2012, June). Child maltreatment—Clinical PTSD diagnosis not enough?!: Comment on Resick et al. (2012). *Journal of Traumatic Stress, 25,* 258–259.

Lanktree, C. B., Gilbert, A. M., Briere, J., Taylor, N., Chen, K., Maida, C. A., ... Saltzman, W. R. (2008). Multi-informant assessment of maltreated children: Convergent and discriminant validity of the TSCC and TSCYC. *Child Abuse & Neglect, 32,* 621–625.

Laor, N., Wolmer, L., & Cohen, D. J. (2001). Mothers' functioning and children's symptoms 5 years after a SCUD Missile attack. *American Journal of Psychiatry, 158,* 1020–1026.

Levendosky, A. A., Huth-Bocks, A. C., Semel, M. A., & Shapiro, D. L. (2002). Trauma symptoms in preschool-age children exposed to domestic violence. *Journal of Interpersonal Violence, 17,* 150–164.

Maitra, B. (1996). Child abuse: A universal 'diagnostic' category? The implication of culture in definition and assessment. *International Journal of Social Psychiatry, 42*(4), 287–304.

McNeil, C. B., & Hembree-Kigin, T. L. (Eds.). (2010). *Parent-child interaction therapy* (2nd ed.). New York, NY: Springer.

Milner, J. S. (1986). *The child abuse potential inventory: Manual* (2nd ed.). DeKalb, IL: Psytec.

Nader, K. O., Kriegler, J. A., Blake, D. D., Pynoos, R. S., Newman, E., & Weather, F. (2002). *The Clinician-Administered PTSD Scale, Child and Adolescent Version (CAPS-C).* Available from www.ncptsd.org

Ohan, J. L., Myers, K., & Collett, B. R. (2002). Ten-year review of rating scales IV: Scales assessing trauma and its effects. *Journal of the American Academy of Child & Adolescent Psychiatry, 41*(12), 1401–1422.

Olafson, E. (1999). Using testing when family violence and child abuse are issues. In A. R. Nurse (Ed.), *Psychological testing with families* (pp. 230–256). New York, NY: Wiley & Sons.

Olafson, E., & Connelly, L. (2012). Child abuse assessment strategy and inventories. In L. Sperry (Ed.), *Family assessment: Contemporary and cutting-edge strategies* (2nd ed., (pp. 265–308). New York, NY: Routledge.

Osher, T., Garay, L., Jennings, B., Jimerson, D., Marcus, S., & Martinez, K. (2011). *Closing the gap: Cultural perspective on family driven care.* Retrieved from https://gal2.org/library/documents/volunteer/continuing-education/closing-the-gap-cultural-perspectives-on-family-driven-care.pdf

Pelcovitz, D., van der Kolk, B., Roth, S., Mandel, F., Kaplan, S., & Resick, P. (1997). Development of a criteria set and a structured interview for disorders of extreme stress (SIDESNOS). *Journal of Traumatic Stress, 10,* 3–16.

Putnam, F. W. (1997). *Dissociation in children and adolescents: A developmental perspective.* New York, NY: Guilford Press.

Putnam, F. W. (2003). Ten-year research review update: Child sexual abuse. *Journal of the American Academy of Child and Adolescent Psychiatry, 42*(3), 269–278.

Putnam, F. W., Helmers, K., Horowitz, L. A., & Trickett, P. K. (1994). Hypnotizability and dissociativity in sexually abused girls. *Child Abuse & Neglect, 19,* 645–655.

Putnam, F. W., Helmers, K., & Trickett, P. K. (1993). Development, reliability and validity of a child dissociation scale. *Child Abuse & Neglect, 17,* 645–655.

Putnam, F. W., & Peterson, G. (1994). Further validation of the child dissociative checklist. *Dissociation, 7,* 204–211.

Raman, S., & Hodes, D. (2011). Cultural issues in child maltreatment. *Journal of Paediatrics and Child Health, 48*, 30–37.

Sachser, C., Berliner, L., Holt, T., Jensen, T. K., Jungbluth, N., Risch, E., … Goldbeck, L. (2017). International development and psychometric properties of the Child and Adolescent Trauma Screen (CATS). *Journal of Affective Disorders, 210*, 189–195. doi:10.1016/j.jad.2016.12.040

Saigh, P. A. (2002). The Children's Post Traumatic Stress Disorder-Inventory (CPTSD- I). Available from Phillip A. Saigh, Ph.D., Department of Educational Psychology, Graduate Center, City University of New York, 365 Fifth Avenue, New York, NY 10016.

Saylor, C. F., Swenson, C. C., Reynolds, S. S, & Taylor, M. (1999). The Pediatric Emotional Stress Scale: A brief screening measure for young children exposed to traumatic events. *Journal of Clinical Child Psychology, 28*, 70–81.

Sebre, S., Sprugevica, I., Novotni, A., Bonevski, D., Pakalniskiene, V., Popescu, D., … Lewis, O. (2004). Cross cultural comparisons of child-reported emotional and physical abuse: Rates, risk factors, and psychosocial symptoms. *Child Abuse & Neglect, 28(1)*, 113–127.

Straus, M. A., Hamby, S. L., Finkelhor, D., Moore, D. W., & Runyan, D. (1998). Identification of child maltreatment with the parent-child conflict scales: Development of psychometric data for a national sample of American parents. *Child Abuse & Neglect, 22*, 249–270.

Stockhammer, T. F., Salzinger, S., Feldman, R. S., & Mojica, E. (2001). Assessment of the effect of physical child abuse within an ecological framework: Measurement issues. *Journal of Community Psychology, 29*(3), 319–344.

Stover, C. S., & Berkowitz, S. J. (2005). Assessing violence exposure and trauma symptoms in young children: A critical review of measures. *Journal of Traumatic Stress, 186*, 707–717.

Thaber, A. A. M., & Vosantis, P. (1999). Post-traumatic stress reactions in children of war. *Journal of Child Psychology & Psychiatry, 40*, 385–391.

The National Child Traumatic Stress Network. (2005). *Complex trauma.* Retrieved from http://www.nctsn.org/traumatypes/complex-trauma

Valera, E. M., & Berenbaum, H. (2003). Brain injury in battered women. *Journal of Consulting and Clinical Psychology, 71*, 797–804.

van der Kolk, B. A., Pynoos, R. S., Cicchetti, D., Cloitre, M., D'Andrea, W., Ford, J. D., … Teicher, M. (2009). *Proposal to include a developmental trauma disorder diagnosis for children and adolescents in DSM-5.* Retrieved from http://www.traumacenter.org/announcements/DTD_NCTSN_official_submission_to_DSM_V_Final_Version.pdf

Weiss, D. (2002). *The impact of events scale-revised.* Available from Daniel Weiss, Ph.D., Department of Psychiatry, University of California at San Francisco, CA 94143-0984.

Weiss, D. S., & Marmar, C. R. (1997). The impact of event scale-revised. In J. P. Wilson & T. M. Keane (Eds.), *Assessing psychological trauma and PTSD* (pp. 399–411). New York, NY: Guilford Press.

Wilson, K. R., Hansen, D. J., & Li, M. (2011). The traumatic stress response in child maltreatment and resultant neuropsychological effects. *Aggression and Violent Behavior, 16*, 87–97.

Wilson, J. P., & Keane, T. M. (Eds.). (1997). *Assessing psychological trauma and PTSD.* New York, NY: Guilford Press.

Wolfe, V. V., Gentile, C., Michienzi, T., Sas, L., & Wolfe, D. A. (1991). The children's impact of traumatic events scale: A measure of post-sexual abuse PTSD symptoms. *Behavioral Assessment, 13*(4), 359–383.

Zuberi, A., & Teixeira, S. (2017). Child health in low-income neighborhoods: The unexpected relationship with neighborhood disorder and other aspects of distress. *Journal of Community Psychology, 45*, 459–472.

INDEX

Note: **Bold** page numbers refer to tables and *italic* page numbers refer to figures.